WAR IN THE PACIFIC

Volume III

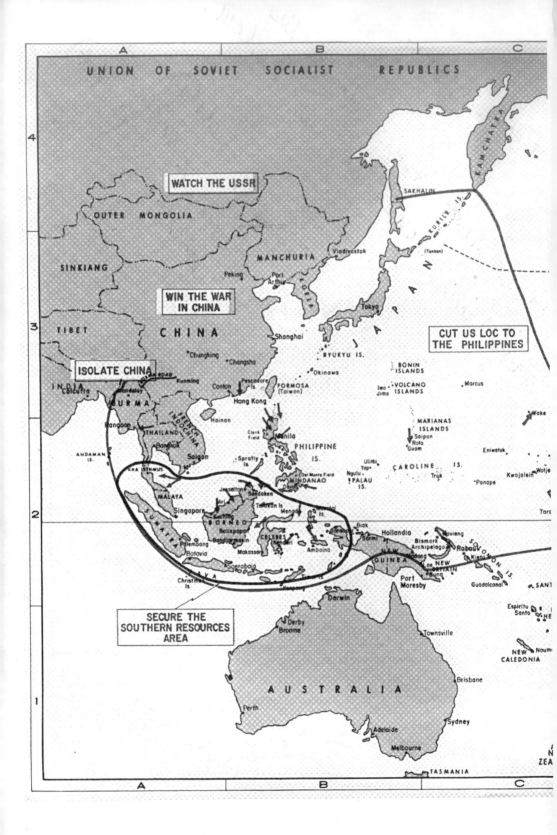

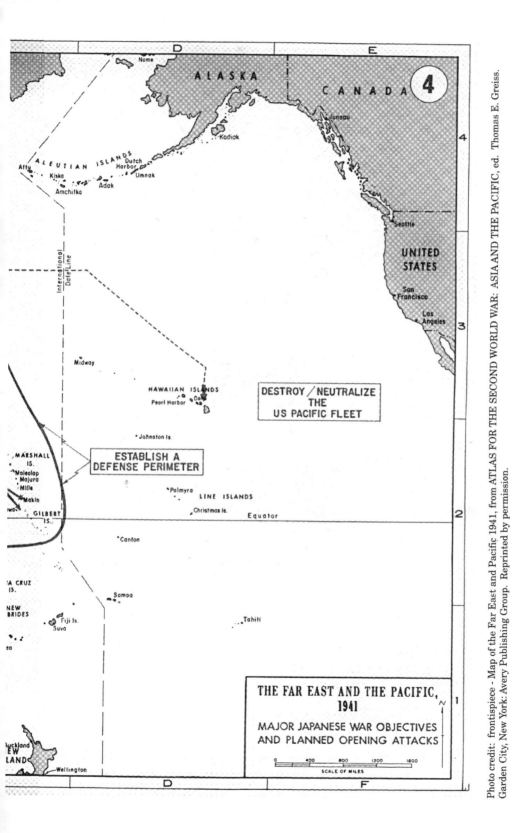

THE FAR EAST AND THE PACIFIC,
1941

MAJOR JAPANESE WAR OBJECTIVES
AND PLANNED OPENING ATTACKS

DESTROY / NEUTRALIZE
THE
US PACIFIC FLEET

ESTABLISH A
DEFENSE PERIMETER

Photo credit: frontispiece - Map of the Far East and Pacific 1941, from ATLAS FOR THE SECOND WORLD WAR: ASIA AND THE PACIFIC, ed. Thomas E. Greiss. Garden City, New York: Avery Publishing Group. Reprinted by permission.

太平洋戦争

WAR IN THE PACIFIC

Jerome T. Hagen
Brigadier General, United States Marine Corps (Retired)

Volume III

HAWAII PACIFIC UNIVERSITY
Honolulu

Copies of the book are available from the author at 47-446 Lulani St., Kaneohe, HI, 96744 (Fax: 808-239-1053)

Printed in the United States of America by Malloy, Inc., Ann Arbor, Michigan

Library of Congress Cataloging in Publication Data

Hagen, Jerome T.
    War in the Pacific / Jerome T. Hagen.—1st ed.
        p. cm.
    Bibliography:
    Includes index
    ISBN: 09762669-2-X
    1. World War, 1939-1945-Campaigns-Pacific Ocean.
    2. Islands of the Pacific. 1. Title.

    D767.H34 1996   96-77738
    940.54'26-dc   CIP

Photo credit: cover- Task Group 38.3 entering Ulithi anchorage near Palau after conducting air strikes against Japanese positions in the Philippines. Leading are carriers *Langley,* and *Ticonderoga.* Following are battleships *Washington, North Carolina, South Dakota,* and cruisers *Santa Fe, Biloxi, Mobile,* and *Oakland.* The photograph was taken in December 1944, and is reprinted with permission of the National Archives.

Frontispiece- Map of the Far East and Pacific 1941, from *ATLAS FOR THE SECOND WORLD WAR: ASIA AND THE PACIFIC,* ed. Thomas E. Greiss. Garden City, New York: Avery Publishing Group. Reprinted by permission.

PREFACE

Readers of Volumes I and II know that I have tried not to burden the reader with excess maps and unnecessary unit designations. I believe that the many history "buffs" that desire such additional information can surely find it in the numerous 600-to-700 page books written about most of the chapter titles.

This volume is a bit different. The four chapters on Burma contain a number of maps and unit designations. This is because Burma is so large, the action so widespread, and the duration of the fighting so long, January 1942 until May 1945, that I believe the maps and unit designations are necessary for the reader to properly track the conduct of the war in Burma. The chapters on internment of Japanese Americans, and Japanese Canadians during WW II, and Douglas MacArthur also require more than the usual maps and photographs. The chapters about Tarawa and Peleliu are overdue and in response to your requests.

Since publishing Volume II in 2003, my good friends Richard Fiske (Chapter 22, Volume II), and Jimmy Daniels (Chapter 9, Volume II) have passed away. They were heroes during the war and quality individuals afterwards. Many of you met them at the USS Arizona Memorial where they volunteered to escort visitors to the Memorial. They will not be forgotten. I am delighted that their story was put into print before they left us.

Volume III also contains chapters of WW II heroes. Joe Foss of Sioux Falls, South Dakota, an ACE flying off Henderson Field on Guadalcanal, later governor of South Dakota and first president of the American Football League. Foss was awarded the Medal of Honor by President Franklin Roosevelt. He was a special person who passed away before I could get this volume in print.

The story of John D. Bulkeley, another Medal of Honor recipient during WW II for his evacuation of General MacArthur from the Philippines, and my boss during the Cuban Missile Crisis is in this volume. What a fabulous career Bulkeley had during 59 years of active duty in the U.S. Navy.

Thanks for your kind comments about both volumes of the book and for taking the time to write. I will continue to search out living veterans to tell their stories, and to research the events, battles, and personalities of WW II that we must all remember.

As in the earlier volumes, Japanese names appear in the western style: i.e., personal name followed by family or surname.

ACKNOWLEDGEMENTS

Every author owes thanks to those folks behind the scenes that take the draft pages and turn them into coherent, meaningful works of literature. My sincere gratitude for such work goes to Rick Stepien, Vice President at Hawaii Pacific University, George Moyer, at Hawaii Baptist Academy, and Robert Carlson, President of Dynamic Data Designs. These three friends, plus hundreds of readers that took the time to suggest titles for volume III made this book possible.

Stepien and Moyer edited every chapter in the book and made significant improvement to the draft pages. They did this after their already long work days with their organizations. Carlson did the typesetting, layout, composition, and graphics for this volume. He was able to do this via long distance following his move to Missouri. He also worked closely with the printer, Malloy, Inc., to produce the book. It is no understatement to say that without their assistance, this volume would not have been published.

For those readers that have waited since the first of the year for volume III, I apologize for the delay. We wanted to ensure that we had a quality product when it was published and that takes time. After publishing of the earlier volumes of *War in the Pacific*, I have found that researching and writing go faster than editing, making changes, insertion of pictures, maps, charts, and the notes, bibliography, and index. However, it is these laborious duties that eliminate mistakes and ensure excellence of the book..

I doubt there will be a volume IV, although there is yet much to write about the Pacific war. There have been many requests for a large print volume and some interest for a Chinese language version. Perhaps these challenges will be next.

CONTENTS

ILLUSTRATIONS

Photographs

Maps and drawings

1

THE MERCHANT MARINE IN WWII

The only thing that really frightened me during the war
was the U-boat peril . . . The Admiralty, with which I
lived in closest amity and contact, shared these fears.[1]
Winston Churchill

Every student of military history understands that logistics,
the supply of bombs, beans and bullets, is the necessary ingredient
for victory. The merchant marine provided the logistics for the
Allies in WW II. Supplies flowed from the United States, Canada,
Australia, and England to Allied forces in Europe, Africa, Northern
Russia, the Mediterranean, Indian Ocean, and the Pacific. In the
Pacific theater, the merchant marines took part in every
amphibious operation starting with the invasion of Guadalcanal.

Five thousand American merchant marines died violent
deaths during WW II when their ships were torpedoed, bombed,
shelled, or hit mines. For too many years, these men were forgotten
and received few, if any, honors from their fellow citizens. After
the war, no GI Bill of Rights awaited them to provide loans, free
education, or continuing life insurance, such as was provided to
7,800,000 military veterans. The U. S. Department of
Transportation, Maritime Administration did provide, upon request,
a list of vendors where medals, emblem, and button could be
purchased. One wonders why a merchant marine, or his survivors,
should have to purchase their medals and emblems themselves
when all other veterans do not. The sad answer is that these men
and their service were truly forgotten.

Early on Sunday, Sept. 3, 1939, Germany's submarines in
the Atlantic received the message that Britain and France had
declared war on Germany. A few hours later, Admiral Karl Donitz,
commander of German submarine forces, notified his submariners
to execute hostilities immediately and reminded them of the
agreements concerning merchant ships. Such ships had to be
stopped and searched. If they were found to be carrying enemy
cargo, they could be sunk after the crew had been safely put into
lifeboats.

At 4:30 P.M., submarine *U-30* discovered the outline of a large ship off the northwest coast of Ireland. Captain Fritz-Julius Lemp, the 26-year old *U-30* commander, elected to follow the ship until dusk and then move in for a closer look. He found the ship to be blacked out (no lights showing), and following a zigzag course. He determined that it was a British merchant cruiser, and, at 7:40 P.M., fired two torpedoes.

One torpedo exploded amidships and the ship began to sink. Lemp had struck the first blow in the Battle of the Atlantic, although not a blow in which he or Germany could take pride. The ship that was sinking was the ocean liner *Athenia*, a passenger ship of 13,581 gross tons, bound for Canada with 1,418 passengers and crew including 316 Americans. As Lemp listened to the SOS being sent by *Athenia*, he realized his horrible mistake. But, he rationalized, what was he to do? He had no room to take the survivors on board and did not want to risk staying in the area to help save lives. Slowly the sinking ship faded in the darkness.

British and American newspapers carried graphic accounts of the helpless *Athenia*. Eyewitnesses told of children trapped in cabins and bodies scattered across the upper decks. Among the dead were 28 American civilians causing East Coast papers to call the sinking an act of total war on civilians.[2]

Survivors of the passenger liner *Athenia*, which sank just hours after the declaration of war on September 3, 1939.

Imperial War Museum

2

German Propaganda Minister Joseph Goebbels denied German responsibility for the sinking, stating that it was a British torpedo that sank Athenia, and that it was part of Churchill's plan to bring America into the war. Few people believed him. The German U-boat once again, as in WW I, had established itself as a terror weapon and would continue to build on such a reputation.

By mid-October, the Germans lifted all restrictions on their submarines operating in the North Sea and then the area to the west that included American-escorted convoys. By June of 1940, eight months later, German U-boats had sunk 300 ships of 1.1 million tons.

On June 10, Italy entered the war on the side of Germany and made 26 modern submarines available to Germany. During the period July to October 1940, the German submariner's "happy time," another 217 Allied merchant ships were sunk.

During September 1940 Admiral Donitz implemented his plan for group submarine tactics called wolf packs. The first submarine to locate a merchant ship convoy sent a message to German U-boat headquarters giving the speed, course and position of the convoy. The submarine continued providing such information until enough additional submarines could arrive on scene and commence the attack. Attacks were made on the surface at night. By gathering several submarines around a convoy, the U-boats could penetrate the convoy escort protection and sink ships at close range. The convoy escorts were never sufficient to locate and attack several submarines simultaneously. Even when they did locate a submarine, they found that most of the U-boats, when surfaced, could outrun the old escort vessels.

In theory at least, it was far easier for an escort vessel to force the U-boat to dive, fix the position of the U-boat, maintain position over it for 36-48 hours until the U-boats air supply ran out, and then destroy it when it surfaced. The problem that faced convoy escorts was that every hour they were away from the convoy, it was more vulnerable to other U-boat attacks. By operating U-boats in packs, it became virtually impossible for the escorts to pursue a submarine for more than an hour. Even then, it would take the escort as much as two hours to regain contact with the convoy.

An example of the carnage inflicted by the German wolf pack tactics occurred during the evening of October 16, 1940.

Just before midnight, Commander Heinrich Bleichrodt (*U-48*) discovered a 35-ship convoy from Nova Scotia bound for England. He reported the sighting to Admiral Donitz's headquarters at Lorient in occupied France. U-boat headquarters diverted six more "wolves" to join the hunt.[3]

U-48 attacked rather than wait for the pack, and sank two of the merchant ships while surfaced. Forced to dive by the convoy escorts, *U-48* was joined by *U-38*, which damaged a freighter before being forced to dive. Shortly thereafter, the wolf pack arrived, and by morning the convoy was no longer a convoy but rather a few ravaged merchant ships fleeing in different directions and hundreds of oil-soaked sailors clinging to anything that floated under the smoke from burning wood and oil. The convoy lost 20 of its 35 ships while the U-boats had no losses. In just three nights in October, wolf packs sank 38 merchant ships. By the end of 1940, the Germans had sunk 1,281 ships, mostly British, totaling 4,747,033 gross tons. The loss was equivalent to five years of peacetime ship construction.[4] Wolf pack tactics were so successful that they became the standard attack method for the U-boats for the next three years.

Better training of convoy and escort commanders, the introduction of surface radar, and breaking of the communication code used by the U-boats, helped the British save ships and inflict greater casualties on the submarines. In May 1941, the British captured Commander Lemp and U-110 complete with its top-secret code machine. Priority was given to decoding the machine and in less than 36 hours, ships were being routed away from German U-boat locations.

Two weeks later, two of Germany's top U-boat aces including Lieutenant Cdr. (Kapitanleutnant) Englebert Endrass (*U-46*) with 22 sunken ships to his credit was killed, Captain (Korvettenkapitan) Gunther Prien (*U-47*) with 21 sinkings was killed, Captain (Fregattenkapitan) Otto Kretschmer (*U-99*) 45 sinkings, was taken prisoner, and Lieutenant Cdr. (Kapitanleutnent) Jaochim Schepke (*U-100*), 39 sinkings, was found on the surface by radar while attacking a convoy. *U-100* was rammed and sunk.[5]

Many of the merchant ships plying the North Atlantic route in convoy were American ships and in March 1941, the United States assigned three destroyer flotillas and five flying-boat squadrons to patrol areas of the Western Atlantic. From March to May 1941, the tonnage of merchant shipping sunk by the German submarine fleet exceeded British ship production by a ratio of 3 to

1, and the combined British and American production by 2 to 1. Something had to be done to reduce merchant ship losses. The answer was to convoy the merchant ships with armed escorts.

In May, the U.S. established a naval and air base in Newfoundland to service and assist convoys and in July, sent a military force to Iceland. Finally, in September, the U.S. Navy took responsibility for escorting all convoys in the Western Atlantic that included American ships.

A convoy-escort procedure was established whereby American armed vessels escorted the convoys to a point south of Iceland, where they were relieved by British vessels that shepherded the convoy to England. During September 1940, the U.S. loaned Great Britain 250 WW I "four-stack" destroyers for use as convoy escort.[6] On March 11, 1941, the U.S. Congress passed the "Lend-Lease" bill that essentially provided the British with their wartime needs so long as the goods could be shipped safely to England.

Admiral Ernest King, chief of naval operations, initially refused to escort maritime ships off America's East Coast, believing it to be a waste of armed vessels. After losing hundreds of ships within sight of East Coast ports, he agreed to escort the convoys during the day, and put them into protected anchorages by night. This system slowed movement of the convoys, but reduced ship losses from 40 in January to five in May and three in July. Similar convoy methods were adopted in the Gulf of Mexico after 41 ships were sunk in May, and maritime ship sinkings in the Gulf stopped completely.

During 1941, German U-boats sank 432 ships with cargo exceeding 2,000,000 gross tons. U-boat losses were 35; with 27 of them sunk by British escort vessels. During 1942, U-boats sank 1,160 ships with a gross tonnage of 6,000,000. Other German forces (aviation and surface navy) sank an additional 1,500,000 tons of shipping. The Allies had lost a total of 14,000,000 tons of shipping since the war began and were in serious danger of losing the battle for merchant shipping.

One must remember that Britain was an island nation completely dependent upon its maritime force to bring food and raw materials from its far-flung empire, and export finished goods to the world. Without sufficient merchant shipping, Britain would starve, and its economy would collapse.

A success story of the maritime war was the shipbuilding capability of American industry. The United States built 60 ocean-type cargo ships for Great Britain before Pearl Harbor was attacked. Once in the war, the U.S. capacity for construction of ships, tanks, planes and guns was remarkable. The famed Liberty cargo ships (EC-2) were produced at an astounding rate. One such ship was launched in four and-a-half days after the keel was laid. These were 7,200-ton ships powered by diesel engines capable of 11 knots. In all, 2,710 Liberty ships were built, more than replacing Allied losses to the U-boats.[7]

Another success story was the emergence of the Canadian Navy. At the start of the war, Canada had six ships. Knowing it had to do its share in the North Atlantic, Canada began to build a modern navy. By the end of the war, Canada had a navy of 400 ships, all built in Canadian shipyards, and 90,000 men, nearly all from Canada. Many of the escort vessels that left Halifax with maritime convoys were Canadian.

Although the war against the U-boats was improving, by D-day in Europe (May 1945), 53,556 seamen aboard British merchant vessels had lost their lives in 2,828 ships sunk by U-boats[8]. The numbers are shocking but they only tell part of the story. The remainder of this chapter describes the conditions under which the merchant seamen worked and the stories of some of these brave men.

The British government call for volunteers to reinforce their merchant navy in 1938 was successful. Within a year 13,000 men had been processed. The men ranged in age from teenage deck boys, to apprentices and pensioners. Initially, seamen were required to sign up for a minimum of six months and a maximum of 12. Once signed on, they received an allotment note as an advance in pay. These notes were cashed by pub owners with a discount of 10 percent. Until 1943, there was no such thing as paid leave. Before then, a seaman whose contract expired was paid his wages, plus train fare home. Men who were in no hurry to sign on again, bought their train tickets and spent the remainder of their back pay at the local pub.

A British Able Seaman's pay was 12 pounds ($45.00) per month, less than half of that received by their American counterparts. American merchant seamen were insured by their government for $5,000, and received an overtime rate of pay of 85 cents for every hour worked over 44 hours per week. They also

6

received a bonus of 100 percent of their pay for service in the North Atlantic and the Mediterranean. Not so the British merchant seaman. His only insurance was what he paid for himself and there was no such thing as overtime. [9]

The Allied Merchant Seaman's Club, Hollis Street, Halifax.

Canadian War Museum

Merchant seamen shared a life full of hardships and dangers. Most came from seafaring families where fathers and grandfathers left a rich naval heritage for their families to follow. Many of the younger men would have quit the merchant service after a particularly dangerous mission but did not, because if they did, they were immediately drafted for service in the military. They preferred a life at sea, doing something they knew, as compared to life in the army.

At sea, living conditions were cramped and unhealthy. In the lower decks of the ships, portholes could not be opened for ventilation. Usually eight men lived in a small cubicle with iron frame bunks. They ate, slept, smoked, and cursed their ill fortune in damp smelly clothes until they could go ashore at the next port. The air was thick and the odor of tobacco and sweat was always heavy. It was a major event to be allowed to go topside and stand on the deck to breathe fresh air. The food aboard ship was unsatisfactory at best. Most of it was canned or dehydrated with very little fresh food. Those seamen who were captured and became prisoners of war found no great difference between their accommodations aboard a merchant vessel and a German POW camp.

Felix Riesenberg, well-known author of books about merchant marines tells about American seamen this way. ". . . sleeping on a narrow bunk on a dirty mattress crawling with bedbugs, in a deep, dark hole in the aft part of the ship, over the screw, where the fumes from showers and the toilet permeate the air, with no ventilation and little light. . . Meals in a smelly mess room just off the hot galley, while facing a not too clean wall with a slovenly mess boy shoving a plate of greasy stew over your shoulder. . . . living conditions are the cause of much of the discontent and rioting that have occurred the past two years along our waterfronts and aboard our merchant ships."[10]

Many of the seamen that manned the merchant vessels came from the fishing fleets, while some of the commanders were right out of college with no experience. Sometimes it was necessary to use less conventional methods to enlighten the crew with the commander's leadership attributes. Commander Colin Warwick had served for a time in the merchant service, was commissioned and pushed through a two-month commander's course in seven days. He reported to a coal-burning trawler with 250 tons of coal in its bunkers, enough coal for a month at sea.

He learned that the seamen ate and slept in the old fish hold while the commander had his own cabin beneath the wheelhouse. Warwick recalled his own group commander, named Turner, telling him how he gained the respect of his crew. During his initial inspection of the ship, Turner asked one of the seamen in the engine room what his job was. The man replied that he was f———— greaser. "When you speak to your captain, you say sir," said Turner. "Oh," the greaser replied, "there's none of that bloody nonsense about me." [11] Turner knocked the man down and continued his inspection.

Back in his cabin, Turner heard several new men talking outside his cabin. "What's the old man like," one asked. "Oh, he's all right, he'd as soon knock you down as look at you."[12] Warwick received a quick lesson from his commander on how to handle men in the merchant navy.

The merchant ship sailor was looked upon as a bum by the American public.[13] They thought of merchant sailors in terms of cheap whiskey, waterfront brawls, brothels, and unauthorized strikes that delayed large passenger ships on both coasts and New Orleans. Even the captains of the ships and ships masters were looked down upon. They held no position in society, owned one uniform, and, considering their responsibilities, were poorly paid. A master mariner, after 20 years at sea, earned less then $350.00 per month, bought his own clothing, and received no pension or insurance. [14]

Every merchant seaman that made the Murmansk run will tell you it was a nightmare. Added to the continuous attacks by German ships, U-boats, and aircraft, was the most severe weather conditions experienced anywhere.

Murmansk was Russia's ice-free seaport and the main source of supplies for the defense of Leningrad and Moscow. Once a lazy fishing village, Murmansk quickly grew to a population of 100,000 when Germany invaded Russia. The people were mostly strong women, old men, serious-faced children, and military personnel. The people all worked at the piers unloading cargo from Allied convoys seven days a week, in shifts that continued 24 hours a day. The people were without a sense of humor and refused to communicate any more than necessary with the seamen who survived the dangerous convoy trip from America's east coast.

After watching the muscular Russian women unload the ship, more than one American seaman decided he was better off staying on board ship than trying to find female companionship on shore. Russian women did not fraternize with the seamen; there were no houses of prostitution, and vodka was often limited to one drink per day to visiting seamen.[15] Those seamen that did go ashore, often subsisted on a diet of black bread, with barley and grass soup. Unfriendly Russian guards monitored their every move, and ensured that the merchantmen understood they were not welcome to come ashore in Murmansk.

The creaky, patched docks and buildings near the piers were constantly bombed by German planes based only 35 miles away. Soot and oil permeated the urban area which seemed to consist of more anti-aircraft weapons and sandbags than buildings. The dirty ground and water cover would turn white when the frequent blizzards roared down from the Barents Sea area, and then turn ugly again when the snow melted from bomb explosions and fire.

From 1942 to 1945, 48,000 merchant vessels in 1,134 convoys crossed the Atlantic bound for Murmansk.[16] The largest such convoy, PQ-13 with 167 ships left New York in March 1944, in nineteen separate columns covering nine miles. As the convoy approached Russia on March 19, in heavy seas, blinding snow squalls, and spray that instantly turned to ice, three German destroyers appeared in front of them. The convoy quickly become a collection of individual ships traveling the same direction, rather than a well-organized and defined convoy.

A submarine delivered the first blow, putting torpedoes into the two escort ships, HMS *Trinidad*, a cruiser, and HMS *Eclipse*, a destroyer. The next ship to sink was the convoy commodore's ship, *River Afton*, which carried a cargo of mines in her after hold, the same spot where she was torpedoed. The British ship disintegrated and sank in 40 seconds.[17]

Aircraft depth charging and machinegunning a U-boat.

Imperial War Museum

During the attack by surface ships and submarines, the weather cleared a bit and PQ-13 was also attacked by German land-based bombers flying from Banak and Petsamo air bases, 70 miles from Murmansk. After the war it was learned that the convoy had been spotted by a German long-range patrol plane near Iceland. Five merchant ships, totaling 30,000 tons, were sunk by the combined German attack.[18] Many of the survivors of the ships that were sunk, died of exposure and frostbite

During the first week of July 1944, only 13 of the 36 ships in PQ-17 made it to Murmansk. The 23 ships that were sunk carried 125,000 tons of much-needed cargo for the Russians. Ships that did make it to Murmansk during the war delivered more than a million tons of cargo including 7,400 aircraft, 5,200 tanks, 5,000 anti-aircraft guns, 14 minesweepers, and four submarines.[19]

Most Atlantic convoys formed in Halifax Harbor in Nova Scotia and followed a north easterly course to Liverpool, England. A lesser number of convoys formed in New York and followed the Liverpool route. Other convoys formed at Norfolk, Virginia, and followed a south easterly course to Gibraltar. A 45-ship convoy leaving Halifax would move in columns, with perhaps 10 columns abreast, 1,000 yards between ships. Such a convoy might be seven miles wide and 30 miles long. Armed escorts, as were available, operated 3,000 yards in front and to the sides of the convoy. Many North Atlantic convoys contained more than 100 ships.

Atlantic convoy duty, especially in the winter was cold, wet, and miserable. Low overcasts with ice, sleet, and snow reduced visibility, and the wind and wave action kept everyone uncomfortable and irritable. Well, perhaps not everyone. One young seaman said he was fascinated by the raging seas and gales. He did not mind the green water, or the rain and hail that dumped upon him because he felt that this was the way the Atlantic was supposed to be. He would have been disappointed had it been any different.[20]

In contrast, an American officer of a convoy ship reported, "I did not enjoy convoy work in the Atlantic. It was cold and miserable duty under the very worst possible weather conditions most of the time with very little feeling of accomplishment."[21] Most navy men shared that sentiment.

As many as 75-percent of the crew might be seasick at any given time. The constant pitch and roll made life uncomfortable and dangerous to move about. In addition to the constant shifting of the ship, water seeped into the berthing and feeding compartments. Below deck was always wet with the smell of mildew on everything. When the weather did permit, the commander might authorize a fishing expedition whereby a depth charge would be dropped and the men would haul in fish with nets, buckets, boots and anything else that was handy. The fresh fish made an enjoyable change to the canned meat ration. British sailors also had their daily rum ration to enjoy, one shot of rum mixed with two of water.

Temperatures aboard ship could range from one extreme to another. For those that worked in or near the engine room, heat exhaustion would set in within a matter of hours. On deck, seamen suffered from frostbite and hypothermia. Injuries due to handling heavy equipment aboard the tossing and rolling surfaces were common. When injuries did occur, seamen were dependent upon their captain for treatment until the next port visit.

Lady sickness, a venereal disease, was considered to be a "self inflicted injury" for which the seamen received no treatment while afloat.[22] Despite these hardships, most seamen were not overly unhappy with their lot. They loved the call of distant places and new horizons. For some, there was always the suggestion of adventure and even romance in these far off places. Simply stated, most merchant seamen found their lot as good as or better than if they had stayed home.

Merchant seamen were much appreciated by Great Britain, if not especially respected. Both Liverpool and Halifax operated Seamen's clubs, and canteens. Relief organizations provided mittens, scarves, socks and shoes. Live entertainment was usually scheduled, young ladies were available to dance or talk, reading and writing rooms were provided, and the seamen were always made to feel at home. Halifax has established several Seamen's clubs as historical places and maintains them as memorials of those dangerous days.

American merchant sailors came from such major port areas as Boston, Philadelphia, New York, Norfolk, Baltimore, Mobile, and New Orleans. They were attracted to the merchant service by high wages and a bonus for serving in a war zone. American liberty ports were prized by all merchant sailors, with New York City being the best place for a three-day liberty.

Weather was not just the enemy of the convoys. Submarines could do nothing on the surface during the heavy storms and would have to go deep to avoid the waves and strong wave action. Underwater attacks were impossible even if enemy ships were sighted. The survival of the ship and submarine became the prime considerations during such times. For the convoy, it became one more day closer to their destination and safety; for the U-boats, it was one day less to attack and destroy the merchant convoy.

No chapter on the Merchant Marine of WW II would be complete without a report on the March 1943 convoy battle in the North Atlantic. Three Allied convoys sailed from New York bound for England. Admiral Donitz sent 42 U-boats to trap the convoys. In the ensuing battle, 21 merchant ships were sunk in what the Germans called "The greatest convoy battle of all time."[23]

Convoy SC.122 (SC indicates slow convoy), with 50 merchant ships, left New York on March 5, escorted by four escorts. Ships in the convoy were destined for Iceland, Scotland, Belfast, and Bristol. By late afternoon when the weather turned rough, the ships had formed into eleven columns and began their trip at an average speed of 6.94 knots.

As the weather deteriorated, squalls of heavy rain and wind reached gale force, and ships began to lose their place in formation. A Canadian officer on one of the open bridges reported that, "It was sheer unmitigated hell."[24] It was impossible to move anywhere about the ship. The mess decks were a shambles. "But, we were young and tough, and in a sense, we gloried in our misery and made light of it all."[25]

The following day, as escorts rounded up the stragglers, 11 ships were missing. This was nothing out of the ordinary. No ships had sunk. Two ships returned to New York, six went to Halifax, and two trailed the convoy. The other ship, the British cargo vessel, *Clarissa Radcliffe* remained a mystery for much of the voyage.

Three days after SC.122 left New York, HX. 229 with 40 ships, and one day later, HX.229A with 27 ships left the same harbor with plans to join SC.122 at the midway point of the 3,000-mile crossing. The two convoys were escorted by Canadian, British and American armed escorts. Both convoys entered heavy fog and snow shortly after departing. HX.229A was in fog for two and a half days and lost 19 ships in its convoy. All but three were able to rejoin the convoy when the weather cleared.

The first few days and nights were routine, and when weather permitted, off-duty hours were spent playing cards or sleeping. British sailors enjoyed their rum ration. Most of the escorts were Canadian and manned by reservists with little experience. One evening a signalman yelled at his lieutenant, "Ship in trouble astern." The lieutenant observed one of the rear ships silhouetted against a bright glow. Thinking the ship to be on fire, he called the

13

chart room to have his discovery verified. "Damn it, haven't you ever seen the moon come up before?" was the salty navigator's response.[26]

On March 9, 13 merchant ships and one rescue vessel from Halifax with three escorts joined SC.122. Two of the convoy's original escorts departed with two merchant ships for Halifax, so that the convoy now consisted of 51 ships and five escorts. Other departures and arrivals occurred at St. John's, Newfoundland, so that the composition of the three convoys on March 14 was SC.122 with 50 ships and 10 escorts/rescue ships; HX.229 with 38 ships and five escorts; and HX.229A with 37 ships and 6 escorts. This is a total of 146 ships carrying 860,000 tons of cargo and 1,000 passengers. The ships were manned by more than 900 merchant seamen.

The first non-battle casualty was HMS *Campobello*, a 545-ton trawler from SC. 122. Campobello was receiving more sea water in her hull than she could pump out. Soon her boilers flooded and the commander gave the order to abandon ship. The Belgian corvette, *Godetia,* rescued the crew.

The convoy passed through a severe storm on March 13 and 14. Forty-foot waves destroyed many life boats and all loose gear was swept overboard. The storm passed on the 15th, and the following day *U-653* sighted and reported the location of HX.229.

Convoy headquarters became aware of a large U-boat patrol line across their projected path on March 14 and routed HX.229A well to the north of the patrol line, and the other two convoys due east to miss the patrols. HX.229A was passing Newfoundland on the 15th, with no U-boat contact. SC.122 and HX.229 followed an easterly course with HX.229 closing the distance between the two convoys. The Germans were able to intercept and decode the course changes and were busy establishing a U-boat patrol line across the convoy's new projected path.

The Admiralty in England intercepted the U-boat message and plotted the locations of the U-boats and the convoys. They messaged the convoys to take direct routes to England and to fight their way through the U-boat line. The total distance between the 42 U-boats awaiting the convoys was 42 nautical miles. This was close enough to permit the smoke of the convoy to be seen by at least two U-boats.

U-653 sailed into the middle of the convoy on the 16th and continued to report its location, speed and direction to U-boat headquarters. Eighteen U-boats were directed to proceed immediately to intercept the convoy and to attack that night. The gap in the patrol created by the departure of the 18 U-boats was filled by new boats within 24 hours.

Full darkness came at 10:00 P.M. The sea was still rough, but a full moon permitted visibility to ten miles. The U603 commander guided his boat on the surface through a huge gap in the convoy and was not spotted by convoy lookouts or the escort's radar. U-603 fired four torpedoes at two American ships but missed. Instead, one torpedo struck the *Elin K*, a modern Norwegian ship carrying 7,000 tons of wheat and manganese, and 339 bags of mail. The *Elin K*, with 40 men onboard, started to sink immediately, and the order to abandon ship was promptly given. The last ship in the convoy, the Dutch cargo ship *Terkoelei*, was tasked to pick up survivors, but she sailed by without stopping. Fortunately, a corvette sighted the survivors and rescued the Norwegians.

A short time later, U-758 fired four torpedoes at the convoy. The Dutch cargo ship *Zaaland*, loaded with fuel, sank immediately, but the crew was able to abandon ship. The American Liberty ship *James Oglethorpe* lost its steering but continued to steam in huge circles at the end of the convoy. The captain did not order abandon ship, believing that he could save it. Ninety of the crew had other ideas, however and dove overboard. Thirteen of them drowned trying to reach the lifeboats. The ship's captain, was left with 31 men to put out the fires, keep the engines running, and plug the hole. Once again, *Terkoelei* steamed past the survivors in the water without stopping. *Zaaland's* survivors were rescued by the *Godetia*.

The captain and 31-man crew repaired *Oglethorpe's* steering and headed for St. John's, Newfoundland, but were never heard from again. Perhaps the ship was damaged more than suspected and sank quickly without time to send a SOS message. None of the U-boats reported sinking this ship. Shortly thereafter, *U-435* fired two torpedoes into the convoy and scored two hits on the American Liberty ship *William Eustis*, a cargo ship of 7,169 tons. The entire crew of the ship was able to get away in four lifeboats, but once again, the last ship in the convoy failed to stop to pick up the survivors. This meant that the convoy commander in the lead escort vessel, *Volunteer*, had to leave his escort position and return to rescue the survivors. As a result, there remained only one escort for the convoy since the corvette was making depth charge attacks on the U-boat *U-89*.

Three hours after the U-boat attacks began, three U-boats had made attacks on the convoy, torpedoing four merchant ships and forcing all the convoy escorts to be away from their escort duties picking up survivors or attacking submerged U-boats.

Shortly after midnight, two torpedoes fired by *U-91*, struck the American freighter *Harry Luckenbach*. The old freighter went down in four minutes. Three full lifeboats of survivors were seen by four separate convoy ships but none stopped to pick up the survivors. None of the *Luckenbach* survivors were ever seen again.

U-600 attacked the convoy next, hitting three ships, the American freighter *Irenee du Pont*, the British refrigerator ship *Nariva,* and the 30-year old, 12,156-ton British tanker, *Southern Princess*. The crew of the *Irenee Du pont* panicked and jumped into the ocean without waiting for the lifeboats to be lowered. They left codebooks and 17 diplomatic pouches on board. *Nariva* remained floating, and the commander kept his boats nearby in order to reboard the ship if it was still floating in the morning. *Southern Princess* was carrying 10,000 tons of fuel oil which ignited and formed a towering inferno visible for 30 miles at sea. Of the 100 men aboard, 96 got away safely. The last ship in the convoy, *Tekoa* stopped to pick up the *Irenee du Pont* survivors, and one of the escort vessels picked up the others.

The morning of March 17, found the HX.229 convoy missing eight merchant ships and 11 U-boats in contact. SC.122 with 44 ships and three escorts was 110 miles ahead of HX.229 on the same course with *U-666* and *358* reporting their every movement to U-Boat Headquarters. Twenty miles behind SC.122, the U-boat *U-439* discovered the merchant ship, *Fort Cedar Lake* burning and sinking. The ship had been torpedoed the previous evening and was still afloat. As *U-439* examined the ship, prior to firing another torpedo, it was surprised by a Liberator aircraft from Aldergrove, England. *U-439* crash dived and avoided the depth charge attack. The Liberator departed England more than eight hours earlier and was still able to remain on station for an hour. During the hour, the Liberator attacked and depth-charged U-boat's *U-338* and *U-666*. The Liberator returned to Londonderry, England after 18 hours and 20 minutes of flight time.

From top to bottom: A British Liberator bomber, a B-17 Flying Fortress, and a Sunderland Flying Boat.

U.S. Navy and Imperial War Museum

One hour after the liberator departed, *U-338*, in broad daylight, put a torpedo into the hull of the old Panamanian steamer *Glanville*, which was loaded with military stores for Iceland and 500 bags of mail for American forces in Iceland. The corvette *Lavender* rescued 31 of the 43 men aboard. Twenty-seven depth charges were dropped by two escort vessels without damage to U-338.

About this time, another long-range Liberator arrived and surprised the *U-305* on the surface. *U-305* dove but suffered minor damage from the bombing. The Liberator circled the convoy for two hours and prevented any further U-boat attacks on the convoy.

At 10:30 A.M., *U-384* torpedoed the Dutch ship *Terkoelei*. She was an East India ship, manned by a mixed crew of Dutchmen, Lascars (Indian seamen), and British gunners. Many of the Lascars were stunned by the event and refused to row their lifeboat. Two such lifeboats capsized and 38 of the Lascars died in the frigid water. At the same time, *U-631* torpedoed merchant ship, *Coracero*. The ship did not sink immediately, and all but five of her crew escaped and were rescued by escort vessels. Some of the rescued seamen later died from exposure.

Later in the day, another Liberator aircraft from England arrived and flew patrol around the convoy for two hours. Shortly before dark, (5:05 P.M.), the aircraft spotted three U-boats on the surface in front of the convoy. The first attack damaged *U-221*. *U-608* stayed on the surface and engaged the Liberator with its machine gun. The Liberator dropped a depth charge alongside the *U-608*, and damaged it. The third U-boat survived because the Liberator was out of depth charges. It sprayed the U-boat with machine gun fire and dropped some harmless marker flares to scare the boat. One such flare was a direct hit. Before the Liberator departed, it sent a message to the convoy stating, "Six Hearses in Sight Bearing 180 Degrees Twenty Five Miles."[27]

Hearses was the code name for submarines, so the message caused great concern to the escort commander. The Liberator was leaving, darkness was fast approaching, and six U-boats were in attack range of the convoy. At this time, SC.122 passed the halfway point in its journey and HX.229 was ninety miles behind. The men in both convoys and the U-boats prepared for the second night of battle.

U-305 claimed the first hits on ships of SC.122. They were the 8,789-ton refrigerated ship *Port Auckland* with 8,000 tons of cargo and 129 bags of mail, and the smaller cargo ship *Zouave*, with 7,000 tons of iron filings. Both were British ships. *Zouave* sank immediately, but most of her crew escaped. *Port Auckland* remained afloat for some time, but lost 21 of her crew. This was the only attack on SC.122 during the evening.

HX.229, now 80 miles behind SC.122, had only three destroyers to escort the convoy. Thanks to bad weather and high seas, and the fine work of the Liberator aircraft during the day, the 30 U-boats had dispersed and no attacks occurred during the night. Liberators arrived again in the morning, spotted and attacked four U-boats with no noticeable damage, and spent 10 hours providing cover for the convoy.

During early evening, one of the escorts made radar contact with a U-boat (*U-642*), and scored several hits with her 4-inch gun before the submarine dove. After two depth charge attacks, the destroyer was rewarded by an oil slick on the surface. At the very least, the U-boat was put out of action for the forthcoming night.

The captain of *U-221* positioned the boat in front of the convoy and torpedoed the *Canadian Star*, a refrigerator ship with 24 civilian passengers, and the liberty ship *Walter Q. Gresham*, loaded with 9,000 tons of sugar and powdered milk. Thirty of the 87 passengers and crew of *Canadian Star* perished after abandoning ship. *Gresham* lost 27 of 69 crewmembers.

Later in the day, HMS *Highlander* joined the convoy and her captain took command of convoy HX.229. At this time only 70 miles separated the two convoys. The weather began to moderate, making easier attacks for the 24 U-boats still in contact. To date, 19 merchant ships had been sunk, 12 from HX.229, and seven from SC.122. Five U-boats had been damaged, none sunk.

During the evening of March 18, *U-666* fired four torpedoes at ships in SC.122 but had no hits. *U-441* fired five torpedoes and scored no hits. U-606 fired three torpedoes at HMS *Highlander*, one of the escorts, but they also missed. Finally, *U-666* torpedoed the old Greek cargo ship *Carras*. All 34 crewmembers of *Carras* were rescued by the rescue ship *Zamalek*, which had ample beverages on board to toast their rescue.

The morning of March 19 brought calm seas and good visibility, interspersed with showers and sleet. B-17s arrived to escort the convoys and morale improved noticeably. The convoys were now only four days from England. SC.122 received the U.S. Coast Guard cutter *Ingram* to assist in escort duties, and USS *Babbitt*, an old American destroyer joined HX.229. *Babbitt* immediately attacked *U-190* and seriously damaged the submarine.

The battle continued on March 19. Shortly after daylight, *U-527* torpedoed the freighter *Mathew Luckenbach*. *Luckenbach*'s captain had become disenchanted with the nine-knot progress of the convoy and decided to steam ahead at 15 knots. It was a bad decision. On the morning of the 19th, *Luckenbach* was 40 miles ahead of the convoy when it was hit by two torpedoes. The crew made it into the lifeboats but were without a convoy, escorts, or rescue ships. Fortunately, *Luckenbach*'s course took them close to SC.122 and the American Coast Guard cutter *Ingham*. Together with destroyer USS *Upshur* as an escort, *Ingham* was able to rescue all survivors.

Luckenbach stayed afloat and consideration was given to boarding her and trying to get her underway. In the meantime, no less than five U-boats were positioning themselves to sink the ship.

On the same morning, a B-17 surprised a surfaced U-boat astern of HX.229. The aircraft dropped four depth charges and sank *U-384*. Another B-17 damaged *U-666* so severely that it was forced to disengage from the battle. Two other U-boats were found and attacked by aircraft, forcing the U-boats to discontinue their attack on the convoy. Later in the day, Liberators relieved the B-17s, and the escort ship *Abelia*, having traveled 1,000 miles from St. John's, joined HX.229.

Fifteen U-boats were still in contact with the convoys on the evening of March 19, but much of the fight had gone out of them. Many had mechanical problems due to the depth charging and the crews were exhausted. The additional escorts also made the U-boat's job more difficult. HX.229 now had eight escorts in its screen. SC.122 enjoyed the luxury of night-time air cover for two-and-a-half hours after sunset. Perhaps this explains why the U-boats did not pursue the convoy as aggressively as they had previously. *U-642* was tracking SC.122 while *U-631* was following and reporting the position of HX.229.

At dawn on March 20, Coastal Command arrived in force with aircraft and escort vessels. All U-boats were ordered to return along the path of the convoys and destroy any crippled ships they found. Not all the U-boats retreated fast enough. U-527 and U-598 were found on the surface by one of the Liberator aircraft and depth charged, damaging both boats. A Sunderland flying boat also bombed and damaged U-631. The final battle of this convoy took place well behind the convoys when a Sunderland surprised U-631, trying to make its escape.

The conning tower of the U-boat had jammed and the submarine was forced to remain on the surface and fight it out with the attacking aircraft. The Sunderland strafed and depth-charged U-631, which was able to repair the jam, dive and then pump out tons of sea water that entered through the conning tower. Although the U-boat survived, it was in no shape for aggressive action.

HX.229A enjoyed a crossing free of U-boat attacks but suffered damage and loss of ships due to their extreme northern route. For three days the convoy plowed through blizzards, fog, and icebergs, a hazard almost as frightening as the U-boats. Convoy formation was lost as the escorts tried to illuminate the icebergs with their searchlights. Two escort ships were damaged early and five of the merchant ships had to turn back to St. Johns.

Early on March 19, *Svend Foyn*, a 14,795-ton freighter with 195 men aboard was leading the convoy and hit an iceberg. The ship was badly holed and had to secure her engines. The ship remained afloat, but there was no tug available so a rescue ship, the sloop HMS Hastings was detached to save the crew. There was no light from the disabled ship as two more rescue ships arrived to take survivors aboard. Much to everyone's surprise, the Captain of *Svend Foyn* refused to let any of his crew or passengers leave the ship. His final signal was that, "Impossible to do anything until morning."[28]

The wind came up during the night and *Svend Foyn* sank, quickly and quietly. It was difficult for the escort ships to rescue survivors in the dark and among the icebergs, but 128 were saved. Had they been rescued during daylight, it is likely that all would have survived, including the captain, who perished.

Destroyer *Mansfield*, the first HX.229 convoy ship to reach Londonderry, England, logged a trip of 18 days, 10 hours, and 10 minutes after weighing anchor in New York on March 8. The two convoys, SC.122 and HX.229 lost 22 ships of 146,596 tons with 161,000 tons of cargo. U-boats required 90 torpedoes to sink the 22 ships. The lost ships carried 1,494 crew and passengers, of which 1,122 were rescued (75 percent). Germany lost one submarine, U-384, and 47 crewmen. The convoy expended 378 depth charges, although they also damaged a large number of U-boats.

The story of convoys SC.122, HX.229 and HX.229A, as exciting as they are, could be the story of hundreds of other convoys that plied the North Atlantic during this period. The Allies owe these merchant seamen and their military escorts their sincere gratitude.

During May 1943, Admiral Donitz lost 41 U-boats in exchange for 50 merchant ships sunk. As the direct result of these unsustainable losses, he was forced to withdraw his boats from the North Atlantic. By summer 1943, American shipyards launched more tonnage than the U-boats were able to sink. Thereafter, the survival of Britain and the merchant navy was never in doubt. New escort vessels, including the carrier USS *Bogue*, fast destroyers and destroyer escorts were added to the fleet as well as long-range patrol and attack aircraft.

Escort aircraft flew from the coasts of both countries and Newfoundland, creating a sense of security for the merchant navy and destroying Admiral Donitz's U-boat command. Hitler was unwilling or unable to construct submarines to meet the numbers of those destroyed, and experienced submariners were nearly all lost or disabled.

It is now clear, that the sailors engaged in convoy warfare were impacted far more than suspected by the code-breaking analysts of both sides. U-boats and convoy positions were rapidly plotted on operational charts within hours of intercepting enemy communications. Locations of U-boat supply ships and patrol lines were updated frequently as were the location, speed, and headings of convoys even as they left their outbound harbor.

Following the war, Admiral Donitz was tried and convicted as a war criminal on the rather vague charge of "waging aggressive war, and crimes against peace."[29] He was sentenced to ten years in prison and served his entire sentence. He left imprisonment as a well-adapted man, friendly, cheerful, and approachable.

Merchant shipping in the Pacific was vastly different than the Atlantic due to moderate weather, distances between ports, and fewer ports at which to unload cargo. Distances between ports were usually twice those in the Atlantic. With so few ports available to the Allies, amphibious craft were often used to move the material from the merchant ship to land, doubling normal off-loading time.

The merchant marine supported every amphibious operation in the Pacific after the Battle for Guadalcanal. More merchant seamen lost their lives at Mindoro than did members of the armed forces in the D-Day invasion of Europe.[30] Kamikazes took a heavy toll of merchant ships and men at Leyte Gulf and Tacloban anchorage in the Philippines and Okinawa.

Because distances were long, and port facilities few and far away, merchant ships in the Pacific often ran short of food. Glen Trible, a seaman from Kansas, made five trips in merchant ships; the first three were aboard SS *Cape Constance*, an ammunition ship home ported at San Francisco. On one such trip, the ship hauled ammunition to Espiritu Santo, Guadalcanal, Bougainville, New Caledonia, and Tulagi.

They returned to San Francisco for another load of bombs, and then to Finschhafen in Milne Bay, Hollandia, New Guinea, Tacloban, Port Moresby and back to San Francisco. Thanksgiving dinner consisted of canned stew, beets, dehydrated potatoes, and apple pie. From then until they reached Hollandia on December 22, three meals per day consisted of Australian chile with mutton.[31]

During the time SS *Cape Constance* was at anchor in Leyte Gulf and Tacloban, the ship underwent more than 300 air raid alerts and 114 actual attacks by Japanese aircraft and kamikazes. The ship suffered two kamikaze near-misses and one crash. Damage to the ship's propeller shaft required a diversion to Pearl Harbor for repairs.

Trimble's fourth trip was to Okinawa aboard a new liberty ship, SS *Grinnell Victory*. Kamikaze attacks were greater than at Tacloban, but the ship spent less time at Okinawa and had one near miss bomb hit (300 feet away), and one close call with a kamikaze (60 feet away).

Trimble's last ship was SS *Joplin Victory*, another ammunition ship. The ship departed San Francisco on August 12 to support the Allied invasion of the Japanese mainland. Following Japan's surrender, the ship waited at the anchorage in Ulithi harbor in the Caroline Islands until November, and then unloaded its cargo at Saipan.

Cruelty and atrocities between enemies were commonplace in the Pacific. In the Atlantic, it was not unusual for a German submarine captain to surface and offer some assistance and directions to crewmembers that survived the sinking of their merchant ship. Not so in the Pacific. The Imperial Navy order to the commander of Japanese submarines stated: "Do not stop with the sinking of enemy ships and cargoes. At the same time you will carry out the complete destruction of the crew of the enemy's ships."[32] For a graphic description of Japanese atrocities against merchant seamen in the Pacific, read Hagen's chapter "Lord James Blears."[33]

The Tower Hill Memorial, London. Commemorated here are 37,701 British merchant seamen lost at sea during both World Wars.

Commonwealth War Graves Commission

The American Memorial, Cambridge, England. The names of 1,371 U.S. Navy men and 201 U.S. Coast Guard men lost in the Battle of the Atlantic are inscribed on the memorial wall on the right.

American Battle Monument Commission

Movement of people of Japanese descent involved all kinds of transportation.

National Archives

2

INTERNMENT OF JAPANESE-AMERICANS DURING WW II

This chapter was written in the spring of 2004, at perhaps the height of contention concerning The Patriot Act, and the resulting abridgement of individual liberties enjoyed under the American constitution. Many of us support our government's belief that curtailment or suspension of certain rights is a necessary evil to defeat terrorism. Others are not so sure. Sixty years ago, the United States and Canada faced another challenge to our constitution and individual liberties. Few Americans or Canadians under the age of 70 remember the tragic events associated with the evacuation and internment of Japanese-Americans/Canadians in 1941. It seems appropriate to recall these events and apply them to our present situation.

According to the 1940 census, there were 126,000 Japanese-Americans living in the United States mainland, 67% of these were American citizens by birth. California was home to 93,000 Japanese-Americans, while 19,000 lived in Oregon and Washington. Another 157,000 Japanese-Americans (one-third of the Hawaii population) were living in Hawaii.

During the opening months of World War II, the United States government imprisoned almost 120,000 Japanese-Americans. The action was deemed necessary because the government believed that Americans of Japanese ancestry might commit acts of treason against the United States. Japanese-Americans were apprehended and processed at assembly centers in the western states, and then moved to internment camps throughout the mainland. The U.S. government spent $80 million to intern Japanese-Americans during WW II, although not a single case of espionage or sabotage was ever knowingly committed by Japanese-Americans.

Most Japanese-Americans were forced to sell their homes, businesses and property at great financial loss and leave their friends, schools, and jobs for an indefinite period. Unlike the mainland, there was no mass internment of Japanese-Americans in Hawaii because they were needed to work the sugar and pineapple plantations. Less than 1,800 Japanese-Americans from Hawaii were sent to mainland internment camps.

FBI agent searches the belongings of a Japanese American family in December, 1941.

National Archives

Initially, Hawaii internees thought to be security risks were processed at Sand Island and Honouliuli on Oahu, and the Kilauea Military Camp on the Island of Hawaii. Those determined to be security risks were later transferred with their families to mainland internment camps.

Detention of Japanese-Americans was swift. FBI agents began rounding them up the day after the attack on Pearl Harbor. They were questioned and initially held at hastily constructed assembly centers where they were "detained" for months, until shipped under Justice Department orders to internment camps in New Mexico, North Dakota, Texas, and Montana. Subsequent detainees would be sent to War Department internment camps which were constructed in the western states.

All Japanese branch banks were closed, and the U.S. Treasury froze all bank accounts of anyone born in Japan. All Americans of Japanese Ancestry (AJA) and Japanese nationals were required to carry special identification and a mandatory curfew was imposed on them. Cameras, weapons, and radio transmitters were seized to prevent espionage.

It was February 19, 1942, ten weeks after the attack on Pearl Harbor, before President Roosevelt signed Executive Order 9066.[1] The order excluded all persons of Japanese descent from specified areas of Arizona, California, Oregon and Washington. The areas included airports, dams, power plants, railroads, shipyards, and military installations.

In all, there were 16 assembly centers and ten internment camps located in eight states. The name and location of these camps are at the end of this chapter. The Japanese words, Issei, Nisei, Sansei, Yonsei, and Kibei are used in this chapter. Issei means first generation. An Issei emigrated from Japan to the United States or Hawaii to find work. Nisei means second generation. These are the sons or daughters of the Issei. Since they were born in the United States, they were United States citizens. Sansei or third-generation Japanese-Americans were born during or after WW II. Yonsei are fourth-generation Japanese-Americans. The Kibei are Japanese-Americans born in the United States, but educated to some degree in Japan.

Newspapers in California's Bay Area broke the news February 27, 1942.

National Archives

Horse stalls at San Bruno, California's Tanforan racetrack were converted into living quarters for Japanese-Americans.

Tanforan

The Tanforan assembly center near San Bruno, California, was one of the earlier camps used to house the Japanese-Americans. Yoshiko Uchida, her older sister, and Issei mother, were interred at Tanforan while their father, designated a dangerous enemy alien, was sent to a Justice Department camp in Missoula, Montana.

FBI agents came to each AJA house searching for anything that might qualify as contraband or illegal activity. Sometimes a model airplane might qualify as an excuse to arrest the man of the house. After all, why was he studying American aircraft? Perhaps to provide aircraft plans to the Japanese government. He would be hauled away with no word to the family as to what would become of their husband and father. The next day, the rest of the family were told to prepare to move to a processing center within a few days.

The women, left without a man to help them, were easy prey for the junk dealers that flooded the Japanese sections of the cities. New or nearly new household appliances and electronic equipment sold for a few dollars. At first, the women would refuse such offers, but as their deadline to leave approached, they were forced to accept whatever offer they received. They would pack as much as they could into bundles formed from sheets, blankets, backpacks, and suitcases and wait for the truck that was to move them to the processing center. There was scarcely any time to tell friends or relatives where they were going and no one knew how long they would be gone.

The Uchida family was taken to a central collection point and then transferred to a caravan of trucks and busses that took several hundred Japanese to Tanforan. When they arrived they were processed and assigned to Barracks 16, apartment number 40. Some friends that arrived at Tanforan earlier helped them trudge through the mud to find Barracks 16.

Everywhere there were black tar-papered barracks that had been quickly erected to house 8,000 Japanese but there seemed to be no Barracks 16. Finally someone spotted a sign that proclaimed a long row of horse stalls as Barracks 16. Each stall was numbered, and after a search, they found number 40.

The horse stall was ten by 20 feet and empty except for three army cots lying on the floor. A single light bulb hung from the ceiling. Dust and dirt covered everything and the stalls reeked of horse manure and urine. Lye had been thrown on the floor but it could not hide the stench. Earnest Uno, a fellow AJA, described the situation as degrading.[2] A broom was borrowed from neighbors, the floor swept, and some mattress covers and straw obtained for bedding. As they finished sweeping the stall, it was time for the evening meal.

The way to the mess hall, which was under the grandstand of the racetrack, was along the muddy race track. A cold piercing wind was blowing in from the bay. When the trio got to the grandstand they found six long lines of internees waiting to get into the mess hall. The line moved very slowly. Yoshiko felt degraded, humiliated, and longed for their home they had been forced to leave. Why were they being treated like this? After all, they were American citizens and had done no wrong. Yoshiko felt even worse when she saw the sadness on her mother's face.

When they reached the serving area of the mess hall, they held out the plates they had borrowed from neighbors and were rewarded with two canned sausages, served by the fingers of the attendant, a boiled potato, and a slice of unbuttered bread. They found a place at a large wooden picnic table and tried to eat but could not. Let's get out of here, Yoshiko's sister suggested. They agreed that it would be better to go back to the stable than stay in the depressing mess hall.

They had just returned to their stall when a truck stopped outside and a voice said, "Hey Uchida, apartment 40."[3] Their baggage had arrived. As the bundles were moved into their stall, Yoshiko and her sister began to untie the knots and pull the familiar objects from the bundles. As soon as the tea kettle was unpacked, Yoshiko ran to the washroom, filled it with water and brought it back to heat on the hot plate they had just received. Their mattresses were unpacked and put on the army bunks, and they sat near the hotplate to keep warm while their tea boiled. Now they felt much better and sat up most of the night talking about the future and worrying about their father.

The next day they explored the camp and found there were 25 stalls facing north and 25 stalls facing south. One hundred feet from the stables were two latrines and two washrooms. The latrines were crude wooden devices with eight one-holers separated by partitions but no doors. The washrooms consisted of two sections. The front section had a long trough with spigots of hot and cold water for washing and brushing of teeth. There were eight showers in the rear, separated by partitions but no doors or curtains. As one might expect, the showers were difficult to adjust and one was often scalded by extremely hot water or shocked by an icy blast of cold water.

Toilet paper was a premium. As soon as new rolls were placed in the latrines they would disappear. One learned to "make-do." Across from the latrines was a double barracks, one contained laundry tubs and the other had clotheslines and ironing boards. It became common practice to get up at 4:00 A.M. to do laundry and get it on the clothes lines to dry before long lines formed.

The Uchidas went to the main mess hall for their meals for four months. They never had a meal they liked. Then, they learned that smaller mess halls had opened in several parts of the camp. They were excited because they thought the smaller facilities would have better food. They eagerly went to the new mess hall in their area only to find a menu of chile con carne, a soggy ear of corn, and bread without butter. Disappointed, they went to the old mess hall expecting to find the same food, but, they found small lettuce salads and the first fresh vegetables they had seen for a long time. The food gradually improved, and by the time left they left Tanforan, fried chicken and ice cream were served at least once on a Sunday afternoon.

Five months after the Uchidas arrived at Tanforan, their father was sent there to join them. The family was elated and all the neighbors came to welcome Mr. Uchida to Tanforan. Now four cots took the space formerly occupied by one race horse, but no one complained. They were together as a family. Their father told them about life in Missoula, Montana, with temperatures that dropped to 30 degrees below zero and how the "men only" group of "dangerous enemy aliens" organized themselves and got by from day to day. Later, the Uchida family was moved to the internment camp at Topaz, Utah, where they spent the remainder of the war.

Chiura Obata and his family were in a different situation than the Uchida family. Chiura was an assistant professor at the University of California Berkeley campus, He was economically secure, with many friends and colleagues. The Obatas owned a nice home with a beautiful Japanese garden, and their two children were actively involved in the Berkeley community.

As 1940 approached, Berkeley was home to more than 300 Japanese families and 70 businesses. Although Japan was making aggressive moves in the Pacific, Berkeley seemed a safe place to live with excellent educational opportunities for the children. During early fall of 1941, the President of UC Berkeley invited Obata and other faculty members to a meeting in his office to discuss a confidential government plan to "evacuate" Americans of Japanese ancestry (AJA) from certain designated areas in California. The meeting was scheduled for 30 minutes, but lasted for two hours. Obata argued long and loud about the illegality of "evacuating" anyone that is obeying the law and earning an honest living.

Following Roosevelt's signing of Executive order 9066, a curfew and five-mile travel limit was placed on all Japanese in the California "exclusion" zone. Chiura, now age 57, and his wife were registered and fingerprinted as enemy aliens. By mid-March, the mass evacuation of AJA from California began, and on April 20, orders were received to evacuate the 1,300 AJA from Berkeley.

Chiura, a well-known and successful artist, sold many of his paintings at a loss, stored some paintings with friends, and gave some of their household appliances to friends. Chiura's prized paintings, on display at UC Berkeley, were stored at Berkeley for the duration of the war. Because their bank accounts had been frozen, Chiura borrowed money from friends, pulled a lot of strings, and was able to get his son on a train to St. Louis, Missouri to attend Washington University. Their daughter accompanied them to the detention center.[4]

The Obata's closed their house, packed one suitcase plus blankets, sheets and pillows, and were driven to the First Congregational Church for processing. Members of the church acted as host for the AJA, assisting them to make phone calls, write letters, find home for pets, and places to store possessions, including the cremated remains of family members, and the thousands of things that need to be done at the last minute. The church also provided rest areas and refreshments for the evacuees.

Buses arrived to take the evacuees to the Tanforan assembly center, which was only 20 miles from Berkeley. When they arrived at Tanforan, it was raining and everyone on the bus was sad and depressed. The Obata family was assigned a horse stall, the size of their dining room, as their apartment. There were two army cots on one side of the stall and another on the other side. Mrs. Obata cried until she had no more tears to cry.

After five days in the stable, the Obata family was moved to barracks-type quarters. They shared a 400-square foot room with five other people, a total of seven people in the room. Their food at the mess hall was lima beans, boiled potatoes, and bread without butter. Because of recent rains, the mud outside the stables was so deep and thick that it was very difficult to travel to the mess hall, toilet or wash room. Vehicles that tried to drive by the stables became stuck, and several trucks would have to come with cables to pull them back out.

Chiura refused to fall into the daily routine of depression and sorrow. He arranged for an art program affiliated with the University of California and began to recruit a faculty of college graduates to teach art in the camp. Sixteen instructors, many with master's degrees in art and architecture, put together a program of 23 courses. Generous donations from the American Friends Services Committee provided art supplies, and the art school opened. Once classes were underway, enrollment grew to 600 students.[5]

The Obatas stayed for five months at Tanforan and were then sent to an internment camp at Topaz, Utah. Their internment at Topaz is described in the section titled Topaz.

Chihura Obata, wife Haruko, daughter Lily, and son Gyo, in the living room of their home in Webster Groves, Mo., in 1944.

National Archives

Manzanar

Manzanar, California, was both an assembly center and War Department internment camp. It was located near the California-Nevada border at the 4,000-foot elevation level. Jeanne Wakatsuki Houston and her family were evacuated from southern California directly to Manzanar without adequate clothing for the cold temperatures and winds flowing down the back sides of the Sierras.

Jeanne recalls the "apartments" at Manzanar were in a small wooden building, with bare floors, blanket partitions, and a single light bulb hanging from a roof beam in each compartment. The ceilings were open allowing youngsters to climb along the rafters and look down on each of the families below.[6]

The War Department was in charge of the camp and issued WW I surplus clothing to those in need. Olive drab earmuffs, pea coats, canvas leggings, wool trousers, and caps soon adorned the internees. Of course, the clothing was several sizes too large for the internees, which resulted in flopping, dangling, and droopy clothes that no one seemed to mind since they kept them warm.

A dust storm sweeps through the Manzanar Relocation Center, in the shadow of the Sierras and Mount Whitney, the highest peak in California.

National Archives

A greater problem was the food. Many of the internees were continually sick with stomach cramps and diarrhea. Initially, many internees became sick from the shots given for typhoid and other illnesses, but then it was the food that made them sick. Food left out too long would spoil, refrigerators kept breaking down, and the cooks were novices. The "Manzanar trots" became a daily ritual and one simply hoped that there would be a space available at the latrine when you got there. Oftentimes the latrines were plugged up, with feces covering the floor and all toilet bowls erupting like small volcanoes. When this happened, the internees searched through the camp for a latrine that was working.

Elaine Yoneda was a white American, born in Connecticut, who married Karl Yoneda, a Japanese-American. They had a two-year old son, Tommy, when Karl was sent to Manzanar. Elaine insisted that she and Tommy would follow him and arrived at the camp on April 1, 1942, before it was ready for habitation.

The three of them were forced to share a 20-foot by 25-foot room with a 75-year old blind man and his 15-year old nephew. The room contained five army cots, five straw mattresses, and two thin army blankets each. There were no chairs, no partitions, no doors, and no toilet or washing facilities. There was one cold water spigot at the end of each barracks and six portable toilets for use by the construction crews. The water spigot stayed frozen until noon, when the sun heated it enough to thaw out. In the meantime, the internees were unable to wash or brush their teeth.

Conditions slowly improved. Toilets without partitions or doors became available and shower facilities with hot water were in place by April 18. Karl was appointed Block 4 Leader and received $16.00 per month for a 48-hour work week. Elaine worked as an assistant librarian for $12.00 per month.

Elaine's parents sent them some sheets for use on the cots and for curtains. In time, the straw mattresses were replaced by army quilts. During May, visitors were allowed, and with proper notification, could stay overnight.

On October 6, Karl left for Idaho to work in the sugar beet fields. He returned at the end on November and was inducted as a private in the U.S. Army. While undergoing training in Minnesota, Elaine and Tommy became victims of the "Manzanar Riot," and were moved from their "apartment" to more secure areas.[7] Then, on December 10, 1942, along with 67 others, were moved to an abandoned Civilian Conservation Corps (CCC) camp in Death Valley

Because Elaine was Caucasian, and Tommy had asthma and allergy problems, they were given permission to move back to San Francisco in the spring of 1943. They were able to visit Karl during Easter weekend, and remained in the area until Karl was released from military duty. Their 1952 "evacuation" claim for $1,355.00 was reduced to $460.00.[7] This was their total payment for their automobile, property, and private possessions that were seized when they were evacuated to Manzanar.

Manzanar was designated a national historic site in 1992.

Topaz, Utah

After several months at Tanforan, most San Francisco Bay area evacuees were sent to Topaz, an internment center in Utah.

Topaz, nicknamed "the jewel of the desert," was 140 miles south of Salt Lake City in an old lake bed near the desert. Summer temperatures reached 106 degrees while the mercury plummeted to 30 degrees below zero in the winter.

Topaz functioned from 1942 until October 1943 and had a peak population of 8,000 internees. Families were housed in small rooms, each having a single ceiling light, a coal stove, and a cot, one mattress, and two blankets per person. The barracks, showers, toilets, mess halls, and laundries were insufficient for the number of internees, and there was no such thing as privacy.

Chiura, Haruko, and Yuri Obata arrived at Topaz on September 24, 1942, with hundreds of other AJA from California. It was hot and dusty. When the wind blew, dust covered the entire camp, which was not yet completed. The barracks had no electricity, there were cots in their barracks, but no mattresses. The camp construction process had removed all vegetation leaving powdery alkaline dirt that caused the dust storms that engulfed the camp.

Despite the heat during the day, cold at night, and constant dust storms, Chiura began to establish an arts program at Topaz, similar to the one he left at Tanforan. By December 1942, 3,250 students were studying art, music, flower arranging, English and other courses.

The first winter was severe. Strong winds and freezing temperatures severely tested the internees, many of whom had never experienced outdoor toilets. The internees burned newspaper, wood, and coal in potbelly stoves to keep warm. The Obata's son, Gyo, was able to spend Christmas with the family at Topaz.

Gyo left, profoundly aware of the conditions under which his family was forced to survive. Chiura represented the internees when a Spanish consul, serving as mediator, came to the camp to hear grievances. Chiura asked only for better housing conditions.

During March, 230 internees from Hawaii arrived at the camp. Chiura was there to meet them. He learned that most of the Hawaii internees spent several months at the processing facility at Sand Island, across the harbor from Honolulu, before they were sent by ship and train to Topaz. As a group, they seemed willing to accept their fate. They dragged their only belongings in rice and flour sacks as they were led to their "apartments."

Early in 1943, the U.S. government demanded that each Japanese internee sign a loyalty oath. This was a tremendous problem for the Issei. The United States had refused them citizenship. If they signed the loyalty oath, they would lose their Japanese citizenship, without the offer of American citizenship. They would be people without a country.

The Kibei were quick to point out this problem to the Japanese and focus their anger against the United States. Many of the Kibei at Topaz refused to sign the loyalty oath, but Obata and his family had no problem doing so. They were Americans and their future was in America.

Late on the evening of April 4, 1942 Chiura stepped out of the shower room, planning to walk back to his barracks, when he was struck by a blow to the face by a blunt metal instrument.[8] He could only attribute the attack to someone that disagreed with his decision to stay in America and not return to Japan after the war. He was treated in a medical facility at Salt Lake City, and subsequently, he, his wife, and daughter were all released from the Topaz camp.

The Obata family then moved to St. Louis to be close to their son, and both Chiura and Haruko found work there. However, it was not home. In January 1945, when the military exclusion order was lifted, Obata wrote to the University of California asking for reinstatement. His request was approved and they arrived at Berkeley for the fall semester.

In 1965, Chiura received the prestigious Emperor's medal in Tokyo for his contributions in promoting understanding between Japan and the United States. Haruko received the medal in 1976. Chiura died in 1975 at age 90 and his wife Haruko died in 1989, at the age of 97.

As WW II neared an end, camps like Topaz were gradually closed. Internees were given $25.00, a $3.00 per day meal allowance, and train fare to their point of apprehension. When the internees arrived home, many found that their homes and possessions had been confiscated, stolen or destroyed.

Japanese-Americans work the beet fields at Tule Lake, California.

National Archives

Tule Lake

Camp Tule Lake, was a maximum security segregation camp for those Japanese who were considered disloyal to the U.S., and for those that chose repatriation to Japan. The term "disloyal' was applied to 12,000 Japanese that answered "No" to either question #27 or #28 of the loyalty questionnaire, or that refused to answer question #28. Question #27 concerned a person's willingness to serve in the armed forces of the U.S. Question #28 asked for unqualified allegiance to the U.S., and the foreswearing of allegiance to Japan. It was one of the most turbulent internment camps, with frequent protest demonstrations and work stoppages. Gangs of militant Japanese, organized groups such as the Black Dragon Society, and terrorized other internees.

The Tule Lake camp was a cold, dry, windswept lake bed near the California-Oregon border at the 4,000-foot elevation level The barbed wire was heavy wire mesh, the guard towers were manned with machine guns at all times, and the perimeter fence line was patrolled by tanks and armored jeeps. Half of the "dangerous" population of Tule Lake were children.

Camp facilities were similar to those of other internment camps except families had the luxury of two rooms. The internees watched movies most evenings and spent the days patching holes in their floors and walls. The comic characters, Superman (mild-mannered Clark Kent and Lois Lane) visited the camp during June through August 1943. Their daily adventures were reported in all newspapers that carried the comic strip. While at the camp, Superman used his x-ray vision to discoverer a plot wherein some Japanese prisoners were planning to kidnap Lois Lane and the military head of the camp. Superman made short work of the villains.[9]

Hawaii

Immediately after the Japanese attack on Pearl Harbor, Hawaii was placed under martial law. Only a small number of Japanese families (59) were collected, processed, and shipped to mainland internment centers. This was due to the lack of shipping to send families to the mainland, and because the Japanese were needed to work in the pineapple and sugar cane fields.

If you were one of the 59 families, however, numbers meant little. FBI agents had their lists prepared and collected the AJA individually. Shoichi Asami, age 47, answered a rap on his door at midnight on December 7, 1941, and found two FBI agents waiting for him. He was ordered to get dressed and come with them. He was told that he was an alien internee of war. When he asked about the welfare of his family, he was told, "Don't worry, everything will be all right."[10] Shoichi had reason to expect the call from the FBI. He was the managing editor of the Hawaii Times newspaper, a Japanese language newspaper with pro-Japanese editorials.

Shoichi was processed at Sand Island, and then moved to a camp on the mainland. Sixteen months later, Shoichi and his family were reunited at the Crystal City, Texas, internment camp. They spent six months in the camp and were then sent to New Jersey, where they were put aboard the ocean liner, Gripsholm for transportation to Japan. The trip took two months before arriving in Japanese-occupied Singapore. Mr. Asami made a decision to take his family ashore in Singapore where he processed newspaper dispatches. His two youngest children attended school there, but his 13-year old son was sent back to Japan to live with relatives and attend school there. His 18-year old daughter, Jane, was put

41

to work monitoring telephones, was inducted into the Japanese army.

During March 1945 the Japanese began evacuating Singapore. Shoichi, now 51, and his youngest son, Harold, age 11, were sent to Japan aboard the vessel, *Awa Maru*. The *Awa Maru* was torpedoed and sunk in the Formosa Straits by U.S. submarine *Queenfish*. There was only one survivor. Mrs. Asami, her daughter Jane, and, Morris, age 13, reached Japan on a separate vessel and were put to work in a division of the suicide corps that would defend Japan on the beaches if the Allies invaded Japan. When they were not working in an arsenal in Hikari, they spent their time in the hills searching for food. Their diet consisted of roots, nuts, wild greens, a few sweet potatoes, and once in a while, a small fish.

When the war ended, Jane translated for the U.S. Counter Intelligence Corps, earning 3,000 Yen per month (about U.S. $200.00). American servicemen also volunteered chocolate, meat, and canned goods for the family.

The Asami family, less Kinichi, Harold and Shoichi (died during the submarine attack), returned to Hawaii in 1947. Their home had been confiscated by the U.S. government, so they had to start life anew. Kinichi was not allowed to return to the U.S. because he served in the Japanese army. Jane died in 1981 and Mrs. Asami in 1984. Harold, and daughter, Alice, live in California and Kinichi lives in Tokyo.

Mrs. Haru Tanaka of Wahiawa, Hawai, was arrested at gunpoint on the afternoon of December 7, 1941. Four FBI men came to her house and made her accompany them with nothing more than the clothes she was wearing. Mrs. Tanaka was the principal of the Showa Japanese language school in Wahiawa, succeeding her husband in 1928, when he died.

Mrs. Tanaka and several other Japanese language teachers and Buddhist priests were kept at the immigration station in Honolulu and the Sand Island Processing center for two months before being evacuated to a girl's reformatory near Dallas, Texas. After a year, they were moved to the Crystal City, Texas, detention camp with a population of 3,500 AJA. While at Crystal City, Mrs. Tanaka received a letter from her son saying that he enlisted in the U.S. Army. Haru felt so helpless as she read the letter. She was enclosed by barbed wire and feared she would never see her son again. Her emotions alternated between anguish and despair for her son, to a deep sense of pride for his volunteering to serve his country.

Haru's daughter Muriel had been in Japan since 1939, studying at the Women's Art College. She was not able to come home when the war started, and was assigned to monitor English broadcasts during the war. Following the end of the war, she was employed by the U.S. Civil Information and Education Section of the occupation forces. She was reunited with her brother, Akira, in November, 1945. Akira returned to Hawaii in 1946 after being discharged from the U.S. Army. Muriel returned in 1947.

Mrs. Tanaka returned to Hawaii in January 1946. She found that her home had been confiscated by the government and was forced to begin the long upward climb to rebuild her life and restore her possessions. At age 74, she became the vice president of Wahiawa Japanese Language School, retiring in 1982, after 60 years of serving the Language School. In 1990, at age 97, she became one of the first to receive the $20,000 in reparations from the U.S. government for the illegal detention of AJA during WW II.[11]

During June 2000, a monument with the names of 800 Japanese-Americans who died fighting in WW II was dedicated in Washington, D.C. The National Japanese American Memorial also bears the names of the ten mainland detention camps where Japanese-Americans were interned during the war. The sculpture at the memorial is that of two cranes, fighting free of barbed wire atop a stony column. The sculpture was designed by Nina Akamu, who never knew her grandfather, a Japanese immigrant on Kauai who died in the Sand Island detention camp in Hawaii. Nina's vision of the sculpture sees the cranes as symbols of happiness and prosperity, breaking free of the barbed wire that surrounded the internees. The twin cranes grip the barbed wire in their beaks in an effort to free one wing pinned against the wire. The other wings are pressed together and raised toward the sky.[12]

During April 2002, 500 people traveled to the Manzanar National Historic Site, a former internment camp for Japanese-Americans. The visit and ceremonies marked the 60th anniversary of Executive Order Number 9066 which authorized the expulsion and internment of Japanese-Americans along the west coast and in Hawaii.[13]

The camp cemetery at Manzanar remains as a silent testiment to the relocation and internment of Japanese-Americans during World War II.

National Archives

3

INTERNMENT OF JAPANESE-CANADIANS
DURING WW II

By 1900, there were 4,700 Japanese in Canada, mostly in British Columbia (B.C.), and they dominated the fishing industry. By 1907, Japanese in B.C. numbered 10,000 and the B.C. government began to cut back on their fishing licenses. In response, the Japanese went up the Fraser Valley and into the Okanagan and cleared land to plant berries, fruit, and vegetables. A census in 1921 listed 15,006 Japanese in B.C., with 5,143 women.[1]

By 1931, the Japanese population numbered 24,205, and Canadian politicians were saying that the Japanese were forcing everyone else out of the agriculture industry. Regulations were put into effect limiting Japanese from clearing land for agriculture and restricting Japanese from the logging industry. At this time, there were 2,000,000 people in B.C. These Canadian citizens of Japanese ancestry (CJA) did not have the right to vote, and were barred from all government positions. They suffered bigotry much like the black Americans did in the south at that time. The issue came to a head on December 7, 1941.

Following the Japanese attack on Pearl Harbor, the White Canada Research Committee, a group of racists in Canada were able to say, I told you so, and have legislation enacted to ensure that the Japanese-Canadians were denied the rights of citizenship and interred for the rest of the war. Memos from as early as 1938 detail Canadian government plans for the detention of Japanese and CJA in B.C., and a 100-mile protected area along the coast.[2]

Two hours after Pearl Harbor was attacked, Mr. Suzuki from the Japanese Fisherman's Association in Vancouver was told to turn over all Japanese fishing vessels in the Fraser River to the authorities.[3] The fishing boats were how the Japanese made a living. They carried no radar, radio, echo sounder, nothing, just a small motor and a hold for the fish. Suddenly the Japanese were spies, and the boats were spy equipment.

Initially, the authorities gathered all the Japanese intellectuals and businessmen in the Vancouver area and outlying islands, confiscated their homes and most of their businesses. They were held in the Immigration Building in Vancouver, sent to a POW camp in Alberta, and finally to Petawawa and Angler in Ontario. During the gathering process, Japanese were required to wear an identification badge and obey a curfew from dusk until dawn. The last Japanese were moved out of the protected coastal area by early October 1942.

A decision was made to ship Japanese-Canadians between the ages of 18 and 45 to the wilds of northern Ontario to build roads. Men in this age group were thought to be the most likely to give assistance to any Japanese invasion of Canada. About a thousand CJA were given the opportunity to move to non strategic areas of B.C. so long as they did so at their own expense.

Movement of the family seemed like a good idea until you stopped to realize that there was nothing 100 miles east of the coastal protection area, only mountains. So, one had to move 400 miles east to find land to live on and try to make a living. Few made such a move. The wiser CJA began to sell their homes, possessions and businesses for whatever they could get, but most continued to function as best they could until they were forcibly moved to detention camps. Then they signed over their homes and possessions to the government Custodian of Enemy Alien Property for safekeeping.

The first collection area for about 22,000 of the CJA in Vancouver was Hastings Park, the exhibition grounds and racetrack east of the city. The men were separated from their families and all were guarded by armed soldiers. Conditions at Hastings were much like those at Manzanar in California. The internees were housed in horse stalls and cattle barns that smelled of cattle and horses. Hundreds of army cots, row upon row, filled the buildings. Everyone was issued two blankets and many of the women would hang blankets in the barns to make partitions affording a small degree of privacy.

There was a shortage of everything, toilets, toilet paper, mess halls, water, and heat. Dysentery became epidemic and diarrhea was common. Everyone had it. People were too weak or it was too dark to go to the uncovered toilets at night, so many defecated at the far end of their stall and then cleaned it up in the morning. The smell was terrible.

Food in the mess halls was adequate but hardly palatable for the Japanese taste. There were long lines for every meal. Almost every meal consisted of stew, potatoes, and bread, usually with butter. There was a store at Hastings where those with money could purchase candy or soft drinks, to supplement or replace the mess hall food.[4]

Internees watch for familar faces as trucks bring another group to Tashme in 1942.

UBC

By summer, people began leaving Hastings in large numbers for work camps in Sandon, Tashme, Kaslo, Kananaskis, New Denver, Jasper, Kamloops, and Roseberry. No one knew where these places were so it was impossible to prepare for the new destination. Only 24 hours notice was given to those about to depart, and they were only allowed to take what they could carry. Those who refused to go to a work camp were sent to prison in Ontario.

Perhaps the worst part of the Hastings experience was the uncertainty and despair. Families were torn apart, friends were lost, and there was no way to plan for the future. The internees simply waited day after day for their number to be called so they could be shipped off to some unknown place where they would likely not know anyone. The men were sent to work camps in the interior of Canada while most of the women and family members were sent to abandoned towns (ghost towns) in the interior.

On March 24, 1942, the Canadian Custodian of Enemy Alien Property was given authority to liquidate or otherwise dispose of such property.[5] Few Japanese were ever informed of this new law, and many served out the war in camps believing that their homes, businesses, and property were in the safe hands of the Custodian until they returned for them. Homes, business, boats, cars, and property were sold at auction for a few cents on the dollar. What did not sell was looted, stolen and destroyed. The equity many had worked 20 years for was gone, and they were left penniless.

The Ghost Towns

By late September 1942 some 2,000 men had been sent to work camps in the interior, and 3,400 Japanese families were working on farms in Alberta and Manitoba. A decision was made to evacuate 12,000 Japanese, mostly women and children, to renovated ghost towns in the interior of B.C. These towns had been mining towns at the turn of the century, but places such as Sandon, Kaslo, Greenwood, Slocan, Tashme, and New Denver, were economically destitute. The remaining residents of these towns asked for the Japanese to come, to live there, and to work there.

Road gangs like this one worked for 25 cents per hour, building roads with hand tools.

The ghost towns near Slocan Lake were not depicted on many of the maps at the time. Kaslo was reached by steam wheeler from Nelson up the river to Kootenay Lake. Slocan was just a tent city when the first Japanese arrived, as was New Denver. Both were located in the mountains with a view of Slocan Lake. Two Japanese doctors from New Denver served 2,500 Japanese in New Denver, Roseberry, Sandon, and Kaslo. Sandon, a ghost town when the Japanese arrived, returned to a ghost town after the CJA dispersed at the end of the war.

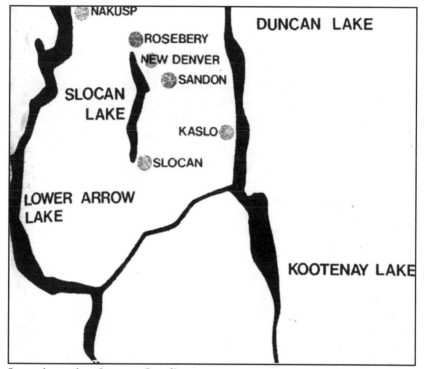

Some places where Japanese-Canadians were sent were not even on any maps.

JCCC

The Canadian government built 700 houses to accommodate the Japanese in these ghost towns and some kind of work was found for them. Many earned only 25 cents per hour for work on the railroads, sawmills and construction, but they were treated as Canadian citizens, without voting rights, by the people in the communities.

Greenwood, a ghost town 350 miles from Vancouver, provides an excellent example of how the system worked. Greenwood once had 6,000 people but by 1940 had a population of less than 250. Only two small stores were operating. The people of Greenwood saw the Japanese as saviors to their problems. Soon, 1,356 Japanese arrived in Greenwood.[5] Jobs were scarce and paid only 25 cents per hour. Most of the Japanese lived in the old hotel in rooms measuring 10 by 14-feet. A single coal stove on each floor was all there was for heat, and there was a single latrine on each floor. During the winter of 1942, the temperature dropped to as much as 39 degrees below zero and many of the Japanese suffered frozen fingers and toes.

Japanese doctors, dentists, educators, and other professionals soon arrived at Greenwood and the town began to show a new character. Starting work at the sawmill increased to 47 cents an hour and the new inhabitants began to build their own homes in and around Greenwood. A community association, including the Japanese, was formed and a library and swimming pool were constructed. Proper food was the one thing that eluded the Japanese at Greenwood. Instead of rice, fish, pickles, fresh green vegetables, and tea, the food consisted of beef steak, bologna, potatoes, and turnips. Why the stores did not bring in rice, fish and tea is still unknown. To make up for this lack of their ethnic food, the Japanese would play the food game. This game consisted of arranging Japanese dishes, including sake cups, and simulating a Japanese meal.

The Work Camps

The Angler camp in Ontario was a former German POW camp east of Thunder Bay. It is a bleak place with cold winters and swarms of mosquitoes in the summer. Angler was a prison, not a work camp. It housed 700 Issei and Nesei men, most of which had protested the way they were treated. The Japanese word is *gangari,* (a rebel). A few of the men accepted transfer to work camps in Ontario, but most refused to work and spent their time behind barbed wire in absolute boredom.

Yellowhead was a work camp near Jasper where men were sent to build and maintain roads. There was a little machinery so most of the work was done with shovels, pickaxes and Japanese diesels (wheelbarrows).

Solsqua, Taft, Yard Creek, and Three Valley were camps in B.C. that housed men working on the road that later became part of the Trans-Canada highway. The work consisted primarily of breaking trail for the road. This meant blasting rock with dynamite, moving rock with wheelbarrows, and felling trees. Bulldozers were used to build the road. Food was adequate in the camps, but everyone contracted diarrhea from food poisoning due to unsanitary kitchen conditions.

Princeton was a camp for 45 Japanese nationals. There was no machinery, so all work was done with picks, shovels, axes and other hand tools. The men moved rock, gravel, and cut down large trees.

The Schreiber camp in northern Ontario was home to 130 CJA. The camp was already prepared when the men arrived. The buildings were in good shape; army cots, toilets, washbasins, and a kitchen were ready for use. The men worked to cut a trail along the line surveyed for the Trans-Canada Highway. The men were paid for their work, had free run of the camp, and enjoyed access to the town of Schreiber for shopping. The winters were bitter cold and many of the men volunteered to move to south Ontario near Chatham in the spring, to work in the sugar beet and tomato fields.

Lemon Creek was another camp that was hidden in the mountains. Most Canadians did not know about the forced relocation of thousands of Japanese-Canadians.

JCCC

Family Farm Work

By fall 1942, there were 3,600 Japanese volunteers working in the sugar beet fields of Alberta and Manitoba. The number swelled to 3,500 in Alberta alone by 1945. The reason for this increase in volunteers was because the Canadian government needed workers to keep from losing the beet crop. The transient workers left the hard work of the beet fields and moved to the cities where they worked in war plants for considerably more money.

To save the beets, the government gave the Japanese the opportunity to take their families with them to work in the fields. This was the first opportunity for the families to be together since most of the women had been sent to the ghost towns while the men were sent to work camps along the Trans-Canada Highway trace.

It was not easy for the Japanese families in the beet fields. Their accommodations consisted of the thin shacks formerly used for summer transient workers and were not fit for habitation in the winter. The whole family worked in slave labor conditions. One family of nine was forced to live in an old railroad caboose on a farm. One end of the caboose was the bedroom for all nine, while the other end contained the coal stove, table and cupboard.

Another family of nine was forced to live in three granaries, each measuring about 12 by 14 feet. Two granaries were used as bedrooms, the third as a kitchen. High school education was not free for the Japanese. The family had to pay seven dollars per month per child for them to attend high school, so few of the beet picker's children went to school. There was no welfare, no unemployment, and no government assistance of any kind.

The Japanese faced open hostility in St. Pierre, Manitoba, Lethbridge, Diamond City, Picture Butte, Calgary, McGrath, and Edmonton, Alberta. The people in Edmonton, Calgary, and Lethbridge wrote letters to the Canadian government asking the government to keep the Japanese out of their cities. Yet, the Japanese families managed to survive.

The CJA found that they liked Alberta. They worked hard, were good citizens, and became part of the community. When, in 1945, they were offered repatriation to Japan, only nine Japanese-three Japanese nationals, three naturalized Canadians, and three Canadian born citizens-decided to return to Japan. In Manitoba, only one Japanese national returned to Japan.[6]

It is likely that the Japanese in the camps were never aware that the Canadian government planned to scatter the CJA across Canada after the war, rather than let them return to British Columbia. Even so, many of the CJA choose not to return to B.C. Their homes, businesses, and possessions had been confiscated, most of their friends had moved, and they had no desire to return to the bigotry they experienced in B.C. before they were moved east.

By the first of January 1943 the number of Japanese in Ontario had grown from 130 to 1,650. A year later there were 2,424. By 1955, the number had grown to 3,742 in Toronto with another 532 in Quebec.[7] The CJA were finding a new life and the freedom they lacked in B.C.

The government was so eager to move the CJA east that they paid for the train tickets, provided food for the trip and arranged for jobs when they arrived. As the CJA moved east they found little, if any, racism. Often people at the train station would ask them what nationality they were but there was no hostility. Prairie people seemed different than the east coast city people. Finding jobs in Toronto was not difficult, the pay was good, and there were no racial problems for the CJA. For the younger Japanese, the freedom to go to movies and dance with non-Japanese was a new experience. They began to think they really were Canadians.

The interment camps did not provide education for CJA of kindergarten or high school age. Consequently there was a certain amount of catching up to do. Parents were delighted to find that their children were welcomed into the public schools at all levels. They could use the public libraries and join the YMCA or YWCA. For work, there was only one standard of pay regardless of one's nationality, and the only thing that mattered was how well you did your job. The CJA began writing to their friends in the camps and on the west coast encouraging them to come east. And so they did.

CJA Military Service During WW II

No Japanese-Canadians living in B.C. were accepted for military service prior to December 7, 1941. As the processing area at Hastings filled, many CJA volunteered for military service but were refused. By 1944, the British needed men that could speak Japanese and came to Canada to recruit them. They were to be enlisted into the British army and sent to the Far East as interpreters. About 150 volunteers were immediately selected but then problems arose.

It was discovered that most of the Japanese-Canadians could not speak Japanese, or if they could speak a little, it was insufficient for the army's needs. Ironically, it was decided to send the volunteers to a language school in Vancouver to teach them

Japanese. While in the school, the Canadian government decided that their citizens could not go to war as British soldiers.

They would have to be enlisted into the Canadian army. The British did not care, they needed the men. Therefore, the only way a Canadian citizen of Japanese ancestry was allowed to serve his country was because of the need for his services by another country. Perhaps it is not so strange. Japanese-Canadians that served in WW I and WW II earned the right to vote. This was true in all the provinces except B.C. Perhaps the refusal to enlist CJA was to prevent such persons from gaining the right to vote.

CJA served in combat in the Pacific under strict secrecy. They did their job well, as their medals for valor attest. It would be September 1945, before the Canadian government acknowledged that these "enemy aliens" of 1942 played a small but important role in the Allied victory in the Pacific.[8]

Where Was Home?

One wonders where home really was for the CJA of B.C. In 1949, when the last bans on Japanese-Canadians were cancelled, B.C., which was home to 22,000 CJA in 1940, had only 7,000 CJA. Ontario was home to 7,800, Alberta, 3,900, and Manitoba and Quebec, 1,300 each. Smaller numbers of CJA called Saskatchewan, and even the Yukon home.

Those who did return to B.C., some fishermen from the river and farmers from the Fraser Valley, received no government assistance and found resentment still existed. Some of the CJA fishermen who were able to get financial backing from small canneries were beaten by white Canadians who drove them out of the area. The returnees quickly learned that they could not go home again.

In June 1948, The House of Commons passed a bill that gave the Japanese- Canadians the federal right to vote. British Columbia was the first province to pass such a law and the other provinces followed. Some CJA were able to sue the government and recover some of the money due them for confiscation of their homes, businesses, and property. By 1979, 90 percent of the Japanese Canadians were marrying non-Japanese.

54

4

INTERNMENT OF THE ALEUT
PEOPLE DURING WWII

(By Gordon E. Castanza, Ed.D.)

The story of the evacuation and internment of the Aleut peoples of the Aleutian and Pribilof Islands is no secret, but due to the small numbers of Aleut people involved, it is not widely known.

One might think to blame Admiral Isoroku Yamamoto, commander of the Japanese Combined Fleet, for what happened to the Aleut people. Or, perhaps more to the point, one might blame Lieutenant Col. Jimmy Doolittle, leader of the B-25 raid on Tokyo on April 18, 1942. Following Doolittle's raid on Tokyo, Yamamoto made the decision to extend the Japanese outer defensive line from the Aleutians through Midway Island, to Port Moresby, Papua New Guinea. If Japan controlled these vital areas, Yamamoto believed, it would be impossible for the United States to raid the Japanese mainland again.

The Japanese fleet attacked Dutch Harbor on June 3, 1942, as part of their plan to seize Midway Island. Yamamoto also hoped to lure vital components of the Pacific Fleet to the Aleutians to defend against his attack, thereby lessening the forces available to defend Midway. The feint did not work as Admiral Chester Nimitz deployed all his forces to defend against the Japanese invasion of Midway.

Japanese submarines reconnoitered the Aleutians on May 29, 1942. Submarine *I-15* scouted Kiska in advance of a landing force of 550 Japanese marines, construction equipment, and 700 laborers. *I-17* scouted Attu for a landing force of 1,120 troops, and *I-19* scouted Dutch Harbor. *I-19* subsequently patrolled Unimak Pass off Dutch Harbor, while *I-26* patrolled off Seattle. Submarines *I-25* shelled Astoria and *I-26* bombarded Vancouver. On the morning of June 3, eleven torpedo bombers and six *Zero* fighters from carrier IMS *Ryujo* and a similar number of aircraft from IMS *Junyo* attacked Fort Mears at Dutch Harbor and the Dutch Harbor Naval Air Station. The *Zeros* shot down a navy PBY aircraft on patrol. In addition, 25 soldiers were killed in the barracks at Fort Mears.[1]

Vice Admiral Moshiro Hosagaya, commander of the Northern (Aleutians) Attack Force, launched a second attack on Dutch Harbor on June 4. Seventeen bombers and six fighters bombed and strafed the fuel storage tanks, destroying four large fuel tanks, but alerting the U.S. Army Air Force at nearby Fort Glenn. Eight P-40 *Warhawks* scrambled from Glenn and shot down four of the bombers and one *Zero*. American casualties for the two days were 43 military killed and 50 wounded, plus 64 civilians, including Aleuts, wounded.[2]

Japanese marines occupied Kiska on June 6. There was only a ten-man navy weather reporting station on Kiska and the Japanese captured nine of the men. A single American sailor, William House, elected to hide in the 110 square miles of rugged mountains that comprised Kiska. He lasted for 50 days, but on July 28, starving and near death, he was forced to surrender.[3] The Japanese began immediately to construct antiaircraft positions and moved 20 ships, including cruisers, destroyers and corvettes into the harbor. Among those captured were 45 Aleuts, a Caucasian school teacher, and her husband. The school teacher and her husband attempted suicide but the woman failed in the attempt. The 45 Aleuts and the school teacher were taken to Otaru on the west side of Hokkaido, on the Japanese mainland. They became POWs for the duration of the war. Only 20 of the POWs survived captivity.[4]

A few hours after the landings at Kiska, 1200 Japanese troops stormed ashore in Massacre Bay, Attu. Admiral Sentaro Omori's troops lacked maps and got lost on their way to Chichagof village. Some of the troops were near starvation in the snow-drifted passes before they found their way out. A small group of defenders could have prevented them from seizing Attu, but there were no defenders, only 39 Aleuts and a Caucasian couple, Etta Jones, the school teacher, and her husband Charles Jones, Attu's weather observer and radio operator. Charles Jones was the only person killed while trying to flee the Japanese invaders. The Japanese immediately began to install antiaircraft guns and improve the ship harbor.[5]

Justification for the internment of the Aleuts is unclear, but stems from a March 19, 1942, correspondence from acting Governor Bartlett to Brigadier Gen. Simon B. Buckner Jr., which stated that evacuation of native people (was) strictly a military problem.[6] Evacuation, if necessary, would be to protect the Aleuts from harm in the event of a Japanese attack.

Within a few days after the Japanese occupation of Kiska and Attu, the U. S. Navy began forced evacuation of Aleut people. Eighty-three Aleuts were ordered to leave their village of Atka at Nazan Bay on Atka Island. On June 12, the Aleuts were notified that they would be evacuated and a navy demolition team burned the village. At 5:22 A.M., 62 Aleuts were evacuated on board the seaplane tender USS *Hulbert*. Twenty-one Aleuts did not receive the evacuation order and were left behind. The evacuees arrived at Fort Mears in Dutch Harbor on June 16, and the remaining 21 Atka villagers were subsequently rescued and flown to Fort Mears.

Philoman Tutiakoff, Harriet Hope, and Alice Petrivelli recalled that they were not told what was happening, where they were being taken or why their village was being destroyed. Their questions were answered by "What is happening to you is for your own protection."[7] Bewildered, confused and afraid, the villagers were not allowed to return to their homes or churches to take away photos, icons or other memorabilia.

On June 15, U.S. Army forces commanded by Sergeant Lyman R. Ellsworth began evacuating Aleuts from the Pribilof Islands. The army transport ship, *Delarof* embarked a total of 544 Aleuts, 19 fish and wildlife employees, and three Russian orthodox clergy from the Pribilof Islands, (Saint George and Saint Paul

Islands) and Nikolski where it embarked the Atkan evacuees, bringing their passenger total to 560 in a ship designed to carry 376 passengers.[8]

There was a long series of confusing and contradicting communications concerning where the Aleuts should be taken and which department was responsible for their welfare. Donald Haggerty, the Indian Service field agent, was able to arrange for the use of the Funter Bay cannery and secured the Fish and Wildlife Service ship, *Penguin,* to load supplies for the Aleut relocation.

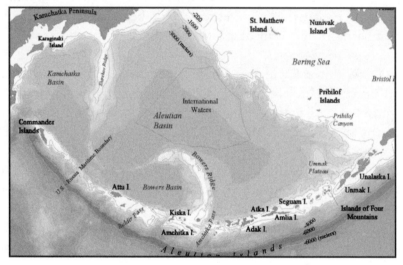

The Aleutian Chain.

National Park Service

The *Delarof* left Dutch Harbor on June 18, and arrived at Funter Bay on June 24. All 477 Priblof Aleuts were initially put in the Funter Bay cannery. On June 26, the Saint George Aleuts were moved across the bay to an abandoned gold mine camp. A baby, Della Kuchutin, was born enroute to Funter Bay but died during the trip and was buried at sea. Anatoly Lekanof, an-11-year old described the burial at sea.[9]

And that baby was wrapped up, and put a weight
to it, a little weightless little child baby body, and

slipped down on the plank through an American flag, and splashed into the . . . sea.

The living conditions at both camps were deplorable. Both medical doctors resigned before going into the camps, leaving the evacuees with no medical treatment. The Funter Bay cannery consisted of two, two-story wood-framed buildings, a warehouse building, and 15 small cottages without doors. The abandoned goldmine camp consisted of two cottages, a two-story bunkhouse, an old mess hall and some other decrepit buildings. Both facilities lacked plumbing, sewage disposal, running water, laundry, bathing facilities, cooking equipment, bedding and partitions in the bunkhouses. Many windows were missing or broken and the roofs leaked. There were no building supplies and only such food as the *Delarof* was able to leave. The supply ship *Penguin* did not arrive until August 9.

The supply ship brought building supplies, food, and a supply of wire, large safety pins, and blankets. The wires were strung end-to-end and sideways throughout the bunkhouses to create 10-foot by 10-foot cubicles. The blankets were pinned to the top of the wires to give a small degree of privacy within each cubicle. The *Delarof* contributed mattresses and a few blankets to cover the inhabitants. All 16 members of the Lekanof family were required to occupy a single cubicle. There were no pillows or sheets, just mattresses to walk and sleep upon and a few blankets to share.

As primitive as the conditions were, the youngsters enjoyed Funter Bay. Anatoly Lekanof Jr. described his experiences this way.[10]

And with that way of living like that and not seeing trees living in our lives in the Pribilofs and now we see, kids now see beautiful trees and Sitka deer, salmon in the season in the creeks at Admiralty Island. So we used to eat salmon for the first time, and Sitka deer for the first time and salmonberries for the first time. We had a joyous time. Beautiful scenery and beautiful weather. But, . . . for the parents it was a horrible, terrible life. And what an embarrassing situation for children when night come and young parents have to do their love nesting scene or whatever. Kids were in an unhealthy environment. And then when we have to go out to nature call to go to the bathroom, the country was our bathroom, because there was only, for entire two villages, there was only one outhouse with four holer. The outhouse hanged over the dock (pier).

Saint Paul Seal Division agent Lee C. McMillan reported on the conditions of the evacuee camps to his supervisor as follows:[11]

Most of the buildings at the cannery have been unused for 12 years or more and are all dry-rotted. . . All the cooking for the entire village was accomplished on two old stoves, and it was a miracle how the natives could get the meals for some 290 people on such small cooking space. . . The Territorial Department of Health officers visited the camps and declared them both very much unsanitary. . . Pipes around the cannery are laid helter-skelter on top of the ground, patched with rubber hose, and will soon have to be discontinued on account of cold weather. . . All the water for washing clothing is now heated on the cook stove. . . . Many of the people are sleeping so many in a room that they have to sleep in relays as there is not sufficient room for them all to lay down at the same time in their cramped and stuffy quarters- no bunks, no mattresses.

When conditions did not improve by October 1942, McMillan resigned his position in protest. Before the internment was over, 32 Aleuts died at the Funter Bay camp.

As Haggerty was coordinating the evacuation to Funter Bay, he was informed by Vice Admiral Charles Freeman, commandant of the Naval District in Seattle, that two more villages of Aleuts were to be evacuated. The number of villages to be evacuated rapidly increased to six, causing Haggerty serious problems in locating accommodations for the evacuees.

The additional six villages that were evacuated were Akutan (35 miles northeast of Dutch Harbor), Biorka (15 miles east of Unalaska), Kashega (40 miles southwest of Dutch Harbor), Makushin and Unalaska on Unalaska Island, and Nikolski on Umnak Island. Camp locations were unknown except that some would go to the Wrangell Institute in Wrangell, and some to the North West Trading Company (NWTC) facility at Killisnoo Island.

Tlingit village at Killisnoo in 1887.

Gordon E. Castanza

The *Delarof* arrived near Killisnoo on June 25 with 83 Aleuts and Ruby Magee, a school teacher, and her husband, both had been evacuated from Atka. A fish scow took the evacuees from the *Delarof* to the North West Trading Company facility on Killisnoo Island. The conditions at Killisnoo were slightly better than those at Funter Bay. There were three houses (the schoolteacher and her husband took one), five small cabins, a bunkhouse, warehouse, shed, machine shop, and a generator shed. The most significant difference between the camps was that the NWTC facility at Killisnoo had a watchman living in one of the houses so the condition of the buildings was much better. Three pit toilets constituted the sewage system. There was a small laundry but no bathing facilities. The drinking water came from a small pond which was contaminated. The captain of the *Delarof* left four days supply of food, mattresses and blankets from his ship's stores. By the end of their internment, 17 Aleuts died at Killisnoo.

North West Trading Co. at Killisnoo in 1887.

Gordon E. Castanza

SS *Columbia,* a ship chartered from the Alaska Steamship Company, evacuated 160 Aleuts: 41 from Akutan, 18 from Biorka, 20 from Kashega, eight from Makushin, 72 from Nikolski, and one from Unalaska to Wrangell, arriving there on July 13. Initially the evacuees were housed in a tent camp on the institute grounds and later transferred to a cannery. On August 1, the SS *Alaska,* an Alaska Steamship Company vessel, arrived at Wrangell with another 137 Aleut evacuees. On August 12, the first load of evacuees were moved by barge to an abandoned cannery on Burnett Inlet on the western shore of Etolin Island, 45 miles west of Wrangell.

On August 14, *Penguin* offloaded another 122 Aleuts (72 from Nikolski) at the Burnett cannery. Harriet Hope, one of the evacuees, described life at the Burnett camp:[12]

> We were herded like cattle. We were dumped ashore and told to shift for ourselves. Our elders took charge. We fixed the hole in the roof of the bunkhouse where we all lived first. We had to build outhouses. The first thought was, why are they bringing us here? You know, there's nothing here. It (the cannery) was just totally abandoned. And there weren't any habitable buildings. And yet, we were just put ashore and told to live in them. There was no plumbing in the buildings. Each house had an out house, and a rain barrel out front.
>
> The people were coming to my mother because they had infected boils. There was huge break-out of boils. She sewed up people, set broken bones. She just generally took care of any medical emergency. We just prayed to come home. (Five Aleuts died at the Burnett camp).

On August 23, an army ship moved 125 of the Aleuts from Wrangell Institute to a Civilian Conservation Camp (CCC) at Ward Lake. A few days later, *Penguin* towed a barge of building supplies and 25 more Aleuts from Wrangell to Ward Lake, near Ketchikan, Alaska. A Nikolski school teacher, Pauline Whitfield, and her husband were placed in charge of the camp. Aleut carpenters constructed 16 new cabins, but the sewage system consisted of a slit trench and there was no running water.

For the 200 Aleuts there were nine small cabins, and four communal buildings. Each cabin had a wood stove, table and benches. An adjoining room contained two bunk beds. A large tin basin was used for washing clothes and one cold water tap provided water for drinking and bathing. Before their internment ended, 20 Aleuts died at the Ward Lake camp.[13]

During May 1943, 151 Aleut males from Funter Bay were moved back to the Priblofs to harvest seals under supervision of the Fish and Wildlife Service. The men were promised high pay, bonuses, and a speedy return to their homes after the war. A total of 95,342 seal skins were taken by August 8, the end of the sealing operation. This was the greatest number of skins ever harvested in a year.

The U.S. Treasury made a profit of $1.58 million from the harvest. After four months of hunting seals, the most any Aleut made was $19.00. Many were not paid anything. Despite being promised that they would be returned to Funter Bay as soon as the harvest was over, they were not returned to Funter Bay and their families until October 4. In the meantime they were forced to work or not eat.[14]

Despite promises from the secretary of war to return the evacuees to their homes in the summer of 1943, many were not returned until June 1945, and the government refused to fund the return of evacuees from Akutan, Biorka, Kashega and Makushin.

In 1980, the 96th Congress of the United States established the Commission on Wartime Relocation and Internment of Civilians (CWRIC). On June 23, 1983, the CWRIC submitted a report to congress that concluded "that the expulsion and incarceration were not justified by military necessity, and the decisions to do so were based on race, prejudice, war hysteria, and a failure of political leadership."

The attorney for the Aleutians/Priblofs' Islands Association (APIA), Mr. John C. Kirtland, testified that:[15]

> Once a decision had been made by the United States to relocate the people out of a doctrine of "military necessity," it was necessary to take care

that they be properly cared for, to insure that they had adequate food, adequate shelter, adequate medicine, and that their property was protected while they were away from their homes. None of those things were done, and moreover, there was no compensation paid for the use of their homes and community buildings while they were interred in the camps in Southeastern Alaska. There was no justification that more than 10% of them died in the camps because of the lack of adequate care, shelter, food and medicine. And there was no justification that their priceless religious icons from the Russian Orthodox Church had been looted and stolen from their homes and churches. It was on the basis of restitution that we made our fundamental case. And we were successful in that respect.

Senator Ted Stevens of Alaska co-sponsored the Aleut reparations amendment and knew that passage would be a hard fight. "There were people who objected to the apology that was in the bill. There were people who objected to the compensation that was in the bill. And there were people who objected to the findings that the United States had made a mistake in World War II."[16]

During August 1988, President George Bush signed legislation that provided for restitution to Aleut residents of the Priblof and Aleutian Islands. On November 2, 1989, he signed Public Law 101-162 that funded $9.7 million for restitution of personal and community property and provided for each eligible Aleut to receive $12,000. The U.S. government made more than 500 restitution payments to Aleuts.

The Aleuts were unique in that, unlike the Japanese-Americans and Japanese-Canadians interred during the war, the Aleuts were U.S. citizens. Many of the Japanese-Americans and Japanese-Canadians were citizens of their country, but not all. The Aleuts

65

were also unique in that they were the only ethnic group interred by both American and Japanese governments.

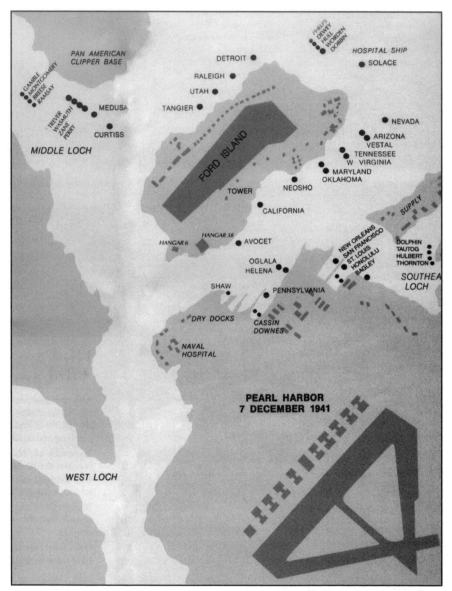

Ships and their positions inside and around Pearl Harbor at the time of the air attack on December 7, 1941.

U.S. Naval Institute

5

SALVAGE OF THE BATTLESHIPS AT
PEARL HARBOR

One of the more interesting aftermaths of the Japanese attack on the Pacific Fleet at Pearl Harbor was the effort that went into salvaging that portion of the fleet that was sunk or severely damaged. Not much has been written concerning this tremendous effort, carried out at the same time the navy was going to war.

Eight of the Pacific Fleet battleships were in port on Sunday, December 7, 1941, and berthed at piers to the southeast of Ford Island. They were USS *Arizona, California, Maryland, Nevada, Oklahoma, Tennessee*, and *West Virginia*. USS *Pennsylvania* was in dry dock at the naval shipyard. USS *Utah*, a training ship, was berthed on the northwest side of Ford Island. Three of the battleships entered port the day before, the other five on Friday. They had been on training maneuvers.

Soon after the attack, flames continued to envelop USS *Arizona* and *West Virginia*. They lay on the bottom of Pearl Harbor, with only their mainmasts and upper works above water. *West Virginia* had been torn open by torpedoes and *Arizona* had been pounded by bombs until her forward magazines exploded in a gigantic eruption. Thick, black, foul-smelling oil was everywhere. It floated on the water in the harbor, flowed out to sea, and coated the shoreline. The oil came from thousands of gallons that gushed from the sides of the damaged ships. Much of the oil burned on the surface of the water, adding its smell to that of smoke, gunpowder, and burned flesh.

The bodies of American sailors and marines, coated with oil, floated in the harbor, washed ashore, or drifted down the channel to the sea. Small boats began scurrying across the harbor long before the last Japanese aircraft departed. They carried ammunition for the operational ships, and pumps and diving equipment for those ships in distress. In addition to bodies, the harbor was covered with burnt pieces of wood, oil-soaked life vests, mattresses, canvas awning material, and clothing. Sailors on the small boats could be seen leaning over the side and pulling large limp forms towards the boats. From a distance, the objects could not be identified. To the sailors in the boats, they were the bodies of friends and shipmates.

The minesweeper *Tern* pulled alongside *West Virginia* at 10:50 A.M., and sprayed five separate streams of water on the superstructure while *West Virginia's* hull filled with saltwater. From what could be determined at this time, *West Virginia* had been hit by four torpedoes and a bomb.

By Monday, December 8, the fires on *West Virginia* were extinguished, so *Tern* moved to the *Arizona* to fight another blaze that continued for 24 hours.[1] Details of the damage to *Arizona* were vague. The thunderclap of the Arizona's explosion had rocked the area for miles. Debris and body parts rained over Pearl Harbor. It was known that Admiral Isaac Kidd, the battleship division commander, and Franklin Van Valkenburg, captain of the *Arizona* had died, but other details were sketchy. Rumors indicated three bomb hits, a torpedo hit, and a bomb was seen to go down the stack. Heavy, oily smoke continued to pour from the hull, making work difficult and dangerous. The navy yard declared USS *Arizona* a total loss and initially did not concern themselves with repair or recovery of the ship.

The crew of USS *Maryland* was trying to stop the flooding from a bomb hit that exploded below the waterline at the bow of the ship. The ship had sunk five feet after it was hit. Another bomb exploded on the forward deck, but caused little damage. Once the flooding was controlled, *Maryland*, as the most lightly damaged battleship, would be ready to fight - - if she could free herself from behind the capsized hull of USS *Oklahoma*.

The battleships were not the only ships sunk or damaged. On the same side of Ford Island as the *Utah,* the light cruiser USS *Raleigh* lay in danger of rolling over. A bomb had gone through her port side and exploded on the harbor bottom. She had also been hit by a torpedo that flooded both fire room compartments and the forward engine room. Sixty tons of equipment had been removed or tossed overboard to lighten the ship and pontoons and a barge were brought alongside to keep *Raleigh* from capsizing. Four two-inch steel hawsers were run completely around the ship and pulled tight to the barge. Despite these efforts, a significant shift in *Raleigh's* weight would cause the ship to roll on her side and sink to the bottom of the channel, just as USS *Utah* had done astern of *Raleigh*.[2]

Utah, an old battleship launched in 1909, had been serving as a target ship for the fleet. Her guns had been covered with steel sheds, and her decks covered with a double layer of 6-inch by 12-inch timbers to shield her from aircraft practice bombs. *Utah* entered the harbor on Friday, and her crew had been busy removing the wooden planks so the ship could go into dry dock on Monday for maintenance. *Utah* was hit during the first few minutes of the attack, two torpedoes puncturing her hull. She rolled over almost immediately, loose timbers crashing and mooring lines snapping, as her mainmast disappeared under the water. Some of the crew were still trapped below decks, but *Raleigh's* crew was able to cut open a portion of the hull and rescue one sailor.[3] Fifty-eight of *Utah's* men died in the attack.

The upturned hull of USS *Oklahoma* now lay a few hundred yards ahead (west) of *Arizona*. No one knew how many times she had been hit. Torpedoes had caused her to capsize 150 degrees to port, stopping only when her mainmast and superstructure contacted the bottom of the harbor. Some reports said she took three torpedoes, others five, and some seven. The first torpedoes tore open her side, flooding her, and starting a list. The final torpedoes exploded at her water line, caving in the hull, and sending her to the bottom.

Work on *Oklahoma* was especially difficult because of the heavy smoke from *Arizona*. Divers were forced to work in near darkness. Bodies lay everywhere. Four hundred of the crew were unaccounted for, but some were still alive, tapping on the hull of the black, inverted maze of hatches, compartments and passageways. Lieutenant Cdr. William H. Hobby, *Oklahoma's* damage control officer, was on top of the hull at 9:15 A.M. on that Sunday morning rescuing shipmates, while Japanese planes continued their attack. Now, sailors and civilian welders worked frantically to cut holes in the hull to rescue them.

During the next 24 hours, and with the help of nearly every department at Pearl Harbor, 31 sailors were rescued from their "would be" tomb. Two sailors died of suffocation caused by the fumes of the cutting torches and the torches using up all the oxygen in the tight spaces. No one knows how many more men might have been trapped and praying for rescue, but there would be no more survivors from USS *Oklahoma*.[4]

USS *Pennsylvania* shared the dry dock with the mangled remains of destroyers *Downes* and *Cassin*. The four screws and tail shaft of *Pennsylvania* had been removed before she was placed on her keel blocks. A single bomb penetrated her superstructure, plunged through her deck, and into the 5-inch gun casement. The fire was quickly extinguished and repair work was begun immediately.

USS Cassin, right, lies toppled next to *USS Downes* in Dry Dock 1.

Salvage of *Downes* and *Cassin* would be quite another matter. Bombs, burning fuel, and exploding ammunition ripped open both destroyers in numerous places. The topside of *Downes* had been demolished, and as she rolled, she turned *Cassin,* so that *Cassin's* starboard side lay against *Downes*. The flooded dock was filled with wreckage and the inescapable oil coated everything.

Heavy mooring lines secure *USS Oglala* to Ten Ten Dock and keep her from sliding into the channel Dec. 9, 1941.

Near the dry dock, light cruiser *Helena* suffered a torpedo that tore open her starboard side, killing 20 men. Behind her, only a bit of hull, some superstructure, and masts lying across the dock revealed USS *Oglala*, a minesweeper, and flagship of the mine force. Now, *Oglala* was a derelict, blocking some of the most valuable piers in Pearl Harbor. Not far from *Oglala*, floated part of destroyer *Shaw*. *Shaw* was a sister ship to *Downes* and *Cassin*. A magazine explosion tore *Shaw's* bow off, and now the ship lay at the bottom of the floating dry dock. The remainder of *Shaw's* hull was still afloat, but her bridge structure consisted of melted metal. Her ordnance and dead crewmen had been removed and a crew of one officer and four men manned the pumps that kept *Shaw* afloat.

USS *Nevada* lay aground at Hospital Point. She tried to leave the harbor but came under a ferocious attack and was forced to go aground rather than be sunk in the narrow channel, thereby blocking the harbor to other ships. Fires still burned and her crew was trying to stop the flooding from a torpedo hit that opened up her port side. Bomb hits and near misses burst seams and tore more holes in *Nevada's* bow. *Nevada* was slowly flooding with her bow three feet below the waterline. All day Sunday, damage control parties were forced to retreat in the face of the rising water. By Monday afternoon, only 300 sailors remained on the main deck. *Nevada* was drawing 51 feet of water, and the bottom of the channel was 54 feet. No one answered the diver's tap of hammers against the hull of the ship, so it had to be assumed that no survivors were inside the hull.

USS Shaw lies smashed and burned on Dec. 8, 1941. To the right is *USS Helena*.

Naval Historical Center

On the south end of the battleship piers, the crew of USS *California* was forced to watch helplessly as their ship sank. Numerous pumps were delivered to try to stay ahead of the flooding, but it proved impossible. Divers reported two torpedo holes in the side, each 12 feet square. *Widgeon* was alongside, as was the seaplane tender *Avocet*. The tug *Nakomis* was moored to *California's* starboard side attempting to put out the fires and a fuel barge came alongside to pump fuel from the ship. Later, the minesweeper *Bobolink* tied to *Widgeon* and added her hoses to the pumping effort. Throughout the day and night, other yard craft tied up to *California* and pumped water from the ship. Numerous manhole covers on the deck of *California* had been left open and un-dogged because the ship was to have been inspected the following morning for possible leakage. As the water reached this level, flooding increased to such an extent that it was impossible to save the ship, but efforts to do so continued through Sunday night and into Monday morning.

To illustrate how Pearl Harbor was a functioning port despite the destruction just described, the USS *Enterprise* task force pulled into Pearl Harbor on Monday at 5:43 P.M., took aboard 463,000 gallons of fuel oil, 61,000 gallons of gasoline, provisions, supplies, and was underway at 4:20 A. M., the next day. With *Enterprise* were cruisers *Northampton, Chester, Salt Lake City*, and nine destroyers.

Commander Homer Wallin, battle fleet material officer, made a survey of the cruisers on Sunday afternoon to determine how many were ready for sea. He found *San Francisco* needing another two weeks of yard work. USS *New Orleans* could go to sea with three of four shafts working in 24 hours. USS *Honolulu* needed pumping but was otherwise seaworthy. USS *Helena* was in the worst shape and was given priority for the dry dock as soon at it was available.

Wallin's survey of the battleships termed *Arizona* as a total wreck, *West Virginia* sunk and burning, and *Oklahoma* sunk. *California* had a list of ten degrees and a serious fire amidships. *Pennsylvania's* damage was superficial and she could be quickly repaired, as could *Tennesse*. Other ships such as *Cassin* and *Downes* were total wrecks. *Shaw* was gutted by fire and lacking a bow, and the *Oglala* appeared to be a wreck that needed to be moved.[5]

Besides the Herculean job facing the salvage and repair facilities at the yard, one must appreciate the effect of the attack upon the morale of the military and civilian workforce. The sight of the gutted battleships and the smoke and fire covering the harbor created a pessimism among many that the ships could never be recovered. There was also the knowledge that the U.S. was now at war. Japan had struck the first blow. Would they deliver an additional blow at any time? Would the sailors of Pearl Harbor have to fight with one hand, and repair ships with the other? Perhaps most damaging was the feeling that somehow each man was in some way responsible for what happened. This feeling of guilt would last until Admiral Chester Nimitz arrived to take command of the fleet on Christmas Day. Nimitz quickly put to rest any thought of guilt. He praised the men for their dedication to duty and asked each of them to remain with the Pacific Fleet until the war was won. Morale improved significantly.

There was some good news in the aftermath of the attack. Overall damage to the base was slight. Except for the floating dry dock that sank with the bow of *Shaw*, the others were relatively undamaged. The marine railway was operational, and the oil storage tanks had not been hit. The cranes and floating derricks were undamaged, basin piers usable, and the repair ship *Medusa* and destroyers *Dobbin* and *Whitney* were undamaged.

Lieutenant Cdr. Lebbus V. Curtis, a salvage expert from the San Diego salvage base, was passing through Hawaii at the time of the attack. He stayed at Pearl Harbor, and provided immeasurable assistance.[6] Perhaps the best news was that the submarine base had not been damaged and submarine patrols were already being sent to war.[7] Now the real work at Pearl Harbor was to begin

Commander James M. Steel was a former submariner before taking command of *USS Utah*. Now with no ship to command, he was designated commander of the Base Force Salvage Organization. His job was to get the sunken ships off the bottom of Pearl Harbor and deliver them to the shipyards for repair. Steele had no previous experience with ship salvage.[8]

Salvage operations began on Tuesday, December 9. Many of the officers and men assigned to the organization came from

USS *Utah*. On December 10, *Helena* was pushed by tugs to dry dock. *Helena* was extensively flooded, but once inside the dock, pumps and a suction dredge removed the water. A continuing problem was the thick layer of oil that accompanied each opening of the docks. The oil would rise and fall on top of the water, coating the entire sides and bottom of the docks and the blocks as well. Hoses discharging steam and hot water cut some of the oil and an oil-collection system was developed to trap and skim oil for removal. Oil removal remained a dirty, time-consuming job throughout the salvage and repair effort.

On December 14, Steele issued the first daily salvage bulletin intended to advise workmen of priorities and progression of salvage work. Lack of storage space for salvaged material and a shortage of manpower were two items that slowed the salvage effort. Men were quickly assigned from other non-operational ships, and storage space was found at Magazine Island and 4,000 feet of space near the docks where repair work was ongoing. Next, project officers were assigned to *Tennessee, California* and *Nevada* to oversee and supervise the salvage efforts of those ships.

USS West Virginia, outboard, pins *USS Tennessee* to the forward quay at F-6 on Dec. 10, 1941.

US Naval Intitute

Morale rose again on December 15, when USS *Saratoga* and her escorts arrived from San Diego. The task force remained at Pearl Harbor only long enough to refuel before sailing for Wake Island with marine fighter aircraft. The aircraft were essential if Wake was to continue to resist the Japanese invasion attempt that had been ongoing since December 7.

USS *Tennessee* had relatively minor damage, but was pinned between the quay and the sunken *West Virginia*. Various ways to try to free the ship were discussed, and the plan settled on was to remove the large concrete quay, without damaging *Tennessee*, and tow the ship from astern. By December 14, 60 percent of the quay had been removed, repair work was being done to the inside of the ship, and thousands of gallons of fuel oil had been removed. It now appeared that there would be about six feet of water between the ship and the quay, and once USS *Maryland* was removed, *Tennessee* could be towed forward. At 4:00 P.M., on December 12, USS *Tennessee* was pulled free. She began her trip to San Francisco on December 20, for repair at the Puget Sound shipyard. *Tennessee* was restored to the fleet in time to participate in the Iwo Jima and Okinawa campaigns.

USS *Maryland* also had light to moderate damage and, once free of the USS *Oklahoma's* hull which pinned her to the pier, could be ready for major repair. Divers reported a bomb hole 23 feet below the waterline, split seams at the hull, and hatches blown clear that permitted 1,000 tons of water to flood the ship. Another bomb detonated on the forecastle and main deck, wrecking the anchor chains and destroying electrical wiring. Much of the necessary repair was done as *Maryland* lay slightly flooded at the quay. After carefully sounding the depth of water around and forward of *Maryland*, she was towed forward on December 10, and sent under destroyer escort to San Francisco on December 20. She then went to Puget Sound with *Tennessee* for more overhaul work.

USS *Pennsylvania* was in dry dock when the attack occurred. The yard quickly reinstalled the three propeller shafts and screws, renewed and repaired superstructure and upper decks, and she was ready for operations on December 14. She departed Pearl Harbor on December 20, in company with USS *Tennessee* and *Maryland*. *Pennsylvania* went to the Mare Island repair facility.

76

Pennsylvania was returned to the fleet and participated in the Battle for Okinawa, where she suffered a torpedo hit. She was the last major ship damaged in action.

The remaining battleships would require the major effort of salvage operations but lesser ships were also salvaged. Cruisers *Helena, Honolulu,* and *Raleigh* were salvaged and sent to the West Coast for permanent repair. Destroyer *Helm,* repair ship *Vestal,* and the harbor tug *Sotoyomo* were raised, salvaged, temporarily repaired, and sent to California for permanent repair.[9]

Destroyer *Shaw,* which was originally reported as a total loss, remained afloat, its machinery was found to be in good condition, and it was put into dry dock on December 19. It was pumped dry, the forward part of the hull cut off, and a false bow fitted,. *Shaw* sailed for Mare Island on February 9, 1942. *Shaw* participated in 11 battle actions during WW II, and was back in dry dock for repair of battle damage on VJ-Day.

Floating dry dock number two was patched, pumped, and returned to service on January 25. Full operation of the dock was available on May 15, 1942. Destroyers *Cassin* and *Downes* were scrapped. Machinery and equipment from the two destroyers were salvaged, and sent to Mare Island where it was used in new hulls, named after each of the destroyers.

With USS *Maryland, Pennsylvania,* and *Tennessee* on their way to California, and USS *Arizona* and *Utah* deemed unsalvageable, salvage personnel were left to determine the best way (if possible) to salvage *California, Nevada, Oklahoma,* and *West Virginia.*

Nevada had been beached, was flooded throughout, and suffered extensive bomb and fire damage. Weight was removed, the hull patched and pumped, and she entered dry dock on February 18. The divers did a major portion of the repair work on *Nevada,* with more than 400 dives, totaling 1500 diving hours of repair without accident. *Nevada* left the dry dock on March 15, 1942 and sailed for Puget Sound under her own power and arrived on May 1, 1942. She reentered the fleet, and fought in the Aleutians, and the Normandy invasion. Following Germany's surrender, she returned to the Pacific theater and fought at Iwo Jima and Okinawa,

The "Big Patch" for *USS Nevada* is brought to Waipio Point.

The window-frame patch that divers secured to the hole in *USS Nevada's* port bilge. The ship had just been dry-docked when this photo was taken.

The size of the patches is apparent as one is lifted from the water. The lower wales were spaced closer together than those near the surface to resit the greater water pressure.

National Archives

California was partially coffer-dammed (A coffer-dam is a watertight structure for making repairs below the waterline of a ship), weight was removed, and the hull pumped out. Bodies found on *California* were floated into body bags without being touched. The remains were then transferred to the Naval Hospital at Aiea for identification and burial. *California* entered dry dock on April 9, 1942, and sailed for Puget Sound on October 10. *California* was returned to the fleet, and earned seven battle stars before WW II ended.[10]

West Virginia was also partially coffer-dammed and patched extensively with concrete. Weight was removed and she was floated with compressed air. After pumping, she went into dry dock for temporary repair on September 6, 1942, and sailed for Puget Sound as the *Oklahoma* was being righted. She returned to the fleet, and spent 223 days in battle action..

Captain Homer Wallin replaced Jim Steele as the salvage officer of the Salvage Division of the navy yard on January 9, 1942. Steele had been recently promoted to captain and had done an excellent job as salvage officer, despite having lost his ship (USS *Utah*), and suffered the loss of many men from the ship. Wallin could not find a suitable officer for his position as material officer, so he volunteered to do the salvage job as extra duty.[11]

The two salvage efforts that were especially noteworthy were the salvage of *Oglala* and the righting and refloating of *Oklahoma*.[12] *Oglala* on her side with her superstructure resting on the dock, clearly blocking access to the dock area and needing to be removed. Plans to cut up the hull were rejected because too few divers were experienced in explosive cutting and there was danger to the surrounding areas from the explosions. Lifting the *Oglala* with four barges was rejected because of the personnel and materials that would be needed to make the barges suitable as lifting vehicles. Pumping and floating the ship on its side with compressed air was rejected because the hull would not hold the necessary air pressure. The plan that was decided upon was to right *Oglala* where she lay, float her and move her into the dry dock.

Ten 80-ton submarine salvage pontoons were sunk on the inboard side of *Oglala*. Chains from these pontoons were then passed under the hull and attached above the water-line on the starboard side. Compressed air at three pounds-per-square-inch was pumped into the hull and jacks were positioned between the hull and the dock.

As *Oglala* was being raised, with Admiral Nimitz and other distinguished visitors in attendance, the chain connections to the hull failed, the pontoons rose to the surface, and *Oglala* returned to the bottom. A second try was made and was successful. *Oglala* was righted to a list of seven degrees. A coffer-dam was constructed and extended upward along the entire deck edge. Pumps were employed and the water level reduced substantially. Then the coffer-dam failed. The coffer-dam was repaired and the ship finally refloated. Two days after *Oglala* was refloated, a primary pump stopped overnight and the hull flooded, *Oglala* settled by the bow, began flooding throughout, and returned once again to the bottom.

The original plan was just to move *Oglala* from the dock area, but not return her to duty. Some in the salvage crew vowed if they ever did get her moved she would return to duty, or else. Another effort to float the ship was unsuccessful when the coffer-dams failed a second time. Once again, repairs were made and the ship was refloated for the third time. Finally, a gasoline-driven pump on *Oglala's* deck caught fire when some fuel splashed on a hot exhaust line. The fire spread quickly to the oil-soaked coffer-dam timbers and a major fire ensued. The fire was extinguished by professional fire fighters from the base.

Between 15 and 18 divers worked constantly to salvage *Oglala*. They made 542 dives totaling nearly 2,000 hours under water. They did this without a single injury or casualty. *Oglala* was finally moved by tug to the dry dock for temporary repairs. She then sailed for the West Coast where she was converted to a diesel repair ship. In February, 1944, an almost new *Oglala* sailed for the South Pacific and participated in the fleet advances to Hollandia and Leyte. *Oglala* is still part of the Maritime Reserve Fleet at Suisan, California.[13] If work on *Oglala* was unpredictable, salvage of *Oklahoma* proved to be the most complicated job ever accomplished at Pearl Harbor, and possibly, anywhere during WW II.[14]

USS *Oklahoma* was not intended to return to service. She simply had to be moved, and the most efficient way to move her was to raise her to an even keel, refloat, patch, and pump her. The job would be difficult. *Oklahoma* capsized to port and rested on her side in 25 feet of mud. Work was divided between the navy and the heavy engineering contractor, Pacific Bridge Company. The work was carefully planned and models used to simulate the movement of the ship at all times during the salvage effort.

The power to right *Oklahoma* would come from 21 electric winches anchored on concrete foundations on Ford Island. The winches would pull three-inch wire ropes guided over 40-foot high headframes, and fastened to 34 strong points on the ship's hull. (The reader is encouraged to study the following photographs that depict the *Oklahoma* on her side, the electric winches, and the headframes.) The headframes were intended to increase the righting arm during initial pulling of the wire ropes. Strain gauges determined the pull being done on each cable and allowed for a balanced pull.

Commencement of righting operations on March 8, 1943. The twin drums of the winches reeled in the 1-inch wires of the fixed and moving tackles which were connected to the 3-inch wires run over the tops of the headframes to the starboard side of *USS Oklahoma*.

National Archives

Construction of the winch foundations on Ford Island on Oct. 28, 1942.

National Archives

Placing a headframe on the hull of USS Oklahoma on Jan. 8, 1943. There would be 21 in all, braced against the docking and centerline keels.

National Archives

Weight and fuel had been removed from the ship, and divers had divided the hull into seven compartments that could be made watertight with manifolds to control the air pressure. To prevent the ship from sliding sideways, 2,200 tons of coral soil was deposited near the bow to stabilize the soft mud. The righting procedure began on the morning of March 8, 1943.

Righting was a slow, controlled process, with frequent stops to clear the wire from the drums, and make minor repairs. When the hull reached 68 degrees, the headframes were removed and floated clear. On June 6, with the ship inclined only two degrees, the effort was declared completed and the refloating phase begun.

The capsized USS Oklahoma was righted by building headframes on her side and pulling with purchases and winches mounted ashore on Ford Island.

US Navy

Oklahoma was now upright and resting on the bottom. The next effort involved restoring buoyancy and floating the ship. Patching included large steel and wood open–topped coffer-dam patches and the bottom sealed in concrete. A wooden coffer-dam similar to the one used on *Oglala* was also constructed. The hull was pumped and *Oklahoma* floated on November 3, 1943. Not counting the drydock period that followed, the salvage took 18 months. The work was a testament to the skill and resolve of the officers that planned and supervised the effort, and to the troops that did the work. Captain Wallin was still the salvage officer, and Captain Francis H. Whitaker, the salvage superintendent.

Oklahoma went into dry dock, her turrets and superstructure were removed, and she was towed to the repair basin. There she was stripped of her guns and remaining upperworks, and remained afloat in West Loch at Pearl Harbor for the remainder of the war. She was decommissioned and was being towed to the West Coast on May 17, 1947, when she sank under tow. *Oklahoma* lost 415 men of her complement of 1,354 on December 7.

Preparations for righting USS *Utah* took 13-months, mostly due to the lack of equipment that had to come from the mainland. There was not much enthusiasm for floating *Utah*. Admiral Robert Ghormley, commandant of the 14th Naval District, said it should be towed to sea and sunk. The Bureau of Ships said all work should cease, and the sailors were weary and wanted to be done with salvage work. But, Captain William F. Furlong, commandant Navy Yard, Pearl Harbor, wanted to float *Utah*, patch her, and return her to the West Coast for scrap. The chief of naval operations concurred, and so the righting effort commenced on February 9, 1944.[14]

USS Utah alone and abandoned. She was not recoverd, and remains a memorial.

Naval Historical Center

Initially, *Utah* rolled easily and reached a position of 68 degrees. Then suddenly, *Utah* began to sink in the mud rather than roll on top of it. The soil under the ship could not support her weight. The hull rotated so far and sunk so deep that the cable assemblies, cables, and headframes became embedded in the mud and could not be removed. They had to be blasted off with dynamite later. Continued pulling failed to stop the sinking and a determination was made to leave *Utah* where she was. Her remaining upperworks were removed, and she now lies where she was left, a memorial to those men who reside in her and to their shipmates.

On May 6, 1942, the toppled, blackened foremast of the *Arizona* was cut down and placed on a barge. The mainmast was cut away on August 23, and the number three and four turrets cut away and given to the army for shore batteries. In 1943, the second turret and the superstructure were moved. Over time, the hull settled into the mud so that only the barbette of turret number three was visible. USS *Arizona* was stricken from the register of navy ships on July 7, 1944.

The USS *Arizona* Memorial was constructed using funds donated by individuals, the U.S. Congress, and the State of Hawaii. It was dedicated on Memorial Day 1962. The bodies of more than 1,100 men are still entombed in the memorial. When the visitor center was completed in 1980, the National Park Service began operating tours to the memorial.

6

HIDEKI TOJO

General Hideki Tojo, Premier of
Japan, 1941-1944.

US Army

Most Americans believed Hideki Tojo to be responsible
for the war in the Pacific, and for all evil things that happened
during the war. Not only was Tojo the prime minister of Japan
when Pearl Harbor was attacked, he also held the posts of minister
of war, education, commerce and industry. Without question, Tojo
was the most visible of the Japanese leadership during the war,
and commanded the most print in American newspapers, but his
actions paled in contrast to the atrocities committed by Masanobu
Tsuji and Shiro Ishii. Yet, Tsuji and Ishii were never charged as
war criminals, while Tojo was hanged as one. Other chapters in
War in the Pacific explain why Tsuji and Ishii were never charged;
this chapter will describe Tojo's guilt.

Tojo was born in Tokyo on December 30, 1884. He was
the son of an army general who served in both the Sino-Japanese
and Russo-Japanese wars. The senior Tojo published a book on
the art of war which was recognized as a work of distinction.

When he retired at the age of 53, he was promoted to the grade of lieutenant general.

Like his father, Hideki did well in the area military and central preparatory schools. Hideki's final schooling and training was interrupted by Russia's war with Germany. Japan stationed forces in Manchuria, near the Soviet border, to take advantage of any Russian setback at the hands of the Germans. Due to the "emergency," Tojo was commissioned a second lieutenant in half the time normally required.

Tojo married Katsu Ito, aged 19, in 1909. Ito was attending Tokyo Women's College and planned to complete her education. By the time she finished raising seven children, however, it was much too late. The war was over and she was a widow.

Tojo attended the army war college from 1912 to 1915 and graduated with honors. Following a series of short assignments, he was sent to Berne, Switzerland, where he was the military attaché at the Japanese Embassy. Also assigned to the embassy at this time was Shigenori Togo. Togo would later become foreign minister in Tojo's cabinet and one of the "doves" seeking peace with the United States.

Tojo returned to Japan in 1922 amidst a clamor for change. Political parties were being exposed as corrupt and young army officers were resorting to direct action in defiance of civil and military authority. The military initiated actions abroad and assassinated public figures in Japan. Tojo was not a maverick and did not participate in the internal uprisings or the Kwantung Army's fabrications in China. He was assigned to the army general staff shortly before the assassination of Marshall Chang Tso-lin in Manchuria in 1927. This event led to the "Mukden Incident" of 1931, and Japan's subsequent occupation of Manchuria.[1]

In 1937, while chief of staff of the Kwantung Army (Japan's army in China), Tojo sent an urgent top secret message to the vice chief of staff of the general staff in Tokyo. The message advised that Japan should deliver a knock-out blow against Chiang Kai-shek's nationalist government in Nanking to eliminate Chiang's government and military.[2]

Tojo's recommendation was acted upon in mid-December 1937, when the reinforced Japanese army committed the Rape of Nanking.[3] Tojo's message became available after the war and was

88

used by the prosecution during Tojo's trial for war crimes. Tojo argued that his message did not initiate the attacks upon Shanghai, Wanping, Peking, and Tiensin. The judges believed otherwise.

Tojo actually led two Kwantung army brigades in a flanking movement against Chinese troops in the Peking area. This was the first combat experience for the 53-year-old general and he was credited with a highly successful operation.[4] One Japanese triumph followed another until the entire area of outer Mongolia came under Japanese control.

During March 1938, Tojo was recalled from China to serve as vice-minister of war under Lieutenant Gen. Seishiro Itagaki, his successor as chief of staff of the Kwantung Army. Following the war, both Tojo and Itagaki were found guilty of war crimes in China. Tojo was one of the few that believed Japan could wage a simultaneous war with China and the Soviet Union. Tojo was forced to resign his position in the war ministry because of his views, and was assigned as inspector-general of the army air force.

In July 1938, the folly of Tojo's two-front offensive became apparent. A small point of land along the frontier bordering Manchuria, Korea and the USSR, became the site of a confrontation between Russia and Japan. Japan demanded that the Soviets remove their border guards along the disputed territory or Japan would use force to dispose of them. The Soviet's increased their guards and number of patrols until fighting broke out on July 29. By August 11, the Soviets reinforced their ground and aviation components in the area to such an extent that the Japanese had to back down and accept the boundary lines as they were with the Soviet armed border guards.

The action was an embarrassment to the Japanese army and festered until May 1939, when the two countries again came to blows over the border region. By May 28, the fighting escalated to a war with artillery, tanks and aircraft. By September, Japan lost 50,000 men to the Soviet's 9,000.[5] Again, Japan resorted to diplomacy to end the conflict. Lieutenant Gen. Itagaki was in charge of the Japanese forces in both conflicts.

The Japanese Army was becoming increasingly displeased with the actions of the cabinet led by Prime Minister (Admiral) Mitsumasa Yonai. The army was committed to Japan's colonization of the Far East, and felt the Yonai cabinet was reacting too slowly if at all. During July 1940, the Japanese Army toppled the cabinet and replaced it with one more to their liking. Tojo became war minister in the new cabinet headed by Prince Fumimaro Konoye. As war minister, Tojo announced that he intended to settle the China Incident.

Tojo's idea of settling the China Incident was to force the French to halt supplies to Chiang Kai-shek through French Indo-China, obtain permission for the passage of Japanese troops through French Indo-China and to use the airfields and raw materials in the country. In similar manner, Great Britain was to be forced to terminate aid to China along the Burma Road, from Burma to Kunming, China. With China isolated from all sources of supply, Tojo believed Chiang would be forced to negotiate with Japan.

Once the China Incident was settled, Japan would take advantage of the war in Europe to seize an empire in Asia. This was the initial planning that led Japan to attack Pearl Harbor less than 18 months later. Behind every initiative in the Konoe cabinet was the philosophy of obtaining everything possible through diplomacy; but when diplomacy failed, resort to force. Konoe established the Imperial Rule Assistance Association (IRRA), the intent being to form a one-nation, one-party system of government to help settle the China Incident. His hope was to keep the army out of the government decision-making process, but it was far too late for that.

The IRAA was also intended to permit the government to do what it wanted at home and abroad without opposition. Under the system, anyone who disagreed or questioned the decisions of the IRRA would be arrested and prosecuted. The IRRA announced that Japan would march "one-hundred-million strong" in whatever direction the government chose.[6]

Initially, Tojo was content to be overshadowed by the foreign minister and to cooperate with members of the cabinet and the army. He was not greatly involved with the planning or signing of the Tripartite Pact in Germany on September 27, 1940. The Pact, so Tojo believed, would serve notice to Russia to leave the Manchurian border area alone since such a provocation would involve Germany. Five days after signing the Pact, Japan began occupying bases in French Indo-China and moving forces and equipment through Indo-China into China.

When Chiang would not sign an agreement with Japan, a puppet government was installed in Nanking by the Japanese army, and a basic treaty signed with Wang Ching-Wei, the puppet leader.

As a result of the agreement, China became a province of Japan, at least in the eyes of the Japanese army and the Konoe cabinet. During this period, pressure was also put on Thailand to allow the movement of Japanese forces through Thailand and into Malaya. During the fall 1940, Japan placed demands upon the Dutch East Indies for increased exports of bauxite and oil. The Dutch balked at the demands and negotiations continued into 1941.

At the time that Japan was occupying Hainan, annexing the Spratley Islands, dispatching troops to French Indo-China, leveraging Thailand, and demanding more exports from the Dutch East Indies, they were caught completely by surprise on June 22, 1941, when Germany invaded the Soviet Union. The surprise illustrates the lack of coordination between Germany and Japan. A similar relationship continued for the duration of the war.

Japan decided not to enter the German-Soviet war, but rather to prepare to strike south into Malaya, Singapore, and the Dutch East Indies. Obviously, the United States and Great Britain stood in her way. Britain was seen as being fully occupied with the war in Europe and only the U.S. Pacific Fleet posed a deterrent to Japan's plans for Asia. It was decided to negotiate with the U.S. to keep America out of the war. If the U.S. should go to war against Germany, Japan would attack the U.S.

Events moved at a faster pace in the summer of 1941. On June 17, Japan broke off negotiations with the French over occupation of Indo-China. On July 26, the United States froze all Japanese assets in their country. Great Britain and the Netherlands followed suit. Japan faced the possibility of a total economic blockade. Tojo saw this development as justification for going to war. Japan was only exercising its right to self defense.[7]

Tojo was concerned with more than the economic blockade, American aid to China, and the Pacific Fleet. He cited Roosevelt's "arsenal of democracy speech," American spending of $33 million for military expansion, and the upgrading of military facilities throughout the Pacific.

Relations continued to deteriorate between the two countries with the Japanese military pushing the cabinet for a deadline to go to war with the United States. On September 20, the military submitted a demand for a date of October 15 for Japan to resort to war. On the evening of October 5, Konoe advised Tojo that he intended to continue negotiations with the United States to the very end. Tojo advised that the demands of the military had to be met if the cabinet were to continue. A continuation of negotiations would place Japan at the mercy of American interests.

Following an inconclusive but noisy cabinet meeting on October 12, Konoe resigned as prime minister and dissolved the cabinet three days later. The Emperor designated Tojo to form a new cabinet the following day. Thus, Tojo would forever be known as the man that led Japan to war. The fact is that it was the military, and especially the army, that led Japan to war. Tojo's job was to coordinate the military and civilian plans and efforts in order to win the war.

As prime minister, Tojo's character became well defined. He was blunt and decisive, forthright and aggressive. Once a decision had been made to go to war, he would allow no interference with such a decision. In addition to being prime minister, he kept the posts of commerce, education and industry. He was promoted to full general on active duty, an obvious implication that the army gained and accepted full responsibility for the policies and conduct of Japan.

Less than two months later, Japan attacked Pearl Harbor. At the war crimes trial, Tojo admitted that he knew of Japan's plan to attack Pearl Harbor but did not know the date. Japan went to war in December, because they could not wait. Every day they delayed, the shortage of oil for the navy became more acute. If they were to resort to force, they had to do so by December 7. After that, the navy would not have sufficient fuel to engage in war. Some say that Japan's military must have been reading Shakespeare's attitude of Brutus:

> There is a tide in the affairs of men,
> Which taken at the flood, leads on to fortune;
> Omitted, all the voyage of their life
> Is bound in shallows and in miseries.
> On such a full tide we are now afloat:
> And we must take the current when it serves,
> Or lose our ventures.

Tojo served as prime minister through Japan's impressive military successes. Parades, the ringing of bells, and distribution of presents hailed the victories at Pearl Harbor, Wake Island, Hong Kong, Singapore, the Philippines, Malaya, Singapore, and Rangoon. A euphoria filled the air. Tojo enjoyed the successes but knew there would be difficult days ahead. Even during the "success" period, he reiterated that the 100-million people of Japan must devote their entire energies, and even their lives, to the service of the state.

Tojo was correct. The successes were relatively short-lived. Reverses at Midway on June 4, 1942, and Guadalcanal later in the year, stopped the Japanese advance and sent their military on the way back to the home islands. It would still be a long war, but Japan was now losing it. Perhaps in atonement for the military atrocities at Hong Kong, Bataan, Manila, Singapore, and Burma, the Japanese people that survived the war, suffered through four hard years of back-breaking toil.

All Japanese male civilians were expected to work full-time, and to wear the national uniform, consisting of khaki trousers and leggings, and a peaked cap. The women of Japan also worked full-time and wore a baggy and unattractive bloomer-looking garment called a *monpe*. Children were pressed into military production on a part-time basis initially, and then full-time near the end of the war. Schools were used to store military supplies and school yards were converted into vegetable gardens. As the war progressed, food became scarce, all metal was confiscated for defense, there was no fuel for heating, and all imported materials were reserved for the military.

Starting in 1943, Tojo's speeches began to stress the seriousness of the situation facing Japan. Air raids could be expected and an Allied landing on the heartland was a possibility he told the public. In a more closely held speech, he told the cabinet that Japan was suffering from the Allied submarine attacks on merchant shipping. Rationing was necessary to fully utilize what Japan could import. As always, however, he boasted that hard work and the national spirit would overcome all difficulties.

In early 1944, Japan's strategic base at Truk in the Caroline Islands was destroyed by the largest carrier-based aircraft attack in history. Japan lost 20 ships and 200 aircraft. This loss of a strategic base in the Pacific forced Tojo to relieve General Hajime Sugiyama and assume the post as army chief of staff himself. Simultaneously, Admiral Toshio Shimada was designated to replace Navy Minister Admiral Asami Nagano. Both cabinet changes amounted to the same routine as changing baseball managers or basketball coaches when the team is losing. There was little anyone could do to change the eventual outcome of the war.

Tojo was beginning to find the existing political system more than he could handle. He had never been able to resolve the inter-service squabbles and failure to communicate between the army and navy. The power of the army, even though he was the chief of staff, was beyond his control. Militarily, Allied forces were advancing throughout the Pacific, culminating in the Allied seizure of Saipan in mid June 1944. From Saipan, American long-range bombers would deliver air attacks on the homeland. As if these problems were not enough, Japan's army in Burma was retreating in disorder before the British advance led by General William Slim.

Japan's problems gave some degree of hope to those who opposed a continuation of the war. Although it was impossible to openly oppose the army, a small group of concerned Japanese leaders were determined to find a way to negotiate an end to the war. These men were former Prime Ministers Prince Fumimaro Konoe, Admiral Mitsumasa Yonai, and Admiral Keisuke Okada. The three knew that if peace was to be obtained, they must first obtain Tojo's resignation. For a year they worked carefully and circuitously in order to not arouse resentment or dissension. Their solution was for Tojo to resign his position, rather than an overthrow of the entire cabinet. It was believed that the impact of such an overthrow would have disastrous implications for the country in light of Japan's current situation.

During February 1944, Japan's elder statesmen met with Tojo to convince him to resign. Tojo refused to resign, believing the problem to be the way the cabinet was organized, rather than him. He attempted to reorganize the cabinet instead. The three former prime Ministers spread the word of their dissatisfaction with Tojo and their work was so effective that when Tojo appeared in the Diet, he was greeted with silence rather than the usual applause, a hint of trouble that did not go unnoticed by Tojo.

The climax came on July 17, 1944, when the statesmen, led by Konoe and Kido, drafted a statement for the emperor calling for a unified cabinet, a typical Japanese oblique way of saying that Tojo should step down. The emperor signed the document and it was delivered to the cabinet. Tojo realized he had lost support and resigned his cabinet on July 18.

Tojo was gone but not completely forgotten. He resigned his cabinet after serving nearly three years in the highest ministerial position in Japan. Tojo's resignation was overshadowed by the death of President Franklin Roosevelt and the attempted assassination of Adolph Hitler. Although Tojo disappeared from public view, he remained as an elder statesman and continued to influence policy. During February 1945, he was given a private audience with Emperor Hirohito. Tojo briefed the emperor that the United States could be expected to step up its attacks against Japan significantly once Germany had been defeated. The date set by the Allies for defeat of Germany was April, two months away. Tojo explained that the only way the army and navy could be expected to work together was if they both came under the emperor's direct administration and command. Tojo said he did not believe that the Soviet Union would attack Japan, and that the special attack *(kamikaze)* corps seemed to promise excellent results in the future.

Hirohito listened to many elder statesmen as conditions worsened. Prince Konoe told the emperor that he believed the war had already been lost. Unless hostilities could be terminated soon, he expected the Soviets to invade and foment a communist revolution. The new prime minister, General Kunaiaki Koiso, lacked the moral strength and will to free himself of the army's political power. He was replaced by Kantaro Suzuki, who had a mandate from the emperor to end the war.

The battles for Iwo Jima and Okinawa took a heavy toll on both sides, but the Americans were able to reinforce their manpower and produce additional ships and aircraft, whereas Japan could not. From Okinawa, the Allies could pound Japan into submission whether the military agreed to surrender or not. The dropping of the two atomic bombs was, in reality, a positive thing, saving millions of casualties on both sides. The emperor agreed to surrender on August 15 and Japan signed the instruments of surrender on September 2, 1945.

It took two weeks after Japan's surrender before the occupying powers found time to arrest Tojo and 39 other suspected war criminals. During this period, numerous war correspondents found their way to Tojo's home and insisted upon interviews for their papers. Tojo's home was guarded by a few Japanese policemen and soldiers who were there to protect Tojo from fanatics rather than American journalists. Tojo was available and polite during such visits. He usually invited the correspondents to come into his garden, provided cigarettes and tea. Speaking through an interpreter, Tojo declined to discuss political or military affairs, but willingly answered questions about his responsibility for the war. Tojo said he accepted full responsibility for the war, but insisted that did not make him a war criminal. He said it would be up to a third party to decide if Japan's fight was just.

On Tuesday, September 11, MacArthur ordered the suspected war criminals arrested. Many correspondents, photographers, and curiosity seekers went to Tojo's home to view his arrest. While Tojo sat at his desk in his house, the activity outside the house increased. Tojo asked his wife to take the maid and go to the home of some relatives that lived nearby. Mrs Tojo left, with an admonition for her husband not to do anything rash. She then circled around the house and waited in the yard of a neighbor's house (Dr. Suzuki) across the street, where she could observe what happened. Tojo had expected the arrest and ironically, such an event to occur and had asked Doctor Suzuki to draw an x over his (Tojo's) heart with charcoal so that he would not miss the spot when he used his small .25-caliber pistol to commit suicide.

Major Paul Kraus, a Nisei army captain, a special agent, and three lieutenants arrived at 2:00 P.M. to arrest Tojo. A former *kempeitai* (military secret police) officer answered the door and went to tell Tojo he had company. Six minutes later, the agent returned to ask if the officers had credentials. Six minutes later, Tojo sent word that he would see only the person in charge. Then, Tojo suddenly appeared at an open window at the side of the house. He could only be seen from the waist up. He identified himself as General Tojo and asked Krause if this was an official arrest. Kraus told Tojo that he was directed to bring Tojo to Yokohama and that he should prepare immediately for the trip.

At 4:17 P.M., a shot was heard coming from inside the house. Kraus and his men kicked the outside door down, kicked out the inner door, and threw aside the furniture which had been piled against the door. Tojo was seen sitting in a stuffed chair, bleeding from a wound just below the heart. He was still conscious and waved the pistol towards the soldiers. Kraus ordered Tojo to drop the gun and he did. One of the arresting officers retrieved two weapons, a .32 caliber Colt pistol, a .25 caliber pistol, and a Japanese "*hara kiri*" (ritual suicide) sword.

A Japanese doctor arrived at 5:15 P.M. Tojo was still conscious and refused treatment, but bandages were placed on the entry and exit wounds. An hour later, an American medical team, headed by an army surgeon, James B. Johnson, Jr., and an ambulance arrived. Dr. Johnson had the room cleared of spectators and examined Tojo. He found a weak but steady heartbeat. The Japanese doctor was still on the scene and told Johnson that "the general was shot through the heart-would soon die-and nothing could be done for him."[8]

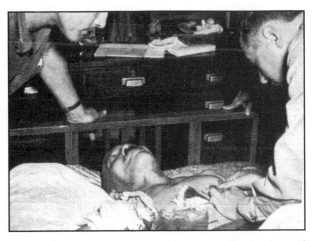

General Hideki Tojo, about two hours after he shot himself Sept. 11, 1945. He is being examined by Dr. James B. Johnson, the first US Army medical officer to arrive at the scene.

US Army

When Johnson removed the bandage from the entrance side of the wound, he recognized the sucking sound of a punctured lung. Tojo was breathing air into his lungs and exhaling it through the hole in his chest. Johnson started administering blood plasma and noticed that Tojo's pulse began to increase. He stitched the wound closed with some white thread, a dull curved needle, and well-worn scissors. He then applied airtight bandages to the wound and injected some morphine into a vein. Tojo was ready to travel.

Doctor Johnson gave Tojo another plasma transfusion and, after posting a Nisei interpreter at the side of the bed, retired for the night. It was 10:30 P.M. In following days it was found that Tojo had lost half of his normal blood and required six transfusions. Slowly, Tojo was nursed back to health against his will. The United States wanted to save Tojo so they could try him and hang him properly.

Tojo became a scapegoat for the Japanese people. The entire country seemed to echo the sentiment that, "Tojo is to blame for everything. He got us into war. He is a miserable bungler. He should have used a knife."[9] When it became known in Japan that Tojo would be tried as a war criminal, a flood of letters addressed to MacArthur was received. One letter respectfully requested that Tojo's entire family be executed. Another said that Tojo's head should be publicly displayed in Hibiya Park in Tokyo, and that Mrs. Tojo be given a life imprisonment sentence.[10]

Tojo was quietly transferred from the army hospital to the Omori prison camp. The camp had been a POW camp where Allied prisoners were held, tortured, and murdered. It was a foul, filthy place where the *kempeitai* had plied their special torture skills upon starving, sick, defenseless POWs. Tojo and other suspected war criminals were given adequate food, blankets and hot water for baths, something the Allied POWs never had.

It became apparent that Omori was limited as a detention camp for a long period. A new site, Sugamo prison, was selected in the northwestern section of Tokyo. The buildings were repaired, cleaned and heating facilities installed. Space was made for 1,500 prisoners. Tojo spent his time exercising, smoking cigarettes, and talking to his defense team. He also began composing poems in the Japanese style.

General Tojo at the Omori prison camp in November, 1945.

National Archives

During April 1946, indictments naming 28 defendants (class A war criminals) were presented to the Military Tribunal of the Far East, a court of 11 judges. The indictment consisted of 58

98

counts, arranged in three different categories. Class A criminals included the leadership of Japan. These men were not charged with a single act of atrocity but could be found guilty for the responsibility of leading Japan to war, and for atrocities committed during the war. The tribunal met for the first time on Friday, May 3, 1946. The prosecution began its presentation of evidence in mid June 1946.

On November 4, 1948, the International Military Tribunal for the Far East, commonly called the "Tokyo Trial," convened to deliver its verdict against those tried as war criminals. The verdict was a long time coming. The trials began in the spring of 1946, and, after 417 days and costs of $10 million, (a dollar for every word spoken in the courtroom), the attendees and defendants hoped for a quick conclusion to the event.

They were disappointed. Sir William Webb, the Australian president of the tribunal, took seven more days to read the 1,500-page judgment. Tojo was found guilty of seven of the nine charges filed against him. The charges were:

One: "as a leader, . . . in the execution of a common plan or conspiracy . . . to wage wars of aggression, and war or wars in violation of international law."

Two: "having waged an unprovoked war against China."

Three, four and five: "having waged aggressive war against the United States, the British Commonwealth, and the Netherlands."

Six: "waging war against France."

Seven: "having ordered, authorized, and permitted inhumane treatment of POWs and others."

Tojo was found not guilty of waging war against the Soviet Union and a no-verdict was delivered on the charge of having "deliberately and recklessly disregarded his duty to take adequate steps to prevent atrocities."[11] After a short recess, the defendants returned to the court to hear Webb announce the verdicts. Fifteen of the men were sentenced to life imprisonment. Former foreign minister Mamoru Shigemitsu received a sentence of seven years, and Shigenori Togo, also a foreign minister, received 20 years in prison. [12]

General Tojo hearing his sentence on Nov. 12, 1948.

The remaining seven defendants, The "Seven Samurai," Kenji Doihara, Iwane Matsui, Akira Muto, Seishiro Itagaki, Koki Hirota, Heitaro Kimura, and Tojo, were all sentenced to death. The Tribunal adjourned on November 12, 1948.

Tojo and the other condemned men were placed in seven adjoining cells in a cellblock of Sugamo prison. The cellblock was cleared of all other prisoners. The cells were eight feet long, five-and-a-half feet wide, and ten feet high. Security precautions were rigorously enforced, due in part to Hermann Goering's cheating of the executioner at the Nuremberg war trials in Germany.

Each cell contained a desk, washbasin, mattress, and sanitary facilities. The entire cellblock was heated. Guards were constantly present outside each cell and a medical aid army NCO was immediately available. The defendants were given until November 19 to submit appeal petitions. On November 24, General MacArthur, as supreme Allied commander, upheld all the verdicts. On November 30, a stay of execution was ordered pending a Supreme Court review of the proceedings. The petition was submitted by lawyers for Koki Hirota and Kenji Doihara.

On December 20, the Supreme Court ruled that the Tribunal was not a court of the United States, and therefore the Supreme Court had no power to review the petition.[13]

Tojo spent his time in prison working with his defense lawyers, preparing messages to the Japanese people, writing *haiku* and *waka* (Japanese style poems), and talking with Dr. Shinso Hanayama, a Buddhist priest serving as a prison chaplain. During such meetings, Tojo was handcuffed to two soldiers, one on each side.

The commandant of Sugamo prison was notified on December 21 by General MacArthur to carry out the execution of Tojo and the other six men on December 23. The defendants were notified of the execution date on the evening of December 21.

In his final statement to Dr. Hanayama, Tojo reiterated much of what he said during his trial. The vanquished should have been tried by a third party, not by the victors. Since this was a world war, perpetrated by Germany and Japan, one must wonder from where the third parties would have come. It is also interesting to speculate which third parties Tojo would have found to try Truman, MacArthur and Nimitz as war criminals if Japan had won the war.

Tojo went on to lament that America and Great Britain destroyed Japan, which had been a bulwark against communism in the Far East. The Allies turned Manchuria into a base for communists in Asia, and divided Korea, making it a source for future problems. Tojo neglected to praise the Allies for preventing the Soviet Union's occupation of northern Japan, thereby creating just the sort of problem about which he seemed concerned.

Tojo apologized for the atrocities that had been committed (although he had no knowledge of such atrocities at the time). He said America should apologize for the air attacks against Japan and for dropping the atomic bombs.[14]

Shortly after their meeting with Hanayama, Kenji Doihara, Iwane Matsui, Akira Muto and Tojo were led from their cells to a small Buddhist chapel on the first floor of the prison. The prisoners wore army fatigues with the letter "P" stenciled on the back. The men were allowed to light incense, light the altar candles, and sign their names with the traditional brush and black ink on heavy Japanese paper. They removed their dentures, spectacles, prayer beads, hair and nail clippings, and placed them in small boxes for their families.

Matsui led a *banzai* cheer for the emperor and the empire of Japan, after which the well-guarded prisoners were led to the gallows. The nooses and hoods were adjusted, the head executioner saluted the execution detail, and the traps were sprung. All four men were pronounced dead at one-and-a-half minutes after midnight on December 23, 1948.

The gallows prepared for war criminals. Note the 13 steps.

US Army

Shortly thereafter, Seishiro Itagaki, Koki Hirota, and Heitaro Kimura were led to the gallows. Later the same night, the bodies of the "Seven Samurai" were taken to the Kuboyama Crematorium in Yokohama, where they were cremated, and their ashes scattered to the winds.[15]

Tojo wrote his own epitaph several months earlier in prison.

Juyo kyutsu
Ten no mei nari

Whether life is long or short,
Whether we succeed or fail,
Is in accordance with the will of Heaven.[16]

102

7

SUBHAS CHANDRA BOSE

Subhas Chandra Bose was unquestionably a fierce advocate for India's freedom from British colonialism. Bose's militant approach to Indian freedom continues to generate debate within India and the world today, nearly 65 years after he devoted his life to the cause of complete and immediate freedom for India. His cause was frustrated by Indian leaders, such as Mahatma Gandhi, who advocated a non-violent struggle against British rule.

Bose was born on January 23, 1897, in Orissa, India. He was the ninth child in a family of 14 children. He received his BA in philosophy from the Presidency College in Calcutta, finishing at the top of his class. He traveled to England and completed his examinations for the Indian Civil Service, also finishing at the top of his class. Disturbed by the Jallianwalla Bagh massacre, Bose returned to India, joined the Indian National Congress, under Mahatma Gandhi, and began his crusade for India's freedom.

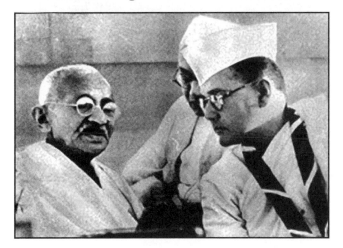

Bose (at right) with Mahatma Ghandi at the Haripura Congress session in February, 1938.

National Archives

103

The Jallianwalla Bagh massacre took place on April 13, 1919. On that date, British Lieutenant Governor, Sir Michael O'Dwyer, authorized fire on 20,000 unarmed Indians who had congregated at the Bagh in Amritsar to protest against the imprisonment of Gandhi and other Indian independence leaders. The troops at the scene gave no warning for the crowd to disburse. Revolutionary leader, Lala Laipat Rai, in the United States at the time, returned to India and charged O'Dwyer as responsible for the entire blood bath in Punjab, not only in Amritsar, but also in Lahore, Gujranwalla, Kasur, and Shaaikupura.[1]

Lajpat Rai went on to tell the Indian people that ". . . no man in India has done such a great disservice to the British Empire and brought such a disgrace on the good name of the British nation as Sir Michael O' Dwyer."[2]

Bose was even more outspoken in his anti-British stance. He was jailed eleven times between 1930 and 1941 for his opposition to British rule of India. His imprisonment sentences varied between six months and three years. He led the youth wing of the Congress Party and organized trade unions in opposition to the British government.

Bose split with the National Congress Committee (headed by Gandhi), which advocated freedom for India in phases. Bose wanted complete freedom for India immediately. Other younger leaders, such as Jawaharlal Nehru, supported Bose and were able to get the Congress to adopt "Complete Freedom" as its motto during the historic Lahore Congress convention. Bose opposed the Gandhi-Irvin Peace Pact, was imprisoned, and expelled from India. He returned and was imprisoned again.

In 1937, Bose warned the Indian people and the British that war was imminent and India should not be dragged into a war on the side of the British. He was elected president of the Indian National Congress twice, in 1937, and again in 1939, defeating Gandhi's nominee in the process. In 1939, he delivered a resolution to the British demanding that Great Britain give India her independence within six months or India would revolt against British occupation. Bose did not have the necessary support for his position and was forced to resign from his post as president. He formed a progressive group named Forward Block, and continued his freedom-now policy.

World War II began in September 1939, as predicted by Bose, and Britain declared India a warring state. The declaration

104

was made without consulting Indian leaders, and all Indian state governments resigned in protest.

Bose began a mass movement against Britain's mobilization of Indian men and resources for the war. Indian response to his movement was tremendous, and as a result, the British authorities imprisoned him. Bose began a fast to protest his imprisonment on November 29, 1940, and due to his failing health, he was released after the 11th day. The British feared massive uprisings should Bose die in prison, so he was placed under house arrest with an attending physician and constant guards.

On January 26, 1941, the authorities realized that Bose was no longer in the house where he was kept under arrest. He left in disguise on January 17 with his nephew, Sisir Kumar Bose, under an Italian passport with the assumed name of Orlando Mazzota. He traveled by foot, car, and train, and crossed the Kabul River using leather bags as flotation devises. He next appeared in Kabul. From there, he made his way to Berlin, via Moscow, arriving on March 28, 1941.[3]

In November 1941, Bose began a series of broadcasts from German radio stations aimed at the Indian people. His radio messages energized the Indian masses and gave them strength to challenge British rule. Bose went on to make alliances with both Germany and Japan, receiving promises of military and economic assistance in his war against the British. Bose traveled the Atlantic, the Indian Ocean, the Middle East, and Madagascar, and as he sought to develop an Indian army to fight the British in India. Early in 1943, his army was formed with Indian Army deserters from British units in the middle East. The army numbered 2,000 men, and was trained in Frankenberg, Germany. The Indians received the same pay, clothing and food as the German military units.

There were numerous Foreign Legions in Hitler's army. Most were defectors from the Soviet bloc such as Cossacks, Turkmens, and Georgians. The Indian Legion was unique in that it was intended to fight against British forces as propaganda for the "Free India" cause espoused by Bose. While the German government army supported Bose's legion, many of their leaders did not. General Erwin Rommel refused their services in North Africa and Adolf Hitler was quoted as saying, "The Indian Legion is a joke. There are Indians who can't kill a louse, who'd rather let themselves be eaten up. They won't kill an Englishman either. I consider it nonsense to put them against the English.[4]"

Always an opportunist, Bose traveled to Tokyo following Japan's defeat of the British in Malaya and Singapore. He was recognized as the head of the Indian army, and was able to form additional units from Indian deserters from the defeated British Army in Malaya and Singapore. Bose termed his army, the Indian National Army (INA), declared an independent Indian government on October 21, 1943, and declared war on Great Britain and the United States.

Bose in his military uniform in 1943.

Recognition of the Provisional Government came quickly from nine countries, Japan, Burma, Croatia, Germany, the Philippines, Nanking China (Japan's puppet government in China), Manchuko (Japan's puppet government in Manchuria), Italy and Siam. The Japanese Army promised all-out support for the provisional government.

When the Japanese navy seized the Andaman and Nicobar islands in the Bay of Bengal early in the war, Prime Minister Tojo of Japan placed the islands under the jurisdiction of the provisional Indian Government thus giving Bose's government sovereignty over its first territory. Bose's government was composed of all Indians. German or Japanese interference was not tolerated in either the government or Indian army. Bose formed three army brigades, Subhash, Azid, and Gandhi.

Bose flew to Singapore from Tokyo on June 27, 1943. He was given a tumultuous welcome by the resident Indians. His speeches kept the listeners spellbound. By now, a legend had grown around him, and he mesmerized his audiences. Addressing representatives of the Indian communities in East Asia on July 4, he said:[5]

> Not content with a civil disobedience campaign, Indian people are now morally prepared to employ other means for achieving their liberation. The time has therefore come to pass on to the next stage of our campaign. All organizations whether inside India or outside, must now transform themselves into a disciplined fighting organization under one leadership. The aim and purpose of this organization should be to take up arms against British imperialism when the time is ripe and signal is given.

On July 27, 1943, Bose left Singapore for a 17-day tour of East Asian and Southeast Asian countries. The objective of this tour was to enlist moral and monetary support for his movement from other countries, as well as the resident Indian communities. He was given a rousing reception in Rangoon, where he attended the Burmese independence celebration. He enlisted the support of Prime Minister Phibun and received a tumultuous ovation from the Indian community. He then flew to Saigon and addressed Indians there. Returning to Singapore for a brief rest, he flew to Penang to address a rally of 15,000 Indians. Besides good will for his cause, Bose raised in excess of $2 million.

During early 1944, Bose made plans to join the Japanese invasion of India from Burma. He moved his provisional government headquarters to Rangoon, provided an Indian division for the Japanese assault on Dimapur, Kohima, and Imphal, India, and established a women's brigade within the INA.

Dimapur was the strategic objective for the Japanese army. It sat astride the only railway linking Calcutta to Ledo, India. Ledo was the base for all airlifted supplies to Chiang Kai-shek in China. If the railroad at Dimapur could be captured, the Allies would be unable to supply nationalist China. Although Gandhi advocated non-violent opposition to British rule, it should be remembered that Bose's supporters, especially in Bengal, made frequent attacks on the railways, stations, signal facilities, and on the trains themselves. Often, Indians stopped trains, removed Europeans and hacked them to death.[6] Lieutenant Gen. William Slim, commander of the British 14th Army, had to deploy 57 battalions to fight against sabotage of the trains. Internal security was an even greater problem. Once in India, though not publicized, Japan hoped that the Indian masses would welcome Bose's Indian army, rise up in revolt against the British, thus permitting both Japan and Bose to enter Delhi in triumph.

Lieutenant Gen. Renya Mutaguchi commanded the 15th Japanese Army, and had three divisions for his drive into India. Bose provided another division, the Subhas, although in size it was more of a regiment. Mutaguchi's total force numbered 130,000 men.

The town of Imphal, the capital of the state of Manipur, was situated on a flat treeless plateau just inside the Indian border from Burma. The town was at the 3,000-foot elevation level, and surrounded by impassable mountains on all sides. For Bose and the INA, the importance of the Imphal campaign was that it was the only major battle in which it would participate with the object of achieving freedom for India. The Imphal Operation became the final Japanese offensive of the East Asia War. The campaign lasted from March 15 to July 9, 1944, and resulted in the defeat of the Japanese army in Burma.

The execution order for the operation was issued on January 7, 1944. That evening, Lieutenant Gen. Masakazy Kawabe, commanding the overall Burma headquarters, held a welcome party in honor of Bose and his staff officers. Bose spoke, and concluded his speech with these words. "My only prayer to the Almighty at this moment is that we may be given the earliest opportunity to pay for our freedom with our own blood."[7]

Mutaguchi set March 15 as the D-day for the beginning of the Imphal campaign. He deployed 130,000 troops along the Chindwin river, over a front of 200 kilometers, undetected by British spies in the area. On D-day, Mutaguchi assembled the war correspondents at his headquarters in central Burma and declared: "I am firmly convinced that my three divisions will reduce Imphal in one month. In order that they can march fast, they carry the lightest possible equipment and food enough for three weeks. They will get all the supplies they need from British supply dumps. Boys! See you again in Imphal at the celebration of the Emperor's birthday on April 29."[8]

The Japanese-Indian offensive took the British by complete surprise. The Japanese and INA troops moved quickly through mountains and jungles pushing the 17th Indian Infantry Division back to Imphal. On March 22, Japanese forces swept past the India-Burma border, and advanced from the north and west to encircle Imphal. On April 8, Japanese Imperial Headquarters issued a communiqué which said: "Japanese troops, fighting side by side with the Indian National Army captured Kohima early on April 6." A jubilant Bose started talking with the Japanese about the administration of the liberated and soon-to-be-liberated territories in India. In response to a call by Bose, Prime Minister Tojo made an announcement clarifying that all areas of India occupied as a result of the Japanese advance would be placed under the jurisdiction of the Indian Provisional Government.

Japanese declarations about the capture of Kohima were premature. Kohima did not fall to the Japanese, nor did Imphal or Dimapur. Readers are directed to separate chapters describing the battles for Imphal and Kohima.

As the INA and the Japanese forces attacked Imphal, Allied air superiority gained strength and the British prepared for a counterattack. Shah Nawaz, commanding two battalions of the Subhas Division in the Chin Hills, later told of the hardships his men were suffering as a result of disease, supply and transport difficulties. However, owing to communication problems, the news of difficulties his men were undergoing at the front did not reach Bose.

During the short stalemate at the Indian border, Bose collected money and donations in Rangoon to finance the campaign. His offer of additional INA regiments to be sent to the border was accepted and more troops were dispatched. During mid-April, the military balance began to shift against Japan and the INA. Brigadier Orde Wingate's airborne unit had already been attacking Japanese supply routes. British forces were being supplied by airlift into the besieged Imphal, and reinforcements were arriving at Kohima.

Japan had no matching air power to strike back at enemy air operations. By the end of April, the battle strength of Japanese and INA divisions was decreased forty percent. Time for success by surprise attack had already passed and gradually the offensive turned into a defensive battle. The monsoon that followed brought the ultimate disaster. As roads became impassable, all supply routes were cut off. Muddy streams flooded roads and valleys, and rivers swelled to sweep away tanks and ammunition. In the wake of the monsoon, disease became rampant. Cholera, malaria, dysentery, beriberi and jungle sores began to take their toll. The INA and the Japanese started living on rations consisting of rice mixed with jungle grass. The 33rd Division had fought desperately for forty days without being able to penetrate the British lines at Imphal. And now that vast amounts of military supplies were reaching the British garrison at Imphal, there was virtually no hope for a renewed offensive. On July 8, on the recommendation of top-ranking generals including Kawabe and Mutaguchi, Prime Minister Tojo issued the order to halt the operation.

The story of retreat from Imphal is one of the great tragedies of World War II. It is a story of misery, hunger and death. Japanese and INA troops, bottled up in the Kawab valley between the Chin Hills in the west and the Chindwin river in the west, began their long trek back through jungles and mountains, headed by division commanders and guards in jeeps and horses. Officers, and supply, communication and medical units followed. Behind them marched thousands of stragglers: rain-soaked, emaciated with fever and malnutrition. Soon, corpses began accumulating along the trek, only to be left unburied. Of the 230,000 Japanese troops who began the Imphal and Kohima Campaign, only 130,000 survived, and of these only 70,000 remained at the front to retreat. INA casualties were more than fifty percent. It was a disaster equal in magnitude to Dunkirk and Stalingrad.

When Bose heard the order to retreat he was stunned. He made an effort to blunt the defeat by proclaiming, "Though the Japanese Army has given up the operation, we will continue it. We will not retreat even if the advance of our revolutionary army to attain independence of our homeland is completely defeated. Increase in casualties, cessation of supplies, and famine are not reasons enough to stop marching. Even if the whole army becomes only spirit we will not stop advancing toward our homeland. This is the spirit of our revolutionary army."[9] Despite Bose's oratory, the INA retreated with the rest of the Japanese forces.

During the last three months of 1944, Japanese forces withdrew to the banks of the Irrawaddy in Burma, where they intended to make a stand. Bose enthusiastically offered the reorganized INA First Division, when the Japanese 15th division was ordered to oppose the British. Subsequently, the 2nd Division was also readied for action. In February 1945, the INA held some positions in the region of Mandalay in Burma, giving battle to the advancing enemy. This was the second campaign of Bose's army, and it held out tenaciously at Nyaungu for some time. However, allied troops later crossed the Irrawaddy at several points, and the Japanese and INA units were surrounded, and some INA forces deserted.

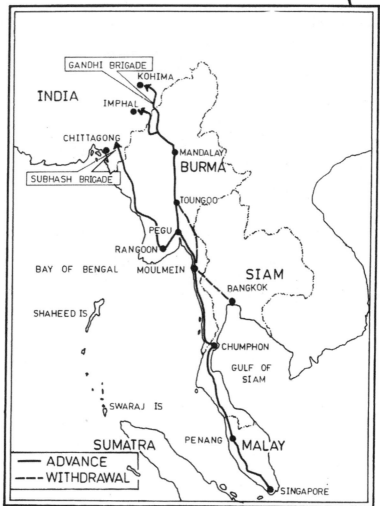

Route taken by the INA.

K.C. Yadav

The subsequent Allied use of the two atomic bombs forced Japan to surrender. Bose was in Singapore at the time, and decided to fly to Tokyo to plan his future course of action in India. His plane crashed at Matsuyama airport near Taipei on August 18, 1945. Bose and his aide, Colonel Habib-ur-Rahman were carried to Taihoku military hospital at 3:00 P.M. Rahman had less serious burns to his face and right arm, but Bose was badly burned over his entire body. He was examined by Dr. T. Yoshimi, an Army doctor. who found that no part of Bose's body was unburnt and did not give him long to live. Despite the severity of his burns, Bose was conscious.

With the help of Dr. Tsurata, Bose was treated with ointment, bandaged, and given medicine. Bose remained conscious and asked repeatedly for water. His entire body except for eyes and mouth was wrapped in bandages. Bose became unconscious at 7:00 P.M. on the 18[th,] and died at 10:00 P.M. Dr. Tsurata, Dr. Yoshimi, several nurses, Mr. Nakamura, an interpreter, and Colonel Rahman witnessed Bose's death. Cause of death was third-degree burns on the whole body.[10] Bose's remains were cremated, and his ashes flown to the Renkoji Temple at Koenji Asagaya, Japan. They remain there today.

I have given some detail to Bose's death because many continue to believe that Bose survived the crash and went underground. Dr. Satish Maikap postulates that Bose was captured, charged, tried, and executed by General Douglas MacArthur shortly after Japan's surrender. Maikap says MacArthur executed Bose without notifying President Truman or General Marshall. Bose was also rumored to have gone to China and Russia after the war.[11] It seems safe to assume that Bose did not survive. He could not have remained silent regarding the British terms for Indian independence. Bose was 48 years old in 1945. Initially, the British government announced they would try Bose's senior leaders as deserters and war criminals at military courts-martial. The trials began at the Red Fort in Delhi on September 8, 1945, and continued until December 31.[12] The Indian nation rebelled against such trials, and the British, in no position to face an open rebellion, were forced to grant amnesty for all INA soldiers.

Bose's "Freedom Now" position continues to be a heated item of debate today within India. His patriotism was perhaps overshadowed at times by his unwillingness to compromise and his recklessness in seeking alliances with the Axis powers. He lives on as a legend in Indian history, a history he helped create.

8

STILWELL'S RETREAT FROM BURMA: MAY, 1942

When the Japanese bombed Pearl Harbor on December 7, 1941, Major Gen. Joseph W. Stilwell was in command of the Third Army Corps at the Presidio of Monterey, California. Three months later, he landed in Chungking, China, to become Chiang Kai-shek's chief of staff.

There were many colorful US military characters in WW II. "Pappy" Boyington, George Patton, John Bulkeley, and "Bull" Halsey to name just a few. Perhaps "Vinegar Joe" Stilwell was as colorful as they came. His friend and boss, Field Marshal Sir William Slim, said of him, "He was over sixty, but he was tough mentally and physically. He could be as obstinate as a whole team of mules: he could be, and frequently was, downright rude to people ... I think it amused him to keep up the 'Vinegar Joe' tough guy attitude ... He was undoubtedly the most colorful character in South-East Asia-and I liked him."[1]

Japan invaded Burma on January 20, 1942, with two experienced divisions of infantry. They moved into Burma from occupied Siam, and drove quickly towards Rangoon, inflicting heavy casualties on the 17th Indian Division that opposed them. British General Sir William Slim arrived in Burma on March 13, 1942, to take command of the two battered British (Indian) divisions. Stilwell arrived on the same day, and was placed in command of all Chinese troops in Burma, the Fifth and Sixth armies.

Although Stilwell was in charge of the Chinese troops on paper, the Chinese commanders did not follow his instructions and retreated on their own initiative. In a conversation with General Tu Li-ming, Stilwell was told, "Ah your Excellency, the American general (Stilwell) only thinks he is commanding. In fact, he is doing no such thing. You see, we Chinese think that the only way to keep the Americans in the war is to give them a few commands on paper. They will not do much harm as long as we do the work."[2]

One Chinese division, the 38th, commanded of General Li-jen Sun, did conduct a skillful defensive action which shielded the British Army of Burma during its retreat, and reached northern Assam in India relatively intact.[3] For his excellent work, General Sun was awarded the Order of the British Empire, Knight Commander (Sir Li-jen Sun). The remaining Chinese forces in Burma crumbled and escaped into India or China as best they could.

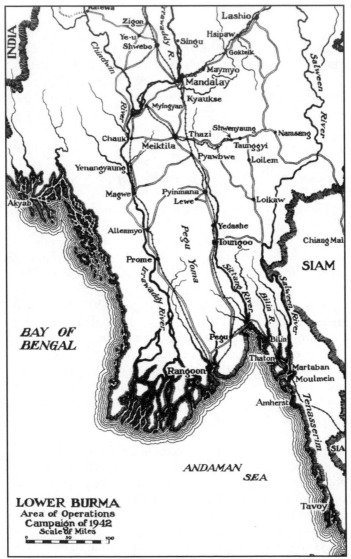

Lower Burma area of operations in 1942.

J.M. Dent

By mid-March 1942, Japanese forces pushed the British 17th Division up the Burmese peninsula past Tavoy, Amherst, Moulmein, Martaban, and finally, the Sittang River Bridge near Rangoon. Disaster struck there. British forces were encircled on the east bank of the Sittang River and cut off from the only bridge. Unable to break through the Japanese cordon, the British blew the bridge, leaving the English, Scottish, Burmese, Indian, and Gurkha forces to their fate on the east bank. The British commander was relieved during the fighting, confusion reigned, and a rout followed. Many Burmese deserted their positions; artillery was left intact; Gurkhas, who were unable to swim drowned by the hundreds; and all semblance of military discipline evaporated.

The Japanese marched into Rangoon unopposed, raised their flag, and seized the huge stores of supplies, ammunition, fuel, and vehicles the United States had brought to supply Chiang Kai-shek in China.

Moving quickly, the Japanese pushed north, past Prome, Toungoo, Magwe, Meiktila, Mandalay and Lashio. General Slim was at Prome, and Stilwell was at Toungoo trying to rally the Chinese forces. British forces fought well at Prome, and Chinese forces did the same at Toungoo, but the Japanese had air superiority and attacked the ground forces with bombs and cannon fire at will. The British and Chennault's Flying Tiger planes were caught on the ground and destroyed before getting airborne.

Slim's forces were defeated at Prome and fell back to Magwe. The Chinese 55th division at Loikaw, south of Mandalay, was defeated and simply disappeared. "It's impossible," Stilwell roared. "You cannot have a division in place one day and disappear off the face of the earth the next day.[4]" But they did. Only the commander, General Ch'en mien-wu, and his personal staff escaped and moved further north. Stilwell tried to have General Ch'en shot for cowardice, but that did not happen. The Chinese Generals answered only to Chaing Kai-shek.

Once the momentum of the retreat by British and Chinese forces got underway, there was little hope of reversing the situation. Stilwell never understood how two Japanese regiments were able to encircle two British divisions, and why the British, with twice as many troops, could not break out of the encirclement. The answer is that there was little fight left in the Allied forces. The commander of the British First Burma Division recommended to General Slim that the entire division be surrendered to the Japanese without a fight.[5]

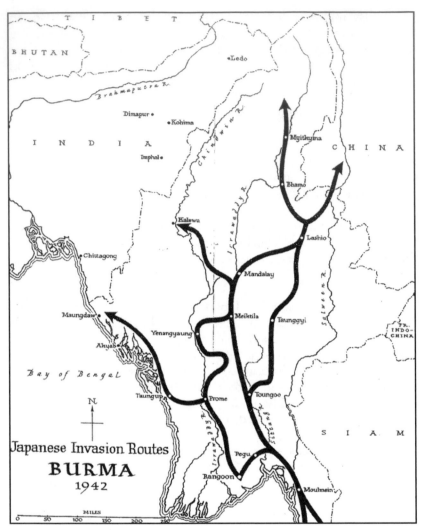

Japanese invasion routesin Burma in 1942.

Papermac

"Hold Mandalay" became the Allied cry, but Mandalay was a doomed city. Japanese bombers had taken a toll of the city in advance of ground forces. The moat surrounding the walls of the royal palace was jammed with bloated bodies. Smoke from fires created by the bombings drifted throughout the city. The streets were clogged with debris and corpses. Black crows were busy plucking out the eyes of the dead. Dogs and stray pigs feasted upon decaying bodies. The stench generated by the heat and the decay was unbearable. The population jammed the streets in their effort to flee the dying city.

116

"Hold Mandalay," the junction of all communication, road, and rail centers in Burma was the order. But the Burmese cut the electric lines, the roads were jammed by refugees, and the trains stopped running. A hasty conference of British and Chinese generals, plus Stilwell, resulted in an agreement that the Allied cause was lost and that the commanders needed to focus their attention on withdrawing from Burma to India with such forces as were still available.

Tens of thousands of British troops, trucks, artillery, and native refugees filled the bridge over the river leading north out of Mandalay. When the time came to blow the bridge, only one span went down. The bridge was still useable. As the troops trudged north, it was apparent that this was a defeated army. The Sikhs, proud of their heritage, were disheveled and dirty. Punjabis, once proud and cocky, were afraid, shoulders drooping and ready to quit. The Burmese merely looked for the opportunity to desert and meld into their own villages. The Chinese were trapped. They had no friends in Burma and did not know how to return to China. That knowledge was apparent in their posture and slow progress.

The British officers tried to maintain face, but knew full well they had lost it. They were quite aware that the natives held no respect for the "Lords" of the country any longer. Dependent upon the British for direction and government, the masses were lost without it. They slogged along behind the military convoys seeking what protection they could find. All Allied troops except Stilwell's group were out of Mandalay by April 28.

Without a command and trapped by the advancing Japanese forces, Stilwell had to escape to India by whatever means he could find. He hoped to take his group on the train from Wuntho (40 miles south of Indaw), to Myitkyina (pronounced mitch-in-ah), 200 miles to the north, and then fly to India. He assembled a group of 80 people, all wanting to travel to India. Major Frank Merrill, an American army officer assigned as an observer with the British army, and later to head the unit known as Merrill's Marauders, elected to walk out of Burma with Stilwell's group. When they started, the group had motor vehicles, consisting of three sedans, nine trucks, four jeeps, a pickup, and more jeeps to carry gasoline, food, baggage, and a radio. There were 28 American military; an American reporter; 16 Chinese guards and interpreters; seven British Quakers (ambulance drivers); nine Malay, Indian and Burmese cooks and helpers; plus the Burma surgeon, Doctor Gordon Seagrave and 19 of his nurses. They started their trek on May 1, 1942.

117

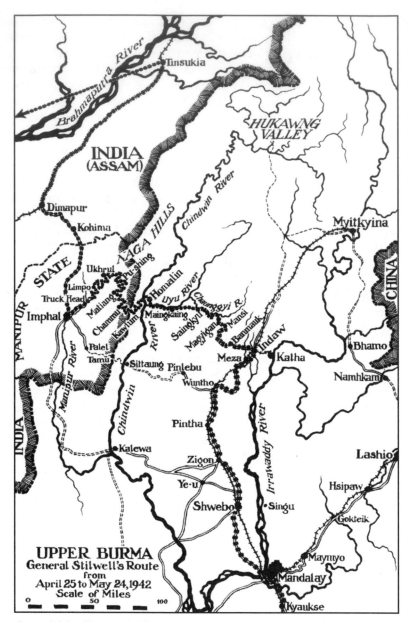

General Stilwell's route in Upper Burma in 1942.

J.M. Dent

Seagrave had worked in Burma as a surgeon all his life. His father and grandfather were missionaries along the China-Burma border before him. Seagrave established a hospital at Namkahem, south of Bhamo, where he treated Burmese who

118

contracted the scrub typhus disease common to the area. When the Japanese invaded Burma, and Chinese casualties became excessive, Seagrave volunteered to establish a field hospital at Pyinmana, 225 miles north of Rangoon. With him were Captain John Gridley of the Mayo Clinic; Captain John O'Hara, a dentist; 40 trained Shan and Burmese nurses; and part of an English Friends ambulance unit (conscientious objectors). Stilwell welcomed their services.

As the group headed north towards Myitkyina, they learned that the railroad had been hopelessly destroyed and blocked at Shwebo and again just short of Indaw. The dozen British officers that recently joined the Stilwell column decided to leave the group and travel west to the Chindwin river, cross the Chindwin at Sittang, and then trek northwest to Assam (India). Before they reached the Chindwin, they were ambushed by Japanese soldiers. Half the group was killed or wounded.

Stilwell decided to try and reach Mitkyina by vehicle or foot, and then fly to India. His group had high morale, led by the nurses singing Onward Christian Soldiers. They traveled for 24 hours and came to a bridge across the Irrawaddy River near Meza, where a Chinese military truck had broken through the floor planking, halting all vehicle traffic across the bridge.

Stilwell found a Chinese military engineer who said he had the necessary troops to repair the bridge, but also learned from two British officers that all the bridges from Indaw to Myitkyina were down and the Japanese were already entering Bhamo and moving fast toward Myitkyina. Stilwell decided to abandon his plan to reach Myitkyina and, instead, travel west to Homalin by whatever roads possible. At Homalin, they would cross the Chindwin and begin the long steep hike through the Naga Hills to Assam.

At Meza, Stilwell was offered 400 elephants to take to India, where he was told he could sell the beasts for a million dollars. Although tempted, Stilwell knew the elephants would slow his pace and the Japanese were closing in fast from the south. He declined the offer and started off in his motor column.

Whenever the convoy came to a downed bridge, they abandoned the road and bridge, searched for the closest fjord, and crossed the shallower rivers in the vehicles. They lost several of their vehicles at these crossings. Tens of thousands of refugees lined the roads and tried to catch a ride on the vehicles. It became necessary to push the refugees away from the convoy. Had they not done so, all the vehicles would have collapsed from the overload.

Burmese soldiers knocked down civilians, stole their food, looted their possessions, and set fire to buildings. Chinese soldiers were observed pulling drivers from vehicles and stealing their trucks. Anyone who fell to the ground was kicked and killed, and then stripped of shoes and clothing. Each person's survival depended on oneself. There was no longer a government to protect the people or manage the situation.

Among the Burmese refugees mingled some British stragglers, both civilian and military. Approximately 900,000 people began the march to India. Less than 9,000 arrived. The remainder of the refugees lay where they fell, their bodies picked clean, and bones bleached by the sun.

The first night after leaving Meza, Stilwell's convoy stopped at Banmauk, 15 miles west of Indaw. The group ate, filled gas tanks, and rested for two hours, now ahead of the stream of refugees. Stilwell determined to remain ahead of the refugees and after two hours, started the convoy for Mansi, another 15 miles to the west. The group now numbered 87 with two British officers and several Eurasian refugee women having attached themselves to the convoy.

As the convoy approached Magyigan, they found a bamboo and rope bridge that spanned a deep ravine. The bridge could only carry one empty jeep at a time. All the vehicles had to be emptied and all baggage and supplies carried across by hand. Then the jeeps, one at a time were driven across. The sedans and trucks had to be left behind. The remaining distance to Imphal, India, was 180 miles, across rivers, gorges, through jungles, and up the steep side of the Himalaya mountains. All excess baggage was discarded at Magyigan.

The vehicle trail ended at Saingkyu, which the convoy reached on May 6. As I researched material for this chapter, it seemed to me that there were at least two miracles (or heavenly interventions) for Stilwell during his trek. The first occurred at Saingkyu. Stilwell's advance party consistently went ahead of the main body to make arrangements for rafts, boats, porters, food, and to ensure the main body was not ambushed by Japanese. When they reached Saingkyu, they tried in vain to arrange for rafts or porters without success.

When Stilwell and the main body arrived, Stilwell bargained with the local chief but could not obtain rafts and only 60 porters could be provided, which was less than half of those needed. The trail at this point was very narrow and rutted. The jeeps would have to be abandoned and there was food for only two meals a day for two days remaining. The 60 porters could not be provided until the next day, and Stilwell worried that the Japanese could arrive about the same time.

Adjusting thatch shelters on rafts at Maingkaing, Burma, on the Uya River.

US Army

As Stilwell and three of his staff officers discussed the gloomy situation, they heard the tinkle of a tiny bell. The sound came from a narrow trail that came down the mountainside from the east. The bell sound grew louder. Suddenly from around a rocky wall, 20 small mules came into view following the bell mare. Two muleteers drove the mules with bamboo sticks and Chinese curses.

Stilwell reacted instantly, "General Tseng" he shouted. "Grab those mules. Take them prisoners. I don't care how you do it, but grab them all."[6] General Tseng and his 16 men raced about wildly rounding up the mules and herding them into Stilwell's camp. The two muleteers ran away, but soon came back to find their mules. Stilwell learned that the mules carried no cargo, were on their way to India, and the muleteers were delighted to be paid to carry Stilwell's supplies to India.

Each night when they stopped, the group sent a radio message to the British in India advising them of their position and requesting assistance. They never received a response and had to assume that their messages did not get through. After sending their last message, the radio jeep and radio were destroyed at Saingkyu before departing with the mule train. The mules were loaded with sacks of rice and grain, a few air mattresses, and the medicine and kitchen equipment. Everyone carried a pack with their personal possessions. The convoy numbered 115 people, 20 mules, and a stray dog.

With the mules, Stilwell's new plan was to hike to Maingkaing on the Uyu river, raft down the Uyu to Homalin, cross the Chindwin river on boats, and then climb the mountains to Ukhrul and Imphal on foot. The Chaunggy river flowed over the trail forcing the convoy to walk in knee-deep water for most of the way to the Uyu river. The daily travel, which had averaged 14 miles per day, fell to five miles. Stilwell was concerned that they would be overtaken by the Japanese and kept the convoy moving even though several members could not keep up.

The temperature was cooler in the late afternoon and evening, so Stilwell kept the convoy moving until they had to stop for a rest, and a meal of rice and tea. For the evening meal, they ate the last of the canned corn beef. Breakfast consisted of oatmeal mush, tea, and a dozen skinny chickens that had been bartered from a native village. From time to time, they were able to purchase eggs and vegetables from the natives to break the monotony of rice.

Before reaching Maingkaing, the convoy encountered a rogue bull elephant on the trail and gave him ample clearance. When they reached the next village, the chief asked them to go back and kill the elephant since he had recently trampled two villagers to death. Stilwell refused to take the time to do so, but did barter for a large number of chickens that were draped over the mules.

At Mainhkaing, reached on May 10, nine Japanese aircraft flew a reconnaissance down the river, but Japanese troops were not seen. Stilwell asked the village chief for 20 rafts to cross the Uyu, but was told that only nine were available. The group worked out an arrangement whereby General Tseng and the Chinese guards, the mule train, and the porters would walk the trail alongside the Uyu river to Homalin. The remainder of the party would cross the river on rafts.

The next morning, the chief provided 13 rafts, although several of them were not seaworthy and required constant maintenance. The river was filled with sand bars and debris that hindered and snagged the rafts and required the occupants to frequently jump in the river to free them.

The next day, a single plane the size of a small bomber flew over the river, turned and flew directly over the rafts. Many in the convoy recognized the plane's insignia as British. The plane circled, and passed just in front of the rafts, dumping many long, brown packages onto a sand bar just in front of them. Everyone on the rafts paddled and some jumped into the waist-deep water to get to the sand bar and claim the packages. Before they could do so, however, a horde of naked, dark-skinned natives came out of the jungle, swam to the sand bar, pounced on the packages, and carried them all back to the jungle.

Fortunately, the plane made a second pass and dropped more packages. Stilwell's group was ashore on the sand bar by this time and secured all the packages. Inside the boxes were cans of corned beef, hardtack and biscuits. Most of the canned milk containers broke on impact. Most importantly, Stilwell now knew that the British had received his messages and had been able to find his group. They could expect similar assistance in the future.

The rafts reached Homalin on May 12. The town was deserted, neglected and dirty. The British evacuated the town several days earlier when they learned that Japanese forces were nearby. The few shops that were still open had nothing to sell. There was no food, no boats, no telegraph or telephone service. While Stilwell's group stopped to consider their options, a column of British refugees, officials, wives, servants, horses, mules, and baggage went by on the way to India. A long line of Burmese soldiers, British stragglers, and natives trailed after the column. Not a word was spoken to Stilwell's column. Homalin was clearly a town waiting for the executioner. Stilwell's convoy left without regret.

As the convoy proceeded west, darkness fell and the night became as black as the inside of a tomb. Men tripped over rocks and roots and fell to the ground. Finally, each person grabbed the belt or strap of the person ahead and held on so that they did not become separated and lost along the track. Hungry, discouraged, and with small hope for their future, they struggled on. After two hours, a Buddhist temple loomed in the darkness. A few coconut lamps glowed dimly so that the walls, buildings and painted plaster animals guarding the gates could be seen. Four priests in dirty, saffron-colored robes stood at the main doors to the temple.

This Buddhist temple could have been the second miracle that I mentioned, but I prefer to think it is yet to come. To be sure, the group desperately needed a night's sleep under roof in order to prepare for the ordeal ahead. The priests of the temple resisted the group's effort to enter. They had to be thrown aside physically and finally retreated to a back area of the temple to glower at the members of the convoy as they took off their packs and prepared to bed down for the night.

The temple interior was impressive. The huge hall held row after row of life-size Buddhas. Before each gilded statue the orange flame of a small, oil lamp cast shadows that seemed to bring life to the still faces. That night, Stilwell's group slept in the temple, the first night they had been under cover since they began their march. They were supervised by the four priests who roamed continuously about the great hall. Sometimes they would bend over the sleeping people, perhaps cursing them and wishing them all sorts of bad luck. Or, perhaps, their whispers had to do with cleansing the temple of the unbelievers.

The next morning while breakfast was being prepared, the four priests moved about the cooking area to beg for food and money. Their resentment of the night before had changed to greed, their angry curses to whining pleas. As the group prepared to move out, the priests stood with empty begging bowls as the group passed them. The convoy had three day's rations of food remaining, and India was about an eight-day march.

The convoy reached the Chindwin river the next morning and not a boat was in sight. As they stood contemplating their fate, five dugout canoes and a freight boat nosed around a bend in the river and moved towards the group. The advance party that walked along the river had reached the Chindwin first and arranged for the canoes to take the group across the river.

Loading dugouts for the crossing of the Chindwin River near Homalin.

US Army

Thirty men and women crossed the fast-flowing, treacherous river first, and then the boats returned for another load. In a short time, the entire party was moved across the river and the convoy proceeded west. Thirty-six hours later, a large detachment of Japanese cavalry galloped into Homalin looking for the American general.

Heavy monsoon rains made the trail a mess of muck and muddy ooze. When a person slipped and fell to the ground, they were instantly covered by gallons of water and muddy soil from head to foot. Everyone tripped often, including the porters who would lose portions of the small food reserve they carried. The mules brayed and tried to group together to avoid continuing up the steep track in the heavy rain. Sudden bursts of heavy rain and wind made it impossible for even the strongest men to retain their footing.

After hours of climbing, the column reached a level spot with a sparkling brook of icy water. Everyone, mules, porters, nurses, and military sloshed the icy water on their heads and shoulders. Some rice, tea, and the last of some air-dropped sardines made up the evening meal. Then it was time to start the climb again. Several times as the group climbed the twisting, steep track, Naga chiefs would appear on the trail. They had heard that a great American chief was approaching and wanted to pay their respects. Stilwell required them to pay their respects on the move since he was still concerned with the Japanese.

General Stilwell cleaning his tommy-gun after exiting the Uya River.

US Army

As evening approached, through the heavy rain, a clearing surrounded by trees began to take shape on the track a short distance ahead. As the column drew closer, the image of half-naked men standing on the track began to take form, surrounded by a half dozen native huts. Stilwell's first concern was that these might be refugees in need of food and medical care, and he had none to spare.

As they drew nearer, the huts (bashas) were identified as government shelters and there were more than enough to accommodate the entire group. As Stilwell entered the closest hut, he was startled by a tall, blonde, Englishman, who introduced himself as Tim Sharpe. He had been sent by General Wood at Imphal to bring food, bearers and animals to Stilwell and to guide his party to Imphal. This was the second miracle. All of Stilwell's messages had been received by the British at Imphal, although Stilwell had no way of knowing.

Sharpe explained that he had 500 porters, a day behind him, with pack ponies, food, cigarettes, whiskey, and medical supplies. After bringing the party up to date on the war (fall of Bataan, Singapore, and Corregidor), Sharpe led the group to a large pork barbecue with all the trimmings that he had prepared. Imphal remained a hard five days walk.

After filling up on the greatest meal they had eaten in more than a month, the party slept securely on the floors of the bashas. The next morning, the rain stopped, and those with raw, blistered feet, or sick with fever were able to ride on horses. There were ample porters to carry everything so Stilwell's group was relieved of their packs.

There still remained a climb of 7,000 feet through thickets of bamboo and jungle foliage before they reached Imphal, but now the morale was high. They had escaped the Japanese, and freedom seemed assured. Naga tribe chiefs would meet the column frequently on the path with wide-mouth, clay jars of local beer. The beer tasted a bit like apple cider and was quickly consumed by the convoy members.

The second day, the group crossed into India. That night was spent in more government bashas, and the evening meal consisted of rice, sausages, kidney pie, and sweetened tea. After four hours of sleep, the group continued on their steep climb, sometimes climbing on all fours. After the long, steep climb, three

Naga chiefs appeared on the trail with more jars of rice beer. Sharpe had arranged for a party and left ample food and tea for the group to stop for the night and enjoy their meal.

The next day, after much steep climbing, the group reached the town of Ukhrul, population 6,000. An honor guard of Assam Rifles waited Stilwell's arrival. The Indians were immaculate in their starched khaki shirts, shorts, and red fez caps. Rifles gleaming from hours of polish, they came to present arms as Stilwell passed their ranks. He returned their salute and complimented the commander for the men's appearance. Then he moved swiftly on. That evening, all the clan chiefs of Ukhrul arrived at the campsite, each bearing jars of rice wine and sides of freshly butchered beef. Another huge cookout ensued.

From Ukhrul, the trail wound 23 miles downhill to a clearing and government post where trucks would be waiting for them. Shortly after leaving Ukhrul, the monsoon struck, bringing not only torrents of rain, but a raging tempest of heavy thunder and gusts. About noon, the convoy reached the village of Limpo. When the convoy completed the final eight miles to a designated truck stop, they were met by a British officer at a clearing containing five barracks like buildings.

Members of the convoy went inside the buildings to dry off while several U.S. Army trucks arrived. The drivers had chocolate bars, cigarettes, and whiskey for the group. They spent the evening in the buildings, and tried to leave the next morning for Imphal, but the roads were nearly impassable. Several of the trucks slid off the road and seven additional British trucks were required to get the convoy moving towards Imphal.

They reached Imphal on May 21, and were taken to an old British fort. Waiting for them was a huge luncheon boasting linen, silverware, and china. After dinner, Stilwell retired early. The effects of leading the group from Burma to India had taken its toll on the general and he would need a few days to recover.

On May 24, Stilwell flew to New Delhi in a U.S. Army C-53. He was billeted at the Imperial Hotel and immediately the press arranged for an interview. He was asked to explain the British press releases about their withdrawal from Burma. Stilwell suggested that the journalists should ask British Generals Wavell and Alexander to amplify upon their statements. The journalists insisted that they wanted to hear Stilwell's explanation because the British described their evacuation of Burma as "a heroic, voluntary withdrawal and a glamorous retreat,"

Stilwell minced no words, "no military commander in history ever made a voluntary withdrawal and there is no such thing as a glorious retreat. I claim we got a hell of a licking. We got run out of Burma, and it is humiliating as hell. I think we should find out what caused it, go back, and retake Burma."[7]

What caused the Allied defeat in Burma was apathy on the part of the British (Indian and Burmese) armies, a lack of attention to defense against an invading army, a lack of training of all the military forces, and a well-trained and-equipped Japanese army that sized the initiative. This was nothing new. The same thing happened in Guam, Hong Kong, the Philippines, Singapore, Java, Wake Island and other islands in the Pacific. The Allies were not willing to pay the price for readiness against the rising Japanese and German threats.

Except for the 200th Chinese division, which fought its way up the Burma Road to China, most of the Chinese forces in Burma suffered through the monsoon season in the Hukawang valley. Air drops of food kept them alive, but many died from dysentery and malaria. After the monsoon, they began to trickle into Assam in pitiful physical condition and without their weapons. General Sun Li-jen's 38th Division arrived carrying all their own weapons and many of the weapons abandoned by other units.

During the summer of 1942, the British gave Stilwell the large training center at Ramgarh in Bihar province to rehabilitate, rearm, and train the Chinese divisions for future war in Burma. Chiang Kai-shek gave his approval for the camp on June 29, 1942. Ramgarh was 200 miles northwest of Calcutta and had been used as a British POW camp for Italian prisoners captured in North Africa. It was not a bad training site. The mosquito population was low, so the malaria rate was significantly lower than other parts of Burma and India.

The base consisted of one-story permanent buildings made from adobe brick with thatched roofs that were home to insects, rodents, and snakes, especially cobras. As the Chinese arrived for training, more and more tents were erected to house the trainees. The base had firing ranges for small arms, mortars, automatic weapons and light artillery. It was astride a narrow gauge railway that took three days to get supplies from Calcutta.

Initially, there were 9,000 Chinese at the camp. These were the remnants of the 22nd and 38th Chinese Divisions that fled from Burma. The troops were well fed, paid in full each payday, received medical care, and trained for the next Burma campaign. In time, 10,000 replacements were flown to Ramgarh from Kunming, China, and the divisions brought back to full strength

The C-47 and C-46 aircraft that ferried equipment, fuel and supplies from Ledo, India, to Kunming could not carry heavy artillery so Stilwell accumulated all the heavy artillery that was shipped to India from the United States. He had an acute shortage of small arms, and it would take some time to obtain sufficient weapons and ammunition to arm each man. By March 1943, some of the units were ready to be moved to forward positions in Assam along the Burmese border.

By mid-1943, Stilwell had trained and equipped two Chinese Armies, the 5th and 6th, and obtained American engineer troops and road-building equipment. He also was allotted more combat and transport planes to escort and carry fuel, light artillery, and ammunition from Ledo to Kunming. Construction of the Burma and Ledo Roads is described in volume I of War in the Pacific.

9

THE BATTLE FOR IMPHAL:
MARCH 6, 1944

The longest retreat in British history, four months and a thousand miles, ended on May 19, 1942, when what was left of the British 17th Division exited Burma and entered Tamu, India. The division lost Burma, 13,463 men, and ceased to exist as a fighting force. Lieutenant General Joe Stillwell and his small band of followers fleeing Burma reached Imphal about the same time.

During the next two years, Burma remained relatively tranquil. British soldiers trained new Indian divisions in the safety of India. Stillwell's American troops trained Chinese troops that had been routed from Burma, coordinated the supply of Chiang Kai-shek's army in China via the "Hump" airlift from Ledo, India, and supervised a new road to China, the Ledo Road. The Ledo Road would go from Ledo, India, to Myitkyina, Burma, where it would join the old "Burma Road".

Both the British and Japanese armies sought to start an offensive in Burma during this period but the summer monsoons prevented it. The monsoon washed away roads, bridges, and communications. Malaria and dysentery took a heavy toll of soldiers from both sides. Soldiers living in tents would find the legs of their cots sinking into the mud. Leeches would suck the blood from patients in hospital tents, and huge water rats swam through the water chewing on anything they could find, including patients and nurses.[1] The 23rd Indian Division had 5,000 men unfit to fight and one 900 man battalion was down to 120 men. When the medical personnel were not caring for their soldiers, they were overwhelmed by the 180,000 Burmese refugees that reached Manipur, India during the exodus. Twice that number died enroute to India and most of the refugees that survived the march were desperately ill.

All written material that has to do with fighting in Burma during WW II include references to the Arakan, but seldom is the term Arakan defined. It is time to do so. "Arakan" is a place. It runs

from the Chin Hills on the edge of Manipur, near Ledo, down to
the south-west corner of Burma, west of Prome, a distance of
460 miles. The conditions in the Arakan are horrible. Arakan is a
land of creeks and *chaungs (streams),* where transportation is primarily
by boat[2]. There are some tracks to follow on land, but only one
road existed in the area, running from the small port of Maungdaw
on the Naf River, across the Mayu range, to the town of
Buthidaung on the Kalapanzin River.

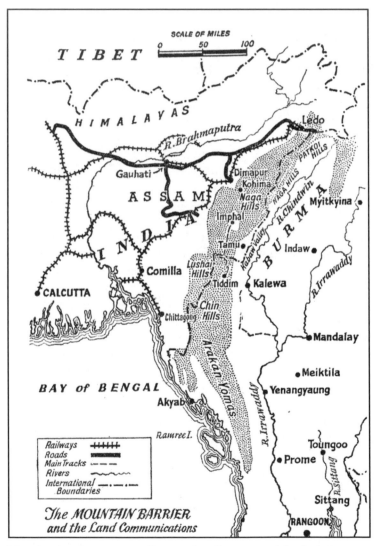

Map showing three avenues of approach to Rangoon and the Arakan.

Imperial War Museum

The Mayu hills are covered with dense jungle, but to their west run a narrow coastal strip varying in width from a few hundred yards to two miles. The coast is part sand, part mangrove swamp, and some of the *chaungs* are tidal. In the flat, the ground is covered with bamboo trees. It was not the heat, hills, monkeys, or tigers that made the Aarakan so inhospitable to the fighting men; it was the monsoon which dumped 200-inches of rainfall per year. The rains brought everything to a halt, except for boat traffic on some of the chaungs. Malaria was rampant and leaches abounded. Only during the dry season could either army conduct warfare in the Arakan

The Arakan was important because the town of Akyab had an airfield and was only 330 miles from Rangoon. If the British were to conduct an overland campaign from India to reach Rangoon, the capital of Burma, Akyab was essential for resupply. The Japanese knew this and captured Akyab on May 4, 1942. The British initially withdrew to Chittagong, and then a hundred miles further north to Feni.

The "First Arakan" offensive started at the end of 1942 and involved the 14th Indian Division. The division moved down the Mayu Peninsula range, between the evil smelling Naf and Mayu rivers. Doing their best to avoid the crocodiles, oozy slime, and hordes of malarial mosquitoes that thrived in the steaming heat, the division reached Donbaik, 20 miles northwest of Akyub, before the rains washed away their roads and Japanese resistance stopped their forward progress. The division was engaged in heavy fighting at Donbaik for 10 weeks. Early on April 3, 1943, a Japanese force landed on the east coast of the peninsula behind the British positions, climbed the steep mountain spine, and ambushed the British 6th and Indian 47th brigades, killing Brigadier R. V. Cavendish in the process. The British force fought its way out, but were forced to fall back 20 miles to better defensive positions.

The desired British victory to raise morale collapsed in failure. The only positive aspect to the offensive was that the operation, coupled with the Chindit penetration, did succeed in pulling a Japanese Division away from their planned offensive into the Arakan. British casualties were 5,057, Japanese losses as reported by the Japanese were 1,775.

The next British advance into Burma occurred on February 13, 1943, while the 14th Indian Division was still engaged at Donbaik. This expedition, termed Chindits was led by flamboyant Brigadier Gen. Orde Wingate. Wingate and 3,000 men, penetrated deep into Burma, well behind the Japanese lines, intending to cut the railway line between Mandalay and Myitkyina, cut the supply line to the two Japanese divisions in North Burma, and to conduct harassing operations against Japanese forces north-west of Mandalay.

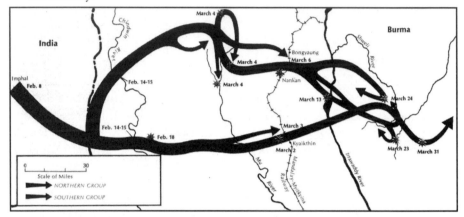

Colonel Orde Wingate's 3,000-man 77th Indian Infantry Brigade, known as the Chindits, set out from Imphal on Feb. 8, 1943, on a raid deep into Burma. The Brigade split into two groups and crossed the Chindwin River. Following a setries of wide-ranging feints and clashes with the enemy, the northern group blew up the bridges of the Mandalay-Myitkyina railway near Bongyaung and Nankan, while the southern group cut the rail line near Kyaikthin.

National Archives

Wingate divided his force into seven columns with specific instructions for each column. Two columns were lost shortly after entering Burma, when they encountered strong Japanese forces and were forced to leave their dead and wounded and return to the Chindwin River. On March 2, two of the columns blew the railway bridge in two places and went on to destroy 70 miles of track. By the end of March, Wingate's forces had been located by superior sized Japanese forces and Wingate was forced to improvise his return to the Chindwin.

The Chindits blew up some railway, most of which was quickly repaired, gathered some useful intelligence, killed a few hundred Japanese, and pioneered the concept of aerial supply of units behind Japanese lines. Nonetheless, the expedition must be considered a failure since 1,000 men failed to return to India. Less than half were known to have been killed in battles, the remainders were left as wounded, and most were killed by the Japanese. The Chindits had walked nearly 1,000 miles, carrying their weapons and equipment. Air drops kept them supplied during the early going, but after they were discovered and hunted by the Japanese, air drops became impossible. Those that returned were starving, had beri-beri and malaria, and most were unfit for future military duty.

Sappers used charges to blow up a bridge on a rail line used by the Japanese. After the blast, they carted off track and railroad ties to reinforce bunkers.

Imperial War Museum

Following top level consultations between Prime Minister Churchill and President Roosevelt, a number of command changes (stream) were made to unify future operations in Burma. Lord Lewis Mountbatten became Supreme Allied Commander of the new South-East Asia Command with General Joe Stilwell his deputy. General William Slim became commander of the new 14th Army, and Brigadier Gen. William Old commanded troop Carrier Command[3].

By 1944, the Japanese were being defeated throughout the Pacific. Allied aircraft and submarine forces were making it increasingly difficult for Japan to supply their widely dispersed forces, especially those in Burma. They decided a successful offensive in Burma would ease the logistics problem, destroy the British forces there, isolate China, and, perhaps, free India from British rule. The opportunities were too great to ignore.

In similar fashion, the British yearned for a major victory in Burma that would destroy the Japanese army, open the supply route to China, protect India from invasion, and free thousand of Allied forces for deployment elsewhere.

The 30-by-20-mile Imphal plain, is the only sizeable area of flat ground between India and Burma. It is located in the mountains in Manipur, India, at the 2,600 foot level and is a natural staging area for military logistics to support operations in either India or Burma. It is surrounded on all sides by jungle covered mountains which rise to 5,000 feet in the Naga Hills and 6,000 feet in the Chin Hills, with peaks reaching 9,000 feet. Imphal lies 400 miles from Calcutta and 70 miles from the Burma border.

By 1944, the plain had changed significantly since British forces were run out of Burma in 1942. No longer did the visitor have to stand in soggy ground, bombed out buildings, and deep muddy vehicle tracks filled with water. Instead there was row after row of neat huts, hospitals, supply dumps, ordnance depots, engineer parks, and wide tarmac roads[4]

Troop billets covered much of the 800 square miles and hard surface roads led north to Dimapur and south to Tiddim. 70,000 Indian non-combatants worked on the roads while others maintained the railway at Dimapur, 130 miles north.

It was the plan of General William Slim, commander of the 14th Army, to lure the Japanese 15th Army, commanded by Lieutenant Gen. Renya Mutaguchi, to the Imphal plain, and defeat Mutaguchi's three divisions there. Slim had adequate provisions for a long siege and could be supplied by air. Logistic support for Mutaguchi's forces would be difficult once he crossed the Chindwin river, and made his way through the jungles and mountains that stood between his forces in Burma and Slim's forces in India.

136

Mutaguchi would have little, if any logistic support once the monsoon set in.

Lord Louis Mountbatten, Supreme Allied Commander of the new Southwest Asia Command, standing between Winston Churchill and President Roosevelt at a strategy conference in North Africa.

Imperial War Museum

Slim had several other advantages. General "Vinegar" Joe Stilwell had finally convinced Chiang Kai-shek to free two Chinese divisions to help open the Ledo roadway from Ledo, India to Myitkyina, Burma. Stilwell also had a regiment of Merrill's Marauders, named after their commander, Brigadier Gen. Frank Merrill. By the end of 1943, Stilwell's forces had moved 103 miles into Burma. By the time Imphal was surrounded, Stilwell had a force of five Chinese divisions and three mobile "Chindit" brigades attacking Myitkyina. His success put great pressure on the Japanese northern forces and prevented them from sending reinforcements to Mutaguchi at Imphal.

Slim had yet another advantage that was still in the experimental stage. In late 1943, he conceived a new strategy to cope with the Japanese tactics of infiltration and flanking movements that demoralized many of his forces. He referred to this strategy as the establishment of "pivots of maneuver."[5] They were more commonly referred to as "Admin boxes," or "The Boxes." These boxes were well stocked strong points capable of supporting units while defending against enemy attacks.

Not every box was the same, but all were sited on level ground along routes the Japanese would have to pass in order to reach the Imphal plain. They averaged 1,200 yards long by 1000 yards wide, and were stocked with ammunition, gasoline, hospitals, and other supplies.

The strategy was that once a British unit was being outflanked or infiltrated, they could enter the box with their weapons and fight a defensive battle until relieved or the Japanese fell back. They would be supplied by air drops as necessary. There could be no thought of surrender once a unit entered the box. Surrender to the Japanese was already unheard of due to the attendant horror associated with capture by the Japanese. Slim made it clear to his commanders that the large numbers of men and equipment in the box, including the wounded, prohibited their surrender.[6]

Some Boxes had a major drawback in that they were surrounded by higher ground which permitted the enemy to observe the effects of their artillery and mortar fire inside the box. The boxes were also crowded with men, mules, tanks, weapons and other supplies which meant that every impact of enemy indirect fire caused casualties.

The Imphal-Kohima battle actually began on March 6, 1944, when the Japanese outflanked the British 17th division near Tiddam, to the northwest of Rangoon, along the Indian border. A week later, the 17th Division was retreating on foot along the Tiddam highway towards Imphal. The wounded, stores, ammunition, and supplies, were moved in 2,500 vehicles and 3,500 pack animals. The division averaged 20-miles per day and blew its bridges behind it.

General Sir William Slim.

Imperial War Museum

The Japanese were experts at outflanking the British by cutting through the thick jungle and establishing road-blocks that had to be destroyed before the division could continue its retreat to Imphal. At mile 109 of the Imphal road, the division was halted by a particularly strong Japanese road-block and was forced to ask for help from Dimapur. The 23rd Indian Division was sent to help them break the roadblock. With the help of air support and aerial resupply, the 17th and 23rd Divisions fought through the road blocks and reached Imphal on April 5.

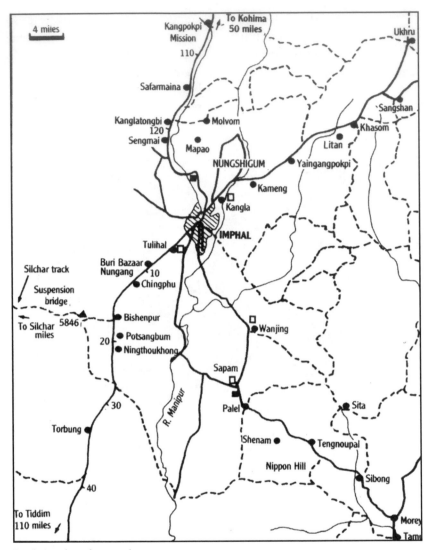

Imphal and road networks.

Imperial War Museum

In their retreat, the British were forced to destroy one of their largest defensive boxes. At Moreh, a base had been established to supply two divisions for a month. The defensive position was two-and-a-half miles long and a half-mile wide. It contained 200 head of cattle for food and large quantities of gasoline, oil and ammunition. As they fell back, the British slaughtered the cattle, fired the petroleum, destroyed a million pounds of equipment, and booby trapped anything remaining.[7] Two additional Admin boxes were similarly destroyed.

Slim had envisioned a single, or perhaps a few, major battles on the Imphal plain where his artillery, tanks, aircraft and resupply capabilities would permit him to soundly defeat the Japanese. However, he made a major mistake, which he acknowledges in his book, *Defeat into Victory*. His mistake was that he left the decision when to fall back to Imphal to his forward positioned commanders, rather than order the units back himself.

As a result, several of units fell back too late and too slowly with the result that there were numerous battles in the jungle forward of the Imphal plain and the British lost considerable forces there. When the units did arrive at Imphal, they were disorganized, in some cases decimated, and already under attack as they moved into defensive positions.

Instead of a single major battle, the battle of the Imphal plain became numerous battles of small units. Companies and platoons, commanded by lieutenants and non-commissioned officers, became the norm. Instead of coordinated artillery and air attacks, preceding infantry assaults, much of the fighting involved flanking movements and direct assaults by small units with rifles, grenades and bayonets.

While the 17th Division was fighting for its life, three Japanese divisions crossed the Chindwin River, and moved quickly through the "impenetrable" jungle and mountains to threaten Imphal, Dimapur, and Kohima. Ukhrul, 15-miles north of Sangshak was captured on March 21 after two days of desperate fighting. What remained of the three British battalions fell back to positions at Sangshak.

The town of Sangshak, 85-miles northeast of Imphal, was astride the main road from Imphal to Dimapur. It lay on a bare hill and consisted of 30 houses and an American mission church. The hill was volcanic rock with only a few feet of dirt on the top. Digging in was impossible. There was no barbed wire for defensive positions and no water in the town. The 50th Brigade of Gurkhas with some British and Indian troops formed a defensive box 800-yards-long by 500-yards-wide. In the box were the 2,000 men and mules of the brigade which included some light (mountain) artillery, a mortar section, and a small engineer unit.

Major Gen. Shigesauro Miyazaki's leading brigade of the 31st Division attacked the defensive box at dusk on March 22. The Gurkhas held their fire until the Japanese reached the clearing in front of their positions. Then they reacted with machine gun and mortar fire, killing 90 of the 120 Japanese in the leading company. A second attack cost the Japanese another 20 men.[8] Sangshak was the first battle where the Jiffs (members of the Indian National Army) made an appearance.[9] The Jiffs were not used in a combat role, but used loudspeakers to try to confuse the Indian troops and cause them to desert the British cause. These attempts were never successful.

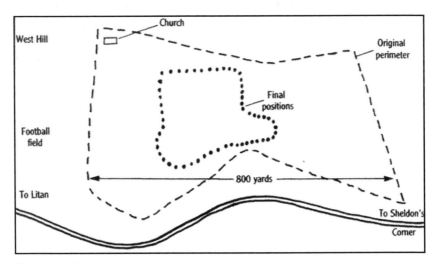

The Box at Sangshak.

By March 23, Sangshak was completely surrounded. The Japanese used elephants to bring artillery and ammunition forward to shell the position. Due to the narrow defensive position and the inability to dig in, every artillery round caused death and destruction, The decomposing bodies of men and mules were constantly hit, blown up, and scattered throughout the defensive box. A nauseating stench permeated the entire area.

The following day, the Japanese penetrated the defensive perimeter before being repulsed. A dead Japanese officer was found to be carrying detailed plans for the 15th and 31st Divisions to include their routes and timetables for their advance on Imphal, Kohima and Dimapur. The brigade intelligence officer slipped through the Japanese lines and delivered the plans to Corps headquarters in Imphal. In the plan, General Slim learned that the entire Japanese 31st Division, not a regiment as he had assumed, was approaching Kohima.

The battle at Sangshak continued around the clock with frequent Japanese penetrations and counter attacks to regain the defensive perimeter. By March 25, 300 Gurkha, British and Indian wounded lay in the shallow trenches fearing that every artillery round would mark their death.[10] As the defensive perimeter began to shrink; Gurkhas burned all buildings, including the church that could be used by the Japanese. At night on March 26, a message was received from Corps headquarters to "Fight your way out. Go south and west."[11] The small force fired all their artillery and mortars at the enemy, and slipped through the Japanese positions during the evening. Left were more than 100 wounded that could not be evacuated. The remainder of the wounded was carried by their comrades.

The "Box" was occupied by the Japanese on the morning of the 26th. It was an appalling sight. The church was in charred ruins, the trees blown away, and the grass burned brown. Everywhere laid discarded weapons and the bodies of mules, British and Indian troops. The wounded were killed, and all the dead were examined for signs of life. That done, Lieutenant Gen. Miyazaki distributed the "Churchill" rations to his units: tinned food, cigarettes, whiskey, trucks, wireless sets, and mortars. It was a significant victory for Mutaguchi, but his casualties were high and he was unaware that his plan to attack Kohima had been compromised.

The remnants of the Gurkha and Indian units at Sangshak had to cross 30-miles of jungle-covered hills, many rising to 4,000-

feet in order to reach Imphal. Water was obtained from mountain streams and the men subsisted on a few tins of cheese and some raisins. One of the British officers, too badly wounded to be evacuated woke up to find a Japanese soldier going through his pack. The officer killed the Japanese and staggered off into the jungle. He found a corpse and took a grenade from a pocket. When he came to a stream, he threw the grenade into the stream, killed some fish, ate, rested, and then continued on alone until he reached Imphal. Of the two battalions defending Shangshak, one lost 80-per-cent of its strength, the other 30-per-cent. Most of the survivors reached Imphal.

Slim's forces on the Imphal plain had a serious tactical disadvantage. Their only line of communication to India was the road from Imphal to Kohima and Dimapur. If the enemy was able to close this road, the only resupply would have to be by air. The Japanese blew a bridge on the highway 30 miles south of Imphal on March 30, and established strong road blocks. Imphal's supply and communications by land were now cut off.

General Mutaguchi expected to capture Imphal and Kohima by April 6, and then to advance to Dimapur. The mauling his 58th Regiment took at Sangshak delayed his advance considerably and allowed Slim to fly in the 5th Indian Division to Imphal and the 2nd British Division to Dimapur before Mutaguchi could attack the Imphal plain. The Japanese 58th Regiment lost two-thirds of its officers and half of its men at Sangshak.

Major Gen. Tsunoru Yamamoto's 33rd Division pushed up the Kabow Valley in two columns and were engaged in daily combat. Following a severe three day fight near the Indian border, the British forces fell back to Tamu, 40-miles south of Imphal. Tank versus tank battles ensued with the Japanese light tanks being no match for the heavier British tanks. On the 16th, two miles north of Tamu, four Japanese tanks were destroyed and one captured. On the 22nd, the Japanese attacked the defensive positions again, but were repulsed with heavy losses including more tanks

By this time it became apparent to General Slim that the entire Japanese 31st Division was closing the ring around Kohima, and threatening Dimapur. He had not believed that the Japanese would mount such an attack with more than a regiment due to the difficult jungle terrain and problems of resupply. He was wrong. The defenses at Kohima were not sufficient to defend against such a large force and he had no forces at Dimapur, the huge British supply base and railhead.

Mountbatten, without authority to do so, diverted 30 aircraft from the "Hump" resupply mission to fly reinforcements to Dimapur and Imphal. His action was later approved by the joint chiefs. By March 24, an entire division with all its transport had been airlifted. Two additional divisions and Wingate's long range penetration brigade were moved to the Imphal area by plane and train from India.

The battle for Kohima is a separate chapter in this volume. The battle was bloody with heavy casualties to both sides. Once the garrison at Kohima was relieved, it was necessary to attack the Japanese defensive positions that ringed Kohima. The British attack to regain the ground outside the Kohima perimeter began on May 4 and continued until May 15 with heavy casualties to both sides.

Japanese troops refused to surrender or retreat and defended each bunker to the death. If British tanks could engage the bunkers, they were brought to within 30-yards, where their 75-mm gun was most effective. When tanks could not be used because of the steep, inclines or slippery jungle hills, pole charges were pushed through bunker apertures to destroy the occupants.

While fighting continued around Kohima, there were continuous battles with intense fighting around the entire Imphal perimeter. The Japanese advanced along routes that enabled them to move their artillery, tanks, and heavy transport. When they were stopped by a defensive position they immediately tried to outflank or infiltrate the British block. The British would counterattack and the battle would spread several miles on each side of the original contact.

Six main routes led the Japanese to Imphal. These routes were: from the north, the broad and improved Kohima road, and a narrow foot-path down the Iril River Valley; from the north-east, the Ukhrul road; from the south-east, the improved Tamu-Palel road; from the south; the rugged Tiddim highway; and from the west, the Silchar-Bishenpur track.

To the north, along the Iril valley and Ukhrul road, the British 5th division, which flew in from India, was in a fight from the moment they landed. They succeeded in pushing the Japanese back to Litan, but the Japanese spread out to menace Imphal from the north. Typical of hundreds of such actions was the battle for Nungshigum.

Nungshigum was a large hill with two peaks that dominated the Imphal plain. Whichever side occupied Nungshigum would have direct observation of the Imphal plain and main airfield six miles away. The Japanese seized the northern peak on April 6, and the southern peak five days later. On the 13th, with extensive support by close air support and tanks that had to be winched up the steep slopes, the British regained both peaks and held them. Fighting in and around the bunkers was with bayonets and grenades as the Japanese fought to the last man. The monsoons submerged the troops in rain, and at the higher altitudes, they were enshrouded in clouds with visibility less than a hundred yards. Trenches collapsed in the deluge and overflowed with rainwater. Forcing the Japanese from the northern sector of Imphal took until May 16, when the Japanese 15th Division was forced back to within 15 miles of Ukhrul.

On the Tamu-Palel road, two brigades of the British 20th Division held a 25-mile front in a country criss-crossed by steep ridges and deep nullahs (valleys), all tree covered and much in deep jungle. The Japanese commander, Major Gen. Yamamoto was under pressure from General Mutaguchi to break into the Imphal plain with his tanks and artillery and destroy the British forces. Yamamoto's assaults continued throughout April and succeeded in capturing objectives around Tengoupal, Shuganu and Shenam, only to be thrown back by determined counter attacks by the British. The "Ghandi Brigade" of the Indian National Army (Jiffs) made an appearance on this front but was ambushed and suffered heavy casualties. After the ambush, Jiffs were found wandering through the jungle without any organization. Indian and Gurkha soldiers tended not to take these "traitors" prisoner and the

Japanese relegated what was left of them to work as carriers. By the middle of May, the British had secured this approach route to Imphal.

Some of the heaviest fighting occurred along the Tiddam road and Silchar-Bishenpur track to the south and west of Imphal. The British commander on this front pulled his forces back to Bishenpur where he could control both approaches. On the evening of April 14 and 15, Japanese 33rd Division reinforced, attacked Bishenpur but was defeated. While the battle raged, the Japanese blew the three-hundred-foot suspension bridge at mile 51 of the Silchar track. The bridge was over an 80-foot deep gorge rendering the track useless to both sides. Destruction of the bridge was a typical Japanese suicide event. While fighting raged around the bridge, three Japanese evaded the engineer unit guarding the bridge and placed explosive charges. When the bridge blew up, two of the Japanese were blown up with the bridge, the third leapt to his death into the gorge.[12]

Lieutenant Gen. Geoffrey Scones, commander of the central front, moved his 17th Division to meet the threat north of Bishenpur. The move was fortuitous since the Japanese were about to attack British forces at the small town of Ninthoukhong in force. For three days, men of the 17th Division attacked the Japanese defenses and were thrown back, losing seven tanks in the process. Although the 33rd Division could not advance, neither could the Japanese. For the moment, the situation was stabilized.

British casualties were extremely heavy during the Imphal fighting, especially among the British officers who could easily be distinguished from the Indian troops they commanded. One officer commanding a battalion that had already lost three-quarters of its officers was severely wounded a second time, this time in the stomach by a Japanese grenade. When asked why he had not turned himself in for treatment he explained that, "The grenade in the stomach was a nuisance as it made my getting about rather difficult, but I could still keep up with his men so there was no need to go back."[13] The second wound was a bullet that passed straight through his shoulder, so "It causes me no inconvenience." The officer was killed later in the same battle.[14]

At Bishenpur, the Japanese Air Force made several successful attacks upon British positions, and bombed and strafed the airfield. Twenty-five Japanese Zeros attacked Bishenpur on May 6 and 10. Many of the Zeros were shot down and the attacks were not repeated.

At Potsangbam, two miles south of Bishenpur, the Japanese erected strong defenses that took two British brigades and close air support to drive the enemy out on May 15. The British lost 12 tanks in the battle. Although the Bishenpur route to Imphal was not secured, intelligence was reporting that the Japanese 33rd Division was decimated. Some regiments of 3,000 men were down to 800 effectives.

On the Kohima-Imphal road to the north, the Japanese occupied a supply depot at Kanglatongbi and fighting continued in the area until May 7. At that time, reinforcements enabled the British to push the Japanese well to the north of Imphal.

By mid May, Slim's greatest concern was Yamamoto's reinforced 33rd Division to the south and west of Imphal. The other Japanese divisions had been reduced to such strength that they were not considered to be capable of major attacks. Scones and Slim agreed that the British should take the offensive against the weakened 15th Division to the north of Imphal. The offensive began on June 3 during the monsoon.

The Japanese immediately counter attacked and positions changed hands several times. Two battalions reinforced the British troops and by June 13, the front lines were reestablished. Two other brigades pushed the Japanese back at least 20-miles from Imphal. The Japanese 15th Division suffered heavily. Its supplies were dangerously low and it was receiving no resupply or reinforcements.

On June 19, despite warnings from higher headquarters, Lieutenant Gen. Kotoku Sato started the Japanese 31st Division back to Burma in a search for food. He was told there were rations at Humine, but as he grew nearer he found that there was only enough rice there for two days. He was forced to divide his men into groups to forage in the mountain villages for food.

The Japanese 31st Division was badly beaten and falling back to the Chindwin River. On June 22, the road from Kohima-Imphal-

Dimapur was reopened and supplies immediately began to flow to British forces by road. This was the first overland supply since the Japanese cut the road on March 30.

Lieutenant Gen. Masafumi Yamauichi was relieved of command of the 15th Division on June 23. He had not displayed the proper offensive spirit. When relieved, Yamauchi was bedridden with malaria and dysentery as were many of his men. He was replaced by Lieutenant Gen. Shibata Ryuichi, but the change of command could not change the ability of 15 Division. There were simply too few men and too many starving and sick men to go on the offensive.

The infantry group of 33 Division (Major Gen. Tsunoru Yamamoto) made their final attack at Palel from mid-June until July 13. At that time, he was ordered to withdraw to Burma. His men were subsisting on a half-pint of gruel per day made by mixing grass and powdered bean paste with small amounts of rice. The rice was obtained from foraging Burmese villages. The Burmese, greatly resented such thefts, and made it increasingly difficult for the Japanese to locate their small amounts of rice. The Division reached the Chindwin on August 2, but there was little food waiting for them.

Although the British had superior forces and could be supplied by road and air, the monsoon made their advance difficult. Since they had superior firepower, they often resorted to heavy and continuous artillery fire, expending thousands of rounds per day into the Japanese positions.

Aviation played an important role during the siege of Imphal and the advance into Burma. Initially, the Japanese had a preponderance of air support but the British Spitfire fighter proved far superior and soon established air superiority over the battle area. Aircraft were used to deliver ordnance on enemy positions and to destroy communications between Japanese commands. Sixty-five Japanese aircraft were lost to Spitfires in the first 13 days of the battle.

Close air support was provided by the Hurricane MK II fighter-bomber generally called "Hurribombers." The Hurribomber was a perfect plane for this purpose since it had excellent maneuverability, two 40mm cannon, and carried large bomb loads. When loaded with ordnance, it had a flying time of only 90 minutes which meant that new airstrips had to be constructed immediately behind the advancing British forces. These airstrips were prepared by leveling the ground, and laid with perforated metal matting.

The Hurribomber performed well until after the battle for Mandalay when they were replaced with the American built Thunderbolt which, with external fuel tanks, allowed as much as five hours of flying time.

It was now time for General Slim's 14th Army to go on the offensive, drive the Japanese forces back to Burma, destroy them, and capture Rangoon. There were no naval landing craft available for a seaborne assault of Burma. Consequently, any move toward Rangoon had to be overland. Slim planned to drive the Japanese back across the Chindwin River, establish bridgeheads on the east bank, and move his forces towards Rangoon as soon as the monsoon ended, and before General Kawabe could reconstitute his battered forces. Slim asked his command for the impossible, and got it. The British troops, weary as they were, pursued the retreating Japanese, despite the monsoon, with unbelievable energy and determination.

Dakotas were the only means of getting supplies and reinforcements to the front lines.

Imperial War Museum

Ukhrul became the rendezvous point for the Japanese 15th and 31st Divisions. Mutaguchi hoped that he could be reinforced there and continue to fight. By July 1, Ukhrul was surrounded by British forces. As the British closed in from the west, north, south and south-east, a separate brigade cut all the escape routes to the east. By July 8, Ukhrul was in British hands, and the Japanese stragglers were being hunted on the perimeter. Many Japanese units lost all their artillery and transportation as they beat a retreat to the Chindwin River.

The terrain, during the monsoon, was difficult for both sides. A diary of one of the British brigades involved in the pursuit of the Japanese states, "The hill tracks are in a terrible state. They are either so slippery that men can hardly walk or are knee deep in mud. . . . Half a company took ten hours to carry two stretcher cases four miles. A party of men without packs took seven hours to cover five miles."[15]

The decimated Japanese divisions that staggered back to the Chindwin were an apathetic sight. They had thrown away their weapons and clutched sticks to assist them to keep their footing in the torrential rain. The only other possession they had was their rice tin in hopes that food would be available at the Chindwin. Some of the non-walking wounded were carried on wet stretchers. The more seriously wounded lay at the sides of the trails begging for a grenade to kill themselves. All were starving, most had dysentery and malaria, and many were too exhausted to even brush off the maggots that squirmed in their eyes, noses, and mouths. They were no longer soldiers.

At Sittaung, as they waited for boats to take them across the Chindwin, British Hurribombers attacked them leaving the river bank heaped with corpses. As the Hurribombers flew away, they were replaced by circling flocks of vultures[16]

The next chapter describes the Japanese seige of Kohima.

Chinese and Korean comfort girls captured during the Sittang breakout.

Imperial War Museum

10

THE SEIGE OF KOHIMA

During March 1944, the Japanese Army sent 130,000 men across the Chindwin River in Burma with the goal of capturing the huge British supply base at Dimapur, India. Dimapur was astride the railway from Calcutta to Ledo, India. Once the railway was cut, the Allies would be unable to supply Chiang Kai-shck via airlift (the Hump), from Ledo to Kunming, China. The Japanese cut the Burma Road in 1942, and since that time, all support for China was flown over the "Hump."

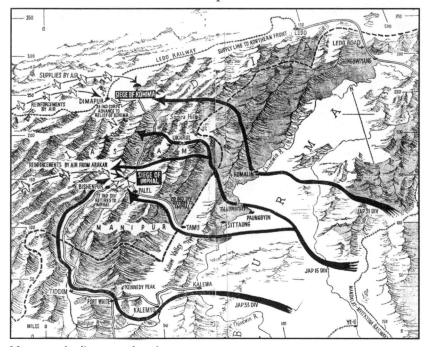

Maneuvers leading up to the seige.

In order to reach Dimapur, it was necessary for the Japanese to defeat the British garrisons at Kohima and Imphal, India. This chapter describes the 16 days during which 500 soldiers of the British Territorial Army successfully defended against 15,000 well-trained, well-equipped and experienced Japanese soldiers.

Kohima, India, was little more than a road junction between Imphal and Dimapur. It had no railroad or airport, and was at the 5,000-foot elevation level. It consisted of a Naga (native Burmese tribe) village, a district commissioner's home and office, a tennis court, a small wooden fort, and a field supply depot (FSD). It was garrisoned by a few fighting troops of the Indian Assam Regiment and Assam Rifles, and 1,500 Indian non-combatants.

Following the siege of Kohima, Admiral Lord Louis Mountbatten, Supreme Commander, South-East Asia Allied Command said, "The Battle for Kohima will probably go down as one of the greatest battles in history. It was in effect, the Battle for Burma."[1] Left unsaid was that there would have been no such battle but for the courage of 500 British citizen soldiers.

Lieutenant Gen. Renya Mutaguchi commanded the Japanese 15th Army in Burma. Mutaguchi was a fierce, brave, and hard-line soldier who loved battles, alcohol, and women. Mutaguchi commanded the regiment that started the Sino-Japanese war and thus the Pacific war, by provoking an incident at the Marco Polo Bridge near Peking, China, in 1937. He had a strong personality and was both feared and respected throughout the Japanese army.[2]

The Japanese, much like the British, assumed that it was impossible to conduct large scale operations across the mountains and jungles of the India-Burma border. They felt secure from a British offensive until the Chindits (named after the fierce sculptured lions guarding Burmese temples) penetrated their lines from India and cut off many of their supply and logistic points. The Chindits were a long-range penetration unit, commanded by the unorthodox Orde Wingate. The Chindits were supplied by air drops and raided Japanese communications, destroyed supply dumps, and created havoc in the Japanese rear. Mutaguchi was not one to let the enemy operate in places his forces could not. Consequently, a decision was made to launch a major strike across the Chindwin River, through the jungle, and to capture the railway near Dimapur, India.

On April 5, 1944, the Japanese 31st Division surrounded Kohima on three sides and was advancing quickly on the small garrison of Indian and Ghurka troops stationed there. The Assam Regiment and Assam Rifles, untried Indian troops from Kohima, met the Japanese forces to the east of Kohima, held up their advance for a time, but had to fall back upon the defenses of Kohima, badly bloodied and dispirited.

That afternoon, 500 soldiers of the 4th Battalion of the Royal West Kent Regiment, a territorial Army unit, pushed through the road from Dimapur and arrived at Kohima. They caught the Japanese road blocks off-guard, or they would never have been able to break through. When the Japanese realized what was happening, they destroyed all the vehicles of the 4th Battalion, and much of their supplies. The unit itself was able to reach the defensive positions of Kohima, however, and settled in for a long siege. A few hours after they arrived, the Japanese division, commanded by General Kotuko Sato, completely encircled the town, terminating all arrivals or departures.

Lieutenant Col. John Laverty commanded the battalion, and together with the sergeant major, the adjutant, Captain Douglas Short, and the executive officer, Major Peter Franklin, comprised the only professional soldiers in the battalion. The company commanders were Majors Tommy Kenyon ("A" Company), John Winstanley ("B" Company), Bobby Shaw ("C" Company), Donald Easton ("D" Company), and Harry Smith (Support Company).

Lieutenant Col. John Laverty.

Imperial War Museum

The battalion was blessed with having Major Yeo and his Indian artillery gunners. Yeo was a career officer and a brilliant forward observer who directed the artillery fire from the Jotsoma defensive box upon the Japanese positions on Kohima. He knew all about guns, especially the 3.7-inch howitzer. He sited what artillery weapons the battalion had and moved them as necessary to keep them from being destroyed. He was always on the move and as soon as Japanese artillery opened fire, he could be seen spotting the flashes through his binoculars and writing down the coordinates. He would scratch out a message, hand it to one of his runners who would take it back to the command post, and, in a few minutes, artillery from Jotsoma would silence the enemy guns.

Laverty's first priority was to have his men dig defensive positions. Existing bunkers and trenches had been poorly located, gun positions had not been established, and a headquarters had not been dug in. Initially, the defensive area was in the form of a triangle, 700 yards, by 900 yards, by 1100 yards. In this space were 2,500 men, with only about 600 of them fit to fight. (Refer to the map of Kohima defensive positions as of April 6, 1944).

Supplies of food and ammunition were sufficient, but drinking water was a serious problem. The only supply of water was in several large metal tanks near the district commissioners (DC's) bungalow. The water tanks and pipelines were vulnerable and could be expected to be destroyed at any time.

The 161st Indian Brigade had been fighting the Japanese on the eastern approach to Kohima but was unable to fight their way back to Kohima. Their commander, Brigadier D. F. W. Warren, decided to establish a defensive position (administrative box) at Jotsoma, two miles from Kohima. He had good observation of the Kohima ridge and established his artillery to support the forces at Kohima. His forces included the 1st Punjabis, 7th Rajputs, and the 24th Indian Mountain Regiment. The 161st Artillery played a major role in the defense of Kohima.

The first Japanese attack came on April 6. Despite heavy losses from small arms fire and artillery fire from the Jotsoma artillery, the Japanese drove the small Gurkha force back, and occupied Jail Hill, which overlooked most of the 4th Battalion positions. Laverty responded with his three-inch mortars, and his men dug even deeper waiting for the next attack. At dusk, the Japanese bombardment began. When it lifted, the Japanese attacked in waves, one after another, and gradually infiltrated Company C positions and the bashas (shelters) on field supply depot (FSD) ridge..

The FSD contained several bashas that had brick walls four feet high, with tin roofs supported by bamboo frames. Japanese soldiers could be heard talking and moving about in the bashas, but the battalion did not have a flat trajectory weapon that would penetrate the brick walls. Laverty organized a counter-attack and asked Lieutenant J. Wright from the Indian Sapper and Miners unit for a way to knock the walls down. Wright devised a bamboo pole with an ammo box filled with slabs of gun cotton on the end. His sappers would crawl forward at night, and just before daybreak, place the charges against the brick walls, and either destroy them or blow large entry holes.

156

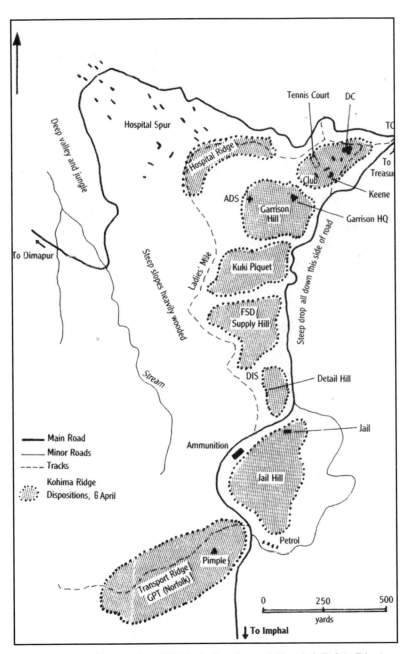

Positions on April 6, 1944. IGH is Indian General Hospital, DC is District Commissioner, FSD is Field Supply Depot, DIS is Daily Issue Store, and GPT is Transportation Ridge.

Imperial War Museum

Major Easton's men of "D" Company then positioned themselves to attack the bashas with grenades, bren guns and automatic weapons. Two Japanese machine guns on the flank raked the men as they started forward and pinned down the attack. Lance Cpl. John Harman saw the threat and told his mate to cover him with his bren gun. Harman then climbed out of his trench, and walked towards the machine gun position. The Japanese gunners saw him coming and fired at him as fast as they could. Harman went on calmly, stopped, removed two grenades from his belt, and, when 30 yards away, lobbed them both into the machine gun position. He then ran forward with his rifle, fired several shots, and emerged with one of the machine guns over his shoulder.

Lance Corporal John Harman.

Imperial War Museum

The action so motivated "D" Company that they charged the bashas, blew in the walls, and shot, stabbed, and bayoneted the Japanese inside. Only one basha remained. It held a large number of cast iron ovens and had refused to crumble under the sapper attack. Harman went into the building, was shot at several times by Japanese popping up from the ovens where they were hiding, and came back out of the basha. He went back to his unit, obtained a box of grenades, and returned. One by one, he lifted the lid of an oven and dropped a grenade inside. He did this nine times and then opened the lids to count the Japanese. He found five dead and two wounded. He picked the two wounded Japanese up, one under each arm, and returned to his unit amid wild cheering. "C" and "D" Companies continued their attack on the FSD until they reoccupied the area. Forty-four Japanese were killed in the battle.

The number of British wounded increased at a rapid rate due to the continuous fighting. There was no place for the wounded that was safe from Japanese observation and artillery fire. The small space being used at Summer House Hill could accommodate 200 wounded. Laverty made the decision to try to evacuate 100 wounded the following night. Major Peter Franklin with a few Indians and a Naga guide, led the walking wounded, and carried 30 stretcher cases from Summer House Hill through the jungle, across the ridge lines, and parallel to the Dimapur road until they felt they had gone past the Japanese road blocks. Travel was difficult in the jungle at night and the wounded men suffered greatly. After five hours of marching away from Kohima, Franklin turned south, found the road, and met some men from the Jotsoma defensive box who were waiting for them. The wounded were taken by the Jotsoma men, while Franklin and his men returned to Kohima, arriving just before daybreak.

While the wounded were evacuated, the Japanese again formed for an attack from Jail Hill. Major Shaw ("C" Company) called for artillery support from Jotsoma and his request was answered immediately by ten 3-inch howitzers. Added to the howitzer fire was the battalion's own mortars. The artillery fire was accurate, hundreds of Japanese were killed, and the Japanese dispersed from Jail Hill.

Easter Sunday fell on April 9. Church service was not possible for the men at Kohima, but Colour Sergeant (mess sergeant) Jack Eaves added sardines to the usual evening meal of stew, potatoes, and tea to make it something special. Jack was determined that the Easter Sunday meal should be a hot meal for everyone, but was hard pressed to do so. When the battle started, he had four mess cooks, but was now down to two. The remaining two cooks found it difficult to collect enough wood, keep the fires burning, and cook food for a hundred men.

Cooking was not the most difficult part of the meal, serving the food was far more challenging. Once cooked, the two cooks each carried two dixies (serving containers), one with stew, and one with potatoes flavored with margarine. Jack followed with two dixies of tea. They staggered down the hill with the meal, pushing the food ahead of them. The soldiers in the trench would hold up their mess tins while the cook ladled the stew and potatoes into one, and Jack poured tea into the other. They repeated this procedure until they fed the entire organization. The cycle took about one hour. As they finished feeding the troops, one of the men said, "Special dinner tonight, Colours: what's the do (occasion)?" Sergeant Eaves replied, "Easter Sunday today, my boy. Sorry there weren't no pink eggs for breakfast."[3]

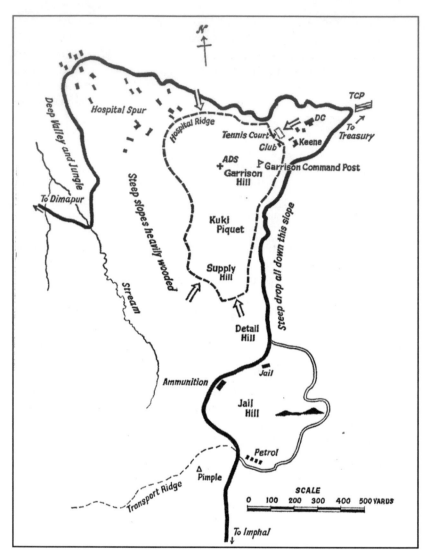

Map of positions on April 10, 1944.

Imperial War Museum

During the evening, a pale, ghostlike figure emerged from the darkness. It was Lieutenant Col. John Young, a doctor who walked from the Jotsoma defensive box to Kohima to help with the wounded. Somehow he evaded Japanese, Indian and British sentries to come to Kohima. Young immediately took charge of the hospital, such at it was, and began to prepare proper conditions for surgery.

160

Another non-combatant who made a difference in the battle was Charles Pawsey, a resident of Kohima for 20 years. Over the years, Pawsey established a superb rapport with the local Naga people. During the battle, Pawsey was without a job, so he organized the Nagas and made them his intelligence section. They brought back daily reports concerning Japanese troop movements in the Kohima area.[4]

Almost every man in the battalion proved to be a hero at one time or another. "D" Company Sergeant Major Haines was wounded in the back of his head and nearly blind. Ordered to go to the aid station he refused and enlisted a trooper named Hills to lead him around the company positions during the fighting. When Major Franklin saw him, he asked, "What the hell are you doing here, Sergeant Major? You should be back at the dressing station. "No Sir", replied Haines, "I'm not going back there. Anyway this will soon wear off. As long as Hills leads me around, I can do my job."[5]

As the Japanese started infiltrating into "D" Company positions, Haines cautioned the men not to shoot too soon. Once it became apparent that the Japanese had reached some bashas behind them Haines gave the order to fire. Most of the Japanese to the front and flanks were killed, but a group made it to the two bashas and was firing on "D" Company from the rear. Haines, with Hills leading him, moved toward the huts with some grenades. As they neared the huts, they found Lieutenant Jack Faulkner from "A" Company preparing to throw a Molotov cocktail at one of the buildings. The missile failed to ignite so Haines and Hill struck out for the company cookhouse where they each obtained a can of petrol. With Hills still leading Haines by the hand, they returned and Faulkner threw the petrol against the huts. In a few seconds, the huts were ablaze, the Japanese ran out, and were promptly killed by the gunners in the trenches.

During the siege, the British Second Division was moving two regiments from Dimapur to relieve the force at Kohima. The Japanese had established a number of strong points and bunkers that controlled the road many miles from Kohima and resisted fanatically at each such position. At one such roadblock, Zubza on April 14, the Japanese lost 96 of the 100 men manning the position. Late on the 14th, the relief column made contact with the regiment in the Jotsoma defensive position, two miles from Kohima. Jotsoma had also been under constant attack but had been able to hold their position with automatic weapon and rifle grenade fire. After five days of battle, the area outside the defensive position (the box) was littered with bloated corpses.

April 13 marked the ninth day of the siege and became a day the Japanese used the aid station as a target for their artillery. For some time Japanese observers from their high ground had been able to look directly down into Lieutenant Col. Young's dressing pit where he performed surgery. Shells had fallen on the wounded before, but the direct hits on April 13 just about put the aid station out of business. Young was completely exhausted, having had no more than two hours of sleep in the past seven days.[6]

He had only one assistant doctor, and ten stretcher bearers to care for more than 200 casualties. He did not have help to move the wounded, dig trenches for them, or bury the dead. Even worse news was that he had precious little water for the wounded or for sterilization of instruments.

Laverty was able to provide some Indian non-combat personnel as litter bearers, and to dig pits and burial sites for the dead. There was nothing he could do to alleviate the artillery shelling and there was no better place to locate the aid station. Water was in short supply and only an air drop could provide the necessary water.

The scheduled air drop arrived at 2:30 P.M. Three Dakota aircraft circled until a green flare gave them the signal to drop. As they passed over British lines, the parachutes opened and the loads descended slowly into the Japanese lines. Frantic radio messages were sent and red flares fired, but during the space of 20 minutes, the planes continued to circle and drop all their supplies within Japanese lines.

The hungry and thirsty men on the perimeter were without water, grenades, mortar shells, medicine and medical equipment: all items necessary for their survival. They watched the heartbreaking air drop unfold, and then ducked back down into their holes as the Japanese artillery shells began to fall.

A second air drop arrived and this time the loads all fell within British lines. Unfortunately, the material dropped was 3.7-inch shells intended for the artillery in the Jotsoma defensive box. Not only was the ammunition not used by the Kohima defenders, it was not available to the artillery unit at Jotsoma who needed it. A third air drop by two aircraft resulted in one of the Dakota aircraft crashing and exploding into the jungle. The single plane remaining dropped medical supplies, but no water, mortar ammunition, or grenades. Laverty covered his face with his hand and said, "The thirteenth of April - Black Thirteen. I hope to God the fourteenth will be brighter."[7]

On the 15th of April, a young Lieutenant from the Rajputs at Jotsoma stumbled into the defensive perimeter of Kohima. He explained that he had led a small patrol through the jungle from Jotsoma to find out the status of Kohima. Laverty thanked him for his assistance and told him to return and tell Brigadier Warren that unless help arrives at Kohima within 48 hours, it will fall. The Lieutenant looked around the dismal landscape, exclaimed, "I see," and disappeared into the steep jungle from the area of Indian general hospital (IGH) Spur.[8]

That night the Japanese attacked through the rain and dark mist against the positions of B Company at the tennis court. They attacked continuously with grenades and dynamite to destroy the defensive bunkers. Major John Winstanley rallied his platoons and they gave as good as they got, frequently throwing back Japanese infantry with their bayonets, knives, and bare hands. They fought valiantly through the entire night, and, in the morning, the Japanese withdrew.

Before dawn, the Japanese attacked again on FSD Ridge. As the Japanese reached within three yards of the top of the ridge, Laverty committed his small reserve force of Assam infantry and they held. They were a hundred yards in front of the defense on Kuki Piquet and surrounded by huge piles of rotting Japanese corpses. A and C companies were manning positions on Kuki and Summer House Hill, and were reduced to 80 men.

During the evening of April 17, the forward positions on Kuki Piquet were manned by Indian soldiers from the Assam regiment and Assam Rifles. These men had fought bravely during the entire siege, but like most of the troops at Kohima were exhausted. Shortly after they were in position, a severe and prolonged artillery bombardment was laid down on their positions. The Assams broke and fled back through the positions of the West Kents.

Laverty was notified immediately, and lacking reinforcements, made the difficult decision to fall back from the positions at Kuki Piquet. As his men left their positions the Japanese occupied them and Major Yeo called in his 3-inch mortars on the position. Laverty's defensive perimeter was now reduced to a few hundred yards from the District Commissioner's (DC's) bungalow to Garrison Hill.

When the sun rose on April 18, the weary defenders of Kohima were staggered by the death and destruction around them. Every tree and building had been blown to bits. The entire area was covered with the rotting corpses of British, Indian and Japanese soldiers, all moving slightly as the black flies and maggots swarmed in and about the bodies.

The stench of death and putrefaction was everywhere. The Japanese were within 100 yards of Laverty's command post and the aid station where 600 badly wounded men lay helpless in shallow slit trenches. Clearly, another artillery bombardment and charge by Japanese infantry would overwhelm the defenders.

At 8:00 A.M., the men noticed a change in the sound and pattern of artillery fire. Instead of the guns from Jotsoma, this fire was coming from the division's 25-pound guns. Quickly, Major Yeo established contact with the leading elements of the division reinforcements, and began calling in artillery fire on all the Japanese positions.

Royal Air Force Hurricane aircraft strafed the Japanese positions on transport (GPT) Ridge, and soon Second Division infantry, supported by tanks and mobile artillery came into view. Behind the tanks came bren carriers, three-ton trucks, and ambulances.

By noon, the First Punjabis made contact with the battalion and began to take over the defensive positions at Kohima. Next came the Royal Berkshire Regiment. There was no elation among the West Kents. The men were too tired to even smile. Most had not washed, shaved, changed clothes or boots since April 5.

They resembled scarecrows as they crawled from their trenches, eyes sunk deep in their sockets and shoulders drooping. Silently, they staggered down to the waiting transports. Japanese snipers took their toll of the newly arrived defenders as well as the wounded as they were moved to ambulances. The battle was not over, but the siege had been lifted.

There would be more fighting and the Second Division would find that the Japanese showed great skill and determination as they shifted from the offense to the defense. They defended each position to the death. It was then April 18, 1944, and it would be June 2 before the Japanese were finally driven from Kohima.

The Kohima siege was the turning point of the entire Burma war. From that point on, the Japanese were on the defensive in Burma until they evacuated Rangoon, almost a year later. Perhaps never before had a lone battalion of 500 men held out against an entire division for 13 days.

By 1991, Kohima had grown to a city of 83,000 people. On April 14 of that year, a group of 3,000 veterans, including 15 Japanese from the 31st Division and 11 British from the Second Division dedicated the new Roman Catholic Church on the lower slope of Andura Spur. The site is just above the Imphal road and overlooks the battle area.

The cemetery at Kohima contains 1,200 graves and many private memorials. For me, the most moving is the Second Division memorial which reads:[9]

When you go home,
Tell them of us and say,
For your tomorrow,
We gave our today.[10]

The Kohima War Memorial.

Imperial War Museum

11

VICTORY IN BURMA

Following Japan's defeat on the Imphal plain, major changes of command occurred on both the British and Japanese sides. Lieutenant Gen. Renya Mutaguchi, commander of Japan's 15 Army in Burma, relieved all three of his division commanders during the unsuccessful attack on Imphal. On August 30, Mutaguchi himself was relieved and replaced by Lieutenant Gen. Hyotaro Kimura, formerly commander of the 54th Division in the Aarakan. On the same day, Lieutenant Gen. Masakazu Kawabe, commander Burma Area Army, was relieved as was most of his staff. Relief of so many high level commanders was unprecedented in the Japanese army.

During the same period, General "Vinegar Joe" Stilwell was relieved as chief of staff to Chiang Kai-shek and replaced by Lieutenant Gen. Albert Wedemeyer. Stilwell's position as the Northern Combat Area commander (NCAC) was assigned to Lieutenant Gen. Daniel Sultan, and Lieutenant Gen. Raymond Wheeler became deputy supreme commander, South East Asia Command (SEAC) under Admiral Mountbatten. Several corps and division commanders were also changed, but General William Slim remained in command of 14th Army. During December 1944, Slim and his three corps commanders, Christison, Scones and Stopford, were knighted on behalf of the King of England. Shortly thereafter, Lord Slim replaced Lord Scones with Major Gen. Frank Messervy as commander 4th

Lord Scones, left, Major Gen. Frank Messervy, center, and General Sir William Slim.

Imperial War Museum

Corps. Messervy previously commanded the 7th Indian Division and Slim liked his dash and spirit.[1]

Without question, Stilwell had the most frustrating assignment of any military leader in WW II. Constantly frustrated by Chiang Kai-shek's duplicity, the evasiveness and cowardice of many Chinese commanders, and his vitriolic relationship with Claire Chennault, Stilwell took his frustrations out on the British commanders and any one else with whom he came in contact. It seems likely that no one was saddened by his departure.

The strategy for the invasion of Burma cried for an amphibious assault but such ships were not available so long as the war in the European theater was ongoing. General Slim was forced to plan for an overland attack of Burma from his bases in India. The distances involved and the difficulty of supply due to the mountains and rivers that had to be crossed caused his staff to wonder if such an invasion could even be conducted.

The entire strategy changed in the spring of 1945 when General "Hap" Arnold, chief of staff of the U.S. Army Air Force in Washington, authorized the transfer of 400 transport aircraft to SEAC. With these additional aircraft, Mountbatten and Slim could transport troops and resupply them while they advanced into Burma. Slim reasoned that the way to Rangoon, the capital, was through Mandalay, the ancient capital of Burma. He was quite certain that Lieutenant Gen. Kimura would force a major battle on the Shwebo plain near Mandalay, and directed three major routes of advance on Rangoon in order to spread Kimura's forces.

The three main routes for the British advance on Rangoon were obvious, since each had been used previously by both British and Japanese forces. One route was along the Kaladin valley in the Arakan, down the coast with Akyab and Ramree Islands as intermediate objectives. Akyab had a major airfield that would be necessary for resupply. Ramree Island would be the launch point for whatever landing craft Slim was able to obtain for the 480-mile trip to Rangoon. This route was assigned to 1th Corps with three divisions.

A second route in the center of Burma, was to cross the Irrawaddy River north of Kalewa and attack Japanese strong points at Monywa and Shwebo, 40 miles from Mandalay. This route was assigned to 4th Corps with three divisions.

The third route was already being pushed hard by troops in Stilwell's NCAC consisting of two Chinese divisions (the 5th and 6th), and one British division. Although Stilwell was replaced by General Sultan, the troops advanced rapidly to Bhamo where they reopened the land link with Kunming, China, via the new Ledo Road and the old Burma Road. The first convoy from Ledo arrived in Kunming on February 4, 1945, carrying 75mm and 105 mm guns, ammunition, and supplies. The drivers were treated to a huge celebration, complete with fireworks and a banquet.[2]

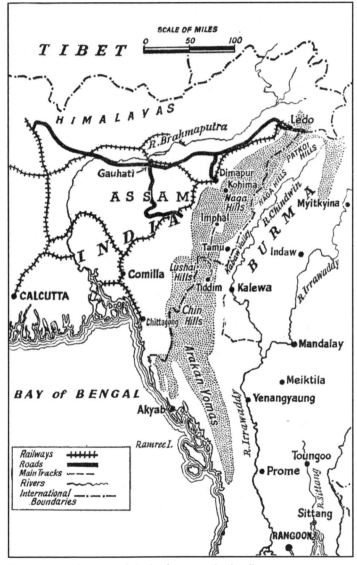

The mountain barrier and the land communication lines.

Imperial War Museum

Frank Owens, the distinguished editor of the SEAC newspaper, described the advance of the NCAC forces as follows:[3]

> Showing considerable ingenuity the 36th British Division adapted a number of jeeps to run on the railway and to pull both wagons and carriages. They advanced through a wilderness, which had been rendered more savage by the Japanese. Burnt out villages, ruined pagodas, broken wagons, rotting equipment, rusting helmets with their stamped white doves of peace, unopened mail, and unburied corpses were the milestones of the advance. Sweating and cursing, the infantryman slogged his way forward through the mud towards the next ruined village with its garrison of death.

The 25th Indian Division moved down the Arakan and approached Akyab with a commando brigade, three cruisers offshore for naval gunfire, and 200 RAF planes for air support. On January 3, 1945, they discovered that the Japanese had abandoned Akyab with its vital airfields a few days earlier. Ramree and Cheduba were captured by January 26, leaving Rangoon only 441 miles away, well within aircraft range.[4] Six makeshift convoys left Akyab and Ramree during early April to carry an India division to Rangoon. They were protected by destroyers and cruisers the entire way.

On December 3, 1944, two divisions of 4th Corps crossed the Chindwin River 30 miles north of Kalewa and moved towards Monywa, 60 miles west of Mandalay. Another division crossed the Irrawaddy at the same bridgehead on December 19, and advanced to Shwebo, 40 miles north west of Mandalay. In five weeks, Slim put three divisions across one of the widest rivers in the world. The feat must rate with best of the European river crossings during the war.

Because of scant Japanese resistance to these river crossings, Slim believed Kimura would not fight a decisive battle on the Shwebo plain. He therefore devised a plan to keep the pressure on Mandalay (and Kimura), while simultaneously sending forces to the south to cross the Irrawaddy west of Meiktila, thereby dividing Kimura's forces between Mandalay and Meiktila, and forcing a decisive battle at Meiktila. The plan required secrecy in order to move forces south to Meiktila, and miracles on the part of the engineers to construct bridges and roads to accommodate the large number of forces being sent there.

Bailey bridges, boats and rafts were constructed by the engineers to move the men, supplies, and tanks down the Chindwin River to a point where it joined the Irrawaddy River. From there, a bithess road was built to move the forces to Myittha. A bithess road involves leveling the ground, laying overlapping rolls of hemp, treating the hemp with a gasoline and diesel fuel mixture, and then packing the surface to form a road. A gallon of gasoline and diesel fuel was required for every yard of the road. Once the road was ready, a hundred miles of bithess could handle a thousand vehicles of all descriptions per day.[5]

Elephants were used to haul logs to the chaungs (streams) where they were emplaced to form roadways. Slim was blessed with 7000 aircraft sorties per day to keep the Japanese aircraft from snooping on his advance down the Myittha River valley towards Miektila. Slim had 1,200 aircraft for his attack on Burma compared to Kimura's 64 aircraft to defend it. On February 28, 1945, while 33rd Corps was attacking the suburbs of Mandalay, 4th Corps attacked Japanese forces at Meiktila.

Mandalay was the religious center and early capital of Burma. It was a key rail, river, road and communication center between northern and southern Burma. Fort Dufferin at Mandalay was the primary defensive position. Dufferin was a medieval castle of 2000 square yards, containing defensive positions, the palace, government house, jail, club and polo ground. The fort was surrounded by a 75-yard moat and brick walls 30-feet wide at the bottom and tapering to 12-feet at the top, 23-feet high.

Mandalay was defended by two divisions, commanded by Major Gen. Seitei Yamamoto. He had been ordered to defend Mandalay to the last man. The British attack on Mandalay commenced on February 28, 1945, with three divisions plus heavy tank and motorized support. By March 12, Mandalay Hill was seized. Howitzers and attack aircraft were used to punch holes through the thick concrete walls of Fort Dufferin, but the 50-foot earth ramparts behind the walls absorbed most of the energy of the shells and bombs.

Major Gen. "Pete" Rees, commanding the British 19th Division, used a "ninja" type tactic to try to gain entry to the fort. During the night, several small units left behind their steel helmets and boots, and were brought across the moat by small assault boats. The men had scaling ladders, flame throwers and a machine gun company to fight their way into the fort. The attack to gain entry began at 10:00 P.M. on March 17. The assault unit established a foothold inside the fort at a point where the railway ran through the fort but was discovered in the early hours of 18th and were driven back. Rees, knowing that any of his forces found on the walls at daylight would stand no chance, called off the attack at 3:00 A.M., and recalled the force.

Major Gen. T.W. "Pete" Rees, 19 India Division, directing the battle for Mandalay on March 9, 1945.

Imperial War Museum

Bombing of the fort with 2,000-pound bombs, shelling by 6-inch howitzers, and tank guns failed to damage the wall sufficiently to permit the infantry to gain a foothold. Rees next ploy was to find a sewer line that he remembered went under the moat and came up inside the fort. A Burmese that knew the plan for the Mandalay sewer system was found and plans were made to wade through the thigh-deep mud, sludge, and feces of the

Mandalay sewers to gain entrance to the fort. Fortunately, the Japanese found and used the sewer line first to escape the fort.

During the evening of the 19th, General Kimura, realizing that he could not defend Mandalay much longer, authorized his forces to withdraw. They did so by using a drain that ran under the moat. On the morning of March 20, four Burmese prisoners of the Japanese emerged from the fort carrying a white flag and announced that the Japanese had left the fort. The British Union Jack was run up the flag pole in quick order in the presence of Slim, Messervy, and the three division commanders

Battle for Meiktila

The 17th Division crossed the Irrawaddy River on February 17, and left the bridgehead four days later. An armored brigade led the advance for the 80 miles to Meiktila. Japanese infantrymen attacked the tanks with boxes of explosives attached to their bodies. They would throw themselves under the front of the tank and detonate the explosives, killing themselves and often stopping the tank. There were about 4,000 Japanese combat troops in Meiktila at this time.[6]

The battle for Meiktila lasted four days and involved heavy fighting. The Japanese defenders were told to fight to the last man and did so. After the battle, 2000 corpses were counted and at least that many more were thought to be buried in bunkers, cellars, and lakes, or blown apart by the massive artillery bombardment. Captured at Meiktila were two large supply depots with stores for two Japanese divisions.

General Kimura reacted too slowly to the British capture of Meiktila. He assembled the equivalent of two divisions of troops that were intended to reinforce his army at Mandalay and sent them to Meiktila. When they arrived at Meiktila, they fought bravely and counterattacked from March 6 to 24. However, the attacks were not well organized and the British were able to use the airports to fly in reinforcement and supplies. The Japanese did destroy 50 British tanks during the fighting but suffered 2,500 casualties and lost 46 artillery pieces.[7]

Staff Officer, Colonel Masanobu Tsuji (see separate chapter titled Tsuji in this volume), did the math to prove that Burma Army could not win the battle for Meiktila. He computed that since Japan lost 50 artillery pieces and 2,500 men to destroy

50 British tanks, and since the British had more than 100 tanks remaining, it would require 100 more guns and 5,000 men to defeat the British. Unfortunately, the Japanese army defending Meiktila had less then 20 guns, and less than 5,000 men in the area.[8] .

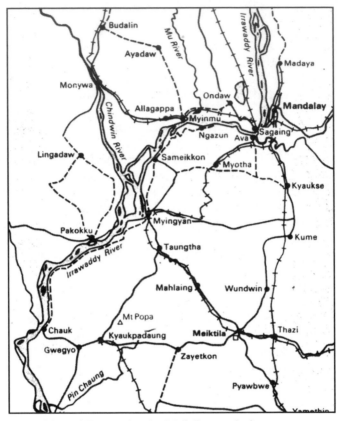

Map of Central Burma, showing Meiktila near the bottom.

Imperial War Museum

As the defeated Japanese moved south from Mandalay, they were ambushed near Toungoo by a British division that had moved quickly from Mandalay by tank and motorized vehicles. Kimura lost another 3,000 men at Toungoo.

Following their victories on all three fronts, (Mandalay, Ramree, and Meiktila), Slim moved fast to capture Rangoon before the monsoon started. Mountbatten was concerned that Rangoon could not be captured before the monsoon set in, especially in view of the spirited battle the Japanese fought at Meiktila. A final major battle was expected at Rangoon.

As the British closed on Rangoon, Bose's Indian national Army (INA) began to surrender in large numbers. One hundred and fifty officers and 3,000 men of the INA surrendered to the 5th Division near Pyu. Many of those surrendering were former deserters from the INA who now saw the chance to rejoin their units and surrender to the British. A deserter could be identified by one or more wounds on his upper arms. Slashing of the arm with a sword was a ritual performed by the Japanese Army to all deserters. The Burma National Army, allies with Japan throughout the war, rebelled against the Japanese on March 27, 1945, and refused to fight.

When the 5th Division reached Penwegon, they found the bridge wired for demolition and the single Japanese demolition man asleep. Both the 5th and 17th Divisions were past Penwegon on April 25. Once past the city, they found a curious mixture of retreating Japanese and their cavalry horses. By evening, the British had killed 100 Japanese, captured 100 horses, two trains and three engines.[9]

The distance from Meiktila to Rangoon is 338 miles. Traveling and fighting overland in 1945 took the British forces all of March and until April 29, to reach Pegu, 50 miles north of Rangoon. The monsoon arrived at Pegu at the same time as the 17th Indian Division, confining tanks and trucks to the main roads, and forcing most of the close support aircraft back to the Imphal area.

Pegu is one of the most important communications centers in Burma. It is adjacent to the Pegu River which has bridges channeling two railways and a road. The whole area was heavily fortified and defended by Major Gen. Hideji Matsui's infantry and engineer units. Matsui's engineers blew the bridges, but the British 48th Brigade walked across the downed bridge girders single file, and after fixing bayonets, charged the Japanese positions. By morning, many of the Japanese had disappeared and Pegu was cleared of all Japanese by May 1.

On the same day, reconnaissance aircraft flying over Rangoon saw a sign on the roof of a suspected POW camp which read "Japs Gone."[10] The following day an RAF pilot landed at Mingaladon airport in Rangoon and found it deserted. The pilot and his navigator made their way to the prison and found a thousand POWs waiting for their rescue. They had been abandoned by the fleeing Japanese.[11]

On May 1, a Ghurka parachute brigade jumped from 38 *Dakota* aircraft into an area several miles from the Japanese coastal defense guns at Rangoon that would contest the amphibious landing of an Indian division from Ramree. The guns were quickly silenced and the landing craft moved upriver and landed in Rangoon on May 3. They restored order in Rangoon and then moved a few miles north on May 6, to link up with units of the 14th Army.

General Kimura ordered Matsui to withdraw from Pegu on April 30, and to fall back to Rangoon where he would defend the city to the death. Matsui withdrew from Pegu, but rather than going to Rangoon where he knew he would be trapped between the British and the ocean, he moved his remaining forces to the Pegu Yomas, a series of low lying hills that rise to 1800 feet and average 80 miles north to south and 30 miles east to west. They are heavily forested, mostly bamboo, and there are few tracks or villages.

The Japanese started stockpiling provisions in the Yomas during April, with the intent of staying there until July when they would break out and engage the British in a final battle. The early arrival of the monsoon delayed the arrival of Japanese forces so that it was the end of July before the army was ready to take the offensive.[12]

Kimura evacuated Rangoon at the end of April 1945. He took his headquarters staff, Ba Maw, the puppet provisional leader of Burma, and Subhas Chandra Bose, the self-proclaimed leader of the provisional government of Free India, and head of the INA, and went to Thailand. Kimura did not tell his forces near Pegu he was leaving, and did nothing to assist them.

There must have been a sense of satisfaction on the part of the British troops following the capture of Rangoon, but the leadership was well aware of the work that remained. There were large numbers of Japanese troops from the 28th Army in the Pegu Yomas that had to be located and eliminated, Operation Zipper, the plan to recapture Malaya and Singapore was being activated, and there remained thousands of Japanese troops in Thailand that had to be accounted for.

The battle for Imphal and Kohima had destroyed the Japanese 15 Army. The Battle at Meiktila destroyed the Japanese 33rd Army. Now the Japanese 28th Army had to be engaged as they attempted to breakout of the Yomas and escape to Thailand. The continuous rain of the 1945 monsoon made conditions miserable for both sides. Whenever there was a break in the rain, the sweltering heat sapped the energy of the soldiers.

Instead of a massive infantry battle along the Sittang River, the strategy of the conflict changed on July 2 when the entire movement plan of 28th Army was captured by a Gurkha patrol who engaged the small Japanese force, killed 19 of them, and brought back the documents in a dispatch bag. Translators and interpreters found that the documents in the bag provided the entire movement plan of the 28th Army, including its ammunition and health status. On July 18, a Japanese officer and a *Kempei Tai* (secret police) sergeant were captured in the eastern foothills of the Pegu Yomas, and their documents provided the date, July 20, of the Japanese breakout. All that remained for the British was to get ready.

Messervy channeled the Japanese breakout into two main killing areas, one between the Yomas and the Sittang River, and the other between the mouths of the Sittang and Salween Rivers. Artillery was placed to command all Japanese avenues of approach and the RAF was alerted to follow the artillery strikes.

Major Gen. Shigesaburo Miyazaki led his 54th Division to the Sittang River on schedule, but as his forces crossed the flooded rice paddy fields, British guns created a holocaust of mud, shrapnel and bodies. The Japanese broke formation and died by the thousands. Miyazaki left the Yomas with 9,000 men and now had less than 4,000.

The remnants of 28th Army reached the Sittang on July 28. The waters rushed by with great force revealing many Japanese dead and dying in the current, victims that tried to cross the raging river and failed. Lieutenant Gen. Shozo Sakurai, commander 28th Army, changed his plans and turned south to find a better place to cross. He covered 50 miles in three weeks, and finally crossed the river into Moulmein and the near sanctity of Thailand. His initial force of 7,000 men now numbered less than 2,000. By the time the Japanese reached Thailand the war was over, following the emperor's announcement of surrender on August 15, 1945.[13]

General MacArthur as Supreme Allied Commander directed that no surrender ceremonies were to be conducted in the field, until the ceremony was conducted aboard USS *Missouri* in Tokyo Bay. This guidance severely limited the ability of field commanders to arrange for Japanese forces to surrender their weapons and to assist Allied POWs under control of the Japanese. Another MacArthur directive was that Allied commanders should not require the defeated Japanese to turn over their samurai swords upon surrendering their units.[14]

Contrary to General MacArthur's instructions, General Slim directed that senior Japanese officers would surrender their swords to British officers in front of their own troops at appropriate ceremonies. Certain Japanese "experts" advised against such a ceremony because the Japanese officer's honor was so bound up with his samurai sword that, rather than surrender it, he would go on fighting. Alternatively, if he did surrender his sword in front of his men, he would never again be able to exercise command over them. He would in fact, rather than be publicly shamed, commit suicide.

Slim's response to the experts was classic and must have bothered MacArthur no end. Slim said that if the Japanese liked to go on fighting, he was ready for them. He could care less about the Japanese soldiers' respect for their officers, he intended to separate them anyway, and he had already broadcast information that any Japanese wishing to commit suicide would be given every assisstance.[15]

Numerous surrender ceremonies were conducted throughout the Pacific following the ceremony on September 2, 1945, aboard USS *Missouri* in Tokyo Bay. In all of them, except the *Missouri* ceremony, the senior Japanese military officer was required to hand over his sword in front of his assembled troops. Lieutenant Gen. Heitaro Kimura surrendered 72,000 Japanese troops in Burma on September 13. With the exception of some Japanese soldiers that escaped to Thailand that was all that remained of the 303,501 soldiers sent to the Burma Area Army from 1941 to 1945.[16]

The final surrender ceremony was conducted in Singapore on September 12, 1945, at the municipal building. Admiral Lord Louis Mountbatten represented the Allies and Gen. Seishiro Itagaki signed the document for Field Marshall Tarauchi. Terauchi suffered a stroke from which he never recovered. Following the ceremony, the same Union Jack that last flew over Singapore during January 1942, was raised to the top of the masthead. The flag had been kept hidden by POWs at Changi Prison during the war. The war in the Pacific was finally over.

Perhaps it is true that the end of all wars is best summed up by the Japanese poet Basho.[17]

> *Summer grasses...*
> *all that is left of*
> *the dreams of soldiers...*

12

MASANOBU TSUJI

The complete fanatic, Col. Masanobu Tsuji displays
the awards his atrocities earned.

Media Masters

Many readers of the two earlier volumes of War in the
Pacific asked me to write chapters about the battles for Tarawa
and Peleliu. These requests were understandable owing to the
tremendous casualties associated with these battles, as well as the
mistakes made during the planning and operational phases.

The next chapter most often requested was Masanobu
Tsuji. I found this surprising. Tsuji never was promoted above the
rank of Colonel, and never held command of army units. He was

best known as the planner and supervisor of executions, cannibalism, spying, and master of disguises. After the war, he had a successful career as a politician. I was surprised at the number of readers that even knew of Tsuji. His role in WW II was that of a staff officer, but certainly a most interesting one.

Tsuji was born in Ishikawa prefecture in Japan in 1902. As the son of a poor farmer, he was unable to attend school, but at age 15, with the help of a benefactor, he entered the Nagoya Army Elementary School. Due to his determination and hard work, he graduated at the top of his class. He also finished first in the Officer's School Preparatory Course in Tokyo which he entered in 1920.

Tsuji was promoted to lieutenant in 1927. He had no interest in sports but became proficient in the art of sword-fighting, known as kendo. At only five-feet-two-inches in height and of a slight frame, he had unusual physical strength and took pleasure in beating his opponents into submission. He shunned alcohol, was disinterested in women, and was described by his peers as scheming, high-handed, and possessing a high degree of energy. He ignored those he did not like and showed favoritism to those he did. He was highly excitable, with a temperament which frequently gave way to fits of violence "almost akin to madness."[1]

Few officers desired to serve for or with Tsuji. He treated his subordinates horribly, and his relationships with his peers were never pleasant. He did not socialize and never attended unit functions. He did eventually marry. His wife was the daughter of a postmaster, and they had five children, two boys and three girls.

Tsuji gained his first notoriety while serving with Japan's Kwantung Army in China. He would go out at night in Shanghai and burn down brothels which were supposed to be off limits to Japanese troops. He was subsequently dismissed from the staff, but managed to show up in many army staff positions thereafter.

When Major Gen. Tomoyuki Yamashita was establishing his undercover network prior to Japan's 1942 invasion of Malaya and Singapore, one of his agents was 31-year old Captain Masanobu Tsuji. Tsuji was a confirmed racist, but was among many Japanese officers that had similar feelings. He belittled the Indian troops who surrendered at Jitra and Alor Star during Japan's invasion of Malaya and Singapore. He compared the Indian's pathetic performance with the British decision to actually use the Indians in the defense of Singapore.

180

Tsuji's military career was a classic example of insubordination (gekokujo) that permeated the ranks of the Japanese Army in the 1930s. Impatient and ambitious junior officers considered senior officers less than intelligent, outdated, and politically compromised. They felt it their duty to provide firm, decisive direction, with appropriate action directed from below. They often openly criticized their seniors and agitated their peers to take action.

Tsuji could have been an excellent staff officer with a talent for operational planning. Instead, his unbridled ambition, violent prejudices, and ruthless lack of regard for human life, marked him as an individualist with no loyalty to his superiors.

In most of his writings, Tsuji takes credit for everything that went well. Insofar as his not being rewarded for such events, he claims to have been misunderstood. "My body," he once boasted, "carried the bullets of five countries: Russian from the battle at Nomonhan, American from Guadalcanal, Chinese from Shanghai, British from Burma, and Australian from the Philippines."[2]

He neglects to tell the reader that he was quickly transferred from each of these commands when his superiors learned that he was operating on his own and in violation of established guidelines. In China, Tsuji was transferred for burning down brothels and lecturing his seniors on the evils of alcohol and womanizing. At Nomonhan, he was blamed for Japan's defeat at the hands of the Russians after providing misleading intelligence information, and urging a Japanese attack against prepared defensive positions.

He tried to take control of the Japanese 11th Army headquarters after the capture of Hankow, China, and was promptly relieved. He was personally responsible for the massacre of native people in Singapore and the Philippines. On Guadalcanal, he consistently overruled objections to his plan for continued attacks against marine corps positions on Bloody Ridge. His objections were responsible for General Hyakutake's disastrous attack and a terrible loss of Japanese soldiers.[3]

No amount of dismissals and transfers could keep Tsuji down for long He kept showing up on the staffs of senior commanders, usually unannounced and unwanted. Woe to the commander that was too busy conducting the war to keep a close eye on Tsuji and his gekokujo.

181

Many operational commanders in the field were reluctant to punish Tsuji because they believed him to be a spy sent from army headquarters in Tokyo. The best they could do was to dismiss him and send him back to Tokyo where he promptly obtained another set of orders to a different staff.

Shortly after Japan's occupation of Singapore, Tsuji came across several junior officers and enlisted arguing with a Chinese shopkeeper, trying to obtain a lower price for some watches on display. "Fools," shouted Tsuji, striking each of them in the face. Tsuji's message was clear, kill the Chinaman and take what you want. Later, the murders in Singapore attributed to Tsuji would be established by the War Crimes Tribunal to be in excess of 25,000.[4]

During the Singapore War Crimes Trials, Lieutenant Gen. Takuma Nishimura, commander of the Imperial Guards, during the occupation of Singapore, testified that Tsuji was a staff officer of the 25th Army under command of General Yamashita. As such, Tsuji requested and was provided with troops from the Imperial Guards Division for duty as auxiliary military police.

Major Gen. Saburo Kawamura, the Singapore garrison commander during the occupation, testified that he received a verbal order from General Yamashita to mop up anti-Japanese elements among the Chinese population of Singapore. When Kawamura went to see Lieutenant Gen. Sosaku Suzuki, chief of staff of Yamashita's 25th Army, he found Tsuji and Major Tadahiko Hayashi in attendance. Suzuki explained how the Chinese males were to be screened, divided into five categories, and killed. The entire operation had to be completed within three days, February 21-23, 1942.

Kawamura stated that he doubted the operation could be conducted in three days, but was cut short by Tsuji, who said, ". . . he and Hayashi would be handling matters, and the garrison commander could set his mind at ease."[5]

Kawamura met with his two battalion commanders, Major Miyamoto and Major Tadashi Ichikawa, plus Lieutenant Col. Masayuki Oishi from the secret police (kempeitai) on February 18, to issue orders for the screening and killings. He testified that he was informed on the afternoon of February 23, that 5,000 Chinese males had been executed.

Changi Beach is an ideal seaside playground now, but was the site of one of the first mass slaughters of civilians by Japanese forces in Singapore .

Media Masters

The Singapore trials were conducted in the fall of 1946, ten months after General Douglas MacArthur had General Yamashita hanged for responsibility for the Rape of Manila.[6] Kawamura and others attempted to implicate Yamashita in the Singapore killings without success. All prosecution witnesses implicated Tsuji and Hayashi in the killings.

Prior to the trial, Colonel Ichiji Sugita attempted suicide by stabbing himself in the throat with a stainless steel table knife. His handwritten note explained that, "I cannot bear to give evidence against my senior officers."[7] Sugita was listed on Britain's most wanted list due to his role as the issuing authority for the list of Chinese to be murdered.

He survived the suicide attempt and appeared in court with his neck heavily bandaged. Sugita testified that there had been two purges conducted against the Chinese in Singapore. The first was on February 21 and 22 when 5,000 Chinese were murdered, the second during the end of February and first of March when 300 more were murdered. The killings, according to Sugita, were planned by Colonel Tsuji and Major Hayashi, staff officers in the 25th Army. By this time, Tsuji was on the run.

On April 2, 1947, the court found all seven defendants guilty and pronounced the following sentences.

Lieutenant Gen. Takuma Nishimura..............Life imprisonment
Lieutenant Gen. Saburo Kawamura.............. Death by hanging
Lieutenant Col. Masayuki Oishi...................Death by hanging
Lieutenant Col. Yoshitaka Yokota,
Major Tomotatsu Jyo,
Major Satorou Onishi,
and Captain Haruji Hisamatsu.......................Life imprisonment

The sentences were confirmed on May 29. Kawamura and Oishi were hanged on June 26, 1947.

During early November 1948, orders were issued to apprehend and arrest Tsuji for trial. On November 23, the Australian Army's legal service noted that Tsuji was underground in Japan, but his arrest was expected any time now.[8]

Tsuji was recalled to Japan in late February 1942, just as the Singapore massacre was at its peak. He was briefed at Army headquarters and sent to Manila on April 1, to prod Major General Masaharu Homma into more aggressive action against General Wainwright's forces on Corregidor.[9] The battle was in its fourth month and the Japanese troops were needed elsewhere.

Tsuji immediately organized a group of junior officers who were impressed with Tsuji's claims that he had direct access to the emperor and was authorized to speak for Imperial Army Headquarters. Tsuji's plan for the prisoners of Bataaan and Corregidor was the same as his solution for the Chinese in Singapore. Kill all. Tsuji argued that Japan was fighting a racial war in the Philippines so the Filipinos should be murdered because they betrayed the Asian cause. American prisoners should be executed because they were white colonialists. General Homma was preoccupied with conquering Corregidor and failed to supervise Tsuji. This was the same situation that happened with General Yamashita in Singapore.

By the end of April, Tsuji was sending orders direct to front line fighting units. He was present for the surrender of Bataan and issued orders to kill all prisoners. Some unit commanders did so, others did not. One commander on Bataan strongly objected to the order. He was told by Tsuji over the phone, that, "The order comes from Imperial Headquarters and has to be obeyed."[10] The colonel was so outraged that he slammed down the phone and ordered the release of all prisoners that had surrendered or been captured. Few commanders had the courage to do such a thing.

Several hundred Americans were decapitated by orders from Tsuji and the Bataan Death March claimed between 7,000 and 10,000 lives. On April 10, the Philippine Chief Justice, Mr. Jose Abad Santos and his son were captured on Negros Island. General Kawaguchi recommended that Santos be given a position in the military administration of the Philippines. Tsuji saw Kawaguchi's message and sent an immediate reply, "His guilt is obvious. Dispose of him immediately."[11]

Kawaguchi refused to obey the order for several weeks, but under great pressure finally had Santos shot. He spared the son. Immediately, Kawaguchi flew to Manila, confronted General Homma, and demanded to know why he had ordered Santos killed. Homma denied having done such a thing. Kawaguchi investigated the incident and determined the messages from higher headquarters were sent by Tsuji.

During February 1946, General Homma was tried for the responsibility for the Bataan Death March, found guilty and executed. Kawaguchi was tried for the murder of Abad Santos, found guilty and sentenced to seven years and three months in prison. Kawaguchi never forgot or forgave Tsuji and would seek revenge several years later.

Tsuji was recalled to Tokyo in July 1942. He now had victories at Singapore, Bataan and Corregidor, and was hailed as a "god of strategy" by junior officers at Army Headquarters. On July 24, he flew to Rabaul to plan for the capture of Port Moresby, Papua New Guinea. Four days later, enroute to Buna, Papua, Tsuji's patrol craft was attacked by Australian aircraft and Tsuji was seriously wounded. He was evacuated to Tokyo where he recovered and then was sent again to Rabaul, to plan recapture of Guadalcanal.

On Guadalcanal, Tsuji came face to face with General Kawaguchi, the man he had duped in the Philippines. Kawaguchi worked with Tsuji as they planned the next attack on Bloody Ridge. Kawaguchi and other commanders argued against more frontal attacks against the American positions, but Tsuji was adamant his plan would work.

Kawaguchi needed more time to prepare for the attack, having already suffered severe casualties during frontal assaults against the marine positions. Tsuji adjusted Kawaguchi's schedule, setting the time for his attack back from the original schedule. Then, without notice to Kawaguchi, Tsuji ordered the attack to proceed on the original schedule. Tsuji then informed headquarters that Kawaguchi refused to advance. As a result, Kawaguchi was relieved of his command. The attack was a disaster. Japan's 2nd Division lost half of its troops in the frontal assault.

Following a bout with malaria, Tsuji became an instructor at the Tokyo Military Academy, was promoted to colonel, and was sent to Nanking, China, on August 20, 1943. During July 1944, he was sent to Rangoon, Burma as the senior staff officer with the 33rd Army, commanded by Lieutenant Gen. Masaki Honda. Tsuji's job was to plan the withdrawal of Japanese forces from the Imphal plain, where they suffered a major defeat. During this time, Tsuji boasted of drinking a mixture made from the livers of captured British airmen on Palau, and offered this "medicine" to fellow officers.

On September 26, 1944, an American pilot, Lieutenant Benjamin A. Parker, was forced to bail out of his aircraft while bombing and strafing targets several miles from Tsuji's headquarters in Burma. Parker landed safely, was captured, and brought to Tsuji's headquarters.

Tsuji had the pilot bound and brought to an area for public execution. In front of his officers and enlisted men, Tsuji struck Parker in the face with what he claimed was a piece of shrapnel from Parker's bomb. The jagged steel made a deep wound from which blood poured. An irate Tsuji then announced that the prisoner would not have the honor of being beheaded by a Japanese sword. He ordered that his personal Burmese sword (Shan da) be brought from his office.

A blindfold was tied over Parker's eyes and he was pushed to a kneeling position. The sword was raised and flashed down on the back of his neck. Parker fell forward on his face from the impact of the blade and a deep wound in his neck. The blade was blunt. Parker was jerked back on his knees and it took two more strokes before his head was severed from his body.

Tsuji then ordered a piece of the flesh to be carved from Parker's thigh. He had the flesh cooked and served it to a group of officers in his hut. Some of the Japanese ate the flesh, others did not.[12]

The butchery of Parker would likely have become another forgotten wartime incident except for the testimony of a 27-year old Japanese named Masao Sasaki. Sasaki surrendered to Allied forces near Mandalay on March 16, 1945, and told of Parker's execution and the acts of cannibalism. Sasaki was in attendance at the beheading.

As a result of Sasaki's testimony, it was decided that Tsuji should be apprehended and tried as a war criminal. On July 8, 1946, the U.S. War Crimes Office in Singapore formally opened a file detailing the atrocity.

During February 1945, Tsuji received a special citation of appreciation from Lieutenant Gen. Heitaro Kimura, the overall Burma theater commander. Tsuji and one other army officer were the only people to ever receive such a citation while alive. Normally the citation was awarded posthumously.

During May, Tsuji was ordered to Bangkok to prepare the city for a final defense against the advancing Allied forces. His work was well along by the first week of August when a B-29 dropped the first atomic bomb on Hiroshima. Very little information about the bomb was provided to units in the field, especially in Bangkok. On the evening of August 9, Tsuji was handed a message quoting a San Francisco radio announcement. The message said another atomic bomb had been dropped, this time on Nagasaki, and that the Soviet Union declared war on Japan, Tsuji refused to believe the message and threatened to disembowel the messenger for delivering such trash.

Tsuji flew to Saigon, and on the evening of August 11, after discussing the situation with General Hidesimi Hayashi, commander of the 28th Army, finally accepted the probability of Japan's surrender. Tsuji was well aware that he would be prosecuted by the British for the atrocities in Singapore and by the Americans for the Bataan Death March. He flew back to Bangkok the next day and began planning for his disappearance.

The Japanese ambassador in Thailand contacted Chiang Kai-shek's government in Chungking, China, to arrange for Tsuji to assist the nationalist army in their fight against the communists. While waiting for Chiang's response, Tsuji donned the robes of a

Buddhist priest and hid in a Buddhist temple in Bangkok. Tsuji took the name, Norinobu Aoki and waited for the embassy to provide him with false documents and a passport. On the evening of August 16, three days after the emperor's unconditional surrender, Tsuji wrote a will explaining that he was committing suicide. Copies of the document were to be sent to Tokyo by the embassy.

Tsuji spent 70 days hiding in the Buddhist temple before a response was received from China. During this period, British forces moved into Thailand and established their headquarters a few hundred yards from Tsuji's sanctuary. Within a few days of being accepted into China, Tsuji departed Bangkok by train for Laos. He was disguised as a Chinese businessman dressed in a pith helmet, white jacket, black trousers and dark glasses.

Tsuji took three months to reach Chungking, arriving there on October 26, 1945. His travels took him through Indo China and finally to Hanoi, where he flew to Chungking. Tsuji was assigned to the Anti-Communist Propaganda Department of the Military Control Bureau. The work was not to his liking as he considered it to be far below his potential. He tried without success to meet Chiang and had little influence on matters in which he was involved.

By mid-1947, Tsuji was homesick, depressed and lonely. Several Japanese military personnel that remained in China after the war had returned to Japan and Tsuji asked them to advise him of the possibility of returning to Japan. One of the returnees was Colonel Takushiro Hattori, a good friend of Tsuji. Hattori advised Tsuji to remain in China for another six months while he attempted to create proper conditions for Tsuji to return.

During November 1947, American intelligence learned that Tsuji was allied with Chiang Kai-shek in the fight against communists in China. Shortly thereafter, American intelligence officer Alva C. Carpenter called on British intelligence officer Richard O. Crewdson, and, after explaining the situation, asked that the United Kingdom drop its plans to prosecute Tsuji.

Crewdson was shocked. He had worked on the Tsuji case since the end of the war and fully intended to prosecute Tsuji for the Singapore massacres. Crewdson went immediately to his superior who was similarly flabbergasted. Together, they drafted a message to British war crimes investigation in Singapore, recommending against dropping the charges against Tsuji. Singapore, possibly assuming the request originated from Chiang Kai-shek, agreed to drop the charges.

Four months later, March 1948, Britain ordered all South East Asian war crime investigations to be terminated. All 50 Japanese suspects held in prison were to be released. On May 16, 1948, Tsuji left Shanghai by ship with papers identifying him as Professor Kenshin Aoki from the University of Peking. Tsuji arrived in Sasebo, Japan, on May 26, without suspicion or notice.

Tsuji's friend Hattori, had worked his way into the US Civil Intelligence Section headed by Major Gen. Charles Willoughby. Hattori was one of Willoughby's closest and most trusted advisors. He enjoyed a private office, a staff in Tokyo, and a network of 60 paid informers spread throughout the country. Hattori was in a perfect position to assist Tsuji to return to Japan, although Tsuji's responsibility for two major massacres, several individual murders, and acts of cannibalism did not make the job any easier.

Willoughby needed little persuasion from Hattori. He reasoned that Tsuji had just the right talent to assist Japan in its re-birth as a nation. Arrangements were almost complete to pardon Tsuji when the British reversed their decision to drop the Tsuji case. New testimony revealed the Singapore massacre of thousands of Chinese to be of such a magnitude that it could not be ignored. New evidence by eyewitnesses named Tsuji as the man responsible for the atrocities.

The British asked the Americans for assistance in locating Tsuji who was moving between safe houses in Yoshinoyama, Tajima, Asama, Kyushu-Omura, and Okutama, while writing his memoirs about his escape from Thailand. Willoughby promised assistance, but instead hindered the British effort. With Hattori doing the legwork, the two provided false information to their British counterparts.

On New Years Day 1950, Tsuji's war criminal status was terminated by the United States. Tsuji could no longer be charged with a war crime. At the time, he was living in a two-story wooden house in Tokyo, writing memoirs about his escape from Burma and underground activities to evade capture. He immediately left his hiding place and joined his family in another sector of Tokyo.

Tsuji's first book, Underground Escape, was published in June 1950, and his second book, Guadalcanal, later that year. Early in 1952, his controversial account of the Malaya campaign, Singapore: The Hinge of Fate, was published and read by millions of Japanese. Later, the book was published in English as Singapore: The Japanese Version.

During 1952, Tsuji gave talks on his WW II experiences. Ten-thousand people attended an outdoor presentation to hear their war hero talk for two hours on the topic, "The Dawn of Asia."[13]

Tsuji denounced both Russia and the United States, declaring Joseph Stalin and Harry Truman as the world's two worst war criminals. Crowds loved him, and mobbed him for handshakes and autographs. On a wave of popularity, he ran for the lower house of the Diet in 1952 and easily defeated the other candidates.

Once seated as a member of the Diet, Tsuji argued for Japan to develop their own military defense and to demand withdrawal of all American forces from Japan. Tsuji had not changed. He glared, remonstrated, and talked down to everyone in the Diet. He was still the glory-seeking, grandstanding, and self-righteous individual that he had been in the army. [14]

By 1953, a backlash of sorts, led by former Army officers was directed at Tsuji. The most vocal and bitter opponent was retired Major Gen. Kiyotake Kawaguchi. Kawaguchi had recently been released from six years in prison for war crimes - crimes that Tsuji committed. On March 4, 1953, the Yomiuri Shimbun (newspaper) ran a story written by Kawaguchi. The title was, "I was innocent but punished for staff officer Tsuji's crime."[15]

Kawaguchi described in some detail how Tsuji ordered the killings of Filipinos in Manila, and Chinese in Singapore. He described Tsuji's disgraceful conduct on Guadalcanal, conduct that resulted in Kawaguchi's disgrace and early retirement from the military.

The military backlash was interesting reading for the Japanese, but did not impact Tsuji's political base in Ishikawa. The following month he won re-election with a slight reduction in votes. Tsuji was re-elected again in 1955. This time he received a record number of votes (83,000) and expected to be named to the cabinet. Instead, he was by-passed by Prime Minister Ichirou Hotoyama for a cabinet post. Stories of his criminal past and foul temperament were too great a risk for the prime minister.

190

Personality conflicts due to Tsuji's overbearing and dogmatic style led to several outbursts and disruptions of Diet business. As a result, he was banished from the inner circle of the Diet. Family problems and unfavorable publicity prompted Tsuji to take a six-week tour in early 1957. Tsuji and his assistant, Shigeharu Asaeda, traveled to Cairo, Belgrade, and Peking. It seems incongruous that these two former army staff officers, both once wanted for trial for suspected war crimes, could be met by heads of state, wined, dined, and pose for photographs with world leaders; but, they did.

Masanobu Tsuji, parliamentarian, walks from the Diet Building in Tokyo before his ouster from the ruling party.

Asahi Shimbum

Tsuji won re-election in 1958, but by a much narrower margin than before. He quickly became embroiled with the new prime minister, Nobusuke Kishi, who served with Tsuji in China. In 1959, during one of Tsuji's tirades against Kishi, Tsuji was formally ejected from the floor of the Diet.

Retired Major Gen. Kawaguchi could stand no more of the despised Tsuji. After spending several days writing about Tsuji's wartime conduct, Kawaguchi traveled to Tokyo and circulated copies of the document to both houses of the Diet. He personally delivered a copy to the Councilor, summarizing Tsuji's activities, and demanding Tsuji's resignation from the House of Councilors.

191

Kawaguchi's charges must be printed in their entirety to be properly understood.

> You, Mr. Tsuji were the planner, instigator, and executioner of the Massacre of Singapore Chinese merchants, the Bataan Death March, the massacre of doctors and nurses at Alexandria Military Hospital in Singapore, and the atrocious murder of the leading Philippine government official, Jose Abad Santos, and many other terrible acts.

> For these acts, many of our superiors, colleagues and men were branded war criminals following the end of hostilities, and were confined to prison for many years and in extreme cases, they were put to death.

> Your actions and statements as a politician in recent years are either playing up to the people or publicity-seeking. There can be found no constructive opinions in what you have said or done. They run counter to our nation's traditional political morality and they are to be despised. You are absolutely without qualifications to be a member of the National Diet.[16]

Kawaguchi went on to tell how Tsuji misrepresented and insulted him in his book, Guadalcanal, and that this was inexcusable behavior for military men. Kawaguchi included an accompanying document that described in more detail Tsuji's responsibility for the atrocities cited, and ended with a statement that "Tsuji has deceived 680,000 good people with his insufferable words, being elected to the House of Councilors. Tsuji should resign in the name of my past friend, Lieutenant Gen. Kawamura, who lost his life because of Mr. Tsuji, in the names of the souls of the people who were executed, in the names of the ghosts of my former men, who gave up their lives on the southern islands, and in the name of their beloved families."[17]

While Japan reeled from these latest Tsuji wartime scandals, Tsuji decided to return to the site of past glories. North and South Vietnam, Cambodia and Laos were experiencing revolution and violence associated with communist expansion. America was supporting President Ngo Dinh Diem of South Vietnam. Hanoi was training, supplying and advising the Pathet Lao insurgency in

Laos and the Khmer Rouge in Cambodia. Communist China supported North Vietnam. The Soviet Union seemed ambivalent to the situation but would change to suit their interest. The situation was simply overdue for Tsuji's abilities.

Tsuji flew into Saigon on April 4, 1961. From there he went to Phnom Penh in Cambodia, visited Bangkok, then was seen in Vientiane, Laos. He was apprehended in Laos on April 16, but released a short time later. Once again he donned his disguise as a Buddhist priest and continued on his journey to northern Laos. On the morning of July 10, he was seen at Vientiane's airport boarding a Russian aircraft bound for Hanoi. He was never heard of again.

Vientiane, Laos, April 21, 1961. Tsuji wearing the saffron robes he disguised himself in when making a trip to contested territory north of the Lao administrative capital.

Mainichi Shimbum

Tsuji's term in the Diet expired on June 1, 1965, and he was officially pronounced dead on July 7, 1968. A shrine was erected in his memory by members of the town where Tsuji grew up.

Many stories have come to light since Tsuji vanished. One having approval of the Japanese foreign office in Hanoi is that Tsuji went to China where he had been a spy for many years. We will likely never know more about his disappearance. What we do know is that this man is one of the most interesting and warped personalities to emerge from the Second World War.

The governments of America, Great Britain, and Japan all bear responsibility for his freedom following the war.

Tsuji's official grave at the Kannon Jigan Temple in Nozaki, Osaka Prefecture.

Media Masters

13

JOE FOSS, USMC
1915-2003

Capt. Joseph Jacob Foss

USMC

Following his service in the Second World War, Joe Foss was elected to the South Dakota House of Representatives, and in 1954, as Governor of South Dakota. He was reelected in 1958. Following his second term as governor, he was elected as the first Commissioner of the American Football League. He served in this capacity until 1966 and subsequently served for two years as president of the National Rifle Association. These are major accomplishments for anyone, but it was Joe's duty in the Pacific during the war that we will examine in this chapter.

Foss was born in 1915 and like most Midwestern farm boys, became an excellent marksman with a rifle and shotgun. He began his college in Sioux Falls, South Dakota in 1934 but was forced to drop out to help his mother run the farm. He did save $65.00 which he used for his first flying lessons. He returned to college and graduated in 1940 with a business degree and completion of a civilian pilot training program.

Following graduation, he enlisted in the marine corps as an aviation cadet. He completed naval flight training, was commissioned a Second Lt., and served for nine months as a flight instructor at Pensacola, Florida. Following the Japanese attack of Pearl Harbor, Foss was ordered to aerial photographers school and then sent to a marine corps photo reconnaissance squadron (VMO-1).

Foss as a newly-commissioned lieutenant.

USMC

Foss wanted to be a fighter pilot and fly the F4F Wildcat fighter. He was told that at age 27 he was too old to be a fighter pilot and had to make numerous requests to become qualified in the aircraft. He finally did succeed and flew 150 flight hours in June and July, 1942. Three weeks after he qualified in the F4F, he was named executive officer of Marine Fighter Squadron-121 (VMF-121), and sent to the South Pacific. While there, VMF-121 was loaded aboard the escort carrier USS *Copahee*.

On the morning of October 9, 1942 the squadron was catapulted off the carrier and landed at Henderson Field on Guadalcanal. This was Foss' first carrier operation. He was impressed with "make-do" atmosphere of Henderson Field and the smaller field where VMF-121 was based, Fighter Strip One (or the cow pasture). Foss recalled that the field was riddled with bomb craters and wrecked aircraft.

VMF-121 claimed their first Japanese planes four days later by shooting down two *Zero* fighters. Later that day, Foss led a dozen wildcats to intercept 32 Japanese bombers and *Zero* escorts. Foss shot down one plane and was instantly engaged from the rear by three more *Zeros*. He barely made it back to Fighter One with a damaged engine. From this first experience, he learned to never give the plane in your gun sights all your attention; you have to keep one eye on your tail to keep from being shot down yourself. He also quickly learned to follow the tactic of "Indian Joe" Bauer, the commander of Marine Fighter Squadron-212, and seven years older than Foss. Bauer flew so close to the enemy planes that he could not miss. Pilots in VMF-121 joked that Foss flew so close that he left powder burns on the enemy planes.

Foss shot down another *Zero* on October 14. On the 18th, he was leading a group of Wildcats that intercepted a flight of Japanese Betty bombers headed for Guadalcanal. Foss quickly shot down one *Zero*, damaged another, and blew up the engine of a third. He then climbed through the fighter escort and shot down one of the bombers. He had been on Guadalcanal for nine days and was already an Ace (five confirmed kills). Foss was the oldest pilot in the squadron and his flights became known as Foss's Flying Circus. The Circus was credited with shooting down 60 Japanese planes.

Bauer and Foss led a flight on the 18th to intercept bombers that were trying to keep Henderson Field inoperable. Foss shot down two more *Zeros*. His total went to eleven confirmed kills on the 23rd but he brought back a badly damaged Wildcat. This was the fourth plane brought back by Foss that was too damaged to fly again. The squadron was having trouble keeping enough aircraft flyable to meet the flight schedule. Bauer earned the Medal of Honor on October 16 when he dove into a flight of Japanese bombers at 200 feet and shot down four of the bombers. Bauer was alone and nearly out of gas when he saw the bombers and took after them.

Major Foss in a Corsair flying over San Diego, Calif.

USMC

Foss shot down two enemy aircraft on the morning of October 25 and three more in the afternoon, becoming the first marine corps' "Ace in a day." Despite the strain of daily combat flying and terrible living conditions, Foss retained his enthusiasm. The pilots and enlisted men slept in soggy tents, ate powdered eggs, and bathed in the Lunga River. Many grew beards because there was no hot water to shave with.

On November 7, Foss shot down a Japanese floatplane (code named Pete), but was hit in his engine by so many 7.7-mm machine gun bullets that he was not able to nurse the plane back to Guadalcanal. He crash landed the Wildcat near Malaita Island and had difficulty extracting himself from the seat and harness. He and the plane were well under water before he finally broke free and rose to the surface. He was able to inflate his life raft and sprinkled chlorine powder in the water to keep the circling sharks away. The chlorine seemed to help.

At dusk, some natives in a canoe found him and took him to Malaita's Catholic mission. There were a number of Europeans and Australians at the mission and two nuns that had been there for forty years. They had never seen an automobile. They fed Foss the best meal he had since leaving the states; steak and eggs. The next day a PBY Catalina picked him up and flew him back to Guadalcanal. Foss learned that the pilots on Guadalcanal shot down 15 enemy aircraft the previous day. His own record was at 19. On November 9, "Bull" Halsey visited Guadalcanal and awarded Foss and two other pilots the Distinguished Flying Cross Medal.

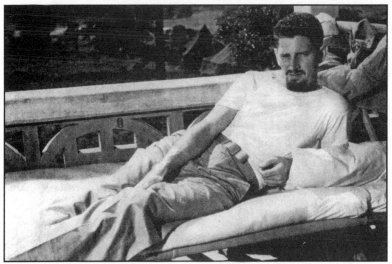

Recuperating in New Caledonia from malari, Foss shows his loss of weight from 195 to 160 pounds.

USMC

On November 12, Foss and his "Circus" intercepted 16 Betty bombers escorted by 30 *Zero* fighters. Foss dived headlong into the bombers, closing to within 100 yards and shot down a bomber, next, he sent a *Zero* into the water. Running at full throttle, he chased the bombers until he was able to shoot down another. His Circus destroyed all the bombers and many of the fighters.

The next afternoon, Lieutenant Col. Harold "Indian Joe" Bauer and Foss went up again to meet the bombers. Bauer did not return from the flight. Foss wrote to his widow and described the flight this way. "I saw Joe shoot down a *Zero* and turn for home. Another pilot and I were chasing a second *Zero* and lost sight of

199

Joe's plane for a while. We went back to the area where we had last seen Joe and discovered him in the water. He waved both arms and seemed to be in good shape. I returned to base as quickly as I could and returned with an amphibian plane to rescue Joe. As we got to within ten miles of Joe's position it got pitch black and we could not see a thing. We returned to Guadalcanal and flew to the area again at daybreak the next day with a flight of 8 Wildcats and the amphibian. The only thing we could find were two Japanese planes which we shot down. We searched the entire area but there was no sign of Joe. Either the Japanese found him or sharks got him."[1]

Capt. Foss completely recovered from malaria and on his way back to Guadalcanal.

USMC

Foss later stated, "To me, Marine Corp's Aviation greatest loss in this war is that of Joe. He really had a way all his own of getting a tough job done efficiently and speedily, and was admired by all, from the lowest private to the highest general. I am certain that wherever Joe is today, he is doing things the best way – the Bauer way."[2]

Bauer was an Annapolis graduate and a football player. He picked up the nickname "Indian Joe" at the academy because of his height, high cheekbones, and dark features. He was credited with destroying 11 Japanese planes and earned the Medal of Honor posthumously.

A statue in the Sioux Falls, South Dakota, municipal airport honors Foss and his career.

USMC

Shortly after the death of Bauer, Foss was diagnosed with malaria and spent six weeks recuperating in New Caledonia and Australia. After a brief relapse of malaria, Foss returned to Guadalcanal on New Years day, 1943. He returned to combat flying on the 15th and shot down three more planes to bring his total to 26.

Enemy aviation action around Guadalcanal dropped greatly after the Japanese forces were evacuated from the island. Foss flew his last mission ten days later when he and his flight intercepted a force of 60 Japanese planes. As additional planes were scrambled from Henderson Field, the Japanese fled.

Foss returned home a few months later to a hero's welcome. In May he was awarded the Medal of Honor by President Franklin Roosevelt. Previously Foss earned the Silver Star, Bronze Star, and Purple Heart Medals. He was a training advisor at Santa Barbara Marine Corps Air Station and became commanding officer of Marine Fighter Squadron-115 in the South Pacific. Following the war, he helped found the South Dakota Air National Guard and was commissioned in the Guard. During the Korean War, he left the Air Guard and returned to active duty with the Air Force as a colonel. Following the Korean war, he became chief of staff of the South Dakota Air National Guard with the rank of Brigadier Gen.

Joe Foss, a true American hero died on January 1, 2003. If you are ever in Sioux Falls, South Dakota, be sure to visit the airport, as the field is named after Joe Foss and there are several impressive memorials to his service.

14

BOUGAINVILLE: NOVEMBER 1, 1943

The battle for Bougainville was substantially different than
most Pacific Island battles. It cut across command structures
between forces in the southwest Pacific (General Douglas
MacArthur), and the south Pacific (Admiral Chester Nimitz). It
involved a joint effort, marines and army, and a combined effort,
U.S., Australian, Fijian, and New Zealand. It was the first time
black soldiers were committed to combat as a regiment or other
infantry unit, and, except for the Burma campaign, it went on for
a longer period than any other battle in the Pacific, November 1,
1943, until the Pacific war ended in mid-August 1945.

In 1943, the capture of Bougainville was considered
necessary to support the invasion of New Britain and reduction
of Rabaul. Rabaul, with its six airfields, excellent harbor, and as
many as 80,000 Japanese troops, was the major barrier to

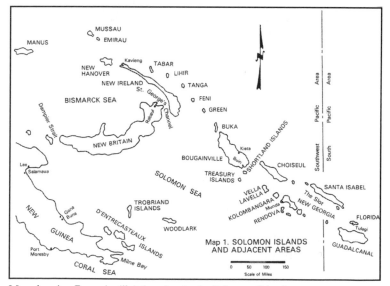

Map showing Bougainville's location in the Solomon Islands.

MacArthur's advance towards the Philippines. By invading Bougainville and establishing airfields there, the Allies would be within 250 miles of Rabaul.[1]

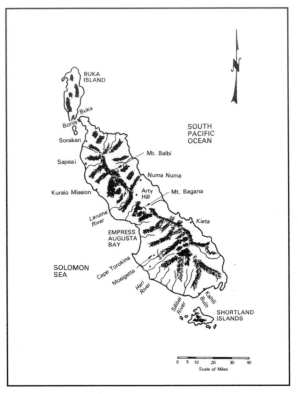

Bougainville Island.

Buka-Bougainville

Bougainville and Buka Islands are separated from one another by a shallow, half-mile-wide strait. Together, they are 150 miles long by 50 miles wide. The islands run on a north west-south east axis and are part of the Solomon Islands chain. Much of the land is mountainous or hilly with the Emperor and Crown Prince mountain ranges running down the center with heights of 10,000 feet. Mount Balbi, at 10,171 feet, and Mount Bagana, 8,650 feet and an active volcano, dominate the ranges. Most of the 800,000 native people lived along the southern coast of Bougainville, with Kieta the major village, and throughout Buka.[2]

204

The indigenous people living inland had little contact with the Japanese during the occupation.

During January 1942, nearly all 4,600 European civilians were evacuated from Buka-Bougainville.[3] The exceptions were a few Marist and Methodist missionaries and several coastwatchers, W.J. Reed at Buka, and P.E. Mason at Kieta. The coast watchers were civilian planters, traders, and administration officials that volunteered to stay on Bougainville after the Japanese occupation. They were given commissions in the Australian navy, provided with radios, and moved inland to observation sites where they could report on Japanese aerial and naval movements that went past Bougainville. They played a major role in Allied victories in all the Solomon campaigns. For more information on the coastwatchers, read chapter 11, *Martin Clemens: Coastwatcher* in volume II of *War in the Pacific*.[4]

Initially, the Japanese were welcomed by the native people along the coastline, and, they, in turn, were treated kindly by the Japanese military. Native food and labor were paid for, Japanese schools were established for the children, and indigenous officials were consulted and given impressive titles and insignia. By summer 1943, especially during the battle for Guadalcanal, it became difficult for Japan to resupply their troops on Buka-Bougainville. The Japanese army took nearly all of the local foodstuffs without payment and forced the natives to produce more garden produce for the army.

As Bougainville became increasingly threatened by the Allies, the Japanese friendliness turned to hostility, and the military became more punitive towards the local people.[5] The Bougainvillian's began to starve and became resentful. Some native people actively resisted the Japanese with bloodshed committed on both sides.

Command Structure

General Marshall, chairman of the joint chiefs, and General MacArthur, wanted a single command for the entire Pacific area, with MacArthur as supreme commander. That proposal was strongly rejected by Admiral Ernest J. King, chief of naval operations. King argued that since the Pacific was largely water, it called for a navy commander, Admiral Nimitz. The joint chiefs of staff ignored both arguments, and placed Admiral "Bull" Halsey (who reported to Nimitz) in direct command of the Solomons campaign under the strategic direction of MacArthur. The result could have been chaos, but Nimitz gave Halsey wide discretion, and MacArthur and Halsey got along and agreed on most objectives for the campaign.

Halsey began the operation by landing troops on Woodlark and Kiriwina Islands, 450 miles west of Guadalcanal during the period June 30 to July 12, 1943. Neither island was defended and the engineers completed construction of an airstrip on both islands by the end of July.

By December 1943, Guadalcanal was secured, after the Japanese removed their remaining forces from the island. MacArthur now felt confident that he could begin the assault on New Britain in the Bismark Sea by invading New Georgia and Bougainville in the Solomon Islands. He planned to use the Army's 43rd Infantry Division to capture Munda airfield on New Georgia, and the Third Marine Division to seize Cape Glouchester in Bougainville. By mid-1943, Halsey had 275,000 men and 1,800 aircraft under his command. Not all of the forces were available for the two campaigns, but he had substantial forces for the operations.

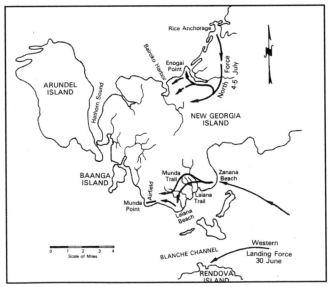

New Georgia Campaign, June 30 to August 4, 1943.

National Archives

New Georgia

Japan had 5,000 men defending New Georgia which was invaded on July 2. The Japanese army, commanded by General Noburo Sasaki, fought well, delaying the 43rd Division advance to the extent that the 37th Division, a National Guard unit, untested in combat, was brought in to reinforce the 43rd, and a force of 2,600 marines and soldiers was landed at Rice Anchorage on the northern tip of New Georgia. The Japanese navy also fought well, sinking two U. S. destroyers, the light cruiser *Helena*, and seriously damaging cruisers *Honolulu* and *St. Louis*. In addition, the Japanese were able to land 1,600 reinforcements.

Major Gen. Oscar Griswold, commander of Army 14 Corps, visited New Georgia on July 11. He found the situation unsatisfactory. Men of the 43rd Division were exhausted, morale was low, and stress symptoms were common. Halsey reacted to Griswald's report by placing Lieutenant Gen. Millard Harmon in charge with orders to do whatever was necessary to capture Munda. Harmon put Major Gen. Griswold in command of the operation and ordered three more regiments (the equivalent of an infantry division) to New Georgia.[6]

Lieutenant Gen. Millard F. Harmon, center, and Major Gen. Oscar W. Griswold, second from left, are briefed on the New Georgia campaign.

National Archives

After the arrival of the reinforcements, Griswold launched a two-division frontal attack of the Japanese defenses on July 25. Heavy artillery, air strikes and naval gunfire preceded the infantry attack. By the end of July, the Japanese had suffered 75 percent casualties and most of their defensive positions were destroyed. Sasaki withdrew his forces to a narrow perimeter around Munda and gave up the airfield. Griswold radioed Halsey that Munda had been captured, to which Halsey replied, ". . . Keep 'em dying."[7]

Army forces turned north to follow the Japanese retreat from Munda, and on August 9, made contact with the soldiers and marines of the northern force. In the meantime, Sasaki was withdrawing his remaining forces to Kolombangara, 20 miles northwest of Munda, and Baanga. On the night of August 6, six American destroyers surprised a convoy of four Japanese destroyers filled with reinforcements for Sasaki. Three of the destroyers were sunk in this battle of Vella Gulf, with the loss of 900 Japanese soldiers. The 25th Army Division landed 6,000 troops on Vella Lavella on August 15 against 250 Japanese stragglers. Baanga was captured on August 21 and Sasaki's troops on Kolombangara were evacuated to Bougainville. Overall, the capture of New Georgia cost 1,094 American dead and 3,873 wounded. Japanese deaths by count were 2,483.[8]

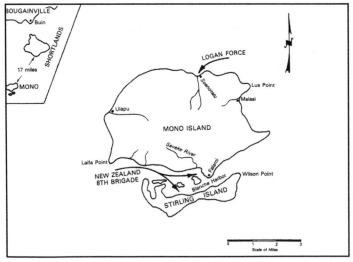

Treasury Islands landings, October 27, 1943.

National Archives

Mono and Stirling

As the battle for Munda was taking place, Halsey and his staff were planning the invasion of Bougainville. The Bougainville battle was complex. It consisted of a landing on the Treasury Islands (two islands, Mono and Stirling) lying 20 miles south of Bougainville, on October 27, to establish a radar station and staging area; a night raid on Choiseul Island (40 miles southeast of Bougainville) on the same evening, to cause the Japanese to think that the main attack was taking place there; and a landing on Puruata Island, simultaneously with the main landing taking place at Cape Torokina in Empress Augusta Bay.

Mono, four miles wide by six miles long, was estimated to have 150 Japanese soldiers, but none were found on Stirling. The 8th Brigade of the New Zealand 3rd Division plus 20 American Seabees and 60 technicians were landed on October 27, and the island was secured on November 6. The New Zealanders killed the entire Japanese garrison of 200 men with casualties of 40 New Zealand and 12 Americans killed and 174 wounded.[9] The raid on Choiseul was far more risky.

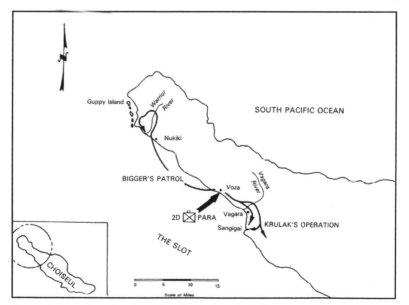

Choiseul Operation, October 28 to November 3, 1943.

National Archives

Choiseul

The 2nd Marine Parachute Battalion was landed on Choiseul the evening of October 27. The island was 70 miles long and 20 miles wide. It was the most rugged island of the Solomons and was protected by coral reefs. Japanese strength was estimated as 3000 men at Choiseul Bay and Sangiagi, farther south. The landing was conducted at night by four APDs that were moved from the Treasury operation. The landing was unopposed, supplies were unloaded, and a hundred natives were hired to assist in moving supplies, to serve as guides and as trackers.

Native guides informed the marines that 150 Japanese were at Sangiagi, eight miles south of the landing beach at Voza. Lieutenant Col. Victor Krulak, commander of the parachute battalion, made the decision to attack Sangiagi. The marines found the forest and swamp to be nearly impassable, and moved closer to the beach. When they did so, they found barges unloading Japanese reinforcements. Several minor engagements ensued with the Japanese losing a dozen soldiers. As the marines approached Sangiagi, the Japanese abandoned it and moved further inland. As they did so, they encountered one of Krulak's rifle companies. The ensuing battle lasted for an hour with the Japanese appearing to be winning until they launched a *banzai* charge and lost 72 killed and many wounded. Marine losses were six killed and 12 wounded.

Other firefights developed during the next days with marines fending off attacks by larger Japanese forces. On November 2, Krulak's force was evacuated by Lieutenant John F. Kennedy (future president) in PT 59 and one additional PT boat to the base at Vella Lavella.[10] The marines killed 143 Japanese, destroyed a major staging base, and sank two landing barges. They also captured valuable maps and charts which revealed the location of Japanese minefields around southern Bougainville. Krulak was awarded the Navy Cross Medal for his leadership and bravery.[10]

A U. S. naval task force arrived early on November 1, 1943, and fired 2700 rounds of five and six-inch shells onto the airfields at Buka and Bonis on Bougainville. Another task force arrived off Buka Passage at 4:00 A. M. the same morning and shelled and bombed the airfields on Buka and Bonis. The attacks continued the following day. In two days, these attacks rendered most, but not all, of the airfields useless, destroyed 30 Japanese planes, and several small ships. The U.S. Navy lost 11 planes during the action.

The Japanese were believed to have 65,000 men on Bougainville, but only 370 were thought to be in the Cape Torokina and Puruata Island area.

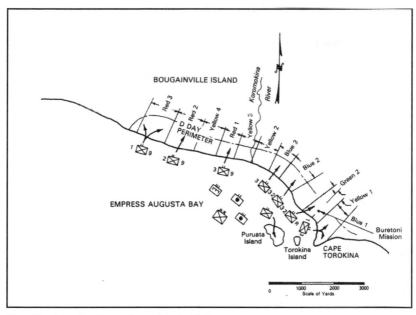

Cape Torokina landings, November 1, 1943.

National Archives

Puruata Island

The Third Raider Battalion landed on Puruata Island, directly south of the landing beach at Torokina on November 1, moved inland with moderate resistance and fought with a ferocity that gained the respect of Japanese soldiers throughout the Pacific. One example will suffice. A marine and his Japanese counterpart fought a one-on-one battle that took them completely across the island. Each used every trick to kill the other until they reached the sea, at which time the Japanese threw down his weapon and jumped in the water. The marine raider recalled:[11]

I don't know where in hell he thought he was going. I was too G—d— mad to shoot him. I threw down my rifle and helmet, took a good run and dove in after him. The little bastard was scared to death. I grabbed him by the neck and pulled him toward the beach. That was the hardest part getting him back on solid ground. I couldn't get him up on the beach but went to work on him in shallow water. Then I dragged him up on the sand and kicked his head apart. The slimy bastard. I'd been chasing him for more than an hour.

By 3:30 P.M. on November 2, Puruata was secured. Twenty-nine Japanese dead were counted. The marines lost five killed and 32 wounded.

Bougainville

The Third Marine Division landed two regiments and the 2nd Raider Battalion abreast at Cape Torokina, on the western coast of Bougainville at 7:20 A.M., on November 1, 1943. They were supported by naval gunfire and close air support. Within a short time, 8,000 troops were ashore and moving inland to secure the beachhead. Japanese aircraft from fields on Rabaul attacked twice during the assault phase but their bombs and strafing attacks failed to damage any ships and caused only a few casualties. The Army's 37th Division was in reserve.

The high surf and beach gradient proved more of a problem during the landing phase than the Japanese defenses. Some landing craft grounded 60 feet from the shore line in three feet of water. Others made it closer to shore and were thrown from the water onto the beach, others broached and were swamped before they reached the beach. Many could not lower their landing ramps after colliding with other craft in the surf. Consequently, marines had to climb over the side into waist-deep water and wade ashore. Before the landing beaches were ordered closed due to the high surf, 64 LCVPs (Landing Craft, Personnel), and 24 LCMs (Landing Craft, Mechanized), were severely damaged, some beyond repair. John Monks Jr., a squad leader in LVCP #62 described the landing as follows:[14]

We were 20 seconds out from the beach when the seaman engineer running the boat turned to a marine sergeant in the rear of the boat and muttered his pathetically ironic valedictory: That's the trouble with you marines. All those fireworks and wasting all that ammunition-and you probably won't see any Japs for a week!" The first shell hit the upper starboard corner of the ramp. Pieces of wood and steel flew into the air. The navy coxswain disappeared. Lieutenant Kirk, one of the two officers on board, wheeled to face the men and shouted, "For God's sake, over the side!"

Two more shells followed in rapid succession. The third shell tore the ramp, detonated against the bulkhead, and exploded in the center of the boat. A shell fragment from the second shell hit me in the left thigh. The boat grounded and I started over the side. It was an awful mess. Bloody men pulled themselves off the deck and forced themselves over the side. One man had part of his back blown off. Everyone kept hold of his rifle. Some of them only had half of a rifle. The water was up to my chin.

As I hit the sand, I looked and saw that Smith wasn't going to make it. He had a wound in his head. He was one of my boys. I went back, pulled him in, and dragged him behind a coconut log. Then a Jap came out from one of the slit trenches. He bent over, armed a grenade-hit it against his knee. As he threw it, I hit the deck behind a ridge of sand. Couldn't have been over three inches high, but it was enough.

Then I threw a grenade. I didn't see it kill the Jap, but Hopkins said it blew the Jap all to hell. Then I got the rest of my squad who were wounded behind the coconut log. All the time snipers were popping away at us. My foot started to hurt, and I pulled off my shoe. There was a big hole where my ankle used to be. I figured it was broken-hadn't noticed it before.

Somehow a few of the troops and a sailor got the boat off the beach and started back to the ship with the wounded. They tried to plug up the big holes in the boat with some of the dead bodies. Then they put life jackets on all the other wounded. The boat sank. Later, when I was evacuated, I learned there were 12 killed and 14 wounded from boat #62. Both of the Lieutenants were killed.

Marines landing on the right side of the landing zone were not hampered so much by the surf, but landed in the face of prepared defensive positions. The most heavily defended positions were on the far right (Blue Beach 1) of the landing zone. The Japanese had 25 large and small log and earth filled pillboxes that ran around the perimeter of the cape. One large pillbox contained a 75-mm artillery weapon. All fortifications were mutually supporting and most had tunnels connecting them. Only three of the positions had been destroyed by naval gunfire.

Japanese aircraft attacked the landing force at Torokina three times during the morning. The initial attack came as the first wave hit the beach, but New Zealand P-40 (Tomahawk) aircraft shot down seven of the 53 attackers with negligible damage to the landing force. The second attack came 10 minutes later and was also beaten off with 12 Japanese aircraft destroyed. The last attack, by 70 aircraft, came just after noon. The attacks caused no major damage or casualties, although unloading of supplies and equipment was set back four hours. The Japanese lost 26 planes from the total of 120 in the three attacks.[13]

Twenty six marines were killed on landing craft and the beach before the lessons learned at Guadalcanal began to take effect. Fire teams provided a high volume of automatic weapons fire at the apertures of the bunkers, while other fire teams ran forward and threw grenades into the bunkers ventilators. One by one, the bunkers were destroyed. The most difficult to destroy, a large bunker with the 75-mm artillery piece, was destroyed practically single-handed by Sergeant Robert Owens. Owens led a group of four other marines in a charge on the bunker, and then directly into the face of the steadily firing cannon. Owens drove the gun crew out the back door where they were killed by his fire team members. Owens was posthumously awarded the Medal of Honor for his actions, the first of ten such medals earned by the 3rd Marine Division.[14] A subsequent count revealed 153 Japanese dead in the landing area.

The landing beaches were crowded with damaged amphibious vehicles and other vehicles trying to bring artillery and supplies ashore. Since Japanese resistance was not heavy, nearly 40 percent of the landing force was sent to the beach to help clear the congestion. Detachments of naval mobile construction battalions (MCB-Seabees) were also landed and helped to clear the beaches.

All eight of the troop transports were unloaded and left Empress Augusta Bay before nightfall. Rear Admiral Theodore Wilkinson, the task force commander, feared a Japanese naval night attack and ordered the four cargo ships to also leave, even though they still had much of the marine division's heavy equipment aboard. The cargo ships got underway, and moved some 30 miles distant when just before midnight, the ships with their destroyer escorts were ordered to return to Cape Torokina and finish unloading on D+1. One cannot help but wonder if the ghosts that haunted Admirals Fletcher and Turner for their abrupt departure from the beach at Guadalcanal (and the intervention by Marine Major Gen. Vandegrift) may have influenced Admiral Wilkinson's decision to return the cargo ships.

By the end of D+1, marines had reached their initial objectives and dug in for the night. A marine described his feelings on the night of D+1 as follows:[15]

> Every officer and man was in his foxhole. These were trained men and they knew the law of the jungle. Anyone out of the foxhole during the hours of darkness was a Jap. Sudden death for the careless. From seven o'clock in the evening till dawn, with only centipedes and lizards and scorpions and mosquitoes begging to get

acquainted-wet, cold, exhausted, but unable to sleep-you lay there and shivered and thought and hated and prayed. But you stayed there. You didn't cough, you didn't snore, you changed your position with the least amount of noise. For it was still great to be alive.

Four significant ship and air battles took place between November 1-11, all in support or defense of the Bougainville campaign. When they concluded, the Japanese had lost a light cruiser, suffered heavy damage to a heavy cruiser and two light cruisers, lost two destroyers with another heavily damaged, and lost 94 aircraft and 86 trained aircrews. Japan was never able to recover from the beating administered by Admiral Halsey's forces in defense of the marine perimeter at Cape Torokina.

Marines, with the help of 24 Doberman Pinschers, continued to expand the perimeter. By November 5, they were almost five miles inland and were sending patrols well to the north to the Laruma River and to the Torokina River to the south. Japanese resistance was slight, the landing beaches were still clogged with vehicles and supplies, but 20,000 marines were ashore.

Members of the 148th Regimental Combat Team (RCT 148) of the 37th Army infantry began arriving at the beach on November 8. They were met by 60 Japanese aircraft that put a torpedo into the transport *Fuller,* killing five and wounding 20 soldiers, and a bomb hit on the transport *President Jackson,* which did not explode. The remainder of the 37th Division, 10,277 men, 8500 tons of supplies and equipment, and a battery of much-needed anti-aircraft artillery, were landed on the beach on November 11 and 12.[16]

During November and December, the 37th Division anchored the left (north) flank of the Allied perimeter while the marines continued to expand the perimeter towards the east. On November 6, four Japanese destroyers landed 800 men two miles off the beach near the Laruma River. Heavy surf prevented the Japanese from landing as an organized unit and they were spread out for two miles on each side of the river. The senior officer chose to immediately attack the U.S. left flank with 100 men. The landing came as a complete surprise to the American forces and a five-hour-long battle commenced.

On November 7, Allied artillery was brought to play and the battle was over on the morning of the 8th. Japanese losses were 377 dead. American losses were 16 killed and 30 wounded. The Japanese survivors escaped to the north into the jungle. At the same time as the beach battle, marines were attacking and being attacked along the Piva track from Cape Torokina to the Numa-Numa track. Tanks, half-tracks and a battalion of men were used to break through the Japanese blocks. By November 8, both sides were forced to pull back to reorganize and resupply. The marines lost 8 dead and 27 wounded. Japanese losses were 125 killed.[17]

During this battle, PFC Henry Gurke, from the 3rd Raider Battalion, was awarded the Medal of Honor for throwing himself on a Japanese grenade and saving the life of his partner in their foxhole. Fighting continued in the same area on November 9, with 12 marines killed and 30 more wounded. Japanese dead were counted as 140. Total Japanese casualties (killed) for the period November 6-9 were 800.

The airstrip near the beach on Torokina was nearing completion but it was not long enough to land bombers. A decision was made to extend the perimeter another three miles inland to build a longer airstrip. A one-mile extension of the perimeter was achieved on November 14, using tanks and air strikes to force the Japanese from their defensive positions. Marines had 59 casualties, the Japanese lost 40 men.

Torokina Airstrip from the northwest, with Empress Bay in the foreground.

National Archives

The most intense battle of the Bougainville campaign was fought by the 3rd Marine Division and began on November 18 as the marines continued to expand their perimeter eastward. The week-long Battle of the Piva Forks began with an attempt to knock out a Japanese road block on the Numa-Numa trail. At the same time, a road block was detected on the East-West Trail. Artillery was used to weaken the Japanese defenses, but the advantage swung back and forth as both sides attacked and counterattacked the positions.

On the morning of November 24, seven battalions of artillery began firing 5,600 rounds of 75-mm and 105-mm shells into the enemy positions. Their fire was joined by corps 155-mm guns and all the 81-mm and 60-mm mortars in the division. It was the greatest concentration of artillery fire seen in the Pacific theater. Prior to the end of the artillery barrage, marines began to assemble for the attack. Just as the artillery barrage ended, a Japanese artillery battalion began a very accurate shelling of the assembly positions. Fourteen marines were killed and dozens wounded in minutes.

A forward observer located the Japanese battery, requested counter fire from the 37th Division 155-mm howitzers, and destroyed the enemy battery. Following the barrage, marines moved forward through an strange silence. At first there was no resistance.[18]

> For the first hundred yards both battalions advanced abreast through a weird, stinking, plowed-up jungle of shattered trees and butchered Japanese. Some hung out of trees, some lay crumpled and twisted beside their shattered weapons, some were covered by chunks of jagged logs and jungle earth, a blasted bunker, their self made tomb.

Japanese reserves moved forward quickly from behind the artillery impact area and put up a strong defense. Accurate artillery and mortar fire caused 70 casualties in one marine battalion while they advanced less than a quarter mile. The Japanese had numerous earth-covered log bunkers that housed machine guns, and all bunkers were connected by interlocking slit trenches and foxholes. By now the Japanese had learned to concentrate their fire on the engineers with flame throwers and marines with explosive charges. Every bunker that was captured was taken at the cost of several lives.

On Thanksgiving day, despite the situation at the front lines, Major Gen. Roy Geiger, commander 1ˢᵗ Marine Amphibious Corps (all forces on Bougainville), organized men to carry the thanksgiving meal to those at the front. Not everyone got turkey. Some marines were asleep beside their weapon in the water, getting a few moments of rest while their buddy stood guard. Dead Japanese floated nearby in the rotting jungle, and the heads and arms of dead Japanese provided the setting for the Thanksgiving dinner. It was not nice, but the tired, hungry men appreciated the fact that the support troops went to the trouble to get them some turkey on Thanksgiving day.

The week-long battle had been costly for both sides. The marines counted 1,107 Japanese dead, while they suffered 115 dead and wounded. Fighting continued on November 26, with 32 Japanese killed and five marines killed and 42 wounded. Fighting continued with losses to both sides until the morning of December 6, when nature intervened with the eruption of the volcano, Mount Bagana. Frazer West, a company commander of the 9ᵗʰ marines, recalled it as follows:[19]

> Being raised in Nevada I'd been through a lot of earthquakes so they were nothing new to me. We had one really severe earthquake on Bougainville. The big trees were just swaying around and we had built this fortification on this ridge, pillboxes, and such out of coconut logs and the roofs fell in on the pillboxes and some of the trenches caved in. The men got down and hugged the ground. It was impossible to stand up while it was going on. They were scared to death when these huge trees were breaking down around them. This went on it seemed for several minutes. The ground really rumbled and shook. It was the worst earthquake I'd ever been in.

The engineers and Seabees did a magnificent job on Bougainville. They cleared the backlog of equipment and supplies on the beach, built bridges over the streams, roads from the beachhead to near the front lines, and completed the airstrip at Cape Torokina. The strip was 220 feet wide and 5,150 feet long with a steel matting. On November 24, a damaged navy dive bomber made the first landing on the strip. On December 10, seventeen F4U aircraft from Marine Fighter Squadron-216 (VMF-216), landed to provide close air support for the ground forces. Other squadrons would use the field including "Pappy" Boyington's VMF-214.

Mount Bagana, an active volcano.

Douglas Oliver

One example of the work done by the engineers was the ration dump. For two months, 400 engineers worked on the project with six bulldozers, two clamshells, and 20 dump trucks. They cleared an area the size of four city blocks and elevated the entire area with dirt. On the elevated area they constructed ten storage platforms each 60 by 30 feet, large enough to hold 100 tons of rations. They also constructed gasoline storage tank areas, a chemical warfare dump, living quarters, offices for the chaplain and the Red Cross, and a movie theater. The work seemed miraculous to the front line troops when they were rotated to the rear.

The 77th Naval Construction Battalion (Seabees) arrived on December 10 and constructed a second airfield for bomber aircraft. The field became operational on January 3, 1944, when the steel matting was installed. Besides bombers and transports, the field became home to P-39s (Aircobras), F4Us (Corsairs), SBDs (Dauntless dive bombers), and TBFs (Avenger dive bombers). The aircraft supported the ground troops on Bougainville but also struck targets on Rabaul each morning before cloud coverage obscured the targets.

Marines continued to expand the perimeter, supported by marine close air support aircraft from the Torokina airstrip, until December 24. By then, the perimeter had been expanded 2,000 yards to each flank, and 8,000 yards forward of the November 6 defensive line. The new perimeter encompassed the area for the two new airfields. Shortly before their last combat action, General Geiger passed command to Major Gen. Oscar Griswald, commanding the Army 14 Corps on Bougainville. Griswald's forces included the 37th Division, which had seen little action in its assigned sector of the perimeter, and the Americal Division due to arrive on Christmas day. The 3rd Marine Division was slated for the invasion of the strong Japanese air and naval base at Kavieng, New Ireland.

General John Hodge, commander of the Americal Division.

National Archives

15

BOUGAINVILLE: THE CONSOLIDATION PHASE

Fiji Infantry Battalion

Perhaps the most successful operation during the consolidation phase was the work of the 1st Battalion of the Fiji Infantry Regiment. On December 28,1942, a few days after their arrival, a reinforced company proceeded along the Numa-Numa Trail 20 miles north of Cape Torokina. The Fijians established a defensive perimeter around the village of Ibu, hacked out a landing strip for small observation aircraft, and began to harass Japanese communications and patrols. They attacked a Japanese strongpoint at Pipipaia, killing 47 Japanese without a single casualty of their own.

By the end of January 1943, the Fijians had so interfered with Japanese operations that it became necessary for the Japanese to eliminate the outpost. A major attack was conducted on February 14 which drove the Fijians back. The withdrawal was well conducted with many rear guard actions that cost the Japanese 120 killed with only one Fijian casualty (a slight wound). The Fijian company reached the main defensive line on February 19 without further casualties.

An American noncommissioned officer poses with Fiji troops of the 1st Battalion, Fiji Regiment.

Americal (194th Infantry) Division

During March 1943, the 194th Infantry (Americal) Division, which fought with and relieved the Marine Corps 1st Division on Guadalcanal, departed Guadalcanal for training, rest and relaxation on Suva, Fiji. While there, they trained, dined, drank, danced, recovered their weight and health, and prepared for the next battle. During December, they were alerted to load aboard ship, did so, and offloaded on Bougainville on Christmas Day, 1943.

In the weeks following arrival of the Americal Division, the daily routine consisted of improving defensive positions and patrolling. Most of the patrols in January and February met no Japanese, but there were exceptions. On January 7, a hundred soldiers on patrol 3,000 yards forward of the front lines were stopped, outflanked, and, after a two-hour firefight, were forced to retreat to the regimental lines. The patrol reported killing 12 Japanese. Two other patrols in late January came in contact with Japanese and drove them from their positions killing 25 of the enemy.

While the Fijians were fighting well forward of the defensive perimeter, General John Hodge, commander of the Americal Division, decided to expand the perimeter east of the mouth of the Torokina River. Early on January 29, 1944, all available mortars pounded the target area. A company, supported by tanks and artillery advanced along the beach area and turned inland at the jungle's edge. They were met by rifle, machine gun, and mortar fire from 21 well-constructed pillboxes 400 yards in depth. Because swamps on both sides precluded flanking attacks, the soldiers were forced to advance into the face of the Japanese defenses.

The tanks were forced to close their hatches to avoid the heavy small arms fire resulting in their inability to locate the pillboxes. Staff Sgt. Jesse Drowley climbed to the top of one tank and talked to the tank commander through a hatch. He then used the tank machine gun with tracer bullets to direct the tanks against the two front pillboxes. Drowley was hit in the chest but continued to guide the tanks until he was hit again, this time in the left eye. Both pillboxes were destroyed by tank cannons. The rest of the company were so emboldened by Drowley's action that they surged ahead and destroyed the remaining 19 pillboxes. For his heroic actions, Drowley was awarded the Medal of Honor, the only Americal Division soldier to be so honored.[2]

The first and final Japanese offensive of any size took place from March 8-27, 1944. Lieutenant Gen. Harukichi Hyakutake, commander of the 17th Army, used 15,000 of his 40,000 troops in the attack. He had an additional 20,000 sailors of the 8th Fleet, without ships, in southern Bougainville. Hyakutake's staff was so certain of victory that they planned the Allied unconditional surrender ceremony to include the exact spot where General Griswold would stand.[3]

The 17th Divisional field commander, Lieutenant Gen. Masatane Kanda, planned to launch his major blow against the 37th Infantry Division positions in two attacks. The first (Iwasa Unit) of 4,150 men would attack the center of the American perimeter at the start of the Piva River, continue forward and capture the two new airfields. The second (Magata Unit) with 4,300 men, would attack the left of the defensive perimeter, drive south and assist in the capture of the airfields. A separate attack against the Americal Division would be conducted by the Muda Unit with 1,350 men. This unit would attack the right defensive line, capture the high ground, and drive south to protect the left flanks of the other forces. The army had rations for two weeks and many objectives, including the two airfields, were planned to be in Japanese hands by March 10.

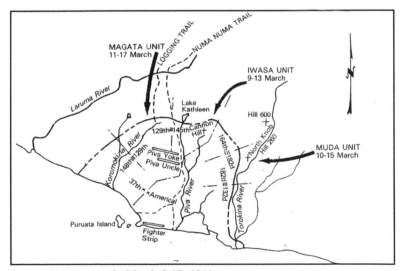

Japanese counterattack, March 9-17, 1944.

The Japanese attack began on the morning of March 8, with bombardment of the beachhead and the Piva airfields. American corps and division artillery began immediate counter-battery fire, as did destroyers in Empress Augusta Bay. Dive bombers and torpedo bombers flew missions constantly and struck the main Japanese troop concentrations around the high ground. When the Piva strips became damaged, the aircraft were moved to New Georgia and continued to support the operation.

During a heavy downpour on the night of March 8, the Japanese Iwasa Unit stormed a steep hill in front of the 37th Division, broke through the barbed wire, and knocked out one of the defensive pillboxes. They set up their machine guns and began to attack other defensive positions along the crest. By morning, they had gained a penetration of 50 yards in depth and 70 yards in width. They continued to expand their perimeter, destroying seven more pillboxes and laying down mortar fire on the supply route for the 37th Division. When this route became unusable, all 37th Division supplies had to be carried by hand to the front lines and all wounded had to be evacuated under direct fire.

Throughout March 9, the Japanese extended their defenses, repaired abandoned positions, and built new ones. A counterattack by the 37th Division reserve failed to drive the Japanese from the ridgeline but did recapture five of the pillboxes. At 6:45 A.M. on the 10th, Iwasa continued his attack in conjunction with the Muda Force attack on the Americal positions.

Lieutenant Charles H. Walker with a 7.7 mm Nambu.

Charles H. Walker

Lt. Charles H. Walker, from Pembina North Dakota, recalled that ". . . wild, vicious fighting trapped their artillery observer up on a tree platform and Company E (Easy) of the 164th Regiment of the American Division took heavy casualties. Flamethrowers, mortars, artillery, everything was used to stop the Japanese." At the same approximate time, General Kanda attacked the 37th Division in two different areas. The fire of the entire corps and division artillery was concentrated on Kanda's troops.[4]

Easy Company suffered the loss of six of their seven officers and 108 of their 143 enlisted during the attack on the 11th. Walker was patrolling upriver on March 11, when he observed wounded Japanese being carried piggyback to the west across the river while ammunition and supplies were being carried to the east. He moved his patrol forward and killed seven Japanese in the riverbed before being ordered out of the sector because it was assigned to the 182nd Regiment and the regiment needed no help.[5]

Both sides attacked and counterattacked during the remainder of March 11 and 12. By 1:00 P.M., on March 12, only one pillbox in the 37th Division sector remained in Japanese hands. A member of the 145th regiment recalls the end this way:[6]

On the second day, the last held enemy pillbox was subjected to everything an infantryman has at his command. Hand grenades by the dozen were thrown at the emplacement. Still there was no responding fire. Flame throwers scorched the hidden Nip into silence. The searching parties entered the charred remains of the emplacement only to hear the click of a Japanese grenade being armed. In the far corner they made out the dim outline of a Jap, eyes bloodshot, mouth bleeding, face seared, clothing burned. His clenched fist held a grenade. Even as the men dove for cover outside the pillbox, the Jap threw the grenade at them in a dying gesture.

General Iwasa admitted defeat on March 13, and moved the remains of his shattered force two miles east of the American perimeter. Fighting in the American sector continued until March 28, when patrols found that the Munda Force had withdrawn.

Magata Force began their attack against the 129th Regiment on March 12. They penetrated the first line of defense and captured seven pillboxes. American counterattacks reclaimed two of the pillboxes but at nightfall, the Japanese still had a forward position and five important pillboxes. Searchlights illuminated the Japanese positions at night and many were killed by artillery and mortar fire. Japanese attacks on the morning of March 13, captured another pillbox, but Sherman tanks were brought forward in the afternoon and blasted the captured pillboxes, forcing the Japanese to withdraw. By the end of the day, American positions were where they had been before the attack.

Magata launched his second attack at 4:00 A.M., on March 15. They penetrated 100 yards into the defensive sector and captured one pillbox. Sherman tanks and close air support enabled the infantry to restore the positions and cost the Japanese 190 killed. The next morning Magata penetrated 75 yards before they were halted. Once again, tanks and artillery drove the Japanese back with 194 killed and one POW captured. The final maneuver came on March 23 when a frenzied attack penetrated the defensive line, destroyed three pillboxes, and reached a position only 25 yards from the battalion command post. Once again the Sherman tanks' 75-mm guns proved the difference as the soldiers rooted out the Japanese from their positions and killed them all.

As the Japanese attempted to regroup, American heavy and medium artillery fired 4,000 shells into the narrow sector that housed the Japanese. Harried by two battalions of the 14th Corps and the Fijians, Hyakutake moved what was left of his 6th Division away from the American lines. He left behind nine 75-mm mountain guns, three 37-mm guns, five 90-mm mortars, two 20-mm antiaircraft guns, 90 light and one heavy machine guns, 52 grenade launchers, hundreds of rifles, and 73 officer samurai sabers. More importantly, Hyakutake lost 5,398 killed and 7,060 wounded during the three-week operation. The 14th Corps lost 263 dead.[7]

The March operation was the last major Japanese attack. The Magata force with 1,500 men used the Numa-Numa trail to withdraw to the north of Bougainville. The Iwasa and Muda forces moved to the safety of southern Bougainville. All Japanese forces became fully occupied with catching fish and growing vegetables in order to survive. The war had passed them by.

The Army 93rd Division

Contact with the Japanese became minimal during the summer of 1943, even though the 14th Corps continued to extend its defensive perimeter. For the senior- decision makers back in Washington, Bougainville seemed the ideal time and place to utilize black troops in combat for the first time. To this time, the army of WW II had been segregated with black troops performing support duties, but not fighting as an all-black unit in combat. That was about to change.

The all-black 25th Infantry Regiment arrived on Bougainville on March 29. General Griswold assigned the regiment to the Americal Division for training and patrolling duties and, when ready, to take over sectors of the defensive perimeter. The first casualties to the 25th occurred in mid-April, when four men were killed during an ambush of their patrol.

During April, the 2nd Battalion of the 25th was detached from the Americal Division and attached to the 37th Division where it was formed into a task force with American and Fijian companies to pursue Japanese withdrawing north along the Laruma River. The task force destroyed a Japanese machine gun and three pillboxes, and Private Wase Fogge earned the Division's first Bronze Star Medal for heroism during the attack. The task force killed 20 Japanese against their own losses of five wounded. The 2nd Battalion performed well and was returned to the Americal Division.[8]

On April 6, a company from the 3rd Battalion of the 25th was directed to move two miles to the east and set up a roadblock. The company was reinforced with a machine gun platoon, four artillery observers, two men from a photographic unit, and a man from the intelligence section to serve as guide. About a quarter mile short of its objective, the company came to a halt while patrols checked out some huts remaining from an old Japanese field hospital. One of the patrols began firing toward the left front and reported killing two of the enemy.

When the company commander went forward, he was fired upon and found two of his own men wounded. He ordered the

229

other two platoons to come forward, one on each flank of the patrol. The patrols moved forward, and then without orders or warning, began firing. Their firing was joined by the machine gun platoon. The company commander ordered "cease fire." The firing ceased briefly, and then continued. Some of the men began to panic and move to the rear.

The company commander ordered the two flank platoons to close upon the center patrol unit, but they began to fire upon the patrol. The company commander now ordered the patrol to withdraw, which added to the confusion. Many of the men, including their first sergeant had already thrown off their packs and disappeared to the rear.

Battalion headquarters ordered the company to fall back and reform, but the men continued firing in all directions and soon there was chaos. The troops continued to fire and caused self-inflicted casualties. The company eventually reached the safety of the battalion, only to find that their weapons platoon leader and nine enlisted men had been killed and twenty men were wounded. No one had seen a Japanese. The company left behind its dead, two automatic weapons, 18 rifles, three carbines, and numerous packs. As the event was analyzed, it became apparent that most of the casualties were the result of the company's indiscriminate firing. It took another three days before the company recovered its own dead and missing weapons.

This was not the first time in the Pacific war that troops panicked and fired indiscriminately at an imaginary enemy. The action was blamed upon lack of experience and failure of senior enlisted to provide proper leadership to the troops. General Griswold appointed a committee to investigate the actions of the company. The subsequent report of May 10, was not favorable to the 2nd Battalion and was forwarded up the chain of command. The Battalion left Bougainville on May 24, for the Green Islands, was later dissolved and integrated into other artillery-defense organizations. Because of the breakdown of one company, the entire regiment was faulted. Senior officials in Washington stifled any attempts for future combat roles for all-black troop units.[9]

Australian II Corps

As early as July 1944, a decision was made to replace the army troops on Bougainville with Australian forces. MacArthur needed both the 37th and 194th Divisions for his invasion of the Philippines. The Australian II Corps seemed adequate for continuing the army's concept of keeping the enemy under surveillance and defending the perimeter against any enemy attacks.

The Australian II Corps consisted of the 3rd Australian Division and two additional brigades, a total of 30,000 men. The Corps commander, Lieutenant Gen. Stanley Savige, was a veteran of several African campaigns and the fighting on Papua. Advance elements of the division arrived at Torokina on October 6, and General Savige assumed command of all Allied forces on Bougainville on November 22, 1944.

We may never know General Savige's strategy for the defense of Bougainville, but we are well aware of the concept directed by General Sir Thomas Blamey, overall commander of the Australian Army. Blamey directed more aggressive patrolling deep into Japanese territory and the destruction of their garden areas with the intent of starving them and eventually destroying them.[10]

The condition of the Japanese soldiers on Bougainville was becoming desperate. There was no way that General Hyakutake's troops could be resupplied, and without a source of resupply, they were starving. Their normal rice ration of 750 grams per day had been reduced to 250 grams after the first of the year, and now in September 1944, was eliminated entirely. Thirty-five per cent of the soldiers worked full time to catch enough fish and raise enough vegetables in their gardens to exist. Thirty per cent were sick, and the remainder occupied with transporting items from one place to another. Only 15-per cent were maintaining defensive positions.[11]

Morale of the Japanese soldiers became understandably low, with many soldiers deserting their units to try and subsist in the jungle by themselves. The native people that had been pressed into service also walked away and returned home. Hyakutake was obliged to relieve several of his subordinate officers for insubordination and in April, he suffered a stroke which paralyzed his left side. General Kanda replaced him.[12]

Under the U.S. Army, both sides adopted a defensive posture that minimized contact in the area between defensive positions. This situation was about to change under the Australians. The unspoken truce was broken by the Australians on November 25, when they made a surprise attack on a hill held by the Japanese. The startled Japanese lost 20 men and fell back several hundred yards to another hill. The Australians attacked the next hill position on December 18, killing 25 more Japanese and discovering a number of recent graves.

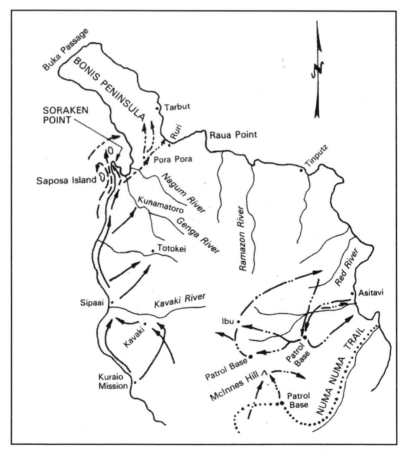

Australian advances in northern Bougainville, January to June 1945.

National Archives

General Savige issued orders on December 23, to destroy the Japanese in southern Bougainville. His campaign was to consist of three simultaneous attacks. The Japanese in the north would be pursued and forced back into the Bonis Peninsula where they would be destroyed. Operations to the east of the current defensive perimeter would be extended to sever lines of communications between the Japanese in the north and the south. His main effort was to be against the Japanese 13th Regiment in the south of Bougainville. The Japanese were believed to be dying at the rate of a thousand per month from illness and starvation. Coupled with the known losses of 18,000 men from fighting and illness, Savige believed one infantry battalion would be sufficient to destroy the Japanese in the south.

Savige's offensive began on December 30, against Pearl Ridge, in the central sector with close air support by New Zealand F4U aircraft. The ridge was defended by 500 Japanese who retreated quickly. The ridge provided views of the sea to both the east and west coasts of Bougainville. Operations in the north began the next day with the use of barges, tanks, and Bougainville natives. The native forces killed 2,000 Japanese soldiers in the eight months they fought them during the Allied occupation of Bougainville.[13]

Australian patrols and company sized actions pursued the Japanese in all three sectors for the next six months resulting in losses of 20 to 60 Japanese during most of the encounters. By the end of June, Japanese forces in the north had been channeled into the Bonis Peninsula. In the south, they were forced into an area 15 by 30 miles. Fighting continued until August 14, when the Japanese ambushed an Australian patrol in the south. Fighting terminated following the emperor's acceptance of the Potsdam proclamation on August 15, 1945.

The long Battle for Bougainville came to a close on August 21 at Torokina when General Kanda and three other senior officers surrendered their swords and 21,090 men to General Savige and other Allied officers. Of the 44,000 Japanese that died from fighting or disease on Bougainville, 18,000 died during the six-month Australian consolidation period. The Australians lost 516 dead and 1,572 wounded during the same period.[14]

General Blamey was required to explain to the Australian government the necessity for a strategy that resulted in so many Australian casualties during a period when Bougainville, Papua, New Britain and Borneo were no longer of any consequence in bringing the war to an end. Australian losses (dead) in the several campaigns totaled 1,048. For Blamey, it seemed to be a matter of pride. For Prime Minister John Curtin and his secretary of the Advisory War council, Sir Frederick Sheddon, it seemed to be apathy. Parents, wives, children, and the Australian Labor Party held Blamey responsible, resulting in his abrupt dismissal from service in 1946.[15]

General Sir Thomas Blamey, front, rides with Major Gen. Robert L. Eichelberger in Bougainville.

National Archives

16

TARAWA: NOVEMBER 20, 1943

It was a time of utmost savagery. I still don't know
how they took the place.

War artist Kerr Eby Tarawa, November 1943

Tarawa (Operation Galvanic) was only one of many
amphibious assaults conducted in the Pacific by the army and the
marines during WW II, but it was the first such operation conducted
against heavily defended beaches and shore defenses. In the space of
76 hours, the atoll and its main island, Betio, became common names
to millions of people around the world, as both Japanese defenders
and American attackers added to the history of amphibious warfare.

The Battle for Tarawa consisted of amphibious assaults on
three separate islands in the Gilbert Island group. The first assault
was against Betio atoll and resulted in 1,000 casualties per day for the
assaulting troops. In the space of 76 horrific hours, 6,000 men died
on this tiny atoll of 300 acres.

The second assault took place against Makin island, 100 miles
to the north of Betio. Makin was defended by 800 men, half of them
laborers. The third assault was against Apamama island, 90 miles
southeast of Betio. Apamama was defended by only 23 Japanese, most
of who committed suicide.

Americans learned much from operation Galvanic as did the
Japanese. Unfortunately this knowledge led to even larger amphibious
operations, stronger defenses, and greater casualties on both sides.

In 1943, Tarawa's strategic value was in its location. It lay
2,500 miles southwest of Pearl Harbor and 1,300 miles southeast of
the huge Japanese garrison at Truk. As such, it became the most
important atoll in the Gilbert Islands. It was the northern most
stepping stone to the Marshall Islands, Truk, Guam, Iwo Jima, and
Japan. It was also the only objective that could be seized, or so it was

thought, with the limited forces available to both Admiral Nimitz in Honolulu and General MacArthur in Australia.

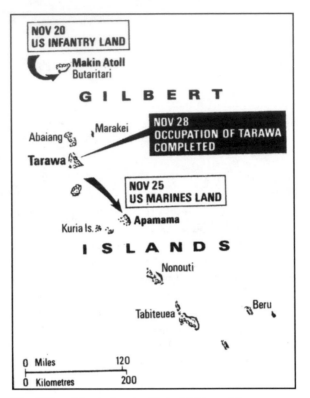

The Gilbert Islands showing Betio, Makin and Apamama.

Admiral Chester Nimitz, commander in chief Pacific, would be in command of the operation, code named Galvanic, and designated Vice Admiral Raymond Spruance as his on scene commander. Spruance was a leader, a man that planned carefully and gained the respect and loyalty of his subordinates. Spruance was in charge of the navy carriers at the Battle of Midway that sank four Japanese carriers and turned the tide in the Pacific.

Spruance's Amphibious Force Commander was Rear Admiral Richmond Kelly Turner, a driving aggressive taskmaster that exploded on enough occasions to be nicknamed "Terrible Turner." Turner would go on to become the most experienced and respected planner of amphibious operations throughout the Pacific campaign. For the Tarawa campaign, Turner's Northern Attack Force was to seize the island of Makin. Rear Admiral Harry Hill with the Southern Attack Force was to seize Betio.

The Ground Force Commander was Major General Holland M. Smith. The marine had a long history of developing tactics and techniques for amphibious warfare and trained both army and marine forces on both coasts. Like Turner, H.M. Smith had a nickname, "Howlin Mad." He demanded and received maximum effort from those who served under him. In return, he "went to the wall" to protect his marines and sailors when he believed they needed more support from the navy. Both Turner and Smith were professionals that trained and inspired those around them, while developing the standards for amphibious operations throughout the Pacific. Our country owes them both our gratitude.

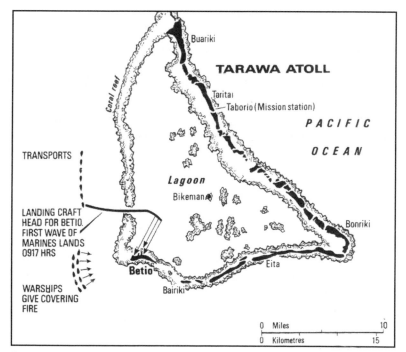

Drawing of Tarawa and Betio Atoll showing the entrance to the lagoon and landing craft approaches to the objective.

National Archives

Betio (rhymes with ratio)

Tarawa atoll was a series of sand ridges lying above sea level with some coconut palms and small trees. The main target of the atoll was Betio with its airfield and access to the lagoon protected by the coral barriers. Betio occupied about 300 acres and every foot of it was defended by the Japanese. The airfield was 4,000 feet long and was defended by the most complex system ever devised. We will learn more about the defenses shortly.

The Second Marine Division was selected to make the amphibious assault to secure Betio and the atoll. The division was rested and ready for action following its fight on Guadalcanal. They recuperated at New Zealand's north island, where the climate cleaned the malaria, dengue fever, jungle rot, and other infections contracted on Guadalcanal. The beer was great, and the girls lovely, prompting hundreds of marriages between marines and local girls. The marines began to hear the British phrase directed against U.S. forces stationed in England. When asked what was wrong with the Americans, the locals responded that they had three problems, "They are overpaid, oversexed, and over here."

Unlike Iwo Jima, Peleliu, and Okinawa, which were yet to come, Betio had no vertical features for subterranean defenses. No part of Betio was more than 300 yards from the beach, which meant that all defenses could be brought to bear against the landing forces. Pillboxes and gun emplacements were completely covered with alternating layers of coconut logs and coral sand. These absorbent layers defied direct hits by bombs and heavy shells. Machine guns were sited in pits, trenches, and nests, with their fires interlocked to sweep the beaches and approaches to the beach. Defenses included:
* mined concrete boat obstacles, with barbed wire and log barricades to channel landing craft into lanes covered by pre registered artillery.
* a barricade a few feet from the beach three to five feet high to slow down the assault and permit pre-registered artillery and machine gun fire on these positions.
* a system of emplacements and trenches, command posts and ammunition dumps with 13-mm and 7.7-mm weapons covered by logs, sand, concrete, and armor plate.
* a system of 14 coast defense guns at the corners of the

island in bomb-proof shelters with underground ammunition storage.

- just inside the beach, a system of 25 field guns, anti aircraft guns, and 14 type 95 tanks dug in with their 37-mm guns. These weapons were all in covered emplacements, immune from all but the largest naval guns.
- finally, a system of bomb-proof shelters that allowed the defenders to move along the horizontal axis of the beaches while protected from explosives and other ordnance.

This view of Betio Island from above gives a clear view of the reefs surrounding the island and stretching 800 to 1,200 yards offshore.

National Archives

Opposing the American invasion of Tarawa, were 5,000 Japanese, under the command of Rear Admiral Keiji Shibasaki. Included among the defensive forces were the 6th Yokosuka Special Navy Landing Force (SNLF), and the Sasebo 7th SNFL. The SNLF units were referred to as Imperial Marines and were considered the elite among Japan's ground forces. Betio would be the first meeting between U.S. and Japanese marines. Lt. Murakami, commanded the IIIth Construction Unit and was responsible for the defenses of Betio and construction of the airfield.

Shibasaki concentrated on defeating the invasion force at the waters edge, and boasted that, "The Americans could not take Tarawa with a million men in a hundred years."[1] To back up his boast, he developed Tarawa into the most heavily defended atoll that the Americans would invade in the entire Pacific.

Besides the defenses listed earlier, Shibisaki had four 8-inch guns (203mm) that were sited to cover likely avenues of approach by an invading fleet. These guns had been shipped from Japan where they had been purchased in 1905 during the Russo-Japanese war.[2]

One of the four 8-inch guns that defended the approaches to Betio.

Jim Moran

Since Betio was a small island, Shibasaki's orders were brief. "Knock out the landing boats with gunfire, tank guns, and infantry guns, then concentrate all fire on the enemy's landing point and destroy him at the water's edge."[3]

The invaders orders were also brief. On November 20, deliver one regiment through the lagoon entrance, and attack the defenses from the lagoon side. The beaches were designated Red-1, Red-2, and Red-3. Another beach designated Green, was on the northern end of the island, but was not planned to be used during the assault phase due to mines and numerous concrete obstacles.

A battalion was designated to land on each of the Red beaches. Major John Schoettel's battalion would assault Beach Red-1, Lieutenant Col. Herbert Amey's battalion would land on Red-2, and Major H.P. Crowe was to land his battalion on Red-3. H-hour was announced as 8:00 A.M. The marine's breakfast of scrambled eggs, steak and coffee at 1:00 A.M. went well, but from then on, execution of the assault plans began to break down.

The first "foul up" actually occurred the evening before the landing when the destroyer USS Ringgold opened fire upon USS Nautilus, which had been reconnoitering Betio for the landing forces. Ringgold's first five-inch shell impacted near the base of the conning tower, rupturing an induction valve, and letting in 30 tons of sea water. Nautilus dived and managed to repair the damage and survive.[4]

D-day blunders occurred at first light when the Army Air Force B-24 bombers based on the Ellice Islands failed to arrive to deliver 500 pound bombs upon the Japanese defenses on the beaches. The subsequent naval bombardment was impressive in terms of light and sound, but many of the shells were fired at such a low trajectory that they skipped off the sand and coral and detonated in the lagoon behind Betio. The concussion from USS Maryland's 16-inch guns resulted in communications and lighting to be lost aboard the ship. Admiral Hill's flagship, Maryland, would have only intermittent communications with the landing forces for the rest of the battle.

By 5:30 A.M., it was obvious that the troopships had been pushed well out of position by a strong southerly current. All naval gunfire ceased as the ships corrected their positions. H-hour, the time the marines were due to land on the beach was pushed back to 9:00 A.M. Admiral Shibasaki was now aware of the landing plans of the invasion force and moved men and equipment from his southern defenses to the northern shore.

Naval carrier aircraft were late in conducting their attack on shore defenses and Admiral Hill was unable to contact the carriers. The Hellcat fighters, and Avenger and Dauntless bombers finally arrived and strafed and bombed the beaches for seven minutes. At 7:35 A.M., the naval gunfire began. It was now daylight and the temperature was passing 90-degrees. Tarawa was only 80 miles north of the equator.

At 9:00 A.M., Admiral Hill ordered the end of the naval bombardment. He was concerned that the landing vehicles approaching the beaches might be hit. Major Gen. Smith and his chief of staff, Merrit Edson protested to no avail. As a result, the Japanese had a full ten minutes to reorganize and pinpoint their defensive fire upon the slow amphibious tractors (LVTs) and Higgins boats (the proper term was Landing Craft Vehicle Personnel LVCPs), approaching the beach. In retrospect, there should have been at least three times as much naval gunfire supplemented by 1000 pound bombs from the B-24 liberators. Without it, the marines would take far greater casualties and be sorely tested.

Many of the 100 LVTs in the first three waves climbed easily over the coral reef surrounding the landing beaches, moved ashore under heavy fire, and unloaded their marines at 9:13 A.M.[5] The Higgins boats grounded on the coral reef 500-800 feet short of the beaches.

The grounding of the Higgins boats was the ultimate mistake during operation Galvanic. Rear Adm. Samuel E. Morison, the official naval historian tells us that no accurate tide tables for the Gilbert Islands existed, but Major Frank Holland had lived in the Gilberts for 15 years and had studied the tides around the islands. He knew and told the planners that they should expect no more than three feet of water over the reefs in November. Since a Higgins boat drew four feet of water when loaded, Holland was appalled to learn that the navy intended to go ahead with the landing in Higgins boats over the Tarawa reefs.

As the LVTs neared their assigned beaches, they came under murderous fire from directly in front and both sides. Automatic weapons fire came from a pier on the left and from a half sunken freighter on the right. Japanese gunners used their type 92 howitzers to drop 70-mm high explosive shells among the landing craft. LVTs began burning and exploding as their fuel tanks blew up. Other LVTs bogged down when their navy drivers were killed; still others disappeared in a ball of fire.[6] Survivors remember explosions, detonations, and bodies falling and bleeding all around them.

A marine that went ashore on Beach Red-1 in an LVT reported the landing this way.

> Bullets pinged off the LVT like hailstones off a tin roof. Large shells hit the water 20 yards off the port side. We got to within 100 yards of the beach and the enemy fire intensified. LVTs were being destroyed on both sides of us. The boats would burst into flames and the survivors would leap over the side looking like human torches. At this point the water was about three feet deep. The boat lurched; I looked up and saw that the driver was dead. The Lieutenant jumped up and drove until he got hit. Now we were 30 yards off shore. Then a large shell struck the boat. I was knocked down and stunned for a minute. Shrapnel was pinging all around us in the boat. My assistant had his pack and helmet blown off. When I tried to talk to him, I found he had a hole in the back of his head I could put my fist through. Another buddy of mine was down, his face all bloody and crushed. As our boat ground to a halt, machine gun fire from a pillbox to our immediate front began. Everyone seemed stunned at the violence of the enemy fire. I yelled, "let's get the hell outa here," grabbed my carbine and ammunition box, and went over the side. Bullets were pouring at us like sheets of rain. Only 12 of the 25 marines in the LVT were able to leave. Only four of them lived to be evacuated from Betio.[7]

When the Higgins boats grounded on the reef, marines were forced to climb, jump, and dive into the surf and wade the

500 to 800 yards of the remaining distance to the beach. The water turned red from the blood of marines that were machine gunned and mortared by Japanese guns pre-registered on their positions. Shells passed overhead, others impacted all around. Only the screams of the wounded rose above the sounds of machine gun and rifle fire that was taking such a heavy toll of the attackers.

Tide changes and miscalculations left the Marines wading to shore for several hundred yards.

National Archives

There was no place for the marines to hide. The LVTs and Higgins boats were ablaze and exploding. The troop's only protection was the shirt on their backs. They could only move forward slowly in water up to their shoulders, waist, and if they made it that far, to their knees in the face of the murderous barrage. It took most of the marines 30 minutes to an hour to make it to shore with their weapons, equipment and packs in the face of the Japanese rain of steel.

Colonel David Shoup reached Betio at 10:00 in an LVT and found only chaos on the beach. Shoup was the newly appointed commander of the 2nd Marine Regiment, the regiment now suffering so badly in the lagoon just short of Betio. He was wounded in his leg and waded painfully towards a long pier between Red-2 and 3, where he saw many of his marines clinging to the pilings. The marines watched their commander and waited for orders.

The pier had been an early objective of the landing force because it dominated the landing area. Japanese on the pier, or in the buildings thereon, could fire upon the flanks of the landing marines. The job of killing the Japanese on the pier was given to First Lt. William Hawkins and his scout-sniper platoon. Hawkins, a Guadalcanal veteran was the first marine to land at Betio. Accompanied by Second Lt. Alan Leslie, an engineer officer, and four of his scouts, Hawkins ran up the ramp to the pier and proceeded down its quarter-mile length, killing the Japanese defenders and burning the structures that might house enemy guns. Leslie used his flamethrower to such advantage that he set portions of the pier afire. This would later delay the landing of supplies over the pier but it was not important at the time. Hawkins team then found an LVT to move them to the beach where they could participate in the assault.

Shoup tried to contact the division commander but communications with the *USS Maryland* had been spotty all morning. As he tried to radio his battalion commanders, he saw an LCM (Landing Craft Medium) with a desperately needed light tank approach the far end of the pier at full throttle. One of the large Japanese guns sounded, the front of the LCM exploded, and the tank slid forward and disappeared into the lagoon.

Shoup, recently promoted, was the junior colonel in the corps. While he talked with Major Schoettel, the commander of the battalion that was to land on Red-1, he must have wondered, Why me Lord? The battalion commander reported that he was still afloat, unable to land on Red One. "Heavy fire all along beach . . . Issue in doubt. . . We have nothing left to land."[8]

However, the battalion in front of Shoup was making progress over Red-2 and were about to cross the taxiway to the airport. The battalion to his left received several Sherman medium tanks and was on the move on Red-3. Shoup ordered his reserve battalion to land on Red-2, and then move to their right to relieve the Schoettel's battalion that was stalled and demoralized. Twenty-five LVTs that were placed in reserve were released and started to replace the destroyed and damaged tractors. Order was taking the place of chaos.

As Shoup moved toward the beach from the pier he was

245

wounded again, but the stubborn commander had the bit in his mouth and was not about to let go. Since he could not communicate with the division commander or task force commander, he sent Lieutenant Col. Evans Carlson back to the USS *Maryland* in one of the returning LVTs with instructions, "You tell the general and admiral we're going to stick and fight it out."[9]

Only 500 yards to the south of Shoup, stood Shibasaki. The Japanese commander was also having problems. He expected all the landing craft to ground on the reef. Instead, the "little boats on wheels," the LVTs, climbed over the reef and proceeded all the way to the beach. This was the first time LVTs had been used in the Pacific. Their use was a first for both Shoup and Shibasaki. Shibasaki also did not expect the landing to be inside the lagoon. He had prepared his defenses facing seaward and was now hurriedly transferring men from the north and west shores to the south.

Bodies of marines killed on D-Day litter Red Beach and await collection.

National Archives

Like Shoup, Shibasaki's lines of communications were almost nonexistent. The naval bombardment and aerial bombing had destroyed most of his communication wire and he was able to talk to only a half dozen subordinates. He did not expect to survive the assault and had the unit colors burned early in the morning. His commanders were told to fight to the death and to kill as many of the enemy as possible. If he could hold out for a week, there was a possibility that the Japanese fleet from Truk would charge to their defense.

On Red-1, Major Michael Ryan led his company from the reef to the beach littered with dead marines and damaged or destroyed LVTs. His company suffered 35-percent casualties walking through the surf to the beach. His battalion commander and staff were still afloat.

Lieutenant Col. Amey, commander of the battalion assigned to land on Red-2, was killed by machine gun fire while walking the last 200 yards to the beach. On Red-3, marines were able to get ashore and proceed to the airstrip before enemy fire forced them to stop and dig in.

Initially, there was close, bloody fighting along the entire beach for several yards inland. Then the marines found that their rifles and hand grenades were of no use against the well dug in enemy. They had to wait until a few flamethrowers could be brought forward. Then, along with blocks of TNT they learned to use at Guadalcanal, they began to destroy the pillboxes and bunkers.

For another two hours the situation remained critical and in doubt. Most of the LVTs had been destroyed or damaged. At least 20 LVTs, Higgins boats and two LCMs full of dead and wounded were stuck on the reef in front of Beach Red-1. Reinforcements were unable to land and some 1,500 marines were pinned down on the first few yards of beach.

Shoup set up his regimental command post on the seaward side of a Japanese coconut-log bunker. The Japanese were still inside with their weapons pointed seaward, so Shoup posted a few sentries with orders to shoot any of the Japanese that tried to leave the bunker.

Abandoned LVTs and floating bodies bear witness to the effectiveness of the defenses.

National Archives

Most of the fighting was being done on Red-3 where Major Henry Crowe and his battalion held a front of 250 yards by 100 yards deep. Much of the credit goes to Lieutenant Hawkins and his sniper platoon. They fired their weapons quick and sure, moved and fired again. They shot Japanese out of the trees and blew them out of their holes. Those Japanese they could not shoot, they killed with their knives. The 34 scout-snipers were credited with killing ten times their number of Japanese. Hawkins continued fighting with bullets in both shoulders and died the following day from loss of blood.[10]

By the end of D-day, some 5000 marines had been moved ashore, with 1500 of them killed or wounded. Marines controlled the beaches for about 400 yards in each direction from the pier and to a depth of 300 yards. Water, blood plasma, ammunition and reinforcements were being landed at the end of the pier and carried to the beach. On the western end of Red-1, Major Michel Ryan's battalion and reinforcements extended their control of the western end of the island to an area 150 yards wide and 500 yards deep. They had been cut off from the marines on Red-2 since they landed, and a strong Japanese counterattack may have pushed them back into the lagoon. At this point, Shibasaki had no troops to counterattack. Half his men had been killed, naval gunfire destroyed his communication wire, and he had no control of his troops outside of his command post.

During the night, several Japanese swam out to the sunken freighter along the edge of the atoll on Red-1 and to several of the disabled LVTs and Higgins boats. They set up machine guns and caused heavy casualties among the first waves to land on D+1. Navy carrier based aircraft attacked the Japanese positions but were unable to destroy them. Three hundred forty four marines were killed or wounded trying to land on Red-1 the morning of D+1.

At noon, Major Ryan's men broke out of their beachhead on Red-1, and overran three 80-mm coast defense guns that commanded the beach approaches. They moved to the western end of the island and radioed that they now commanded the beach approaches. General Julian Smith immediately ordered the regimental reserve to land on the southern half of the western tip of the island (Green Beach) and advance to the airstrip. The regiment landed in rubber boats in the afternoon, called for air strikes on their assigned objectives, and dug in for the night.

Marines on each side of the pier had fought their way forward to the airfield and some light tanks had landed and were blasting the apertures of pillboxes and bunkers. Colonel Shoup now felt confident enough to radio back to General Smith that, "We are winning."[11] Colonel Merrit Edson, the division chief of staff arrived in the early evening to take command of all marines on Betio. Colonel Shoup could now have his wounds treated and concentrate on control of his regiment.

Early on November 22, D+2, a Japanese radio message to Tokyo was intercepted that said, "Our weapons have been destroyed and from now everyone is attempting a final charge... May Japan exist for 10,000 years."[12] The message was sent by a staff officer since Shibasaki was killed on D-day when naval gunfire was directed against a group of Japanese officers standing in the open.[13] Shibasaki decided to give up his command post for use as a hospital and was moving a few hundred yards away with his staff when he was seen by a naval gunfire spotter. His death probably prevented a massive counter attack the night of D-day, which may have been successful.

Marines continued to use tanks, flamethrowers, and explosives to destroy or close enemy defensive positions in front of Red-3. During the evening, Japanese counterattacked at the eastern end of the island, but were beaten back. Some 325 Japanese dead were counted the next morning. Major Gen. Julian Smith estimated that 500 Japanese remained at the eastern end of the island with a lesser number in a large bombproof bunker at the western end.

By 1:00 P.M., on November 23, D+3, all Japanese resistance on the eastern end was destroyed. The final storming of the bombproof shelter by flamethrowers, tanks and explosives was witnessed by correspondents, photographers and ships personnel that had come ashore. Marine engineers and Seabees repaired the main runway and at noon a F4F from one of the navy carriers landed on the strip.

Tarawa was secured on November 27, when elements of Colonel Murray's battalion chased the remaining Japanese to Buariki, the northern most island in the chain. During a fierce fire fight, Marines suffered 32 dead and 59 wounded while killing 175 Japanese.

The Japanese defenders suffered 4,690 killed, or 97-percent of their strength. Only 17 Japanese and 129 Korean laborers were taken prisoner. Marine losses were 3,301, with 960 dead. Some units loses were dramatic. Two regiments suffered 35 percent casualties, the tractor battalion had 49 percent casualties and 66 percent of flamethrower personnel were killed. Half of the marine dead were killed in the water while wading ashore. Of the total of 129 LVTs, committed to the invasion, 72 were destroyed before reaching the shore.

Four marines were awarded the Medal of Honor for heroic action on Betio. Staff Sgt. William J. Bordelon died fighting on D-day. His LVT was stopped 15 yards short of the beach by an enemy 40mm gun and machine gun positions. Bordelon left the assault boat and attacked the enemy positions. He was hit by machine gun fire four times and had a blasting cap go off prematurely while in his hand. He refused aid and succeeded in destroying four enemy positions although he was killed destroying the fourth.

First Lt. Alexander Bonnyman joined the marines as a private and gained a battlefield commission to Lieutenant on Guadalcanal. When his platoon was stopped by a sand-covered concrete blockhouse and 200 Japanese troops, Bonnyman led a charge up the side of the blockhouse with explosives and flame throwers. They killed the crew of a machine gun nest, and threw explosives into the entrances of the blockhouse. The Japanese counterattacked but Bonnyman refused to fall back and prevented the Japanese from reaching the blockhouse until he was killed. Bonnyman was 30 years old with a family and could have avoided military service had he wished to do so.

First Lt. William Hawkins was unable to join the army or army air corps due to severe scarring on his body caused by a childhood accident. He enlisted in the marine corps in 1941, rose rapidly in rank, and gained a commission during the Battle for Guadalcanal. Hawkins commanded the scout-sniper platoon at Betio. He and his 34 man unit were the first to land and secured the quarter mile long pier in Red-2. He then led his men in vicious fighting against enemy strongpoint near the airport. Hawkins was wounded in the hand by a mortar round, and in the chest and both shoulders by machine gun fire. He refused aid and died from a loss of blood.

The only Medal of Honor recipient that lived through the battle was Colonel David Shoup. Shoup was the regimental commander and although wounded while coming ashore, refused to be evacuated and assumed command of all marines ashore. He directed operations for the first two days of the battle, and when relieved as overall commander, stayed to assist with the conduct of the operation. Shoup later became Commandant of the Marine Corps. He died in 1983 at age 78.

Makin: Butaritari Island: November 20, 1943

Butaritari Island in the Makin atoll was selected as an airfield site for Allied forces. It was only 250 miles from the Japanese air base at Jaluit and 200 miles from a similar airfield at Mili.

Intelligence indicated that Makin was defended by only a few guns and less than 800 men. Lieutenant (jg) Seizo Ishikawa commanded 284 troops of the SNLF.

Vice Adm. Turner's Northern Attack Force consisted of the 165th Regimental Combat Team with 6,472 army assault troops and a battalion landing team. The division was commanded by Major Gen. Ralph C. Smith. The troops were supported by eight battleships and cruisers, 13 destroyers, and aircraft from five carriers. The heavy emphasis on naval gunfire and aviation assets was due to the proximity of Japanese aircraft and the possibility of Japanese fleet interference from Truk.

The pre-assault bombardment was limited to a 20 minute aerial bombardment and an hour and 40 minutes of naval gunfire. There was no response from the Japanese, but a turret explosion aboard USS *Mississippi* killed 43 men and wounded 19 more. Major Gen. Smith landed two battalions on the western end of the island from the ocean side, and another battalion landed later on the lagoon side.

Unlike Shoup at Betio, Smith had enough LVTs to land his initial assault force without concern for low tides and a coral reef. There was no opposition to the landing force as the Japanese were located about two miles from the initial landing beaches. Within an hour and a half after landing, Smith's forces began advancing toward the Japanese defenses at the western end of the island.

Japanese resistance increased steadily as the two battalions moved through the heavy undergrowth that partially concealed the defenders. At this time (10:40 A.M.), the third battalion landed from the lagoon side of the island. This battalion landed into the main Japanese defensive area, but because the defenses were oriented seaward, and due to a heavy naval gunfire and aerial bombardment, the defenders seemed dazed and offered little resistance to the landing.

As the army assault troops closed the ring on the Japanese defenders, the situation became more difficult. Visibility through the underbrush was poor and the Japanese held their fire until the army forces were nearly on top of them. As darkness closed in, both battalions dug in within grenade range of the Japanese defenders.

This was the first combat for the 165th and the night became a bad dream. Japanese infiltrators made their lives miserable and caused the inexperienced troops to respond to noises with heavy bursts of firing that were wildly inaccurate. Thankful for first light, Smith found that most of the damage from the wild barrages had been to themselves, and that the Japanese remained essentially where they were. It was a valuable lesson in fire discipline.

During the second day, fighting was at close quarters and conducted by engineer units and infantry. Slowly, Japanese defensive emplacements were destroyed and the defenders killed. By the end of the day, only mopping up of the Japanese defenders remained. Ralph Smith reported to Admiral Turner at 11:30 on November 23rd, that "Makin was takin"[14]

The army brigade suffered 66 killed and 152 wounded. Japanese losses were 695 killed, one captured sailor and 104 Korean laborers. A far greater toll was exacted by the Japanese at sea off Makin. The Japanese submarine 1-175 torpedoed and sank USS Liscombe Bay, one of three escort carriers supporting the assault on Makin. Lost with the ship were the task force commander, Rear Adm. Henry Mullinix, 52 officers and 591 enlisted personnel. This was a tragic ending to a successful amphibious assault on Makin, a steppingstone only 500 miles from the huge Japanese garrison and anchorage at Truk.

Apamama

Apamama was seized because of its anticipated use as a forward naval base. It had a fine lagoon, 12 miles long by five miles wide. Since it was believed to be lightly defended, a small marine reconnaissance company of 80 men was landed by rubber boat from the submarine Nautilus. The marines embarked at Pearl Harbor and spent several weeks aboard Nautilus while she reconnoitered Betio, Makin and Apamama. The marines were startled when Nautilus was hit by the 5-inch round from destroyer Ringgold, and most thankful when Nautilus was able to dive and repair the damage.

Captain James Jones landed his small force on the western part of the island during the night of November 22. As they moved east and north along the chain of six inlets, they killed one man from a three man Japanese patrol they came in contact with. The other two Japanese fled. Local islanders told Jones that 25 Japanese were in defensive positions on the next inlet.

The following morning, Jones tried to cross the inlet but was prevented from doing so by heavy rifle and machine gun fire by the Japanese defenders. Jones asked Nautilus to use its five-inch guns to provide covering fire while he used his rubber boats to outflank the Japanese positions. Nautilus complied but their fire did not reduce the Japanese firing. A destroyer arrived on the 24th and took the defensive position under fire with its main battery. It also failed to silence the Japanese guns which by now had killed two marines and wounded two others. On the morning of the 25th, the Japanese gunfire was silent. Upon crossing the channel, Jones found that four of the Japanese had been killed, and 18 committed suicide.

Author Derrick Wright, in his book, Tarawa 1943, tells us that the Japanese commander accidentally shot himself with his pistol while exhorting his men. The troops, helpless without leadership, dug their own graves and shot themselves. The marines filled in the graves.[15]

Tarawa today

Tarawa is now part of the Republic of Kiribati. It can be reached by plane from Hawaii or Christmas Island. When the marines departed Tarawa in June 1943, it looked like a moonscape of craters, stumps, and littered beaches. Thousands of bodies were buried in a one square mile of earth. Now the island is green with new vegetation, the bodies were moved or cremated, and hotels, bars, shops and a movie theater have taken their place.

Admiral Shibasaki's massive concrete bunker is in the back yard of a person's residence. The concrete bunker where Lieutenant Bonnyman earned his Medal of Honor still stands behind the police station, and one of the 8-inch guns still stands guard at the west end of the island. The long pier is only a few rotting stumps, and the cove that was Beach Red-1 is filled in. There still remain many rusting remnants of landing craft, anti-boat guns and steel covered command posts. A cluster of buildings at the end of a new, shorter concrete pier belongs to a Japanese-owned frozen fish plant.

Lessons Learned

• Everyone condemned the use of the old battleships as command centers. The first salvo of USS Maryland's 16-inch guns essentially wrecked ship to shore communication for the rest of the battle. This mistake was not repeated during the war.

• The portable man-pack radio used by the marines lacked waterproofing. Although this problem would continue to some degree throughout the Pacific war, the problem was recognized and improvements were made.

• The use of the LVT to cross the reef was a lifesaver. If there had been more, many lives could have been saved. After Tarawa, all amphibious assaults used LVTs to move troops ashore. The tractors were better armed, armored, and faster with larger engines.

• There was universal criticism of the effects of naval gunfire. There was not enough of it and it was relatively ineffective. Much of this criticism was pointed towards Admiral Chester Nimitz. Nimitz believed that the Japanese navy would sortie from Truk and engage his naval forces near Apamama. He did not want to lose the advantage of surprise by shelling the island in advance of D-day. Such a decision is understandable considering the paucity of naval forces at the time, but does little to indicate Nimitz's concern for the landing forces. Similar decisions were made concerning other amphibious assaults, the assault on Iwo Jima being a classic example. The lack of such support resulted in less than an amiable relationship between "Howlin'" M. Smith and the navy planners, and caused much higher casualties among the assault forces.

• It was agreed that the use of rubber boats to land assault forces was neither prudent nor necessary. The boats provided no protection, were difficult to manage in surf and swells, and occupied most of the effort of the troops that were attempting to land.

• There is a need for better coordination of air strikes. Some also suggested that the naval aviators needed to practice their air to ground delivery on targets before an actual assault on an enemy beachhead.

• Water brought to shore in 50 gallon barrels was tainted by oil. A better way of cleaning the barrels has to be devised.

• More use of available intelligence to avoid the debacle and slaughter on the reef must be accomplished. If mistakes are to be made, they must be made to favor the landing force, not the other way around.

• The image of the Japanese infantryman's fighting qualities as something less than desirable was shattered at Tarawa. Newsreels showing the bodies of dozen of marines floating in the water besides damaged and destroyed landing craft shocked the American public into a realization of the savagery of this war.

Last week a few thousand marines, many of them now dead or wounded gave our nation a name to stand beside the names of Concord Bridge, the Bon Homme Richard, the Alamo and Belleau Wood. That name is Tarawa.

Time magazine, December, 1943

17

PELELIU: SEPTEMBER 1944

The Battle for Tarawa has long been considered one of the most costly amphibious operations in naval history, both in the number of casualties, and in the mistakes that were made. The planners for the Peleliu invasion had Tarawa as a frame of reference for what went wrong and how to correct the problems. Yet, American casualties on Peleliu were three times that of Tarawa. The questions of what went wrong on Peleliu and why an invasion was even necessary continue to be asked to this day.

William Manchester, in his book, *Goodbye Darkness*, says the invasion of Peleliu "appears to have been doomed from the start." Peleliu was a bad battle, fought in a bad place, at a bad time, against an enemy that could have been left to wither on the vine."[1] Time magazine called Peleliu "a horrible place."[2] Few Americans had ever heard of Peleliu. When President Harry Truman pinned a medal on a marine that fought on Peleliu, he could not pronounce the island's name. Samuel Eliot Morison, the official historian for the U. S. Navy wrote, "Admiral Nimitz's order to capture Peleliu should have been countermanded."[4] Peleliu was not worth the price of ten thousand American casualties, three times those of Tarawa.

Peleliu, and its satellite island of Anguar are the southernmost islands in the Palau chain It is located half way between the Mariana Islands and the Philippines. It is a six-mile-long, two-mile-wide chunk of coral. In the fall of 1944, as General Douglas MacArthur and Admiral Nimitz's forces moved toward Mindanao, Philippines, the capture of Peleliu seemed necessary to protect MacArthur's flank when he invaded Mindanao, 650 miles to the west.

This rationale all changed when Admiral "Bull" Halsey radioed Admiral Nimitz and recommended bypassing Mindanao and landing instead at Leyte Gulf. Halsey especially recommended bypassing Peleliu, predicting it would be another Tarawa. Nimitz forwarded Halsey's message to the joint chiefs, recommending approval, except for insisting that the Peleliu operation take place as scheduled. The joint chiefs approved Nimitz's recommendation. We will never know why Nimitz insisted on the invasion of Peleliu. It no longer had any military value and could easily have been neutralized by carrier-based aircraft as was done on Truk and Rabaul. Whatever his motives, the answer went to the grave with Admiral Nimitz. One might only assume the death of 10,000 young Americans lay heavy on his conscience.

The Japanese had an airbase at Peleliu and a harbor at Malakai for fleet support. They also had a communications center on Koror to the north. The value of these facilities changed dramatically starting on March 2, 1944, when Admiral Marc A. Mitscher arrived with Task Force 58. Mitscher's forces had been bombarding the "impregnable" fortress of Rabaul in the Solomons and destroyed the runway and facilities there so thoroughly that Admiral Mineichi Koga, commander of Japan's combined fleet, fled to Palau aboard battleship Musashi. The American task force followed him, and for two days, Mitscher's fighters, dive-bombers and torpedo planes destroyed the runway and airfield facilities, bottled up 31 ships in the harbor, and sank or severely damaged all of them. When Mitscher's task force finished, Peleliu and Malakai were no longer capable of supporting anything. Admiral Koga remained aboard Musashi at Koror, and was not attacked.

Although Peleliu was no longer included in Japanese plans for offensive operations, General Hideki Tojo, Japan's minister of war, predicted that the Americans would seize Peleliu as a stepping stone to the Philippines. He was determined to reinforce Peleliu and make the enemy pay a terrible price for their victory. During April, he sent Lieutenant Gen. Sadae Inoue and the 14th Infantry Division with 12,000 men to Palau. Inoue and the division distinguished themselves during fighting in China and were sent to Palau to kill as many Americans as possible and die for the emperor. They were very willing to do so.

Inoue established his headquarters at Koror, which boasted some commercial facilities and a population of 30,000 civilians, but poor defensive geography. In his tours of the various islands, he determined that only Peleliu and Anguar, seven miles further south, had defensive capabilities. Peleliu had only one suitable landing beach so defensive preparations began immediately. Two battalions (1,500 men) were sent to Anguar to prepare defensive positions and defend the island with a population of 300 natives. Colonel Kunio Nakagawa commanding 6,500 troops of the elite 2nd Infantry Regiment, was the major force on Peleliu.

Colonel Nakagawa knew that his forces, without surface, naval or aviation support, could not prevent an enemy from landing on Peleliu. He was determined to make the enemy landing force pay a terrible price in casualties, both during the landing phase and once they were ashore. Nakagawa had artillery, mortars, tanks, machine guns and anti-aircraft artillery that could be lowered to fire directly at enemy forces on the ground or at landing craft as they approached the beach. He had his engineers pre-register all his artillery and mortars on every square inch of the landing beaches so fire could be delivered accurately on the beach regardless of smoke or restricted vision. In addition, he installed 500 mines a few feet below the surface of the water between the reef that fronted the landing beach and the beach itself. Hundreds of v-shaped obstacles were implanted a few yards offshore, barbed wire was strung, a six-foot-deep tank trap was dug, and machine guns were dug in and sandbagged so that they had a commanding view of the beaches and were mutually supportive. Just getting ashore would be more of a challenge than Tarawa.

Nakagawa's defensive preparations were impressive, but it was his use of the terrain that almost doomed the invading force. American intelligence, gained from reconnaissance flights, pictures from submarines, and navy frogmen reports, all described Peleliu as essentially flat. It had a 30-foot rise about 100 yards inland from the beach and then was flat with a heavy covering of vines and vegetation. Nothing could have been further from the truth.

Peleliu is a horrible landscape. It has continuous sheer coral cliffs, topped by saw-toothed ridges, all covered by the jungle. Deep ravines, with swamps, and heavy undergrowth at the bottoms, that made movement extremely difficult separated the ridges. There were at least 500 coral caves on Peleliu. Nakagawa reinforced them with concrete and camouflaged the entrances so they could not be seen. A 75-mm artillery piece could be rolled out the entrance, fired, and rolled back in again without being seen. Cave entrances were usually small, well-concealed, and had sharp turns just inside the openings. These turns protected against flame-throwers and demolition charges.

The caves provided living, working, and fighting positions for the Japanese. They were well stocked with food, water, ammunition and medical supplies. One such cave was 300 feet long and had five 150-foot-long spokes (tunnels) which harbored thousands of Japanese. Five months after the battle, 13 Japanese were discovered in one of these tunnels. They were well-fed and wore fresh uniforms.

The unit picked to conduct the amphibious operation was the First Marine Division, victors at Guadalcanal, Tulagi, and Cape Gloucester. The division, nicknamed "The "Old Breed" had been recuperating, reinforcing, and training at Pavuvu, in the Russell Islands. They were based on the only portion of Pavuvu that was useable and found land crabs and rats as their only companions in the tropical heat. The marines were spoiling for a fight, and Peleliu would satisfy their needs.

Major Gen. William H. Rupertus.

USMC

The division commander was Major Gen. William Rupertus. He had been assistant division commander at Guadalcanal, and commanded the division at Cape Gloucester. In 1929, while with the U.S. legation in Peking, China, his wife and daughter died in a scarlet fever epidemic that took thousands of lives. Rupertus seemed to never recover from the crisis. He became a demanding introvert with few close friends or associates.

During the planning phase for the invasion of Peleliu, Rupertus was back in Washington heading up a promotion board. His assistant commander, Brigadier Gen. Oliver P. Smith and his staff, drew up the plans for the assault on Peleliu. When he returned, Rupertus was so confident of the division's ability to execute the plan, that he openly predicted that the campaign would be over in a week. "It will be a short operation," he said, "a hard fought quickie, that will be over in four days, five at the most."[5] later he told his troops that they ". . . would be through in three days, it might only take two."[6] When the actual battle approached six weeks, the commanding general's optimistic prophecies became mocking insults for the troops. To make matters worse, Gen. Rupertus broke his ankle before the operation and was forced to hobble about with a cane.

The assault plan for the invasion of Peleliu (code named Operation Stalemate), called for three days of naval gunfire and air strikes on the island. The battleships *Pennsylvania, Maryland, Mississippi,* and *Idaho* were joined by heavy cruisers *Columbus, Indianapolis, Louisville, Minneapolis,* and *Portland.* Light cruisers *Cleveland, Denver* and *Honolulu* plus three heavy carriers and five "jeep" carriers with 400 aircraft also participated in the bombardment.

The order to commence firing was given at 5:30 A.M., on September 12, 1944, D-Day 3. Tons of steel and explosives from the ships' guns tore up the island for 30 minutes. Then the fighter and dive-bomber aircraft from the carriers dropped 500-pound bombs, canisters of napalm, and fired rockets and cannons at enemy positions. When the aircraft returned to their carriers, the surface fleet resumed shelling. This alternate ship and aircraft bombardment continued until sunset.

On the morning of D-Day-2, observers were amazed by what they saw. The flat plateau covered with vines and jungle growth had been stripped of vegetation and revealed an island of steep coral hills and sheer cliffs that extended the length of the island. Also perplexing to the senior officers afloat was the fact that there was no counter bombardment from the Japanese.

At the end of the second day's bombardment, Admiral Jesse Oldendorf, commander of the fire support fleet, announced that he had destroyed all targets on the island and was leaving the area.[7] The next morning, D-Day-1, not a single ship or plane remained in the sea around Peleliu.

261

The troop transports arrived the morning of D-Day. Just as at Tarawa, a coral reef prevented the troops from moving from their transport ships to the beach. The difference in the two operations was that the reef obstacle was recognized during the planning phase for the Peleliu operation. Troops climbed down nets into Higgins boats, which moved them to the reef, where they were transferred to amtracs (amphibious tractors) for travel across the reef and to the beach.

This was probably a fine plan for an administrative move with no one shooting at you. It became a far different situation at Peleliu. Reveille for the assault troops was 5:30 A.M. Breakfast was steak, eggs and toast, washed down with hot coffee, but few of the troops were in a mood for breakfast. Many of them would not eat another hot meal for more than a week.

The plan was to land three regiments abreast over the beach. Colonel Lewis "Chesty" Puller's First Marine Regiment would land on the left (northern) sector of the beach, drive inland for 300 yards, and then turn left to attack the ridges commanding the shoreline. Colonel Herman "Herm" Hannekin's Seventh Marine Regiment would land in the center, move across the island, turn right, and sweep the southern end of the island clean of Japanese. Colonel Harold "Bucky" Harris' Fifth Marine Regiment would be on the right (south) with the mission of seizing the enemy airfield. All three regimental commanders performed superbly, but it was the enlisted marines and junior officers that won the battle for Peleliu.

The fire support fleet returned to conduct pre-landing bombardment at 5:50 A.M., and continued until 7:50, when 16 landing craft fired a series of 5-inch rockets onto the beach just ahead of the landing craft. The weather was perfect, with slight ocean swells and a temperature of 90 degrees. As the amtracs approached the reef, they were met by a curtain of enemy artillery and rocket fire. Huge chunks of coral and landing craft blew skyward as the troops were blown in all directions. All that could be seen from the bridges of the ships was dense black smoke, and flaming debris. Twenty-six landing craft were destroyed in the first 10 minutes. In the next 90 minutes, 50 more were damaged or destroyed. Something had gone terribly wrong. What happened to the commanding general's prediction of a "walkover?"[8]

Two events occurred that enabled the marines to cross the murderous blanket of fire being delivered on the reef. The first

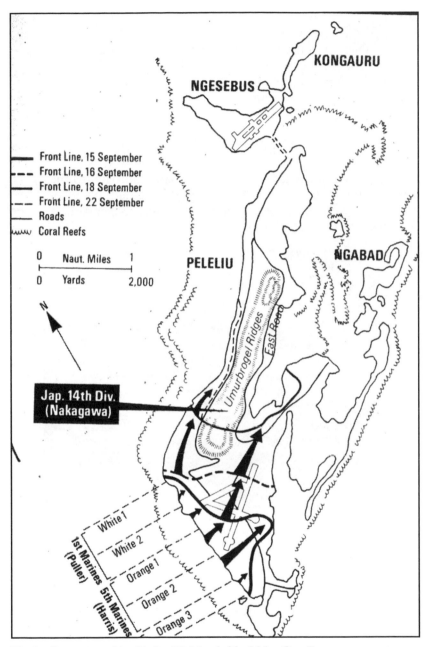

The landing routes of 1st Marine Division led by Major Gen. Rupertus.

was the espirit of the marines in the First Division. They rightly believed that they were the among the elite infantry troops in the world. Their courage and determination under fire would not be denied. The second event was a combination of additional shelling by the fire support ships and the amount of smoke in the beach area. The additional shelling forced Nakagawa to move his artillery back underground or under cover thus diminishing the amount of artillery and mortar fire on the reef and the approach to the beach. The heavy smoke also obscured the Japanese view of the amtracs as they moved toward the beach. It is quite possible that if Nakagawa's bombardment of the reef and approach to the beach had continued, the landing force would have had to return to the transports with whatever landing craft remained, and the landing postponed or canceled.

Marines held down on White Beach by Japanese artillery.

National Archives

With Japanese artillery temporarily silenced, the amtracs loaded their troops, crossed the reef, and, preceded by six new waterproofed Sherman tanks, made their way to the beach, landing at 8:32 A.M. The regiments on the right and center of the landing beach were able to move inland, but Puller's regiment on the left, was pinned down on the beach by heavy artillery fire from their front and left. The scene, as reported by an aerial observer, was mounting chaos. All along the reef marines waited for amtracs to take them across and deposit them on the beach. Burning wreckage, bodies and equipment floated and bobbed along the entire length of the reef and shoreline. The amtracs that did make it to the beach dropped their rear ramp and the marines exited quickly looking for a shell hole to provide protection while their squads and platoons organized the assault.

The first night ashore, the Japanese counterattacked, trying to drive the marines into the ocean. Fighting became hand-to-hand. Men died by the bayonet, knife, grenade, and by the hands of their enemy. When it was over, the marines were still there, deep in their holes, surrounded by dead bodies and parts of bodies.

It is well known by those involved in amphibious operations that the beach is the most dangerous place to be. The troops are reminded of this time and again. Yet, once ashore and facing withering fire from the enemy immediately to their front, many troops forgot the warning, looked for a deep shell hole, jumped in, and stayed there. Officers and non-commissioned officers moved through the withering enemy fire to scream at, order and threaten the troops to get them to move forward. And they did.

Corporal Lewis K. Bausell earned his Medal of Honor less than an hour after landing on the beach. Bausell and several others moved quickly 100 yards inland where they were stopped by enemy fire from a cave in a coral ridge. Machine gun and rifle fire from the cave was frightening, but when a flame-thrower team arrived, the group attacked the cave. While Bausell and his team provided cover fire, the flame-thrower operator moved forward and sprayed the entrance to the cave.

Bausell's team moved to the rear of the cave to be able to stop any Japanese that might try to flee from a rear entrance. The first Japanese to exit charged out with a grenade held to his chest. The explosion blew the Japanese to pieces and wounded four marines. The next Japanese to exit was shot before he could activate his grenade. The third Japanese threw his grenade at the marines as he was killed. There was no place to hide and no place to run. Cpl. Bausell threw himself on the grenade and took the full force of the explosion, thereby saving the lives of his buddies. Bausell earned the nation's highest award posthumously.[9]

By noon of D-Day, the landing beach looked like a junkyard. Wrecked landing craft, vehicles, supplies, boxes of ammunition, and 55-gallon oil drums of fuel lay in disarray along the beach. But, the most critical stage of the amphibious operation was over. The landing force was ashore, moving inland and momentum was on their side.

Puller's regiment on White Beach, the northern end of the beach, was an exception to movement forward. In fact, Puller's troops were in trouble. Five of the amtracs carrying the regiment's radios and operators took direct mortar hits on the reef. Consequently, Puller had no communication with adjacent units or higher headquarters. Minutes after the forward elements landed on White Beach, the beach was bombarded by precisely targeted and timed artillery and mortar fire. Directly in front of the troops was a 50-foot high coral ridge that did not appear on any maps. Japanese machine guns and snipers kept up a deadly crossfire from the caves and dug-in positions facing the ridge. Puller dispatched runners to ask for tank support for his advance.

Three Sherman tanks arrived to lead the advance, but their appearance created such an increase in artillery fire that they were forced to pull back. Marines with only khaki shirts for protection would have to lead the advance. Faced with either dying from artillery fire if they remained where they were, or dying from machine gun fire if they advanced, the marines advanced, only to fall into the six-foot anti-tank ditch at the base of the coral cliffs.

Nearly half of Puller's regiment were casualties. A hundred men from the engineer battalion, 30 from headquarters, a dozen cooks and bakers, and anyone else that could be spared were provided rifles and grenades and hurried into the front lines. Another serious problem facing Puller was a jagged coral projection rising 30 feet above the water edge named "The Point," This was a rocky mass of pinnacles, crevices and boulders, with pillboxes reinforced with steel and concrete. Near the top was a 75mm artillery piece that commanded every inch of Puller's beachhead. Puller recognized the danger of this projection while still aboard ship and asked that it be eliminated. He was told that ". . . the matter will be taken care of."[10] Yet, the 30-foot peak was untouched by naval gunfire or aerial bombardment.

If the regiment was to survive, The Point had to be seized. Many of Puller's men were little more than walking wounded, bandaged, bloodied and mutilated. Marines groaned and writhed in agony, fearing the next artillery round from the 75mm gun on The Point. As often happened during the war, one of those expendable Second Lieutenants, William Willis stepped up to silence the fire coming from The Point. Williams led what was left of his platoon plus some non-combatant reinforcements in a dash around the base of The Point and began to destroy steel-and-concrete positions with head-on grenade attacks. Locating the 75mm gun position that caused so many casualties, Willis dropped a smoke canister into the bunker aperture. The resultant smoke concealed the approach of a marine that took careful aim with his grenade launcher. His grenade went directly into the barrel of the artillery piece, where it exploded and destroyed the weapon. The resultant explosion triggered a large explosion of artillery shells inside the bunker.[11] Screaming Japanese, some with clothes on fire, ran from the bunker and were killed by waiting marines.[12]

While Willis's platoon was seizing The Point, Nakagawa discovered the gap in Puller's lines caused by the platoon's absence. He sent several hundred troops to exploit the gap and cut off Willis from the rest of the regiment. Captain George P. Hunt, Company K commander, was down to 18 men, but managed to beat off the Japanese attacks during the day and throughout the night. Hunt's men, exhausted, low on ammunition and short on water, somehow held their position. After 30 hours, a tank-led reinforcement arrived and eliminated the remaining Japanese.

On D+3, Hunt received a message from his battalion commander to take his remaining men into battalion reserve for a well-deserved rest. As Hunt prepared to leave, he took a last look at his defensive position. Later, he described what he saw.

> Along the shore Jap dead washed in with the tide and bled on the sand. In the countless gullies and basins, the Jap dead lay four deep, and on the level stretches they were scattered in one layer. . . sprawled in ghastly attitudes with their faces frozen and lips curled in apish grins.

> Many were huddled with their arms around each other as though they had futilely tried to protect themselves from our fire . . . horribly mutilated, riddled by bullets and torn by shrapnel . . . Seeing this, I could think of no more scathing and ironic symbol of their disastrous efforts to drive us from The Point. . . On the beach, in the woods, and on the coral rocks, we counted over 500 of them . . . dead.[13]

Hunt's company paid a terrible price for their valor on Peleliu. Of the 235 marines that made it to the beach, only 78 remained alive, many of them wounded. Hunt later received the Navy Cross medal for his bravery. His men believed he deserved the Medal of Honor.

General Rupertus remained aboard USS DuPage, a converted troop ship. The assistant division commander, Brigadier Gen. Smith, was ashore by 11:30 A.M. to establish the division command post (CP) ashore. Smith would have been ashore earlier, but was forced to wait near the reef for 90 minutes before an amtrac became available. Smith sent a radio-wire team to lay wire and establish communications with Puller's CP. Once communications was established, Smith asked Puller about his situation. Puller responded that he was all right. Smith asked if he needed help. Puller said no. Smith asked about casualties. Puller said maybe 40 killed and wounded. In fact, Puller's regiment suffered 500 men killed and wounded on D-Day.

Japanese tanks knocked out by flamethrowers.

USMC

At 4:00 P.M., on D-Day, an observation plane reported Japanese tanks moving forward from areas near the airfield. At 4:50, a force of 500 men supported by tanks attacked portions of Harris's regiment. At this time, one of the marine battalions had reached the edge of the runway. As the Japanese approached the marine positions, marines opened fire with all their weapons. A few of the Japanese tanks penetrated the marine positions, but were quickly located and destroyed. Carrier-based aircraft dropped

500-pound bombs on the advancing tanks and U.S. Sherman tanks destroyed the remainder. The Japanese attack soon began to resemble a banzai charge without coordination or support. Nakagawa lost 19 tanks and 450 of his elite infantry. Major Gordon D. Gayle seized this opportunity to lead his battalion across the airfield and to seize the area all the way to the eastern shore of the island.

Few Americans knew of the battle, because only a few correspondents and photographers went ashore at Peleliu. Six did so on D-Day. By the end of the week, only five continued to report the news. They had been told by General Rupertus that the battle would be over in less than a week so most of the newsmen found ways to join MacArthur's invasion of fringe islands of the southern Philippines. They believed that is where the real action would be. Thus, Peleliu was a forgotten battle before the worst of the horrible struggle began. Private First Class (PFC) Braswell Dean was well aware of the struggle. Forty-five-years later he recalled "Death and destruction were everywhere."[14] Even after fighting the Battle for Okinawa, Dean said, "The first day on Peleliu was a nightmare that will remain with me forever."[15]

Every few minutes casualties arrived at the shell hole on the beach serving as the division casualty evacuation center. Navy Lieutenant Edward Hagan, a navy surgeon who landed with the third wave, did his best to patch up the wounded. Farther down in the crater, Lieutenant Frank Stewart, another navy surgeon, did the same. Chaplain John Malone, kneeling with bible in hand, brought comfort to many of the wounded.

The stream of wounded was endless. Teams of blood-splattered, exhausted corpsmen applied tourniquets, sprinkled sulfa powder on wounds, and gave shots of morphine to relieve the pain. There were no facilities for surgery ashore. The wounded were patched up quickly and evacuated to shipboard hospitals with modern operating rooms. Getting the wounded to the ships was a problem due to the few operational amtracs. Some men went mad among the brutality, savagery, and mind-boggling horror on the beach. One navy surgeon was seen to stand upright on the beach and, while staring into space, slowly raise a pistol to his head. He was stopped, moved to a hospital ship and later recovered. Even men who had been exposed many times to the grisly sights and stench of the dead and dying sobbed with the agony of the situation.

On D+1, a penetration of 700 yards had been made by Harris's regiment to the eastern shore. The shallowest penetration was with Puller's regiment, which was still on the beach. D-Day cost the division 1,298 marines killed and wounded. Puller's regiment accounted for nearly half of this number.

By noon on D+1, the temperature reached 110 degrees. Water was in short supply and troops began to collapse. Someone in the planning phase of the operation decided to substitute 55-gallon drums of water for bulkier water trailers. The plan had merit, since several water drums could go ashore with each amtrac and then be rolled where they were needed. Tragically, the drums had not been properly cleaned and still contained some petroleum. The marines that consumed the water quickly doubled over with stomach cramps, began to cough violently, and to vomit. Diarrhea quickly followed. Hundreds of troops were put out of action by the contaminated water and some had to be evacuated. It would be D+5 before engineers drilled fresh water wells on Peleliu.

Once General Rupertus was established ashore, he quickly put pressure on Colonel Puller to move forward and seize his objectives. "Can't they move any faster?" he shouted in the phone to Puller. When told of the Japanese defense and his own casualties, Rupertus responded, ". . . Lewis, You've gotta kick ass to get results. You know that . . ." [17]

Puller was indeed "kicking ass," but colonels and generals were not about to change the situation facing Puller's men. At 8:00 A.M., one of his depleted battalions advanced in units no larger than a fire team (four men) against the dug-in Japanese. A tank led the way. They were met by the same hail of machine guns, rifles, grenades, and point blank 37mm mountain artillery fire from concealed positions that had stopped them previously. The tank was destroyed immediately. Not a yard of terrain was gained without hand-to-hand combat.

The taller marines clashed with the shorter Japanese in no-holds-barred combat, using rifles as clubs, bayonets, knives, rocks, fists, knees and thumbs. By dark, 200 marines had made it to the top of the ridge. The crest was only 20 yards wide, and it was impossible to dig defensive positions in the coral. Another Japanese position was in full view 500 feet away. Despite mortar fire throughout the evening, the position was held. By doing so, the marines denied Nakagawa direct observation of the beachhead and the airfield. Their control of the position also forced Nakagawa to move his CP further north, reducing communication with his units.

Japanese concrete machine-gun position on Peleliu.

USMC

Puller's second battalion was stopped by intense fire from a large concrete blockhouse with four-foot thick walls. The blockhouse sheltered a company of Japanese infantry and was the hub for a cluster of 12 pillboxes connected by tunnels. USS *Mississippi* responded to a request for naval gunfire and disintegrated the blockhouse. The support was much appreciated, but the marines thought the target should have been destroyed before the landing, not after they suffered 35 casualties assaulting the fortification. The tunnel and pillboxes were also destroyed by naval gunfire and artillery fire, allowing the battalion to evacuate its dead and wounded and focus on the next objective.

Another sheer coral cliff containing caves with more machine guns, rifles and grenades faced the troops. Only a frontal attack could be mounted. As marines cleared a cave of Japanese, they sealed its entrance with explosives. Otherwise Japanese riflemen would travel through the connecting tunnels and reappear at the cave entrance. By evening, marines destroyed 35 fortified

271

caves, none of which were depicted on their maps. The cost of success was heavy. Another 250 marines were killed or wounded.

Lieutenant Col. Ray Davis led the marines against the blockhouse. Davis later earned the Medal of Honor in Korea and retired as a Lieutenant Gen. He described D+1 on Peleliu as "the most difficult assignment I have ever seen."[18] Puller's third battalion was able to advance 700 yards against light resistance. Puller's regiment had 1,000 men dead or wounded. That equates to the loss of one-third of the regiment. The Japanese were suffering terrible losses also, but probably not as heavy as Puller's regiment.

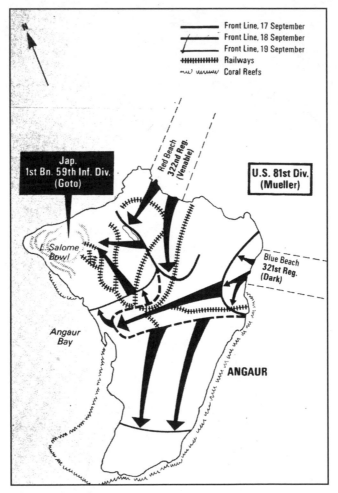

The assault on Angaur.

September 17, D+2, was D-Day for the Army's 81st Infantry Division scheduled to seize the island of Anguar. Anguar was half the size of Peleliu (2,000 acres) and unlike Peleliu was relatively flat with no surrounding reefs. There were excellent landing beaches on all sides of Anguar. It would be an excellent place for the soldiers to get their first taste of combat.

Major General Paul A. Mueller was the commanding general. He sent two regiments (called regimental combat teams) by the army, to land at two beaches on the northeast sector of the island. Intelligence reported strong Japanese defenses at the landing beach on the southeast side of the island.

Major Ushio Goto commanded the island's 1,500-man defense force. He had only enough equipment and manpower to defend against a landing on one beach. He chose to defend the southeastern beach (code-named Green), but his fortifications were discovered by reconnaissance aircraft and Mueller was able to land at beaches that were undefended.

A naval task force bombarded the island defenses for 30 minutes and carrier-based aircraft did the same. The first amtracs landed at 8:35 and met only scattered enemy fire. Within 30 minutes, landing ships began unloading tanks, artillery, trucks, and bulldozers. The soldiers moved off the beach and into the jungle foliage in large groups, making excellent targets for Goto's mortars. The soldiers did as they were trained, they fell back a sufficient distance and called in artillery and tank support. When the Japanese positions had been destroyed or neutralized, they moved forward again, this time in smaller groups.

By the end of D-Day, both regiments had moved forward 600 yards but in the process, they created a 1,000-yard gap between regiments. Goto was quick to recognize and exploit the gap. Infiltrators moved into the gap and throughout the night inflicted casualties upon both regiments. At first light, 30 carrier aircraft arrived to attack the Japanese in the gap, and when they departed army artillery took the Japanese under attack. Sherman tanks finished the fighting and the soldiers were able to continue the advance.

Fighting was strongest on Green Beach, where Goto concentrated his fortifications. By the end of D+2, the island had been split in half by the invaders, and by D+4, Gen. Mueller signaled that the island was secure. One regiment was left to "mop up" the stragglers, one regiment was sent to join the attack on Ulithi, and one regiment was held as a reserve for Peleliu. The battle proved to be an excellent baptism of fire for the two regiments. The 81st suffered 260 men killed and 1,304 wounded. With the exception of 59 men that surrendered, Goto and his 1,500-man force were all killed.

As D+3 dawned on Peleliu, it had became obvious that the landscape was as much of an obstacle to the marine advance as was the enemy. The situation promoted long and deadly guerrilla warfare, the likes of which the marines had not encountered during the entire war.

Before the end of D+3, Harris's regiment eliminated Japanese from the area surrounding the airfield, and men from two naval construction battalions (MCB-Seabees) were ashore and working to restore the airfield. Hannekin's regiment removed mines from the approach to Ngarmoked Island, and killed the Japanese defenders. What remained to be captured was the entire northern two-thirds of the island, the portion composed of steep coral cliffs and rocky saw-toothed ridges.

When the Seventh and Fifth Marines turned north to clear the island of its defenders, they came up against the same terrain and defensive network that had stopped the First Marines. Forward movement was minimal and casualties heavy. Division artillery learned to move their heavy weapons to the front lines and deliver fire directly into the enemy fortifications and caves. The various ridges were given names by the marines such as Bloody Nose Ridge, Five Sisters, and Five Brothers. But, as Sergeant Lisle Shoemaker, a mortar man with the First Marines, explained, "There was no single Bloody Nose Ridge or Five Sisters and Five Brothers." The names were used to identify specific chunks of coral cliffs and jagged outcroppings that were repeated throughout the length of the island.

All three regimental commanders needed reinforcements and fire support if they were to move forward. Fire support was available but no reinforcements were forthcoming. Puller's regiment now had 1,236 confirmed casualties. This was as many casualties as the entire division recorded during the 123-day battle for Guadalcanal.

Each day the three regimental commanders obeyed orders from division to "hurry up" and keep moving forward. Each day, progress was minimal and casualties soared. Heroism was commonplace. Numerous officers and troops received Medals of Honor and the Navy Cross Medal. Most were awarded posthumously. By D+4, Peleliu was a very crowded place. Nearly 45,000 men, Japanese and American, were on the island. Fewer than 10,000 were marine combat troops. The remainder were support troops bringing in supplies across the beach, 400 Seabees constructing the airfields, engineer and medical units, grave registration personnel, and, of course, Nakagawa's defenders.

Progress was being made elsewhere on the island. By D+5, the engineer units cleared large sections of the junk and debris on the beach. Five clearly marked medical evacuation stations were established and navy frogmen blasted several channels through the coral reef, allowing transport ships to proceed directly to the beach with equipment, ammunition and supplies. Not far from the beach, a graveyard was established with crosses bearing the man's name or, in many cases, simply the word, "unknown."

General Rupertus, right, maintains a stoic attitude for General Smith in the tank trap CP as marines complete mop-up of an airstrip a hundred yards behind them.

USMC

By early afternoon, Seabees had repaired a Japanese bunker, which General Rupertus and his staff occupied. Rupertus told his assistant commander, General Smith, to remain in his shell hole that he established on D-Day. "I'll let you know when I need you," Rupertus told Smith.[19] For the first time, some light observation aircraft arrived at the recently secured airfield. Colonel Harris was one of the first to fly over the terrain he was expected to seize. "I was appalled at the sight of those ridges from the air," he recalled. "There were sheer coral walls with caves everywhere, box canyons, crevices, rock-strewn cliffs, all defended by the well-hidden enemy."[20] Harris described the scene to Rupertus and his staff, suggesting that they should see the terrain from the air. They just smiled and said they had maps.

Shortly before noon on D+6, General Roy Geiger, III Marine Amphibious Corps (III MAC) commander, arrived at Puller's CP. "Let's talk privately," Geiger said. The two men moved away and the exchange was heated and brief. Geiger then hailed a passing amtrac and received a ride to division headquarters, where he asked to see the casualty reports. With Rupertus and his staff standing by silently, Geiger saw that his concerns were justified. The First Marine Regiment no longer existed as a combat regiment. Since D-Day, the regiment had lost 1,672 men killed and wounded. These were the heaviest losses ever suffered by a regiment in Marine Corps history.

Geiger wanted Rupertus to relieve Puller's regiment with an army regimental combat team from the 81st Division. Rupertus said no. He did not want an army regiment. Geiger was losing patience, but he listened to Rupertus's obstinate, nonsensical arguments for ten minutes before Lieutenant Col. Lewis Fields, Rupertus staff personnel officer (G-1) spoke up. Fields turned to Geiger and said, "we should bring in the army." Geiger said to Rupertus, "I feel the same way, and we should act immediately."[21] Geiger went further to direct Rupertus to evacuate all of the regiment's survivors to the camp at Pavuvu.

Elements of the army's 321st regimental combat team (RCT) began arriving on Peleliu on D+7 and relieved the First Marines the next day. Senior marines, such as Rupertus understood the differences in tactics, training, discipline, and combat philosophy employed by the army. Such differences did not always work well with marines on the flanks and made control difficult. The first thing that Colonel Robert Dark, the RCT commander did was to move Puller's CP 1,000 yards further back from the front lines.

No purpose will be gained by delving into specifics and examples of these service differences on Peleliu. Suffice it to say that the army moved forward much slower and only after lengthy naval gunfire and artillery bombardment of their objectives. If they met heavy enemy fire after the bombardment, they would fall back, leaving their flanks exposed, and call in more support. Marine units were forced to plug the gaps made by the withdrawal of the soldiers. Rupertus became furious over these frequent problems and told Geiger "That's why I didn't want the army involved in the first place"[22]

By D+12, 4,000 feet of runway was operational and F4U Corsairs and F6F Hellcat aircraft began to arrive to provide close air support to the troops on the ground. The pilots immediately began to attack targets, some as close as 1,000 yards from the airfield. F4U's dropped 1000-pound bombs on enemy positions fifteen seconds after getting airborne and before they had time to raise their landing gear. Their efforts ended Nakagawa's artillery fire on the airfield. On D+15, 25 tons of bombs were dropped on positions facing the marines and soldiers. Little damage was done to the Japanese pocket of resistance. On April 21, 1947, almost three years later, 27 Japanese soldiers walked down from the pocket to surrender. When soldiers examined the cave that the Japanese had occupied for three years, they found it to be 100-feet below a solid cover of coral. It was well stocked with rations, medical supplies and had fresh running water. Small wonder that naval gunfire and air-delivered bombs failed to crack many of the defenses.

September 28, D+13, saw Peleliu-based aircraft fly 50 sorties in support of troops on the ground. Seabees and engineers were erecting Quonset huts to house, and mess halls to feed, the non-combatants. Troops fortunate enough to watch movies complained about the noise from exploding artillery and mortar shells not far to the north where savage fighting continued. Twin-engine "Commando" cargo planes began to evacuate the wounded directly to hospitals on Guam. A day later, an amphibious assault was conducted against Japanese on the island of Ngesebus, 700 yards north of Peleliu. The 500 Japanese defending the island were killed, except for 29 that surrendered, at a cost of 48 marines from the Fifth regiment.

A 155-mm "Long Tom" artillery piece was brought to the front lines on the morning of October 1, and began to fire directly into caves and reinforced bunkers less than 300 yards away. These were the targets that bombs and shells from ships, artillery and aircraft had been unable to destroy. The range was so short that the crew had to take protection from the exploding shrapnel of their own shells.

One target after another was destroyed, with one round igniting an ammunition cache inside a major cave which blew through the entire tunnel complex. Japanese tried to crawl from the cave entrances and were killed by riflemen. The last Japanese stronghold on northern Peleliu had been destroyed. By October 5, D+20, the First Marine division had lost 5,044 men, with 356 missing in action. Japanese casualties were estimated as 9,076 dead and 140 prisoners, mostly Korean and Okinawan laborers.

Action now shifted to the center of the island where Nakagawa and his remaining troops held out in a 900-yard by 400-yard pocket of caves and fortifications in the coral hills. This pocket proved to be the worst mass of rocky ridges, decayed coral rubble, crags, crevices, 200 foot sheer cliffs, and barren saw-toothed ridges on the island. Nakagawa knew every inch of his defensive area and had chosen it well. Not only was his fortress considered to be impregnable, he still had his most experienced troops and officers to conduct his last stand. He would dictate the terms of this final battle.

Puller's men had tried to advance against this pocket since D+2. More than one marine earned the Medal of Honor for bravery attacking the pocket. The remains of more than a dozen marines that could not be recovered littered the ridges. Attempts to recover the bodies had proved too costly. Colonel Hanneken's Seventh Marines were all that were available to lead the assault that would end the battle for Peleliu. As they soon found out, the task was too much for a battered half-strength regiment.

As the assault commenced, a typhoon with winds of hurricane force made its way across Peleliu. Rain cooled the temperature to a bearable 80 degrees, but, 30-foot waves along the shoreline drove several transport ships ashore and isolated the landing forces from their supplies. There were C-rations for only four days ashore, so meals were reduced to two soggy servings per day. As soon as the storm passed, 75 transport aircraft from Guam began landing with all types of supplies. The battle continued.

Baldy Ridge, a steep-sloped, 200-foot coral wall was the first objective. Forty-eight men of L Company moved out to assault Knob Three, a 100-foot high peak looking down on Baldy Ridge. Three hours and fifteen-minutes later, a runner reached the battalion CP to report that only 11 men remained of the 48 who mounted the attack. That night, Japanese infiltrated the remains of K and L companies.

They slipped into the marine lines without a sound and fired rifles, pistols, and threw grenades toward the startled, but alert marines. Within seconds, the fighting became hand-to-hand. Two marines lugged a machine gun to a point where they could take the continuing Japanese reinforcement under fire. In the morning they counted 52 Japanese dead. Eleven marines died in the all night battle. Three marines earned our nation's highest award for bravery during the battle. All were awarded posthumously. They were the last of eight marines to receive the medal for heroism on Peleliu.

The battle for Baldy Ridge was the last fight for the Seventh Marines. Like Puller's regiment, they were shot to pieces. There were not enough men left to continue the fight. General Geiger had been warning Rupertus for several days that he needed to relieve the Seventh Marines. Rupertus did so on D+21, after reading the casualty reports. Of the 3,217 men who landed on D-Day, 1,486 (46-percent) were casualties. The Seventh Marines were headed back to Pavuvu.

The departure of the Seventh Marines left only the Fifth Marines and the army's 321st RCT to continue the fight. Harris's marines began the assault on Baldy with heavy artillery bombardment supported by three Sherman tanks that had been able to approach the objective by bulldozers carving approaches through narrow coral ravines. In 72 hours, the marines seized Baldy Ridge with less than two-dozen casualties.

The next two days were much more difficult as the marines could not advance to within 100 yards of the ridge called the Five Brothers. Harris used howitzers, tanks, and flame throwing amtracs to support his advance, but had to pull back. General Rupertus was on the phone several times a day, prodding and ordering Harris to do the impossible. General Rupertus's concern was obvious. He wanted the First Marine Division to secure Peleliu, not the army regimental combat team.

Most of Nakagawa's troops had lived underground since D-Day. They were always tired, hungry, and thirsty. Their nerves were frayed from the constant explosives delivered upon their shelters. They had no way to dispose of their dead, and the smoke from incoming and their own artillery made breathing difficult. "I still hate the little yellow bastards, but they were damned good fighters,"[23] remembered 18-year-old Herbert Mizner of Chicago. Mizner was a flame-thrower operator and counted 52 Japanese bodies in the incinerated tunnel near Five Brothers.

Nakagawa knew the end was near and gave orders for each man to fight to the death and kill every possible American. He long ago lost radio communications with his remaining troops and was forced to move from position to position throughout each evening. He still retained communications with his higher headquarters.

Fighting continued on D+22 as the marines continued their drive against the pocket. They chipped away at the enemy around Baldy Ridge, China Wall, and the Five Brothers. A few more enemy positions were overrun each day, but like the other two regiments, they had run out of steam. Geiger urged fruitlessly for Rupertus to relieve the marines and let the fully manned, tank-supported, fresh army RCTs finish the job. Rupertus absolutely refused. Geiger realized there were only two ways to accomplish what needed to be done.

The first was to relieve Rupertus, which would end his career. The second was to order him to make the change, which would effectively prevent him from a future command. Geiger could be tough, but he hated to do such a thing at the very end of the campaign.

Geiger's dilemma was resolved on D+ 27, when a dispatch arrived from Admiral Nimitz, declaring the assault phase of the invasion finished, and directing relief of the First Marine Division by the Army's 81st Division. Two days later, Colonel Dark's soldiers relieved the marines in front of Baldy Ridge. The Fifth Marines had lost 1,309 marines, 42 percent of the regiment's strength when the battle began. The 321st RCT fought for another five weeks before Colonel Nakagawa was willing to concede.

Seventy-two days after the marines came ashore at Peleliu, Colonel Nakagawa notified his superiors that "All is over on Peleliu."[24] He burned the regimental colors, and with Major Gen.

Kenijiro Murai, committed sepuku (ritual suicide). Nakagawa had done his job well. The U.S. army and marines respected the courage, tenacity, and willingness to die on the part of the Japanese soldiers. Prime Minister Hideki Tojo posthumously promoted both men to Lieutenant General.

U.S. tanks and infantry move into the Horseshoe on Peleliu and deprive the Japanese of their only fresh water supply.

USMC

Peleliu was never used to support projection of the war to Japan. It became an emergency gas station and motel for a few aircraft and aircrews. By 1990, the reef-fringed backwater atoll supported 500 people living in small shacks built from metal siding salvaged from old Quonset huts.

With the benefit of hindsight, it seems to me that there were two terrible mistakes made on Peleliu. The first is the number of casualties (6,336) suffered by the First Marine Division. This number is three times the casualties that are recognized as reason for relieving the unit. Blame this on General Rupertus. The second is that the battle should never have taken place. Blame this on Admiral Chester Nimitz.

Once a year a Japanese cruise ship anchors at a pier at Ngarmoked Island. Widows and families of Colonel Nakagawa's troops make the trip to honor their dead at services held in a small Shinto shrine at the base of Bloody Nose Ridge.[25] Few Americans go to Peleliu, but through the initiative of several members of the division, a memorial was erected on a cliff at the southern end of Bloody Nose Ridge in October 1984. The memorial's simplicity contrasts with the horror of the battle and the bravery of the men that fought there.[26]

In Memory Of The Marines
Who Gave Their Lives In the Seizure
Of Peleliu and Ngesebus Island
From the Japanese During The
Period 15th September Through
15th October 1944

18

WILLIAM F. "BULL" HALSEY JR.

William F. Halsey Jr. had many nicknames during his 45 years of naval service but "Bull" probably fit him the best. Halsey's barrel chest, James Cagney (hands-on-hips) stance, and huge eyebrows typified a cross between a bull in a china shop and an old "China-hand, sea-dog." His fierce scowl did nothing to ameliorate the nickname.

Admiral William F. "Bull" Halsey.

US Navy

"Bull" Halsey was no spring chicken when Japan attacked Pearl Harbor on December 7, 1941. He was born on October 30, 1882 and graduated from the Naval Academy in 1904. He attended Annapolis at the same time that Douglas MacArthur attended West Point, graduating forty-third out of a class of sixty-two. At age 59, Halsey had the training, operational experience, and motivation to lead the forces in the Pacific in the war against Japan. He would get the chance to start on November 28, 1941.

William was the only son of William F. Halsey Sr., another career navy officer. Halsey the senior received an appointment to the Naval Academy and graduated in 1873. During the summer of 1891, William Sr. was ordered to the Naval Academy as an instructor. The family was provided quarters on the base and attended local schools. Willie, as William Jr. was called, displayed many of the traits that would follow him throughout his career. He shot out streetlights with his slingshot, was hit in the head with a baseball bat, the wound requiring stitches, and was knocked unconscious by a fall broken only by his head.

In 1894, he contracted Bright's disease and was put in bed on a diet of bread and milk for six months. Willie recovered from the disease, but not his dislike for milk. At age 15, he wrote to President McKinley requesting an appointment to the Naval Academy. His letter was not answered. The Halsey family also tried various means to obtain an appointment to the academy without success. Through friends with political connections, Anne, Willie's mother, was able to obtain a personal appointment with President McKinley. Mrs. Halsey explained why her son deserved such an appointment, then added, "I have been praying, I have been praying very sincerely." "Madam," President McKinley replied, "your prayers have been answered."[1]

Halsey accumulated more than his share of demerits at the academy, mostly for smoking, being late for formation, and talking in ranks. During one of his summer cruises, he returned with a fouled anchor and the letters USNA tattooed on his shoulder. Willie passed all his courses, and in his senior year, earned the Thompson Trophy Cup as the midshipman that did the most to promote athletics at the academy. His exuberance at graduating was diminished somewhat by the academy's Chief Master-At-Arms wishing him all the luck in the world, but adding, "you'll never be as good a naval officer as your father."[2] The senior Halsey retired in 1907 in the grade of captain, and died in June 1920.

Bull met Fanny Grandy in Norfolk in the fall of 1905. Fanny was a blonde, blue-eyed, southern belle of good breeding with a family heritage closely aligned with the confederacy. Bull was a pugnacious, outspoken, northerner whose great-grandfather, grandfather and father were seamen without the benefit of "finishing schools." In December 1909, the two opposites were married. Fanny was a good service wife, but one must wonder if her heart was in the job. When asked to describe her years as a navy wife, she replied without hesitation that it was "A series of buying and abandoning garbage cans all over the world."[3] In 1937, while the Halsey's were at Pensacola, Florida, Fanny began to experience spells of depression and character disorder. The problem, coupled with long separations due to World War II, changed their lives forever.

Halsey began his navy career with the battleship USS *Missouri* on the East Coast. The 1904 battleship displaced 12,500 tons, mounted eight-and 14-inch guns, and had a top speed of 18 knots. The modern version of *Missouri* that Halsey ended his career aboard displaced 45,000 tons, mounted 16-inch guns, and could make 32.5 knots. After a brief stint aboard the USS *Don Juan De Austria,* Halsey was ordered aboard USS *Kansas* where he acted as provost marshall during the ship's world cruise. The cruise was part of Roosevelt's Great White Fleet that included 16 battleships.[4] The Fleet departed Norfolk on December 16, 1907, and returned on February 22, 1909.

From 1912 to 1921, Halsey commanded numerous destroyers and destroyer divisions. Following his command of USS *Wyoming* he was selected for the rank of captain in 1926 and was ordered to the Naval Academy as commanding officer. Bull served as officer-in-charge of midshipmen and the sailors who handled the various academy boats. In the spring of 1927, Halsey assumed responsibility for the academy's first aviation detail, and promptly requested aviation training at Pensacola, Florida. He failed the eye exam.

In June 1930, he attended the Naval War College at Newport, Rhode Island. During his year at the war college, the students studied War Plan Orange, the plan for defense of the Philippines should it be attacked by Japan. MacArthur would later shelve War Plan Orange, announcing that he had sufficient forces to defeat a Japanese attack on the beaches of the Philippines.

Following his graduation from the Naval War College, Halsey was selected to attend the Army War College in Washington, D.C. Prior to graduation, Halsey was offered the opportunity to command the carrier USS *Saratoga* if he would complete the aviation officer's course at Pensacola, Florida. Halsey, 51 years old and a grandfather, did not flinch from the challenge. He left Fanny and their daughter in Rhode Island and reported for training on July 1, 1934.

Halsey made his share of mistakes during training and possibly due to his concentrated effort to succeed, his weight dropped from 200 pounds to 155. Fanny was called to minister to Bull, and by the time Halsey earned his observer wings, his weight was up to 175. In order to meet his deadline for assuming command of *Saratoga*, Halsey was forced to fly three flights a day for 28 days to complete the course. He assumed command of *Saratoga* at Long Beach shortly thereafter. In 1936, he assumed command of the Naval Air Station at Pensacola, Florida.

Halsey retook the instrument flying course while commanding the air station. He was promoted to rear admiral in March 1938, and reassigned to command Carrier Division Two, consisting of the two new carriers, *Yorktown* and *Enterprise*.

The carrier division, accompanied by four destroyers conducted spring maneuvers in the Caribbean under the critical eye of Vice Adm. Ernest King, Commander, Aircraft, Battle Force, and the future chief of naval operations. Halsey distinguished himself by disposing of simulated enemy cruisers with his aircraft rather than using heavy surface ships. King held Halsey in high regard. Halsey was selected to command Aircraft, Battle Force on June 13, 1940. He also commanded Carrier Division Two and was promoted to vice admiral. Halsey now commanded all carriers and carrier air groups in the U.S. Fleet.

To the surprise of the operational fleet commanders, the chief of naval operations, Admiral Harold Stark, informed Admiral James O. Richardson, commander-in-chief U.S., (soon to become CINCPAC), that the fleet would be based at Pearl Harbor indefinitely. Pearl Harbor basing did not set well with Richardson. He questioned Stark several times about the decision and went over Stark's head to complain and pressure the administration to move the fleet back to the West Coast.

On February 1, 1941, President Roosevelt relieved Richardson and replaced him with Rear Adm. Husband Kimmell. On the same date, the navy established the Atlantic Fleet (CINCLANT) under command of Admiral King, and the Pacific Fleet (CINCPAC) under Admiral Kimmell. Halsey continued as commander, Aircraft, Battle Force, but was informally known as commander, Carriers, Pacific.

For Bull Halsey, the war began on November 28, 1941, the day he was tasked to ferry Marine Attack Squadron-211 (VMA-211) from Hawaii to Wake Island. Shortly after Task Force 8 with USS *Enterprise* as Halsey's flagship left Pearl Harbor, Halsey issued Battle Order Number One:

U.S. S. Enterprise
At Sea
November 28, 1941

BATTLE ORDER NUMBER ONE
1. The Enterprise is now operating under war conditions.
2. At any time, day or night, we must be ready for instant action.
3. Hostile submarines may be encountered.
4. The importance of every officer and man being specially alert and vigilant while on watch at his battle station must be fully realized by all hands.
5. The failure of one man to carry out his assigned task promptly, particularly the lookouts, those manning the batteries, and all those on watch on deck, might result in great loss of life and even loss of the ship.
6. The Captain is confident that all hands will prove equal to any emergency that may develop.
7. It is part of the tradition of our Navy that, when put to the test, all hands keep cool, keep their heads, and FIGHT.
8. Steady nerves and stout hearts are needed now.

G.D. Murrry,
Captain, U. S. Navy
Commanding

Approved
W. F. Halsey
Vice Admiral, U.S. Navy
Commander Aircraft, Battle Force[5]

Commander William Buracker, Halsey's operations officer gasped when he read the message and asked Halsey if he realized the message meant war. When Halsey answered "yes," Buracker continued "Goddammit, Admiral, you can't start a private war of your own. Who's going to take the responsibility?" "I'll take it," responded Halsey. "If anything gets in my way, we'll shoot first and ask questions afterward." [6]

Task Force 8's trip to Wake Island to deliver the marine squadron was routine, but not so the return trip. *Enterprise* ran into stormy seas and high winds and was forced to reduce speed and delay refueling of the destroyers. Halsey revised his arrival time at Pearl Harbor from Saturday, December 6, to noon, December 7. Unknown to the Americans, Admiral Nagumo's six carriers were on a parallel course to Halsey, several hundred miles north.

Early on December 7, *Enterprise* launched 18 scout bombers to search ahead of the carrier and then land at Ford Island. Four of the aircraft were shot down as they arrived over Pearl Harbor, three by Japanese aircraft. After searching unsuccessfully for the Japanese carriers, Halsey sent six of his fighters to land at Ford Island at the end of their patrol. Friendly fire shot down five of the aircraft and killed three of the pilots. Halsey and his task force spent the next day searching again without success and entered Pearl Harbor at sunset on December 8. They were greeted by the beached and shattered USS *Nevada,* burned out hangars, the superstructure of *California,* capsized *Oklahoma,* the scorched hull of *West Virginia*, and the burning *Arizona.* As *Enterprise* turned west around Ford Island, the upturned hull of USS *Utah* was revealed.

To this point, Halsey had been silent, reflecting upon what he saw. Now, he growled, "Before we're through with 'em, the Japanese language will be spoken only in hell."[7] In retrospect, it is a good thing Halsey did not find the Japanese. Nagumo's carrier aircraft vastly outnumbered Halsey's few aircraft on *Enterprise* and he may well have lost one of the three carriers assigned to the Pacific Fleet.[8]

At Pearl Harbor, Halsey found Kimmell and his staff hard at work though obviously tired. During his visit with Kimmell a report came in that Japanese gliders and paratroopers were landing at Kaneohe. No one seemed to see the ridiculous nature of the report except Halsey who burst out laughing. Kimmell turned on him and demanded to know, "What the hell are you laughing at?" Halsey explained that the report was one of the stupidest he had ever heard. "The Jap's can't possibly tow gliders here from their nearest base, and certainly they're not going to waste precious carrier decks on such nonsense." For the first time in the past two days, Kimmell stopped having his staff track down such rumors and smiled. "You're right," he said.

Enterprise was refueled and replenished by 5:00 A.M., and left with the remainder of the task force to track down Japanese submarines believed to be in Hawaiian waters. No submarine sightings were actually confirmed and Task Force 8 returned to Pearl Harbor on December 16.

The following day, Vice Adm. Kimmell, Halsey's good friend, was relieved of command by Vice Adm. William S. Pye. Pye would fill the position of CINCPAC until Admiral Chester W. Nimitz arrived to take command. Perhaps Pye is most remembered for his decision to abandon the reinforcement of Wake Island. Following a plan devised by Kimmell, the *Lexington* force left Pearl Harbor on December 14 to raid the airfield at Jaluit in the Marshall Islands, location of the bomber aircraft that were attacking Wake Island. The *Saratoga* force departed Pearl Harbor on December 16, carrying supplies, ammunition, equipment, and Marine Fighter Squadron-221 (VMF-221) with 18 F4F aircraft. Halsey, aboard *Enterprise,* left Pearl Harbor with Task Force 8 on December 20 to support *Lexington* and *Saratoga* forces as necessary.

Wake Island surrendered on December 22 and Pye terminated the relief efforts shortly thereafter. Rumor has it that Halsey swore for a full 30 minutes after being notified of the termination of the support effort. He also seriously considered disobeying the directive and proceeding to Wake to attack the Japanese. His staff convinced him not to do so. This would not be the last time that Halsey would be frustrated at his inability to close with the enemy.

The *Enterprise* Task Force returned to Pearl Harbor on December 31, to meet their new commander, Admiral Nimitz.

Halsey had known Nimitz since their academy days together and although they had not served together since, they respected one another. To say that they had contrasting styles would be an understatement. Nimitz was a southern gentleman, polished, urbane, and noted for his self-control. Halsey was rough, outspoken, impetuous and often acted by impulse and emotion. They both shared attributes of dedication, decisiveness, and loyalty to seniors and subordinates.

All dependents of Pacific Fleet personnel were returned to the mainland during the carrier's absence. Due to her poor health, Halsey's wife Fanny was flown to the states and then to Wilmington, Delaware where she moved in with her married daughter. Halsey expressed his appreciation for the consideration afforded his wife by saying that he was now free to pursue one job, "to get those yellow bastards."[9]

During a discussion of possible carrier raids against Japanese bases in the Gilbert and Marshall Islands, Nimitz's staff vehemently opposed his proposal. Nimitz, not being an aviator, was astonished at the degree of opposition to his plan. At the appropriate time, Halsey stood up and denounced the defeatism of the staff. He conceded that the plan had risks but reminded everyone that the war could not be pursued without risk. He not only supported the plan but offered to lead the attack himself. With this display of loyalty, Halsey earned Nimitz's lasting gratitude. Years later when Halsey was being roundly criticized for his decisions, Nimitz defended him by stating, "Bill Halsey came to my support and offered to lead the attack. I'll not be a party to any enterprise that can hurt the reputation of a man like that."[10]

At noon on January 10, 1942, Halsey took the war to Japan. Escorted by heavy cruisers *Chester, Northhampton, Salt Lake City,* seven destroyers, and an oiler, *Enterprise* task force headed towards Samoa, where the carrier *Yorktown* was due to unload West Coast marines to defend Samoa. The American battleships were too slow to accompany the force. Halsey did not want them around in case he might have to run from a superior force. Later in the day, Halsey learned that USS *Saratoga* had been heavily damaged by a Japanese torpedo and was limping back to Pearl Harbor. Loss of *Saratoga* left only *Lexington* to defend Hawaii.

The *Yorktown* force, commanded by Frank Jack Fletcher, arrived on January 23, and unloaded the marines and their equipment at Pago Pago on the 24th. Both task forces then proceeded towards the Gilbert Islands where planes from *Yorktown* raided Jailut, Mili, and Makin, while aircraft from *Enterprise* struck Taroa, Wotje, Roi Namur, and Kwajelein in the Marshalls. Halsey's cruiser division under command of Rear Adm. Raymond A. Spruance bombarded Wotje, and other surface ships fired upon Taroa and Maloelap.

Actual damage inflicted by the *Enterprise* Task Force was one transport and two smaller vessels sunk, eight other ships damaged, three Japanese planes shot down, and an ammunition dump destroyed. Four dive-bombers (SBD's) were lost to enemy aircraft, and eight sailors were killed and 11 wounded when cruiser *Chester* suffered a bomb hit. Fletcher's *Yorktown* force was hampered by bad weather and Fletcher's unwillingness to risk his ships, all of which returned unscratched. Halsey retired all his forces in the cover of a squall line at a steady 30 knots, earning the slogan, "Haul Ass with Halsey." Thanks to Admiral King, *Yorktown* remained with the Pacific Fleet at Pearl Harbor.

Despite the meager damage inflicted upon the enemy, the force was warmly greeted when it arrived at Pearl Harbor on February 5. It was America's first victory of the war and both Nimitz and Halsey were elated to have conducted the attack without greater casualties. Next on the list for Halsey was a raid on Wake Island scheduled for Friday, February 13. *Enterprise* was to sail as the flagship for Task Force 13. The combination of Friday and number 13 was too much for Halsey. He had the task force designation changed to 16, and arranged for a Saturday, February 14, departure. *Enterprise* aircraft bombed Wake while Spruance's cruisers shelled the island. Halsey's group damaged three seaplanes in the lagoon and sank two small patrol vessels at a cost of three aircraft, one of which was shot down by ground fire.

As Halsey prepared to depart the area he received a message from Nimitz asking if Halsey could also raid Marcus Island, 1,000 miles from Tokyo. Halsey refueled *Enterprise* and his two cruisers and made a high-speed dash to Marcus. Before dawn on March 4, Halsey launched 32 bombers and six fighters from 125 miles northeast of the island. The raid gained complete surprise, destroyed facilities and aircraft while losing only one dive-bomber. Task Force 16 rejoined her destroyers and oiler, and arrived at Pearl Harbor on March 10.

Halsey's next mission was a top-secret raid on Tokyo using army B-25s from carrier *Hornet*. The *Hornet* task group under Captain Marc A. Mitsher left San Francisco on April 2 for their rendezvous with Halsey (USS *Enterprise*) and Spruance's cruisers, *Northampton* and *Salt Lake*. The two forces merged on April 13, becoming Task Force 16 under Halsey's command.

On October 17, 1,000 miles from Japan, Halsey left his destroyers and oilers behind, and began a high-speed run with his carriers and cruisers to the launch point 500 miles from Tokyo. The force was detected 700 miles from land on the morning of the 18th. One hour later, the force was in the midst of a Japanese picket line of small boats. Halsey's force intercepted Japanese messages warning of their presence. Halsey could afford to wait no longer. With a "good luck and God bless you," Halsey ordered Lt. Colonel Jimmy Doolittle with his 16 bombers to launch at a distance of 625 miles from Tokyo.

The B-25s dropped their bombs on targets in the greater Tokyo area and flew on to what they expected would be friendly airfields in China. Due to the greater distance they had to fly, it was dark when they arrived in China, the ceiling was low with rain, and all the bombers were out of fuel. Whatever airfields existed, were not lighted. Most of the B-25 crews bailed out, but some crash-landed and one crew flew to Vladivostok, Russia, where the plane and crew were impounded and interned. Seventy-one of the 80 crewmen escaped or survived imprisonment by the Japanese.

Damage to the Japanese cities was minimal; the Tokyo Shinbun (newspaper) reported that it should be called the "do nothing" raid instead of the Doolittle raid.[11] But, the raid was a great psychological victory for the United States. Japan was shown that they could be bombed and that the emperor's life was in danger. The raid was also a personal insult to Admiral Isoroku Yamamoto, commander of Japan's combined fleet. Yamamoto pushed for and received approval from the navy staff to seize New Guinea, the Solomon Islands, and Midway Island in order to extend Japan's outer perimeter and prevent such attacks in the future.

Task Force 16 joined its destroyers and oilers, and arrived at Pearl Harbor on Saturday, April 25. There was no reception for the task force this time because the mission was top secret and had not been leaked to anyone. Even President Roosevelt, at a news conference, announced that the bombers had come from the mythical land of Shangri-La. Of course the Japanese found out where the planes came from once they began torturing the eight captured airmen. As with carrier *Yorktown*, *Hornet* remained with the fleet at Pearl Harbor.

Halsey looked forward to an extended period of rest for his force at Pearl Harbor. Nimitz gave him five days. The staff and troops were in far better shape than Halsey. He had lost weight, painful dermatitis had spread over his entire body, and he could not sleep. The oatmeal-water baths prescribed by the ship's doctor gave him little relief.

Commander Joseph Rochefort and his code breakers (commander Hawaii Combat Intelligence Unit) deciphered the Japanese Navy code (JN25) in early 1942, and advised Nimitz that Japan intended to seize the eastern end of Papua New Guinea and then conduct a major operation in the Pacific Ocean. Based upon this information, Nimitz made plans to defend Port Moresby, New Guinea, and began to look towards Midway Island as the next Japanese offensive in the Pacific. Halsey, eager for battle, concealed his infirmity from Nimitz and departed Pearl Harbor on April 30 with *Enterprise, Hornet,* three heavy cruisers, seven destroyers, and two oilers.

Admiral Fletcher's *Yorktown* force (Task Force 17) was already in the Coral Sea area and was ordered to replenish and then join Rear Admiral Aubrey Fitch's *Lexington* Force, plus one American cruiser, a destroyer, and three Australian cruisers.

The Battle of the Coral Sea did not wait for Halsey. On May 6, Japanese aircraft from carriers *Shokaku* and *Zuikaku* sank destroyer *Sims* and made a wreck of oiler *Neosho.* Fletcher's aircraft located and sank the light carrier *Shoho.* The major action took place on the morning of May 8, when both American and Japanese carrier aircraft located and attacked each other. American planes damaged *Shokaku* and destroyed most of *Zuikaku's* aircraft. Japanese planes hit *Yorktown* with a bomb that penetrated three decks and caused extensive damage to the ship. *Lexington* was hit by two torpedoes that ruptured fuel lines, allowed gasoline vapors to explode, and ignited uncontrollable fires. *Lexington* was abandoned and sunk by one of her escort destroyers. The Battle of the Coral Sea marked the first naval battle where the combatant vessels never saw one another.

Halsey, greatly disappointed at having missed the action, "hung around" the Coral Sea area for several days looking for carrier *Zuikaku* or other Japanese naval forces. On May 14, Halsey received orders from Nimitz not to "risk the two undamaged carriers." The message made Halsey "mad as hell."[12] The message was followed by another on May 16, when Nimitz directed Halsey to expedite his return to Hawaii. Task Force 16 departed at full speed and arrived at Pearl Harbor on May 26. Admiral Nimitz was shocked when he saw the wasted, hollow-eyed Halsey and ordered him to the hospital without delay. Halsey lost 20 pounds during his Coral

Sea trip, seldom being able to sleep due to his dermatitis.

Since Halsey was grounded, he recommended Ray Spruance, a non-aviator, as his replacement for Task force 16 for the Midway operation. Nimitz concurred. Halsey and Nimitz went to the hospital together where Halsey was put to bed. Halsey stated in his memoirs that "this was a sad occasion for me as it prevented my taking part in the Battle of Midway, where I would have been senior officer present. This was my greatest regret in the whole war."[13]

Halsey was sent to the mainland aboard the light cruiser *Detroit,* and from San Francisco to Richmond, Virginia, and placed in the care of Dr. Warren T. Vaughan, the foremost allergist in the U.S. He returned to Pearl Harbor for duty in September. Also arriving in September was Rear Adm. Raymond A. Spruance to take command of the four heavy cruisers of Task force 16.

Nimitz planned to reassign Halsey to command Task Force 16 as soon as *Enterprise* completed repairs necessitated by bomb damage at the Battle of the eastern Solomon's near Guadalcanal. USS *Saratoga* arrived at Pearl Harbor on September 21 needing repair for damage suffered a second time by a submarine-launched torpedo. Halsey accompanied Nimitz to the carrier's flight deck to present awards and was greeted by the crew with a resounding, "Welcome back," that brought tears to the Bull's eyes.

On October 14, Halsey, Spruance, and a few other officers flew from Honolulu to Johnston Island for an inspection of facilities and then to Canton Island. Upon arrival at Canton, Halsey was handed a dispatch from Vice Adm. Robert L. Ghormley, commander South Pacific. The message advised Halsey not to proceed to Guadalcanal because of the tactical situation there. Halsey responded that he would visit Guadalcanal as planned. At 2:00 A.M., Halsey received a message from Nimitz that directed him to proceed to Noumea via Fiji. Thoroughly frustrated, Halsey arrived at Noumea and was handed a sealed envelope with a message from Nimitz. The message read, "Immediately upon your arrival at Noumea, you will relieve Vice Adm. Robert L. Ghormley of the duties of Commander South Pacific and South Pacific Force."

Halsey responded to the news in his patented fashion, "Jesus Christ and General Jackson! This is the hottest potato they ever handed me." Halsey was truly astonished. He had no idea that he might be called upon to relieve his former football teammate and friend of more than 40 years. Halsey was also concerned because he had no experience in handling U.S. Army and New Zealand forces. He was not aware of the problems associated with the Battle for Guadalcanal that both Ghormley and MacArthur pronounced hopeless, and regretted being assigned to desk duty when there was a war on.

Halsey's relief of Ghormley brought great joy to the marines on Guadalcanal. Few marines knew Halsey personally, but they all had heard of his reputation as a fighter. Marines that were so weary they could not climb out of their foxholes were suddenly running around yelling like kids when they got the news. Finally, they had someone in charge that knew how to fight.

Shortly after relieving Ghormley, Halsey asked Major Gen. Archer Vandegrift, commander of the First Marine Division on Guadalcanal, to come to Noumea to update him on the situation. Vandegrift brought along Lieutenant Gen. Thomas Holcomb, commandant of the marine corps, who was visiting his marines on Guadalcanal. After listening to Vandegrift's description of the tenuous situation, Halsey asked, "Can you hold?" "Yes, I can hold," Vandegrift answered, "but I have to have more active support than I've been getting."[14]

Rear Adm. Kelly Turner, commander of the amphibious force, gave a grim recital stating that the navy was already giving all the support it could and were powerless to prevent the nightly Japanese ship bombardments of Guadalcanal and their reinforcement efforts. Although not recorded, it seems likely that Vandegrift may have repeated to Halsey what he told Admiral Nimitz a short time before, "That too many commanders have been far too leery about risking their ships."[15] Halsey was a fighter and here was a fight he was not going to back away from. "You go back there Vandegrift," Halsey replied." "I promise you everything I've got." One wonders if Halsey was aware that the Pacific Theater had only 15-percent of the Allied war resources. The other 85-percent went to the war in Europe.

Vandegrift had barely returned to Guadalcanal when Japanese soldiers launched a massive coordinated attack to capture the airfield. A Japanese carrier fleet was north of the island, waiting to send aircraft to operate from the captured airfield. It was time for Halsey to keep his pledge of support. Immediately he ordered carriers *Hornet* and *Enterprise* task forces to join as Task Force 61 under Admiral Thomas C. Kinkaid, and to oppose the Japanese Combined Fleet in what is now known as The Battle of the Santa Cruz Islands. American search planes located the Japanese force shortly after midnight on October 25, and again at 3:00 A.M. the next morning. Halsey, listening to the search plane reports and hearing nothing from Kinkaid, flashed the general message, "Attack-repeat-attack!" Kinkaid did not receive the search plane reports and had nothing to attack. It was morning before he launched aircraft to locate the Japanese fleet, which had already launched aircraft from three carriers against the Americans.

Hornet was put out of action early by five bombs and two torpedoes. Unable to launch aircraft to protect her, *Hornet* continued to suffer damage until she had to be abandoned. Two U.S. submarines fired 16 torpedoes and more than 400 rounds of shells into the hull but were unable to sink her. The Japanese Navy sank *Hornet* with only four of their long lance torpedoes.[16]

Enterprise was heavily damaged by three bomb hits, and a torpedo plane crashed into a destroyer that had to be scuttled. *South Dakota* and the cruiser *San Juan* were also damaged. The

Japanese Navy lost light carrier *Zuiho,* which was on fire with a 50-foot hole in her flight deck, took severe damage to heavy carrier *Shokaku,* and two bomb hits on the heavy cruiser *Chikuma.* This Battle of the Santa Cruz Islands was clearly a Japanese victory, but Japan lost twice as many aircraft as the Americans, and would suffer the consequences of such losses in the very near future.

This battle, like all Japanese offensives on Guadalcanal, was a combined air-ground-sea effort to overrun the Americans and seize the airfield. The marines, newly motivated by the navy support, held their positions. The Japanese ground attack fizzled out on October 26, with ten Japanese casualties for every American. The final result of the fighting had been too close to call for several days. Although they had been stopped, everyone expected the Japanese to try again.

On November 2, Admiral Tanaka's Tokyo Express landed 1,500 troops near Koli Point, east of the marines' positions. During the next eight days, 65 destroyer loads and two cruiser loads of Japanese troops were landed west of the marines. Coastwatchers reported large numbers of Japanese ships massing at Truk and Rabaul and in the Shortland Islands. This Japanese offensive could well have been the end of the American defense of Guadalcanal had not President Franklin Roosevelt intervened. His memorandum to the Joint Chiefs stated his desire, "to make sure that every possible weapon gets in to that area to hold Guadalcanal, and that having held it in this crisis, that munitions and planes and crews are on the way to take advantage of our success."

Halsey stripped his garrison forces and sent two convoys with 6,000 reinforcements, food, ammunition, and supplies to Guadalcanal. They arrived on November 11 and 12. Halsey, itching to get closer to the action, flew into Guadalcanal on November 8, spent the night there, and found out firsthand about the nightly shelling of Henderson field and the marine positions on Guadalcanal.

The American transports were bombed during the day while unloading and again at night, and had to depart with half their cargo still on board. Admiral's Callaghan and Scott escorted the two convoys out of Ironbottom Sound and returned with two heavy cruisers, three light cruisers, and eight destroyers to meet the Japanese force that included two battleships. The night battle resulted in the death of both Callaghan and Scott, and the loss of most of the American fleet. USS *Portland* and *San Francisco* were heavily damaged, USS *Atlanta* and five destroyers were sunk, and more than 700 sailors died when USS *Juneau* was sunk leaving the battle scene.

Halsey had placed his undergunned force in harms way and suffered great losses including the lives of his close friends, Callaghan and Scott. What he gained from his boldness was the sinking of battleship *Hiei* and two destroyers, and far more importantly, he saved the marines on Guadalcanal from another night of shelling and the landing of 13,500 Japanese replacements. The 11 troop transports were recalled back to the Shortlands to wait for a better opportunity to debark on Guadalcanal.

The Japanese retreat was only temporary. The next day a coastwatcher reported cruisers leaving the Shortlands headed for Guadalcanal. Halsey had no forces that could stop the Japanese fleet; consequently, two heavy cruisers bombarded Henderson Field and the marines the night of November 14. The next morning, search planes discovered the bombardment cruisers with their escort of cruisers and destroyers headed away from Guadalcanal and eleven large transports with destroyer escorts closing on Guadalcanal. The number of troops on the transports was estimated at 10-to-15 thousand.

Bombers from Henderson Field and the patched up *Enterprise* attacked the cruiser force first, sinking one and damaging three others. Then they turned their attention to the troop transports, sinking seven before nightfall. When Halsey heard the news, he exclaimed, "We've got the bastards licked." Archer Vandegrift knew better. A large bombardment force was reported heading south from Rabaul. The marines would have another night of heavy shelling.

The only forces available to oppose the Japanese were those of Admiral Willis A. "Ching" Lee, with *Washington, South Dakota,* and four destroyers. The night battle ended in less than 30 minutes. Japanese gunfire sank all four destroyers and badly damaged *South Dakota*. Only USS *Washington,* Lee's flagship remained to fight the Japanese fleet. In seven minutes, the battleship *Kirishima* was disabled with 50 hits from five-inch and 16-inch guns. *Kirishima* and a Japanese destroyer were scuttled, and the remaining force departed Ironbottom Sound.

On the following morning, the four surviving Japanese troop transports were set afire by Henderson Field aircraft and artillery. Although the troops had been unloaded from the four transports, their food, weapons, and supplies had not.

Halsey was most generous with his praise for the men who fought and died during the November battles. The night surface action of November 12 and 13, the air attacks on the transports on the 14th, and the night surface battle of November 14 and 15 are lumped together as the Battle of Guadalcanal. Halsey was promoted to full admiral on November 26, 1942. He promptly sent one of his three-star rank insignia to the widows of Admirals Scott and Callaghan, with the message that their husbands' bravery earned him his four stars.[17]

Halsey earned his reputation as a tough fighter and proved to be more than a match for the Japanese. He was very outspoken, but not all of his actions were favorable. His brashness probably reached a peak in January 1943, at a press conference in Auckland, New Zealand. When asked by reporters what Japan's next move would be, Halsey replied, "Japan's next move will be to retreat. They will not be able to stop going back."[18] Halsey was then asked if he predicted an Allied victory over the Japanese before the end of 1943. Halsey was at his best in this response, "That is right," he replied, "When we first started out against them I held that one of our men was equal to three Japanese. I have now increased this to twenty." "We have 363 days left to fulfill my prediction (to win the war before the end of 1943) and we are going to do it."[19]

Halsey, not one to clear his press releases in advance, astonished everyone, from the president on down. U.S. production chiefs feared that workers might quit their jobs and draft authorities were concerned that men might ignore their draft notices. Halsey was accused of everything from drunkenness to mental abberation.[20] While Halsey was predicting an end to the war in 1943, the Allied chiefs of staff were meeting with President Roosevelt and Prime Minister Churchill in Casablanca to devise plans for the war in 1944. They paid Halsey little heed.

Halsey went on to gain fame for his command of the 3rd U.S. Fleet, alternating with Admiral Spruance (5th U.S. Fleet). This arrangement permitted Halsey to take his staff ashore and plan for the next operation while Spruance and his staff were at sea conducting operations they had planned. When Halsey went to sea, Spruance and his staff went ashore. Halsey gained the appreciation of his sailors by ordering the hot and uncomfortable necktie removed from daily wear. He also made a point of visiting his sailors whenever possible and personally presenting awards.

As the Allies prepared to advance toward Japan by way of the Japanese stronghold of Rabaul, the forces came under the command of General Douglas MacArthur, commander Southwest Pacific Area. MacArthur had troops and aircraft, but few ships. MacArthur submitted a plan that left him as the overall commander, but gave operational control to Halsey. Pacific Fleet forces would remain under the control of Admiral Nimitz.

Halsey shared the navy's lack of esteem for MacArthur, and must have had grave misgivings about operating under MacArthur's "general directives." However, MacArthur, Halsey, Nimitz, and

Admiral King all shared a desire to "get on with the war" before Japan could further reinforce their gains in the Pacific. Halsey arranged a meeting with MacArthur in Brisbane, Australia, on April 15, 1943. MacArthur had never met the Bull and knew him only by reputation as a hard-fighting, outspoken admiral, ready to take the necessary risks to achieve victory.

"Five minutes after I reported, I felt like we were lifelong friends," Halsey reported. MacArthur, never overawed by anyone reported, "I liked him from the moment we met."[21] The meeting established a lasting friendship between the two that ensured a smooth coordinated advance to the Philippines.

Halsey's 3rd Fleet compiled an envious record in battle, but came out second best in a match with a Pacific typhoon in December 1944. Halsey, with Vice Adm. John McCain's carrier striking force, were supporting the invasion of the Japanese occupied island of Mindanao from December 14 to December 16. Halsey was aboard USS *New Jersey* and ordered McCain's Task Force 38 to rendezvous 300 miles east of Luzon on the morning of December 17 for refueling and replenishment.[22]

Nearly 200 ships would come together on the morning of December 17, for refueling in the path of a mighty typhoon. Task Force 38 had seven huge Essex-class carriers, six light Independence-class carriers, eight battleships, 13 cruisers, and 56 destroyers. The replenishment group had 27 oilers, seven ammunition ships, eight escort carriers, 14 destroyers, 25 destroyer escorts, and seven seagoing fleet tugs.

As replenishment efforts got underway, a refueling hose parted and a collision between a destroyer and oiler was narrowly averted. USS *New Jersey* was unable to refuel destroyers due to the heavy seas and aircraft that had been launched earlier were unable to land aboard their carriers. The pilots were told to bail out and told destroyers would pick them up. Crews worked frantically to tie down aircraft and all equipment on the carrier decks. Refueling was canceled until the following day.

Rather than head north away from the approaching typhoon, Admiral Halsey ordered a rendezvous the following morning 180 miles to the south. Unknown to Halsey or his staff, this put the fleet directly in the path of the typhoon. Several course changes dictated by barometric changes took place but always, the fleet remained in the path of the typhoon. By early morning on the 18th, some ships had to heave-to (reduce speed to steerage speed only). By 10:00 A.M., Halsey's ship captains had begun to depart the ship formation because they could not maintain position and several near misses occurred. By 11:49 A.M., when Halsey did release his ships from formation, he had already lost three of his destroyers. Conditions were near impossible to describe. One could not determine where the sea ended and the sky began. It was impossible to go on deck, due to the heavy rain and winds in excess of 100 knots. Visibility was about three feet.[23]

Green seas swept over the flight deck of *Hancock*, 57 feet above the waterline. Light carrier *Langley* reported rolls of 70 degrees. Cruiser *Miami*, sustained structural damage to her foredeck and hull. Planes broke loose from the carrier decks and hangar decks, smashing other planes and equipment. Loose aircraft started fires aboard the light carriers *Monterey, Cowpens,* and *Cape Esperance.* The escort carriers fared the worse. They wallowed helplessly, hammered continuously by enormous seas that hit them broadsides. Several of the escort carriers narrowly missed colliding with ships that were trying to head into the wind at right angles to the carriers. Most of the 146 aircraft lost during the typhoon were from the escort carriers.

Although the carriers had their problems, they were minimal compared to the problems of the long, narrow-hulled destroyers and destroyer escorts. USS *Alwyn* lay on her side for 20 minutes out of control during the tempest only to right herself and survive. USS *Dewey* lost one of her funnels overboard. The loss of the stack reduced Dewey's speed but reduced her wind resistance just enough to prevent her from capsizing, USS *Hickok* lost steering control, which would not have mattered much except for the need to maneuver to avoid collision with the carriers and larger ships. USS *Hull* went down in winds of 110 knots and rolls in excess of 70 degrees. Two hundred and nine of her crew went down with her.

USS *Monaghan* sank with even a larger loss of life, only six of her crewmen survived. USS *Spence*, a new destroyer, took a deep roll to starboard, and continued her roll to capsize. Only 24 of her crew were rescued. Other destroyers logged rolls of 72 degrees, two were completely de-masted by the storm.

By the evening of the 18th, the worst of the typhoon had passed and Halsey gave orders to search for survivors. There would be an investigation into the disaster and Admiral Nimitz issued a set of "lessons learned," which were provided to all ship commanders. Halsey was not found to be at fault because his errors were "errors of judgment committed under the stress of war operations."[24]

Six months later, June 5, 1945, the 3rd Fleet and Task Force 38 once again found themselves in the eye of a typhoon while refueling. This time there was ample warning of the storm's approach, but neither Halsey nor McCain took evasive action.[24] Six men were lost, four injured, heavy cruiser *Pittsburg* lost 104 feet of its bow, a destroyer was badly damaged, two cruisers, *Birmingham* and *Duluth*, sustained heavy structural damage, and USS *Hornet* was lost for the remainder of the war. Admiral Nimitz censured both Halsey and McCain for ignoring his "lessons learned" from the earlier experience. There were rumors that Halsey was to be relieved, but the salty old sailor had a friend in Chester Nimitz, and the U.S. Navy needed his leadership for a few more months.

Halsey came in for even more criticism for chasing the decoy Japanese carrier force at the Battle of Leyte Gulf than he did for sailing his forces through two typhoons. Perhaps the basis for

Halsey's action stemmed from the Battle of the Philippine Sea, sometime referred to as, "The Great Marianas Turkey Shoot." In that battle, Admiral Spruance led Task Force 58 (Fifth Fleet) to a stunning victory. The battle cost Japan three fleet carriers, 500 aircraft, and hundreds of irreplaceable pilots. Despite Spruance's success, he was criticized for letting the Japanese force escape with an operational navy. One can understand that Halsey might have vowed to never let the enemy escape if he should have them in such a situation.

During the amphibious assault of Leyte, Philippines, on the evening of October 24, 1944, Halsey discovered his chance to destroy the Japanese Navy. He made the decision to leave San Bernardino Strait unguarded and attack a recently discovered Japanese carrier force 200 miles north of his position. Halsey, frustrated by Admiral Nimitz's order not to search for the Japanese fleet, and tasked with defense of MacArthur's landing forces at Leyte Gulf, made the decision to leave San Bernardino Strait and run north at top speed with his ten carriers and a total of 64 warships. He planned to sink all of the reported three enemy carriers and four cruisers with his own aircraft and battleships.

Before sunrise the following morning, a Japanese battleship and cruiser force that had been under constant surveillance by U.S. aircraft and submarines entered the unguarded San Bernardino Strait and attacked the lightly defended "jeep" carriers that were providing close air support for the amphibious assault off Leyte Gulf.

Halsey had already launched his first aircraft strike against the Japanese carrier force when urgent messages of alarm started to reach him. The first message to reach Halsey was from Admiral Kinkaid, commander of the 7th Fleet, tasked with the amphibious assault of Leyte. Halsey received the message at 6:48 A.M., two-and-a-half-hours after it was sent. The message asked if Halsey was still guarding San Bernardino Strait. Halsey responded, "Negative. Task Force 34 is now engaging enemy carrier force."

Kinkaid was dumfounded. No one was guarding the entrance to Leyte Gulf.

At 8:00 A.M., Halsey was handed a second message from Kinkaid. "Fast battleships are needed immediately at Leyte Gulf." Thirty minutes later, a similar message was received from Rear Adm. Spruance, commander of the northernmost escort (jeep) carriers in the Gulf. " Japanese battleships and cruisers were firing on my escort carriers from fifteen miles astern."[25] Despite the emergency, Halsey was not about to give up his opportunity to destroy the Japanese Navy with his long-awaited major ship engagement.

The first report of Halsey's attack on the Japanese carriers included one carrier sunk, two carriers and a cruiser hit badly, one carrier untouched. Halsey launched a second strike and increased speed in hopes of engaging the Japanese fleet with his surface ships.

The next cry for help came at 9:00 A.M., with another message from Kinkaid. "Enemy force attacking our escort carriers (CVEs) composed of four battleships, eight cruisers, and numerous other ships. Request immediate strike by fast carriers." Halsey had all the fast carriers and he was 400 miles away. Other messages from Kinkaid followed. Halsey became infuriated, his stomach tied in knots. Here he was, on the verge of destroying the last vestiges of the Japanese Navy and he was being coerced into returning to Leyte Gulf.

As Halsey formulated a rely to Kinkaid, a message from Admiral Nimitz arrived, "Where is Task Force Thirty-Four RR The World Wonders." Halsey was stunned. He grabbed his cap, threw it to the deck, and broke into sobs. His chief of staff, Admiral Robert Carney, grabbed Halsey by the shoulders, and shouted, "Stop it! What the hell's the matter with you? Pull yourself together."[26]

Halsey showed Carney the message . Thinking he had no choice, Halsey ordered a turn to due south and turned his back on the biggest opportunity of his life. His battleships had traveled 300 miles north and would travel 300 miles south without engaging the enemy.

While Halsey was chasing the Japanese decoy carriers (decoys because they lacked aircraft and crews), the jeep carriers were conducting themselves very well against Vice Adm. Takeo Kurita's battleships and cruisers. They flew 496 missions against the enemy fleet, and so unnerved Kurita that he withdrew his fleet on the evening of October 25. With luck, he could exit San Bernardino Strait and be out of range of Halsey's aircraft by early morning.

Kurita's luck did not hold. Halsey's carrier planes found him at 8:30 A.M., and sank two cruisers and a destroyer. Japan lost 26 ships, including three battleships, four carriers, ten cruisers, and nine destroyers; a total of 305,710 tons. American losses were three destroyers, a total of 37,000 tons of warships, 1,118 dead, and 913 wounded.[27] Despite Halsey's abandonment of the landing force, MacArthur fully supported him as did Nimitz and Admiral King.

During January 1945, Halsey and members of his 3rd fleet staff were able to take two weeks leave in the United States. Halsey and his wife were summoned to the White House, where President Roosevelt awarded Halsey a gold star in lieu of a third Distinguished Service Medal. Following the ceremony, Halsey answered some questions from the press. In response to the question, was the emperor's palace a military target, Halsey answered, "No, . . . I'd hate to have them (B-29 aircraft) kill Hirohito's white horse, because I want to ride it." The comment made headlines and Halsey received hand-tooled saddles, bridles, blankets, spurs, and lariats. There seemed to be no end to Halsey's headline grabbing.

Following the bloody battle for Okinawa, use of the atomic

bombs, and Japan's surrender, Admiral Halsey's flagship, USS *Missouri* was selected as the site for the surrender ceremony. Halsey was the perfect host as he ensured that the ceremony was carried out exactly as General MacArthur desired. He then provided coffee and donuts to the Allied guests, alcohol being forbidden on U.S. ships.

Halsey reached San Francisco on October 15, 1945, aboard USS *South Dakota*. His retirement ceremony from the navy was conducted on November 22, after 45 years of service. A month later, the Senate approved a bill authorizing four fleet admirals (five stars). Several months later, Halsey was named along with Admirals Leahy, King, and Nimitz as fleet admirals. In April 1946, the fleet admiral designation was made permanent and the officers were retained on active duty with pay and allowances for life. Halsey remained active in business and on behalf of the navy until his death of a heart attack on August 15, 1959. He was buried at Arlington National Cemetery with full military honors. He was certainly one of the most courageous, colorful, and loved heroes of the war.

Admirals Nimitz and Halsey were promoted to fleet admirals of the navy in May 1946.

US Navy

Admiral Halsey welcomes Admiral Nimitz aboard Nimitz's flagship, USS *South Dakota* August 29, 1945, as Admiral Nimitz arrived in Tokyo Bay for the surrender ceremony.

US Navy

310

19

SIR EDMUND "WEARY" DUNLOP: 1942-1945

"All men are equal in the face of suffering and death."[1]

Dunlop received a dubbing from Lord Casey in 1969, and became Sir Edward Dunlop.

Imperial War Museum

Many of us have read or heard of the horrible conditions imposed upon the Allied prisoners that were forced to construct the Death Railway from Bangkok, Thailand to Rangoon, Burma in the early years of WW II. For the few prisoners of war (POWs) that survived the ordeal, their sunken eyes and emaciated bodies told us of their starvation, diseases, beatings by cruel and sadistic guards, injuries, and deep despair.

In addition to the captured prisoners of war, there was an Allied volunteer support unit for the POWs working on the railroad. This unit consisted of British and Australian doctors, surgeons, and medical personnel that volunteered to stay with their patients when Java was overrun by the Japanese in March 1942. This chapter pays homage to those men that suffered nearly as badly as the railway workers at the hands of the Japanese.

Lieutenant Col. Edmund E. "Weary" Dunlop, Australian Army, and his 87-man Casualty Clearing Station (CCS) landed at Batavia, Java on February 18, 1942. Dunlop was directed to establish and command an Allied hospital at Bandoeng, Java. Dunlop immediately began scavenging equipment for the hospital from the docks and warehouses that had been abandoned by Dutch and British forces as they went to meet the Japanese or retreated towards the coast. By asking for volunteers, Dunlop was able to expand his hospital staff from 87 men to 206, all of whom elected to stay with the hospital after the British surrender.

Dunlop was informed on March 6 that the Dutch were about to surrender Java and that the British forces would withdraw through Bandoeng on their way to the south coast. Dunlop was told to remain and keep the hospital functioning, knowing that he, his staff, and the patients would be captured by the Japanese. The Allied forces surrendered on March 8, and for the next six weeks the hospital treated 1,351 Allied patients. Dunlop began a diary of each day's activities at this point and, although some of his notes were found and destroyed, much survived the war and was published as a book. His diary provides information for much of this chapter.

Before the Australians surrendered, all documents at the hospital that could be of value to the Japanese were burned, and all weapons were destroyed, buried, or thrown into ponds. Dunlop instructed his staff and patients to give only name, rank and serial number when captured and questioned.

312

As the Japanese occupied the city, a brave Dutch lady drove her car through the parade of Japanese soldiers and to the steps of the hospital where Dunlop and many of his staff waited for the Japanese. The lady implored Dunlop to come with her because the Japanese soldiers were raping young Dutch women. Dunlop dug up two pistols he had hidden in the yard and accompanied the woman to her house. There, many Japanese soldiers were relaxing on the lawn and in the house. Dunlop located the women, and despite being pawed and inspected by the Japanese, put the women into the car and took them to his overcrowded hospital where they were thankful to be able to sleep on the floor.

For the first month, the hospital continued to function without harassment by the Japanese. By April 10, however, Japanese demands became impossible to comply with. All Red Cross identification had to be removed and destroyed. Guards were placed inside and around the hospital, and all Dutch volunteer women were taken by force from the hospital. Contact with persons outside the hospital was forbidden, and the local Swiss Red Cross representative, after having his car confiscated, was told that the Japanese rejected all conventions (Geneva and Hague).

Within two months of their capture, British morale in the hospital dropped to an alarming level. Officers were booed and threatened by enlisted men, there was no leadership. Dunlop, although junior to several other British officers, was asked to accept the role as senior officer of British hospital POWs, and the one person to represent the British in dealings with the Japanese. Reluctantly, Dunlop accepted the role.

During the next three months, an amazing transformation took place in the POW camp. Confusion, bitterness and isolationism vanished. Money was collected from the POW officers, contact with Chinese merchants outside the camp was established and food to augment the inadequate prison rations was purchased. Every man was able to receive a half a duck egg per day to maintain their daily protein requirement. Some greens were also purchased and from time to time a bit of milk. The Japanese guards actually encouraged this trade between the merchants and the prisoners because the guards charged a commission for each item delivered to the camp.

A vast educational system was established with classes for the illiterate on reading and writing, high school topics, agriculture and technical topics, and university level arts and sciences courses to include Greek and Roman classics. A radio was smuggled in by the Chinese merchants and a few men could secretly listen to the BBC to learn just how badly the war was going in those early years.

Dunlop went so far as to establish a mini commonwealth parliament system to investigate charges and countercharges made against prisoners. He also established a model prison hospital in which the most advanced operations were successfully performed on men who would have otherwise died. Morale among the POWs soared.

Dunlop was determined to stand up to the Japanese and to show no fear. This support for the POWs under his command cost him dearly, but set a splendid example for the troops and junior officers. Lest someone think that his rank or status as a medical officer gave him any latitude as a POW, consider this: One evening, Dunlop and three of his officers were relaxing by playing cards and missed the "lights out" bugle. Shortly thereafter, a Japanese sentry entered the canvas shelter and thrust a bayonet towards Dunlop's chest. "Why out of bed?" the sentry demanded. Dunlop took responsibility and was told to report to the guard shack at 8:30 in the morning. He went early and was forced to stand at attention for two hours in the boiling sun. Then, a procession of Japanese guards and other enlisted personnel came by to kick, strike, and hit him with rifle butts and wooden clubs until he was forced to his knees.

He was then made to stand at attention until afternoon when he was told that his insolent manner would require greater punishment. Dunlop rebelled. He broke his position of attention and thundered, "God Almighty, do you not think it not punishment standing in this sun and being kicked and beaten by a pack of bandy legged baboons!"[2]

It took the interpreter a minute to advise the guards what Dunlop had said, and then the pack descended upon him. They smashed him with rifle butts, chairs, boots, boards and anything else they could find, while he tried to roll up into a ball and protect his head and spleen.

Dunlop was beaten unconscious, lying face down in the dirt, with broken ribs and bleeding from lacerations to different parts of his face and body. When he regained consciousness, he was picked up and trussed with rope, with a large log across the back of his legs at the knee level. He was then placed on his knees so the log put tremendous weight and pressure upon his legs. Breathing was difficult and painful because of the fractured ribs.

Slowly, the legs became numb due to the weight of the log and lack of circulation. How long, he wondered, before gangrene would set in due to the tropical sun and no circulation. He was left in the sun until nightfall, and then a guard came to ask if he was ready to apologize for his behavior. Dunlop evaded the apology and said he needed to go amputate a prisoners arm that had been waiting for surgery all day.

Finally, the ropes were untied, and slowly the circulation returned. Dunlop, a bit unsteady from the ordeal bowed to the guards and said, "Now if you will excuse me, I shall go and amputate the Dutchman's arm."[3] Dunlop was determined to show the guards that Australians were tough. Accompanied by a guard, he went to his makeshift operating room where he removed the totally smashed and infected limb of a Dutch prisoner. Dunlop was worried that the Dutchman, seeing the surgeon covered with caked blood, dirt, and sweat, might run away from the operating table, but the prisoner was in no shape to run anywhere. Following the surgery, Dunlop bowed to the Japanese guard, and then moved to his cot where he collapsed for a few hours to recover from his beating.

On April 17. The Japanese commander, Captain Nakazawa, demanded that the hospital be destroyed and that medical personnel and patients be put in prison. The patients were to move at once. Dunlop tried to explain that many of the patients could not move and pointed to a young Australian soldier, who was blind, with a battered face, amputated hands, and a broken leg. Another blind soldier and two more paralyzed from the waist down were next to him. Nakazawa motioned to his guards to use their bayonets on the men.

Dunlop threw himself between the bayonets and the patients, and a long staring match with Nakazawa ensued. Nakazawa then stared at the paraplegics, clearly wanting to have them killed rather than transfer them to prison. Next he turned to patients with chest and abdominal wounds, struck them contemptuously and said, "Man Walk."[4]

Dunlop told Nakazawa that the British, Australian, and American governments would hold him responsible for what he did or did not do. And that he would personally hold Nakazawa responsible and see that he was hanged for his actions. Nakazawa

315

replied, "Good, now you lead the march to prison."[5] Weary was able to have the march delayed until the next day and spent a sleepless night classifying patients as walking, sitting, and stretcher cases. Since no equipment or medical supplies were to accompany the prisoners, plaster casts were put on as many patients that needed them as possible, and equipment and medical supplies parceled out to every man to carry as best he could.

The next morning, 329 patients were transferred to Tjimahi. These men were never seen again. Dunlop and 17 medical personnel and 477 patients began the walk to a penal institution 10 miles away. Other groups left before and after Dunlop's group. When they arrived, they found 107 other patients from the hospital already at the prison. There were also 250 Javanese criminals and 1200 Dutch POWs. The prison was built to house 500 prisoners so many of the POWs had to sleep on the wet earth in the rain.

The Dutch POWs provided a slice of bread and some tea for the Australian prisoners and breakfast the next morning consisted of a slice of bread. A hot meal of rice and vegetables arrived at 3:30 P.M., but there was only enough food for two-thirds of the men, so some of the senior enlisted and the officers went hungry.

Later in the day, Lieutenant Sumiya, the camp commander, called for a formation of British troops and lectured them on their bad behavior and discipline. When Dunlop was told to dismiss the troops, he did so and saluted Sumiya. To Dunlop's surprise, Sumiya swung a fist at him and hit him on the jaw. Dunlop raised both hands to show he was not armed and gave Sumiya a dirty look.

Sumiya drew his sword and lunged at Dunlop's throat. Dunlop avoided the point of the sword, but the shaft hit his larynx with such force that he could not immediately breathe or speak. The Australian troops began to mutter and move toward the Japanese guards who leveled their rifles and thrust bayonets towards them. Dunlop, still unable to speak, put up his left hand to stop his troops, knowing that a massacre of his unarmed men would occur. He then turned to Sumiya, gave a cold, formal bow, and pointed to the sword with his right hand implying that Sumiya was a brave man with a sword.

While Dunlop remained at the position of attention, Sumiya continued to bellow and swung the sword around Dunlop's head, fanning his scalp and ears. Finally, he put the sword in the scabbard, but poked several other Australian officers in the throat

316

with the scabbarded sword. Then the lecture continued until late into the evening. Dunlop was again told to dismiss the troops. Cautiously this time, he did so and retired to his squalor of a cot and floor space to rest for the morrow.

On April 20, breakfast consisted of two slices of bread, a bit of margarine, and some coffee. Dunlop was told that he could expand his unit's living area to the reformatory next to the prison, but would first have to erect barbed wire fencing around the new area. Volunteers quickly erected the required fencing and 196 men were able to move in before the end of the day. Meals seemed to become standardized at two slices of bread for breakfast, rice at 3:00 P.M., and soup about 8:00 P.M. A comprehensive series of lectures and briefings were organized by the prisoners with thoughts of much more to come. The food routine consisted of a moderate amount of rice three times per day.

A few days later, three Dutch POWs were caught trying to escape. They were brought back, lashed to poles, and bayoneted to death in front of their fellow POWs. Japanese justice was sure and swift. Most of the POWs were careful not to break the camp rules, but there would always be some that pushed the rules too far. The Japanese explained that death by the bayonet was most merciful and honorable. It was not a cowardly striking from afar such as a shooting. Officers would always be beheaded, so they need not worry.

Dunlop was informed that on the next day, he would have all his troops in formation, face the northeast, and salute the emperor of Japan on his birthday. Dunlop allowed he was not inclined to give such an order, whereupon the Japanese captain grabbed a rifle and bayonet from a sentry and prodded him in the abdomen. Dunlop looked down and said, "I get your point."[6]

After conferring with his troops and being told, "Please don't get killed for disobeying such an order. If we must live with madmen, then we must humor them,"[7] Dunlop gave the command, "To your front salute." The Japanese guards beamed, while the Australians snickered.

Food was reduced to small amounts of rice three times a day during the month of May with caloric content dropping to 1800. The minimum calories required for continued existence is 2300. The prisoners had lost an average of at least 25 pounds per man since surrendering. Dunlop had lost 38 pounds. Dunlop was told that it would be permissible to purchase fruit, milk, and vegetables on the economy provided the prisoners paid for such food. Since neither the Dutch nor Australian prisoners were allowed out of the camp, arrangements would have to be made for Japanese guards to make the purchases. Such a procedure was started on a small basis using such money as the officers and senior enlisted men had been able to hoard or that were smuggled in to the Dutch prisoners by family and friends.

At the end of May, Dunlop was told that all his troops were to march 17 kilometers to a new camp, called Tijmahi the following morning. Of the total of 559 personnel, Dunlop reported that 96 were unable to make such a march. The Japanese commander allowed 11 litter patients to be taken by truck, but only 46 others would ride. The remainder would have to make the march with all their belongings. The Japanese commander ordered Dunlop to have the troops in formation at 7:15 A.M. If any contraband was found, the person would be executed on the spot.

The march began on schedule, and as the procession wound through Bandoeng, local families lined the way and attempted to pass food and water to the prisoners. Blows and kicks were administered to the civilians, but as the lines grew larger, they were warned that the Japanese would open fire on them if they did not disperse. Shortly thereafter, the POWs were forced to strip naked and stand by their baggage as Japanese guards examined each item. The search was uneventful and the prisoners reached their destination by midafternoon.

The next several days were spent organizing patient care, physical fitness activities, lectures and making plans for future entertainment (skits and musicals). By June 13, the Tijmahi camp was overflowing with POWs. Dunlop was notified that all Australian and British troops were to leave in the morning for Bandoeng. Once the march was completed, there were 1360 Dutch, 846 Australian and British, and 1154 locals (Chinese, Malay, and Ambonese) in one portion of the new camp. Three days later, another 139 Australian and British troops arrived.

Slapping by the sentries became common during July 1942. Because the sentries were much shorter than the Australians, they had to swing wildly upwards with all their might in order to hit the POWs in the face. This extra effort caused serious injuries to the POWs including ruptured eardrums, broken and missing teeth, and broken noses. The intent of the slapping seemed as much to embarrass the POW as to cause pain. Dunlop complained to the camp commander, but the situation did not change.

Through trading with the Chinese merchants, Dunlop was able to ensure that the patients received about 2,173 calories per day. This was enough to sustain life, but inadequate for moderate or heavy labor. As soon as a patient was ambulatory and had all his limbs, he was forced from the hospital and put back to work on the railway.

Life for Dunlop, his patients and staff reached a sense of normalcy during July as the camp became well established and new patients were constantly received by the hospital and treated. Prisoners continued to die, and services and burials were provided by the medical personnel. Card games, and boxing and wrestling matches were organized and the Japanese required the POWs to entertain with a small musical band they had been able to organize. A camp bakery was established which produced excellent bread when sufficient flour could be obtained.

Periodically, the guards or a senior Japanese officer would go berserk over some minor infraction and beat and slap the POWs until he was satisfied that his honor had been satisfied. One of the more common infractions by the POWs was not bowing low enough to the guards. The POWs hated to bow to anyone and would take every advantage not to do so. This might include looking the other way when a guard approached or turning their back to the guard. This refusal to bow usually resulted in hard blows to the POWs with clubs and rifles.

On September 1, local merchants were prohibited from bringing products into the camp. Only Japanese could bring in foodstuffs. This new rule meant there would be no smuggling of additional equipment (radios) or medical instruments. Korean guards replaced the Japanese guards and proved more sadistic than the Japanese had been. The Australian and British prisoners were now dependent upon the Dutch for medical services.

On November 5, 1942, Dunlop and 1054 Australians departed for what they were told was Surabaya, Java, but turned out to be a thatched hut camp named No. 5 Makasura, in a low-lying coconut palm plot of land south of Batavia. As they arrived in the camp, the rain began and the mud deepened. Latrines consisted of an open ditch leading to seepage pits with the overflow going into adjacent rice fields. The POWs were forced to stand in

319

the rain and mud with their meager possessions for several hours until the Japanese were ready to receive their bows and compliments. Finally, well after dark, the POWs were permitted to seek shelter in the camp.

Dunlop was delighted to find several senior British officers in the camp including Wing Commander Alexander from the RAF, Squadron Leader MacGrath, Lt. Colonel Lyneham, and Captain Rees. As he stood, soaking wet and miserable, Weary had reason to hope that much of his administrative and leadership burden would be lifted by these men.

November remained wet, but there was a new outlook on life for the POWs. It was decided that Dunlop would remain as senior medical officer in charge of the hospital, but camp organization would be handled by Lt. Colonel Lyneham who seemed eager to take on the challenge. The population of 1400 POWs plus the rains completely overwhelmed the sewage system which flooded everything in the general area.

Within a few days, education and exercise classes were organized; chess matches, and volleyball games were scheduled; and special rations were being procured for the patients. By the middle of November, all patients were able to receive some soup and one egg per day, in addition to the rice provided by the Japanese. A daily task assigned the POWs by their captors was to kill flies. Every POW was expected to kill and produce four flies and would be in trouble if they did not do so. The quota of four flies was easily attainable and when it came time for the inspection of POWs with their flies, everyone had their quota.

Also during November, many of the prisoners reported failing vision and burning feet and legs. Some of the men were unable to read or even recognize Dunlop when he treated them. The men would suffer a burning sensation in their toes and bottom of their foot, extending up the leg. There was also a dull ache in addition to the burning sensation. The limbs became so sensitive that men could scarcely walk, sleep, or get any rest. Dunlop diagnosed both the optic neuritis and burning feet to vitamin deficiencies caused by a lack of vitamin B. The men needed improved food and yeast tablets, neither of which was available. Dunlop made a thick paste from some black yeast he was able to locate and injected B-1 and nicotine acid into the men most severely debilitated. His efforts helped, but did not cure the deficiency. The Japanese were not helpful in providing the necessary medicines, and seemed interested only in infectious diseases that might spread to them. At the time, Dunlop diagnosed 80 cases of vitamin deficiency, most coupled with chronic malaria and dysentery. Within a month the number of such cases climbed to more than 160.

Christmas 1942 was a special day for the POWs with better food, music, skits, and some small packages of cigarettes, biscuits, peanuts, and sweets provided by the Dutch civilians outside the camp. There were enough "gifts" that each POW received something. The prisoners organized a combined religious service of 1400 men. The lights out order was postponed and singing went on until the early morning hours. A week later, Dunlop and 433 men were told to assemble, and were marched eight kilometers to the train station and then transported to a railway siding near a wharf. Although the POWs did not know it, they were now on their way to the infamous Death Railway, where many of the men would lose their lives.

As they neared the wharf in the darkness, Dunlop's men passed a party of 1000 Australians and a smaller party of about 100 Dutchmen. Embarkation aboard an old, rusty, coal-burning ship of some 6,000 tons began quickly. The group of 1000 Australians was loaded into the foul-smelling, rat-and cockroach-infested hold first. Dunlop's group was loaded next and placed in a hold above the first group. The latrine, which could be used by one person at a time only, consisted of a sheet metal trough washed out with sea water. There was a crude galley adjoining the hold with rice cookers where the POWs prepared their meals. Fresh water was rationed and no soap was allowed. Ventilation was provided by a square vent in the top of the hold practically covered with planks and other debris. When Dunlop asked for better accommodations for the sick, he was told, "no need, only two days to Singapore."[8]

The prisoners disembarked at the main dock in Singapore and were marched past Raffles Square and Changi Prison to a site 24 kilometers outside the city. There, much to their delight, they were assigned to a large three-story stone barracks, capable of holding 200 prisoners on each floor. There were no lights in the building, so movement had to be done in the dark, as well as preparation of their small meal of rice and tea.

The men were only in this location until January 20, 1943, when they were marched to a train station and transported over five days, to a jungle site near the Burma border called Konyu. The bamboo there was 40 to 50 feet high, interspersed with other trees, tangled undergrowth and huge vines. Dunlop was informed that the prisoners must build a camp there. The huts, beds, sheds, latrines and platforms were to be constructed of local bamboo which the men would have to cut and haul to the specified site. Warnings were given about obeying orders and bowing to all guards. Once the buildings, including a hospital and kitchen, were completed, work parties were sent to clear the jungle for the railway being built to Burma.

Dunlop had 837 men including patients but almost no food. The Japanese commander announced that sick men would not draw food. Only those that worked would be fed. A few days later, a party of 626 Dutch arrived, bringing the total POW count at that camp and a British camp a short distance away, to 1875. The Japanese reiterated, "Much work, much food, and much pay; little work, little pay, and little food."[9]

By February 12, the POWs had finished the framework for all huts and the hospital. Some work had been done on the latrines, and the river had been dammed to provide water for bathing. The number of cases of dysentery and malaria began to rise due to the lack of sanitation and protection from mosquitoes. In the next four days, all huts were completed except for the attap (straw) roofs. A perimeter was cleared outside the camp and a bamboo fence was built.

The POWs became most ingenious in their use of bamboo. It was used for bottles, baskets, strips for winding in and around vertical supports, twine, and even ovens and splints when caked with mud and baked. On February 16, Dunlop was escorted to the work site at the railway where bridges were being built across the river. The POWs were moving huge logs across the water with little more than ropes, runners and crowbars.

At the time, the meat ration was 640 pounds per 1000 men for 30 days. That equates to three ounces per day per man. But, seldom was the promised amount of meat, vegetables or rice provided. POWs were lucky to receive half of the rations promised. Malaria and dysentery were on the rise, and some new cholera cases were being diagnosed. When he asked for more food and medicine, Dunlop was told that he would have to start providing 500 men per day for work on the railroad.

The meat, as it was called, was little more than heaving masses of maggots.[10] Prawns and yak meat shipped from Bangkok were dumped by the POWs into large kettles of boiling water, and the maggots skimmed off the top. After a full day of boiling, what remained of the meat was fit to eat.

A sketch by Jack Chalker showing POWs cutting through the Hintok.

Imperial War Museum

On March 20, the work quota became 600 men. This meant that all no-duty and light-duty personnel and those without shoes (224 men) would have to put in a long day of hard labor on the railway. This was the first clear indication that the Japanese had more than enough prisoners in Singapore so that they were not concerned with fatalities on the railway. Fatalities had been averaging one per day, but that was about to increase substantially.

Dysentery and malnutrition didn't keep POWs safe from work.

Imperial War Museum

Some POWs were forced to work 62 out of 72 hours. Men began to die at an alarming rate. The camp workforce that did all maintenance, repairs and medical support for the POWs from the camp was cut from 144 to 80 men. Officers were required to work a full day alongside their men. On March 26, Dunlop was left with only six men to do camp work including cleaning latrines. When he asked for tools to do the work, he was told, "Use hands."[11]

As the tempo of work increased, so did the accidents. The more common injury was rock and steel splinters from drill bits used to bore holes in the rock. Holes were bored using a long metal bit and a sledge hammer. One man held the bit, while another brought down the huge sledge hammer. The bits had a star like protrusion at the head of the bit which often broke, sending slivers of metal into the nearby workers. With proper medicine, the cuts and penetrations would not be overly serious. Without medicine, the cuts became infected, the worker developed ulcers, and soon large sections of the leg, arm, or chest developed huge cavities.

The first Allied bombing of the railway was witnessed by the POWs on April 21, 1943. The bombing and anti-aircraft fire was close, but the aircraft could not be seen through the jungle canopy.

During April, 400 Malays passed through the camp on their way to the front of the railway line. They worked for $1.00 per day and suffered greatly from pneumonia due to the wet conditions in the jungle. Next to pass through the camp were 201 Australian POWs. They had been marching for two days and were worn out. Dunlop and his men made them comfortable, arranged for food, a bath, a place to sleep, and saw them off in the morning. These men were from a group of 500 that left Singapore. Two hundred were thought to be at Konyu South Camp, and the remainder at Tarsau, too weak to move.

Next came a group of 500 Netherland East Indies soldiers enroute to the railway. Dunlop and his men gave them what they could and saw them off in the morning. On April 26, 9,000 British POWs from Singapore began to pass through the camp in groups of about 500 each. They had been marching for seven days with 200 East Indies troops. The British POWs left Changi prison in Singapore on October 27. They had been on the move for six months. A smattering of Dutch POWs (about 250) also passed through at this time. While Dunlop's men sought to provide every bit of comfort and food possible for the transit POWs, they experienced massive theft of their blankets, food, packs, and other items that would be useful to the POWs as they moved forward.

The transit of POWs continued through the first week of May. Most thought they were headed for the 217-kilometer line on the railway. The total rail distance, though unknown to the POWs, was 400 kilometers from Bampong, Thailand, to Thanbyuzarat, Burma. Fifty percent of the POWs at Konyu suffered from vitamin deficiency with the attendant painful feet and legs, and partial loss of vision. Many of the men could not see at all at night and had to be assisted to move about after dark.[12]

On May 9, 1943, after a year as acting as both senior medical officer and camp commander, Dunlop transferred the camp command to Lt. Colonel McEachern. The lack of medical assistants, the greatly increased patient workload, and Dunlop's own malaria and dysentery required that he turn over camp duties to the next senior officer if he was to survive.

Time did not drag for the POWs. There was never enough sleep, rest, or time to think. Prisoners were worked for as much as 40 days in a row for 14 hours per day without a break. When Lt. General Arthur E. Percival surrendered Singapore, he surrendered 100,000 soldiers, half of those British and Australian. The remainder was Malay, Indian, Dutch, Burmese, and other crown colony volunteers. The number of Australian, American, Dutch, and British prisoners forced to labor on the railroad was fixed as 61,000.[13] These prisoners, plus twice that number of native workers, provided far more labor than the Japanese could manage. For the Japanese, there was no reason to feed or care for the prisoners. One simply worked them to death and then replaced them with more prisoners from the camps in Singapore and Java as needed.

The engineers were the most brutal supervisors on the railway. They insisted on a set number of laborers each morning. If that quota was not met, they entered the hospital and forcibly removed sick and wounded patients and forced them to march to the railway. Many of the POWs would collapse from malnutrition or disease on the way to the railway or while at work. The engineers would beat them until they could not move and then leave them to die.

When a collapsed or dying POW was found along the track, he would be brought to the camp and if possible to the hospital. Few of the beaten men survived and when the POWs tried to have a proper funeral with burial at the cemetery, the Japanese refused and told the POWs to bury the corpse in the jungle. Many of the POWs that collapsed along the track were unaccounted for until the next muster (parade). This caused the Japanese to panic, fearing an escape, even though there was no longer any need to worry about POWs escaping. Few were strong enough to even consider it.

On June 26, a British POW, Private H. Bird, was found along the track and brought to the Australian camp for hospitalization. He had been beaten until his face was cut to pieces. His jaw was badly smashed, requiring Dunlop to wire it back together. Because Bird did not return to his assigned British huts, he was absent at the next muster and started a crisis among the guards. Three of Dunlop's patients died earlier that day, all beaten unmercifully by the Japanese engineers. Dunlop had no patience with the Japanese who were trying to account for the POWs. He told them to go look along the track where they left the missing man.

A beating was not something a POW would endure just to escape a work detail. A typical beating started with blows from fists, then beatings about the head and face with bamboo poles and heavy wooden clogs. The prisoner would be repeatedly picked

326

up and thrown to the ground, and then kicked in the stomach, head and scrotum. These brutal, sadistic beatings could go on for hours if the prisoner remained conscious.

During the latter part of June 1943, cholera epidemics occurred in the POW camps at Kinsayock, Konyu, Tonchin, Tarsau, Hintok, Rin Tin, Bangkok, and Kanchanaburi. As many as 70 cases were reported in one camp while Dunlop was treating nine in his camp. The Japanese were especially concerned about the cholera epidemic, less it spread to them as well. One POW, suspected of having malaria, collapsed at work, was beaten with sticks and shovels, pushed into a hole, and the hole ordered to be filled, thus burying the prisoner alive. Only because his fellow POWs refused to comply with the "bury alive" order was the corpse rescued. The POWs all suffered another round of beatings for refusing the order.[14] Konyu had 35 POW deaths in five days from all causes.

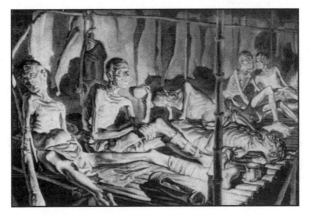

The cholera ward, as sketched by Jack Chalker.

Imperial War Museum

Despite the conditions and evil guards, the POWs tried to keep up a semblance of morale, and the hospital was kept relatively sanitary as conditions permitted. One of the medical personnel devised a way to distill water, and, by using kitchen salt, to produce a saline mixture that saved many cholera patient's lives. Some cattle were brought to the camp for use by POWs and vegetables were made available to the prisoners at several of the camps. Despite the food, by early July 1943, very few POWs were fit for work. British deaths at the Tarsau camp numbered 2,300.

By mid-July, 420 of the POWs at Dunlop's camp did not have boots and had to work barefoot. Clothing consisted of such cloth fastened about the waist and crotch as one could manage. The POWs worked for 62 consecutive days without a break and were required to work for 24 hours straight on July 15. By July 23, the camp was down to 367 POWs, 337 of which were hospitalized with cholera. The Malay laborers were reported dying by the thousands.

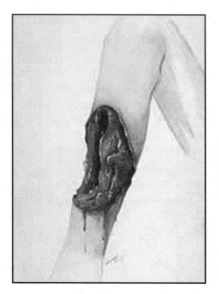

At Tarsau, Dunlop looked at hundreds of POWs suffering from gangrene and ulcers like this.

Imperial War Museum

On September 5, 1943, Dunlop was sent to Hintok camp and then to Kinsayok to augment the medical staff there. His first problem was with the latrines, which had 16 seats for 1,100 prisoners. He set to work putting in more latrines and routing a stream through the latrine and then to the river. Reports from the camp at Tankanoon indicated that 1,500 POWs were in the hospital. Dunlop was severely beaten again on October 3 by a Japanese guard that did not like the way Dunlop bowed to him. After taking away several of the guard's bamboo sticks, Dunlop was about to knock the guard unconscious when they were interrupted by an administrative clerk who put a stop to the fight. Dunlop was glad to get back to his bed without further beating, but anticipated more trouble from this guard in the future.

Dunlop suffered recurrent malarial attacks, some nearly claiming his life. In late October 1943, his temperature reached 106 degrees. Sponging and quinine by mouth finally brought his temperature down and he recovered. Three days later he left for

Tarsau with 50 sick patients. Once at Tarsau, he found 2,461 prisoners in the hospital. Dysentery, ulcers and amputations seemed to be the greatest problem at the moment. Dunlop was appointed senior medical officer and welcomed back to Tarsau by being arrested by the *Kempei Tai* (secret police) and thrown into jail. He was interrogated for four hours, accused of being a spy, beaten, and manacled to a tree. Four Japanese with rifles and bayonets worked themselves into a frenzy in front of him with blood-curdling yells and grunting.

Dunlop was told that he had 30 seconds to confess or he would be killed. The interpreter then said 10 seconds left, and asked if Dunlop had any last message for relatives? Dunlop replied contemptuously, "Last message conveyed by thugs like you - no thanks."[15] As the executioners moved toward him the *Kempei Tai* leader commanded, "Stop. He will suffer a lot more than this before he dies - untie him." Dunlop was severely beaten again, and thrown back into prison. A sentry hit him with a rifle if his posture slumped. In time, he was taken out again for execution. This was a scene similar to the first and ended the same way. This time he was placed in a cell with a Thai prisoner, given enough time to meet the man, and then was forced to watch as the man was hauled out of the cell and executed.

Next, Dunlop was brought before the head of the *Kempei* who said, "Colonel, we know that you are guilty. Even though you have not talked, others have." Dunlop responded, "If they have talked, they are liars." After a short time, the interrogator said, "Is it that you have not really done these things or that you will not talk?" Dunlop laughed and said," "Have I not spent all this time telling you that I know nothing?" "Colonel," the Japanese continued, "if I were to release you, would you have hard feelings against the Japanese? We *Kempis* do but do our duty." Dunlop replied cautiously, "From all I have heard of you *Kempis*, I feel that I have been well treated."[16] Dunlop was released, but was checked on monthly by a *Kempi* who was quick to inform him that they knew he was a dangerous spy.

The remainder of 1943 was spent digging latrines at Tarsau and providing proper cover for them. Dunlop was fortunate to have some excellent personnel in charge of this work. A cholera epidemic that claimed 29 lives made the work necessary and the Japanese, in fear of cholera, allowed more men to work on the project and provided some tools. Despite some improvement in the area of sanitation, 400 sick men still lacked blankets or covering of any kind, or pads for the bamboo beds.

Within a month after Dunlop's arrival at Tarsau, new latrines were in use, the filthy kitchens and wards had been cleaned up, a diet plan had been put into effect, and sick men were being better fed. In addition, a central hospital administration was in place, a new department coordinated all maintenance work and services, and new hospital orderlies were being recruited and trained.[17]

At each of the camps he was assigned, Dunlop put into effect a plan whereby officers contributed a percentage of their meager pay for the purchase of food for the sick. This fund was used to purchase eggs, usually duck, so that each sick POW could have at least one egg per day. This extra food was better than drugs for many of the POWs. Not all officers agreed with such a plan but Weary persisted in implementing it anyway, since he knew it was the right thing to do.

During mid January 1944, Dunlop and 201 medical personnel were moved to Chungkai camp near Kanchanaburi. Chungkai had a population of 8000 POWs. Dunlop was saddened to see nearly a hundred new amputees that he had known before in other camps lining the road to welcome him. The surgeon at Chungkai had performed more than 110 amputations. Thirty of the amputees died.

Dunlop found rations much better at Chungkai than at Tarsau. More rice was available and nearly four ounces of meat per day, a total of 2800 calories.[18] The camp was larger and well organized with concerts, entertainment and sports competition. Dunlop became the senior medical officer for the camp. The camp commander was Lieutenant Col. Cary Outram. Dunlop and Outram got along well together and supported each other. The POW death rate at the camp fell as the POW's diets improved.

Dunlop was aware that he was not to operate on or provide medical treatment for Japanese guards, but was continuously asked to do so. He routinely treated the Japanese for VD and after much hesitation, circumcised a guard who repeatedly asked him to do so. Two hours later, Dunlop was arrested, threatened with death by the commandant, and thrown into a box like prison for two days.[19]

On February 10, 1944 a party of well dressed and well fed POWs (Australian, British and Dutch) arrived from Kanchanaburi with a photographic crew loaded with cameras, musical instruments, and cue cards. The POWs posed for propaganda pictures working and singing in the gardens under utopian conditions. Finally, after many photographs, they all sang "Rule Britannia," and went home.[20] Dunlop's men made mental notes to remember them if they should ever see them again.

Deaths in the camp for October 1943 were 259; November 143; and December 134. Starting in January 1944, the rate dropped significantly to 78 deaths; in February 36; and March 29. Morale was good and everyone was in reasonably good spirits. During April 1944, Dunlop and several of his officers were asked to complete some questionnaires that dealt with Japanese treatment of the POWs. One question was, "What is the kindest action you have seen by a Nipponese soldier." One of the POWs offered the following response. "Before beating me up, the Nipponese soldier let me take off my glasses and did not use a crowbar."[21]

During April and May 1944 hundreds of POWs were sent to Nakom Patom camp for labor. More than a thousand were told to depart on May 18. Dunlop protested to the Japanese commander that these movements were not coordinated with him, that no medical personnel accompanied the POWs, and that he had no knowledge of the facilities at Nakom Patom. The commander had no interest in Dunlop's protest and sent him to see Sergeant Sukarno, a non-commissioned officer who was doing bayonet practice. Sukarno would roar like a rhino, and then charge and impale a straw-filled enemy uniform.

When Dunlop explained his problem and asked to accompany the POWs to Nakom Patom, the sergeant said, "Sick men no work. The more sick die, the better." After more arguing Dunlop lost his patience and said, "You are a black-hearted villain and one day I will have you hanged."[22] It took some time for Sukarno to understand the insult. When he did, he went berserk, and charged Dunlop with the bayonet. Only a Japanese private that stepped between them and pushed Dunlop back saved his life. Three times Sukarno charged Dunlop with the bayonet and three times the private stood between the two men, pushing Dunlop back further each time. Finally, Sukarno wearied and went back to stabbing the straw dummy.

Dunlop was unable to accompany any of the sick that left for Nakom Patom, although nearly 1000 POWs were lying sick, and another 353 required stretchers. Finally on May 18, when only 400 POWs remained at Chungkai, Dunlop was allowed to leave for Kanchanaburi, not Nakom Patom. The movement was by train and foot.

Red Cross packages arrived at the Kanchanaburi camp on May 24, although the parcels were not made available to the POWs. Dunlop called on the commander the next day to try to get the parcels distributed to the men, but was not successful. The Japanese commander was not concerned about the need of sick POWs. Dunlop continued to make improvements in the camp sanitation and medical facilities until June 14 when he was sent to Nakom Patom.

The huge hospital at Nakom Patom is on the flatland of the Bangkok plains. It was designed for 10,000 patients, but was completed too late to help the battered POWs whose care came from the jungle camps of Kinsayok, Tarsau, Chungkai, Tamuang, Non Pladuc, and Kanchanaburi. The buildings were made of wood, not bamboo and accommodations were far superior to the jungle camps.

The chief medical officer at the camp was Lieutenant Col. Albert A. Coates. Dunlop was designated as chief surgical officer and head of the rehabilitation ward. Later, he also became medical economics officer with responsibility for control of camp canteen activity. Air raids and over flights of Allied aircraft became common with dozens of aircraft in each flight, both night and day. During December, POWs began dying at Non Pladuk camp due to Allied bombing of the railroad. On December 18, nearly 20 POWs died from bombing near Tamarkan.

Christmas Day 1944, was celebrated by a special breakfast, lunch and dinner purchased and prepared by the POWs. Religious services were conducted and athletic contests were conducted in the afternoon.

Dunlop observed his 38th birthday on July 12, 1945, and noted a degree of tension in the camp with the Japanese guards seeming to be very trigger happy and the Korean guards moody and disturbed. Dunlop was concerned that the war may be near an end, and his personal record as a dangerous spy and constant surveillance by the *Kempai Tai* would make him a target for elimination if the war should end. Dunlop's concern increased when a Korean guard informed him that if the Japanese were forced to surrender, the POWs would all be massacred. This information seemed to be confirmed when the Japanese registered all their machine guns so that they faced into the camp.

On July 25, Korea informants told some POWs that all fit POWs would be sent on a "Death March" to Nakom Nyak and the sick POWs would all be killed. Dunlop decided it was time to organize resistance to such a massacre. He selected 10 NCOs of high courage and had each of them select 10 trustworthy men, all of whom should devise some sort of weapon for use in an emergency. Dunlop himself devised two molotov cocktails: bottles filled with gasoline, to be used against a machine gun emplacement near his tent.

On August 10, eight truckloads of Red Cross packages arrived at the camp and were put in the Japanese warehouse. The following day, six truckloads of these packages left the camp. On August 13, a small amount of Red Cross products were issued to the POWs. These consisted of 30 kilos of soya beans, four boxes of milk, one box of malted milk, and 200 boxes of soap. The current rumor was that the Russians had entered the war against Japan.

Dunlop gathered his 100 emergency men on August 14, and worked out details for resisting a Japanese attack, and for taking over the camp in the event of a Japanese surrender. Two days later, on the 16th, the Korean guards were tearful and seemed afraid. The Japanese guards remained surly and elusive. Tension was high in the camp.

At 6 P.M., Dunlop and other senior officers were summoned to the Japanese compound. Lieutenant Col. Yamagita accompanied by an interpreter announced that an armistice was in effect. He had been told to release the POWs. "Therefore," he said, "we cease to guard you. Your repatriation will be soon."[23] The Allied POWs assembled on the parade field and raised the long-hidden British, Australian and Dutch flags.

Dunlop remained in Thailand for several months following the end of the war, assisting in the return of the Allied POWs and testifying to war crimes tribunals. He returned and married his college sweetheart, Helen Ferguson, in November 1945. He remained active in medicine and POW concerns into the 1980s and received many honors. In 1977, he was named as one of the 200 Great Australians.

Dunlop and his new bride, Helen Ferguson, are piped out of the Toorak Presbyterian Church after their wedding ceremony in November, 1945.

Imperial War Museum

His name became a legend among Australian POWs as he labored to save wounded, sick, and battered men. On many occasions he put his own life at risk by standing up for his men and denouncing the brutality of the Japanese guards.

Dunlop was asked to speak at hundreds of events around the world and always accepted such invitations. At one of these engagements he paid tribute to his medical personnel with this statement:

> Who could forget one of my devoted medical staff (Staff Sergeant Alan Gibson) who was himself reduced to a near-naked skeleton, shivering with chronic malaria and racked with dysentery, yet when confronted with a man naked and tormented with cholera, dropped his last shred of comfort in the world, his blanket, over the dying man. Only those ill, emaciated and thin, who slept on exposed and rough surfaces in all weather, could comprehend the depth of his sacrifice.

Dunlop died at his home on July 2, 1993. He was preceded in death by his wife in 1988. More than 10,000 people attended Sir Ernest Edward Dunlop's funeral at St. Paul's Cathedral in Melbourne.

20

MARK A. "PETE" MITSCHER

Pete Mitscher is one of the most unlikely admirals I have researched. Certainly he was not gifted intellectually, as he flunked out of the naval academy at Annapolis after his first year. With his father's help, he was allowed to reenter the academy in 1906 and, although he demonstrated few leadership qualities, he graduated four years later, 107th out of a class of 130.

Vice Adm. Mitscher aboard his flagship USS *Lexington* in June, 1944.

U.S. Navy

He was not athletic nor robust, but small (five feet-seven inches), and thin (110 pounds) as a cadet. By age 32, Lieutenant Mitscher was a tired, wizened, balding man. After many of his command assignments, he felt physically unfit for his next assignment, but somehow answered the bell for the next round. After his Guadalcanal tour of duty, his wife described him as a man "with hollow cheeks and dull tired eyes. The skin on his face was pouched and a sickly yellow. He weighed 115 pounds."[1] She could not believe that a dirty little island had so ravaged her husband.[2]

We know Admiral "Bull" Halsey as a dynamic, gregarious, outward leader with charisma and a high degree of self confidence. Pete Mitscher was quiet, spoke so softly that others had difficulty hearing him, and avoided the spotlight whenever possible. He seemed weary and frail, and seldom smiled, causing one to wonder why he looked so worried and serious.

What then caused Pete Mitscher to move up the naval ranks to the grade of admiral and command some of the largest task forces in the Pacific during WW II? The answer is leadership. More specifically, the quality of leadership called "looking after your men." Mitscher was loved by every man he commanded. For just one example of this quality of leadership, consider this article from the Madison, Wisconsin, daily *Journal* newspaper during July 1945.

> Madison was paid a visit the other day by a very distinguished naval officer, Vice Admiral Marc Mitscher. He stopped here to visit with the Reverend E. D. Upson whose son is missing in action in the Pacific. We don't know how many generals and admirals visit bereaved parents but we do know that Admiral Mitscher has the reputation of looking after his men. His gesture in extending that to these Madison parents is one worthy of recognition. We feel safer when humble men like Admiral Mitscher are running the war.[3]

Pete Mitscher died of a heart attack on February 3, 1947; 18 months after Japan surrendered in Tokyo Bay. This is his story.

Mitscher was born in Hillsboro, Wisconsin, on January 26, 1887, and moved to Oklahoma Territory with his family a few years later when it opened to settlement. His father, Oscar A. Mitscher, was elected mayor of Oklahoma City in 1891. In 1900, President William McKinley appointed Oscar as Osage Indian agent at Pawhuska. In Oklahoma, Pete played cards, hunted, rode ponies, and had frequent fist fights in school. He was unconcerned with his low grades and developed a reputation for swearing worthy of a mule skinner.[4] Oscar was unimpressed with local schools and was able to get an appointment for Pete to the U.S. Naval Academy.

Mitscher did not make friends easily. He seemed negative on most topics and often made snide remarks during conversations. Not only was Pete a poor student, he compiled 159 demerits in his first year at the academy. He was directed to resign, did so, and was reappointed to the academy by the same congressional representative, Bird S. McGuire, who appointed him initially.

Mitscher did not do well academically at Annapolis, especially compared to peers such as Chester W. Nimitz, William F. Halsey, Ernest J. King, and Joseph M. Reeves. Pete did develop a passion for flying and would later serve in naval aviation with such classmates as John Towers, Ted Ellyson, Kenneth Whiting, Aubrey Fitch, Frank Fletcher, John McCain, and Ted Sherman. These men pioneered naval aviation and made it what it is today. Among the early naval aviators, Mitscher was the first to be promoted to admiral, and the only one to fill operational command billets. After receiving his commission as an ensign, he served in the fleet until 1915, when he received orders to USS *North Carolina* for aviation training.

Two traits that Mitscher did possess in abundance were serenity and determination. During all his years commanding task forces at sea, no one ever saw Pete Mitscher flustered. He was absolutely imperturbable. The trait of determination is well illustrated by this story.

In May, 1911, Pete attended the wedding of the commanding officer of the USS *Colorado* at Puget Sound, Washington. He was not as impressed with the wedding ceremony as he was with the 18-year old maid of honor from Tacoma. Her name was Francis Smalley, and she cried throughout the entire ceremony. Pete was determined to make her his wife.

Frances was outgoing, loved dancing and parties, Pete was silent, and disliked both. Frances was not ready to marry, but after three meeting, Pete proposed marriage. Frances hedged and dodged the question again when Pete proposed again several months later.

Mitscher resorted to the basketball equivalent of a full court press. He was able to get a month leave and every day sent Frances flowers or a gift. He called upon Frances' mother to no avail and had his parents visit the Smalley family. Frances did not take Pete's attention seriously but eventually consented to an engagement just to gain some breathing room.

When Pete next arrived in Tacoma, he called Frances and said, "We will be married Thursday."[5] Frances replied that she could not possibly get ready so soon, but she did. The couple wed on January 16, 1913, and Pete went to sea for eight months. Frances returned to her parents' home.

Mitscher went to Pensacola, Florida, in 1915 for pilot training and graduated in June 1916 at age 29, as naval aviator # 33. His orders directed him to remain at Pensacola as a flying instructor. He remained there for a year and was then ordered to cruiser USS *Huntington* to command the aviation department. The ship had a catapult on the stern to launch seaplanes and several balloons which were sent aloft on a long cable with an observer aboard to look for submarines. Pete was dumped into the ocean while experimenting with a non-catapult launch of a plane, but was rescued by a small boat from the cruiser.

Six years after graduation, his hair gone, but his wings achieved, Mitscher was flying from Pensacola Bay, Fla., in wood, wire and canvas sea planes with 100-horsepower pusher engines.

U.S. Navy

This was a time of frequent clashes between the aviation community that saw aviation as the future of the navy, and the "old navy" that believed the battleship would rule the waves for the foreseeable future. The chief of naval operations, Admiral William S. Benson, refused to support construction of an aircraft carrier, and made drastic cuts in naval aviation personnel and budget. The navy's first carrier came about because the director of naval aviation, Captain Thomas T. Craven, went directly to the secretary of the navy for approval to convert USS *Collier* into the experimental carrier *Langley*.[6]

In March 1918, Mitscher received orders to NAS Miami as the commanding officer. It was an unaccompanied tour, so Frances, expecting their first child, once again went back to Tacoma to be with her parents. Pete did well at Miami, but Frances became, ill, lost the baby, and nearly died. The doctors told Frances she would never be able to have children, and it would take several years for her to gain back her health. Pete never discussed his sorrow with anyone and never mentioned losing the baby or their inability to have children.

During 1919, Pete was one of the pilots aboard three navy Curtis seaplanes (NC) that attempted to fly across the Atlantic Ocean to England. Only one of the NC seaplanes accomplished the passage and it was not Mitscher. Pete, then a Lieutenant Cdr., had to be rescued from the ocean by a Greek freighter, but earned his first Navy Cross Medal for the attempt.

During his early aviation years, Pete's fitness reports, while outstanding, often contained the words, "He is inclined to work to such an extent and such hours that his health is not excellent." Such remarks would be a part of his fitness reports until his death.[7]

During their first three years of marriage, the Mitschers were together less than three months. Slowly Frances learned that Pete seldom smiled, and when he did it was a thin chilling movement of the muscles around his lips. He was formal to the extent that he seldom removed his coat, even at home or in the privacy of a hotel room. He was so gentle in all their dealings, Frances found it difficult to believe the stories told about Pete's fighting and cursing.

In 1926, Pete became air officer of USS *Langley*, the navy's first aircraft carrier. In 1941, he became commanding officer of USS *Hornet*, a new carrier that just joined the fleet. Three weeks after Japan bombed Pearl Harbor, Mitscher captained USS *Hornet* on her shakedown cruise, and in April 1942, he commanded USS *Hornet* as the launch platform for Jimmy Doolittle's raid of Tokyo with army B-25 bombers. His appointment to rear admiral followed a month later.

At this point, Mitscher was already being recognized as a commander that looked after his men. He also felt their loss personally and keenly. During the battle for Midway, a fighter from USS *Yorktown* crash-landed on *Hornet's* deck. The aircraft's 50-caliber machine guns began firing directly into the ship's control station, killing several sailors. One of the victims was Royal Ingersoll, the son of the commander-in-chief, Atlantic fleet. Pete wrote the admiral about the fatal accident and commented:

> It is my regrettable duty to inform you personally of the death of your son, Royal, on board this ship on June 4th, while we were in action in the so-called Battle of Midway.
>
> As I have said before, Royal was one of the most efficient officers it has been my pleasure to serve with and his death is mourned by the whole ship's company, officers and men, who considered him the Rock of Gibraltar in the Gunnery Department of the ship.[8]

Shortly thereafter, Mitscher was required to notify the wife of Lieutenant Cdr. John C. Waldron, the commanding officer of Navy Torpedo Squadron-8, of Waldron's death while attacking Japanese carriers in the Battle of Midway:

> I am convinced that your husband, together with his whole squadron, will prove to be one of the greatest heroes of the war. His gallant conduct, and that of his squadron, leaves him outstandingly the inspiration for all America.[9]

Mitscher had good reason to be concerned about the death of Lieutenant Cdr. Waldron and his squadron pilots. Shortly before launch, Waldron reported to Mitscher on the bridge of the *Hornet,* and "promised he would press through (attack) against all obstacles, well knowing that his squadron was doomed to destruction with no chance of returning to the carrier."[10]

Out of 30 pilots and 15 crewmen in 30 planes, only one, Ensign George Gay, survived the attack. The remainder of the squadron was shot down by Japanese *Zeros* before they could accurately launch their torpedoes. The heavy casualties suffered by USS *Hornet* took a heavy toll on Mitscher. His sorrow and the burden of command weighed most heavily upon him.

The Battle of Midway, even though flawed by poor attack procedures on the part of navy commanders, changed the course of the war. Japan lost four of their finest carriers and many flight crews. They would not be able to take the offensive in the Pacific again. Upon his return to Pearl Harbor, Mitscher was promoted to rear admiral.

After Midway, Mitscher became commander of Patrol Wing Two, a flying boat organization based in Hawaii. He made several changes to operational procedures, got rid of a chief of staff who could not hear him (Mitscher refused to raise his voice above his normal soft tone), and lobbied for combat command.

On March 31, 1942, Mitscher arrived on Guadalcanal as commander, Air, Solomon Islands, (ComAirSols), a combat command. He quickly instilled a new fighting spirit in the troops and was responsible for the planning of the shoot down of Admiral Isoroku Yamamoto on April 18, 1943.

He contracted malaria in the summer of 1943, and was relieved by Major Gen. Nathan F. Twining of the Army Air Corps. During Mitscher's tenure as ComAirSols, his pilots destroyed 340 Japanese fighters and 132 bombers, sank 17 ships, and had 131 pilots rescued from waters and beaches after being shot down. The rescued airmen were his proudest achievement.

Captain Steven Juricka, flight deck officer aboard USS *Hornet*, described Mitscher as a man that "oozed sincerity. . . . and never used five words when one would do. Quiet, reserved, rarely telling a joke, he demanded no nonsense answers to questions. He smoked a great deal, and the baseball cap he wore failed to prevent his nose from getting burned and freckled."[10] Columnist Howard Morton of the *Baltimore Sun* newspaper reported in April 1943 that, "Mitscher today looks older than his 57 years. . . . Shyness and modesty are his most notable characteristics. . . . Correspondents like him. And if you ask them why, they inevitably tell you that it is because he gives his men credit for everything. With Mitscher, they say, it's always, we, never I."[11]

He had a reputation for being "tough as nails," but scarcely looked the part. He still spoke in a whisper. He was skinny, wrinkled, and bald, reminding some of the village grocer.[12]

Halsey, however, was well aware of Mitscher's fighting skills and wanted him back as soon as possible. When explaining why he asked for Mitscher to come to Guadalcanal, Halsey said, "Pete was a fighting fool, and I knew it."[13] Mitscher returned to San Diego for some rest and recuperation. He was exhausted, having worked continuously without a break while on Guadalcanal. Some senior officers found Mitscher's unorthodox approach to leadership difficult to understand, but not Admirals Ernest J. King (chief of naval operations), Chester W. Nimitz, (commander, Pacific Fleet), or William F. "Bull" Halsey (commander, South Pacific). They wanted him back as soon as possible and sent notice that he was to be given every opportunity to rest and ready himself for the next combat command.

Mitscher left the daily routine to his chief of staff, Captain John Perry, and did some fishing in Alaska, duck hunting in California, fishing in Chesapeake Bay in Maryland, and in the western Sierras. By January 1944, he was rested enough that Nimitz and Halsey ordered him to assume command of Task Force 58/38, a pioneer force consisting of new battleships, cruisers and destroyers clustered around a core of new, huge, fast carriers. The force would often consist of more than a hundred ships, with 100,000 men. When the force was part of Admiral Raymond A. Spruance's Fifth Fleet, it was designated Task Force 58. When it was led by Admiral Halsey's Third Fleet, it became Task Force 38.

The command was what Mitscher lived for. Twenty–eight years since he pinned on his navy wings, he was going to command the largest force ever commanded by a naval aviator. He could not have been happier. He went aboard his flagship USS *Yorktown* on January 13, 1944, at Pearl Harbor, and left on January 19, as commander of four task groups with 61 ships, including 12 carriers. The task groups operated within a radius of 150 miles, allowing quick consolidation for air defense if necessary.

The target for Task Force 58, was the Marshall Islands. Mitscher was not entirely comfortable with serious-minded Raymond Spruance, since Spruance was known as a gunnery and surface sailor. Mitscher's plans did not include fighting surface battles with battleships. Mitscher's staff considered Spruance too cautious, while Spruance's staff thought Mitscher too willing to take unnecessary risks.

Mitscher launched his aircraft against Kwajalein, Maloelap, Roi and Eniwetok as planned on January 29, and by noon achieved air superiority over the objective area. The Japanese lost 155 aircraft while Mitscher's carriers lost 57 planes and 31 aircrews. Japanese aviation was destroyed in the area and could not launch an attack against the fleet or the landing troop transports.

During his after action report, Mitscher credited the quick success at Kwajalein to striking all Japanese bases simultaneously, the use of dawn fighter sweeps against airfields, and the effectiveness of incendiary bullets against Japanese aircraft on the ground. "Jap planes still burn very well," he concluded.[14]

Kwajalein was captured on February 4, and credit for the smooth operation was given to Mitscher and his fast carrier task force. Instead of returning to Pearl Harbor for replenishment, Mitscher took his forces to Majuro atoll, 200 miles south of Kwajalein, which was seized on January 30 and quickly turned into an advanced naval and air supply base. The ships of Task Force 58 would not return to Pearl Harbor until the end of the war. The procedures developed during the assault on the Marshall Islands would be followed for the rest of the war.

Mitscher's carrier groups left Majuro on February 12, with one group scheduled to destroy Japanese aviation on Eniwetok, while three groups attacked the Japanese stronghold at Truk. Within an hour after the attack started, thirty Japanese fighters were shot down, while 40 more were destroyed on the ground. By the end of the day, Japan lost 250 of their 365 aircraft on Truk. Carrier aviation destroyed eight of the 34 Japanese ships sunk or burned. The remainder was destroyed by Spruance's surface forces. Back at Pearl Harbor, Admiral Nimitz remarked that the attack was partial payment for the Japanese attack on Pearl Harbor.[15]

Shortly before 2:00 P.M., on February 21, Mitscher's carrier force of three attack carriers and three light carriers penetrated Japanese-controlled waters approaching the Marianas. The carriers were discovered by a Japanese search plane before they were in range to launch aircraft. The raid on the Marianas was intended to reduce Japanese aviation capabilities that could interfere with planned operations to retake Saipan, Tinian, Rota and Guam.

No carrier task force had ever risked an all-out fight with a land-based air force after the carriers had been discovered. To many of the carrier aviators, Mitscher was still an unknown quality. That was about to change. When informed that the Japanese reconnaissance aircraft had radioed the carrier task force position to the Japanese home base, Mitscher instructed his chief of staff to send this message: "We have been sighted by the enemy. We will fight our way in."[16] The decision was consistent with Mitscher's procedures throughout his command in the Pacific.

Japanese aircraft attacked the carriers throughout the night, locating them by the phosphorous wakes. When morning came, not a single ship had been hit. From 8:00 A.M., until 3:00 P.M., Mitscher's planes bombed and strafed aircraft facilities, and ships on Guam, Saipan, Tinian, and Rota. Seventy Japanese aircraft were destroyed on the ground and 51 in the air. Mitscher lost six planes and six pilots which disturbed him greatly. On the trip back to Majuro, morale among the aircrew was at a new high. Mitscher had made the grade where it counted. Now the carrier people would follow him anywhere.

The role of carrier forces had changed dramatically. Mitscher said it best, "There are just so many Jap planes on any island. We'll go in and take it on the chin. We'll swap punches with them. I know I'll have losses, but I'm stronger than they are. If it takes two task forces, we'll get two task forces. I don't give a damn now if they do spot me. I can go anywhere and nobody can stop me. If I go in and destroy all their aircraft, their damned island is no good to them anyhow." [17]

Mitscher (at left) and his chief of staff, Commodore Arleigh Burke. It took "31-Knot" Burke, a famous surface-navy-man, a long time to win the admiral's confidence. After that, Mitscher relied heavily on him. They are shown here just after an important secret dispatch had arrived in flag plot and at the moment of actual command decision.

U.S. Navy

During March 1944, Captain Arleigh "31-knot" Burke reported aboard USS *Yorktown* as chief of staff to Mitscher. Burke did not want to be there, preferring his command of destroyer divisions to a lesser job aboard a carrier. Mitscher did not want Burke aboard either, preferring an aviator as his chief of staff, and especially his current chief of staff, Captain Truman J. Hedding, The reason Burke was ordered to *Yorktown* was a decision by the chief of naval operations (CNO) that, henceforth, aviation task force commanders would have surface chiefs of staff. Admiral King, the CNO, thought that such a mixture would result in better coordination and thinking within the task force.

Mitscher refused to communicate with Burke for more than a month, including the period while the task force struck the Caroline Islands (Palau, Yap, and Woleai). The task force was discovered on March 25, and began receiving Japanese fighter and bombing attacks on the 29th. Mitscher launched his aircraft at 6:30 A.M., on March 30, and eliminated all Japanese aircraft by the end of the day. At Palau, 26 of the 44 navy pilots shot down were rescued by aircraft and ships. That was not good enough for Mitscher. He tasked his staff to develop procedures to rescue 75-percent or better of all downed aircrews.[18]

Slowly, Mitscher accepted Burke as his chief of staff, and slowly, Burke changed his mind about transferring from this strange admiral and his flagship. Burke would remain with Mitscher until he died.

On June 6, Task Force 58 left the Marshall Islands. Spruance was aboard USS *Indianapolis*, while Vice Adm. Mitscher was on the new carrier, USS *Lexington*. Included in the fleet were 15 attack carriers, seven battleships, 21 cruisers, 69 destroyers, 891 carrier aircraft, and 65 floatplanes. At a substantial distance to the rear was the Fifth Amphibious Force with 535 ships and 127,000 troops. The amphibious forces were on their way to invade Saipan. Vice Adm. K. Kakuta was commander of Japan's land-based aviation in the Marianas with headquarters on Tinian. He promised Vice Adm. Jisaburo Ozawa, commander of the First Mobile Force, 455 land-based planes for his attack on Task Force 58.

Admiral Ozawa was not an aviator and had several disadvantages in a battle against Mitscher. Neither Ozawa, his senior air staff, nor his carrier commanders had fought enemy carriers. Ozawa's carriers had radar, but it was new and his operators were inexperienced. His planes were inferior in quantity and quality to Mitscher's, and he could not operate dive bombers and torpedo bombers from carriers while operating fighter aircraft.

Ozawa knew Spruance was in command of the fleet, and due to Spruance's reputation for caution, he believed Spruance would not take his ships more than 100 miles west of the Marianas. This suited Ozawa just fine. He could launch nearly 500 land-based planes against Mitscher's carriers while rearming and refueling his own carrier planes at Guam and Rota. Ozawa's strategy would prevent the U.S. carrier aircraft from attacking Ozawa's carriers because of the extreme range, nearly 350 miles distant. This was a wonderful plan on paper.

June 19, 1944, forever remembered as the "Marianas Turkey Shoot," dawned clear and warm off Guam for the carrier task force. Mitscher requested permission to start air strikes against the Japanese fleet at 5:00 A.M., but was denied by Spruance. Spruance wanted the carriers close by for support of the amphibious operation on Saipan. Without such a preemptory attack, Mitscher was certain that Japanese aircraft would attack at first light and he tried to make certain the carrier force was ready for the attack.

Approaching enemy aircraft began to be spotted on ships radar at 5:30 A.M. By 7:14 A.M., many enemy aircraft were reporting to be airborne over Guam and headed for the carriers. Mitscher launched *Hellcat* fighters from six carriers and shot down 35 enemy aircraft while losing one *Hellcat*. At 9:50 A.M., ships' radars reported large numbers of enemy aircraft approaching from the direction of Guam, Palau, and Yap. Other enemy aircraft were inbound from Japanese carriers.

Mitscher launched his torpedo and bomber aircraft and sent them to orbit to the east, while his fighters met the incoming Japanese aircraft 90 miles to the west. This procedure allowed the carriers to land fighter aircraft, rearm and launch them without being handicapped by the additional torpedo and bomber aircraft on deck. Some of these procedures seem very simple today, but at the time, they were all firsts in naval aviation.

The aerial dogfight began 90 miles away and continued to the fleet itself. Japanese aircraft were reported to be falling like leaves, but a few bombers got through the combat air control, and scored hits on USS *South Dakota* and *Indiana*. From 11:30 A.M, to 2:30 P.M., Japanese planes were engaged as far as 130 miles out from the fleet and attacked as they proceeded toward the fleet. One pilot commented, "Hell, this is like an old time turkey shoot."[19] From that comment was born the phrase, "Marianas Turkey Shoot." Admiral Ozawa lost 328 of the 430 aircraft he sent against the task force. Mitscher launched 450 fighters, losing 29 planes and 31 crewmembers.

Mitscher spent the following day trying to find the Japanese carriers, sending aircraft as far away as 475 nautical miles. The enemy carriers were sighted at 3:53 P.M., 275 miles distant, and

Mitscher launched fighters, bombers, and torpedo planes to attack them. The aircraft found the Japanese fleet at sunset and sank one carrier, IMS *Hitaka,* and two oilers. It was dark, and the aircraft returned individually or in pairs due to their low fuel state.

Mitscher turned the axis of the fleet and put the carrier's 15 miles apart to make it easier for the pilots to reach any one of the carriers. As the planes came within 70 miles, they started reporting low and empty fuel tanks. One of the worst disasters in naval aviation was becoming possible and probable. As the aircraft reached the task force, the pilots reported their inability to see the carrier lights. Normally carriers keep their external lights dim or off so as not to help enemy submarines locate them.

Mitscher ordered Burke to turn on the lights, increase speed to 22 knots, and launched all the air and ship rescue support he had. Some searchlights streaked up into the sky, others illuminated the deck of the carriers. Cruisers fired star shells, flooding the ocean with light. The effect upon the pilots was electric. Those still on the carrier cheered at the invitation to Japanese submarines to come and get us. Clearly, the navy pilots were not expendable.

Mitscher instructed the pilots to land on any carrier they could find. Some pilots made approaches on battleships and cruisers. Some ran out of fuel and crashed into the ocean. Two hundred and 16 planes had been sent after the Japanese fleet. The following morning it was determined that 80 aircraft had not returned and all but 16 pilots and 22 crewmen had been rescued. Mitscher's decision to light up the fleet in the Marianas ranks with the surface navy's "Damn the torpedoes! Full speed ahead."[20]

In his after action report, Mitscher praised the aviation commanders for the superb performance of their men, but criticized Spruance's decision not to let him steam to the west and engage the Japanese fleet when it was in range. Virtually every other aviator, including Chester Nimitz, did the same. On a more positive note, the battle provided the opportunity for Mitscher and Burke to put aside their petty grievances and cooperate fully with one another. Because the Japanese fleet was not destroyed in the Marianas, they would assert themselves again at Leyte Gulf, with near catastrophic consequences for the U.S. Navy.

Saipan was captured on July 10, 1944, followed by Tinian on August 1, and Guam on August 10. Mitscher would go on to fight his carriers at the battles for Iwo Jima, Leyte Gulf, and Okinawa. Following his release from the Marianas, the fast carrier force launched attacks upon Iwo and Chichi Jima, Wake Island, Yap, the Palaus, and Mindanao for more than a month.

Admiral "Bull" Halsey replaced Spruance on September 11. Normally Mitscher would have gone back to Pearl Harbor with Spruance and Rear Adm. Sidney "Slew" McCain would have relieved Mitscher. After a personal plea to Nimitz, Mitscher was allowed to retain command of Fast Carrier Task Force 58, and McCain was made commander of Fast Carrier Task Force 38.

For the attack on the Philippines, Mitscher had eight attack carriers, eight light carriers, six fast battleships, 17 cruisers, 58 destroyers, and a thousand planes.[21] The Battle for Leyte Gulf is contained in Volume II of *War in the Pacific* and in the chapter on "Bull Halsey" in this volume. During four days in October, the Japanese lost 305,710 tons of combat shipping, four carriers, three battleships, ten cruisers, 11 destroyers, and 10,000 men. Allied losses were one light cruiser, two "jeep" carriers, two destroyers, one destroyer escort and less than 3,000 men. Despite the significant destruction of the Japanese fleet, six battleships and 11 supporting ships escaped.[22]

Mitscher turned over command of Task Force 58 to McCain on October 29, 1944, and took Burke back to San Diego with him. When they arrived at San Diego, Mitscher gave Burke a sealed envelope and told him to go on to Washington alone to brief the chief of naval operations. Burke protested that Mitscher could not do that. "Admiral," Burke protested, "You're ordered back to Washington, what will I tell Admiral King?" "Tell him the truth— I've gone fishing, some place, you don't know where."[23] The envelope was only to be opened if it was absolutely necessary to reach Mitscher.

Mitscher returned to Pearl Harbor in December 1944, to assist in planning for the Iwo Jima and Okinawa campaigns. His task force left Ulithi Harbor on February 10, 1945, and began bombing targets on the Japanese mainland six days later. Iwo Jima was invaded on February 19. The battle for Iwo Jima lasted until March 17, with "mopping up" operations continuing until June 1. Casualties were heavy and *kamikazes* took a toll of Allied ships.

During the battle for Okinawa, USS *Benjamin Franklin* and USS *Wasp* were staggered by bomb hits. *Wasp* lost 101 sailors with 269 wounded. The ship was forced to return for major repairs. *Franklin,* with a deck load of aircraft, took two bomb hits on the carrier deck that set her on fire. Thirty enormous explosions were heard on *Franklin* by sailors nearby on USS *Yorktown.* The ship's

Japan's last, desperate, and brutally effective weapon, the *kamikaze*, suicide attack. This photo was taken from the deck of the *USS Essex*, just before the plane, burning but still in control, crashed into her.

U.S. Navy

captain, Leslie H. Gehres notified Mitscher that "You save us from the Japs and we'll save this ship." Mitscher told Burke, "You tell him we'll save him."[24] Gehres managed to save the most heavily damaged carrier of WW II, but lost 724 men and had 265 wounded. USS *Franklin* reached Ulithi Harbor, initially under tow, and then under her own power. She was given minimal repair and traveled to Pearl Harbor for a brief stop, and then reached the Brooklyn Navy Yard just as the last crewmember's body was recovered from some debris that covered it.

Kamikazes put USS *Bunker Hill*, Mitscher's flagship, out of the war during the Okinawa battle. Between March 19 and May 11, ten Allied carriers were struck by *kamikazes* putting four of them out of action. In just four days, Mitscher lost two flagships (*Bunker Hill* and *Enterprise*). The battle had been costly for the troops on the ground and the ships at sea. Mitscher reported losing 139 pilots and 50 aircrewmen, and 880 planes. Allied ship losses were 11 sunk and 102 damaged.[25]

Mitscher was completely worn out. On May 27, Halsey relieved Spruance and McCain relieved Mitscher. After a stop in Pearl Harbor for debriefing, Mitscher returned to Washington, testified before Congress, chaired several boards, and planned for demilitarization. The secretary of the navy offered the position as chief of naval operations to Mitscher, but he declined, saying that there were admirals senior to him, and besides, he needed a rest. He did accept the position as deputy chief of naval operations for aviation.

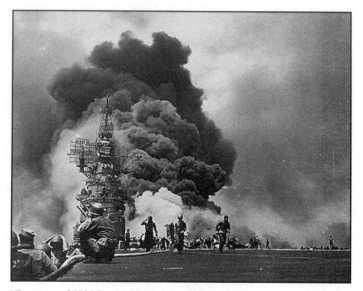

The crew of *USS Bunker Hill* fighting a flight-deck fire after being hit by a suicide plane.

U.S. Navy

On March 1, Mitscher was promoted to full admiral, only the second pioneer naval aviator to be so selected. On the same day, he was directed to assume command of the Eighth Fleet, headquartered at Norfolk aboard USS *Lake Champlain*. Mitscher's first duty was to ask for Captain Arleigh Burke as his chief of staff. During April 1946, when President Truman publicly chastised senior naval officers (for the third time) for "lobbying" against service unification (which Truman advocated), Mitscher submitted his letter of resignation to Admiral Nimitz, telling him that unification of the services would seriously jeopardize the security of the nation. Nimitz agreed with Mitscher, but refused to accept his resignation.

On April 22, Mitscher hosted President Truman, Secretary of the Navy James V. Forrestal, Admirals Nimitz and William D. Leahy, and General Harry H. Vaughan, aide to the president, aboard the carrier USS *Franklin D. Roosevelt*. This was the first time a president of the United States had been aboard an aircraft carrier at sea. Flight operations went well with dive bombing demonstrations and a low pass by a target drone which went out of control and crashed a few feet behind the carrier. President Truman applauded vigorously, not knowing that the close miss was unintentional.

During June 1946, Mitscher and his wife Frances, went fishing in Canada. One day fishing was slow and the weather cold. Mitscher told the guide that they would go in now. "No by God," said the Indian guide, "you'll fish three more drops." Mitscher obediently did so and upon arriving back in the lodge, said with a twinkle in his eye, "You know, I am not used to being given orders what to do, especially in a boat."[26]

Mitscher accepted the position as commander-in-chief Atlantic in the summer of 1946, and began the whirlwind tours of conferences, cocktail and dinner parties, throughout Europe, where he received many honors. Back home on January 26, 1947, he complained to Frances about feeling ill. He was admitted to the Naval Base hospital at Bethesda, Maryland, where his illness was diagnosed as a heart attack.

Mitscher did not have the strength to recover from a heart attack, but the old warrior continued to maintain contact with his staff and answer questions pertaining to future operations plans. On February 1, when he realized that Mitscher was still trying to maintain his operational navy ties, Rear Admiral J.C. Adams, the district medical officer and old friend of Mitscher, went to his bedside and told him the truth. "Pete," Adams said, "We've always been honest with each other so what I'm going to tell you is in all honesty. You've got to realize, once and for all, that you have made your last contribution to the navy. You will not be returned to active duty. There will not be any more staff visits, no more navy talk."[27]

Mitscher did not change his facial expression. Only his grip on Adam's hand tightened. Finally, as if he were failing to answer the bell for the last round, he thanked Adams, said he was "tired as hell," and rolled over as if to sleep. Perhaps the knowledge that his career had ended took as great a toll of Mitscher as the war.

On February 3, 1947, Admiral Marc Mitscher died of coronary thrombosis (a tired heart). Flags throughout the nation flew at half mast in respect for the gallant fighter. He was buried two days later in the snow covered Arlington National Cemetery. Following the 17-gun salute, one of the reporters present, said, "If we have another war we will be a lot less able to win it without him."[28]

351

There were many epilogues by many people and newspapers devoted to Mitscher's passing. Perhaps the most fitting was contained in a letter to his mother by Henry Mustin, Jr., a young man who fought with Mitscher in the Pacific and the son of one of the navy's earliest aviators. Henry was bounced on Mitscher's knee as a youngster in Pensacola, when both Henry Mustin Jr's father and Mitscher were assigned to flight training.

> A bad day. Because of Pete, of course. I found myself pretty moist around the eyes at the news of his passing. This in spite of knowing it could not help but happen before so very long. Men do not live that way and spend a great old age telling grandchildren about it.
>
> How peaceful the passing was in contrast with the fierce, stormy nature of the little man! It was almost a joke of nature that he should have been spared a flaming death in battle to go thus quietly, in his bed, in his sleep.
>
> He will be greatly missed, in a way, and yet I believe it was fortunate in another sense he is gone. He was all fighter, a breed in failing popularity today—though bravery is never out of fashion. He was not happy in peace, having found his ultimate purpose in the holocaust of war. Of all the pictures taken of him, I have seen only one which caught him with a smiling countenance. In it, he stands on a carrier's bridge, looking out over the sea to where his air groups are forming for a strike against the enemy.
>
> How he hated the enemy! Only such a hatred, fierce, bitter, uncompromising, can fit a man to blast and batter others into eternity. Wars are scarcely desirable, but once when waged, such men are needed that they may be waged unremittingly until victory.
>
> I remember very well the lift" (in morale) that came with him to the carrier fleet. One attack with him was all it took to let us know we were sure to win. Until he took command, there still seemed doubt; afterward, none. Surely, there is some Valhalla for him.[29]

21

DOUGLAS MACARTHUR:
JAN. 26, 1880 - SEPT. 2, 1945

Douglas MacArthur had a military career second to none. Consider the following:

He was the youngest division commander in France in WW I, the youngest superintendent of West Point, the youngest active major general in the U.S. Army, the youngest army chief of staff, and the youngest man to become a full general.

He was the only American general whose father was also chief of staff, and the first full general to be awarded the Congressional Medal of Honor. His father also earned the medal. He was the only American to become a field marshal in another nation's army.[1]

His overall scholastic record at West Point was 98.14, and he was the only cadet to earn 100 per cent in several of his classes. He was head of the student body and class salutatorian at West Point. He graduated at the top of his class and was voted cadet most likely to succeed.[2]

In 1912, his father, in the twilight of his life, lamented that that he would not be able to die while leading his troops. Shortly thereafter, his regiment held their 50th reunion and invited the old general to make a brief appearance. Against the advice of his doctors, he did attend and rose to make his remarks. He said that this would be the last time he would ever be able to greet his comrades, made his remarks, and fell dead. His last wish was fulfilled.

The general's aide, rushed across the stage, seized the regimental colors, and threw it over the dead general. "A prayer," he shouted.[3] The veterans rose, knelt and prayed. Two days later, the aide, overcome by emotion, also fell dead.

More than one historian has described Douglas MacArthur as brilliant and the greatest military leader of WW II. MacArthur did have some major victories to his credit, and he ensured that he received full publicity for every victory his troops achieved. But to label him as brilliant and "the greatest military leader in WW II," ignores his inadequacies in the Philippines, and the many hard-fought island campaigns in the Pacific (Midway, Guadalcanal, Saipan, Iwo Jima, and Okinawa to list but a few), that he was not involved in. Perhaps his greatest achievement was not as a military leader but as the ruler of Japan following that country's surrender.

Author John Gunther once asked an illustrious Japanese civilian what he thought of MacArthur. "Not a simple man," was the response.[4] Many books have been written about MacArthur, but perhaps those four words best sum up the man.

Douglas MacArthur was born on January 26, 1880, in Little Rock, Arkansas. He was the third son of Lieutenant Gen. Arthur MacArthur and Mary (Hardy) MacArthur. He lived on army posts most of his life and made a decision early to be a soldier. His mother adored Douglas and raised him as a child of destiny.

Douglas' mother, "Pinkie," is the one constant in MacArthur's life, from his early childhood until she died in 1935. Following her husband's death she became manager of Douglas' career and made constant demands upon senior officers and members of congress for promotions and choice assignments for her son. It is well known that MacArthur felt great stress because of her intercessions, but he did nothing to stop her.

Douglas played baseball and managed the football team at West Point. Because of his high grades and class standing, he was assigned to the engineer corps. His first assignment was Leyte in the Philippines. Forty-two years later he landed at Leyte Gulf, as commanding general of the invasion force of the Philippines. He was an observer for the Russo-Japanese war and first visited Japan in 1905. He then toured the Far East for eight months with his parents, as military aide to his father. Forty years later, following Japan's unconditional surrender, he became Supreme Allied Commander of Japan.

After serving as aide to his father, for an extended eight-month tour of Asia and the South Pacific, MacArthur reported to the Army Engineer School at Fort McNair, near Washington D.C. He was one of 11 officers enrolled in the program. After a month in the school, Lieutenant MacArthur was reported to have little interest in his course at the school. His work was not equal to that of the other officers in the course, and the results of his field work were unsatisfactory.[5]

Mary MacArthur with a picture of her son, circa 1925.

Due to his mother's pleadings, President Theodore Roosevelt asked for Douglas as an aide at the White house. This took him away from the Engineer School, which he would later complete in absentia. He was next assigned to the district office of engineers in Milwaukee. Here he was given a report on his efficiency that said ". . . he exhibited less interest in and put less time upon the drafting room, the plans and specifications for work . . . than seemed consistent with my instructions." "He, (MacArthur), demonstrated and argued verbally and at length against assignment to his present duty" which seemed to detract from his other interests.[6]

When a vacancy occurred at West Point in the engineer department, MacArthur's mother was able to "arrange" a nomination for Douglas to the post. The superintendent, Hugh I. Scott, later to be Army chief of staff, rejected Douglas as not being qualified for the position and reprimanded the officer that nominated Douglas.[7] MacArthur next received orders to the Third Engineer Battalion where he again received unsatisfactory reports on his performance of duty. "I am of the opinion that Lieutenant MacArthur, while on duty under my immediate orders, did not conduct himself . . . and that his duties were not performed in a satisfactory manner."[8]

MacArthur was next ordered to Fort Leavenworth where he was a marked man. He had to redeem himself or face discharge from the army. He did well at Leavenworth, both in command and staff duties. During this period, his mother continued to try to assist his career both within and without the army. In February, 1911, MacArthur was promoted to captain and appointed head of the military engineering department of the Field Engineer School.

When his father died in 1912, Douglas requested special consideration in his assignment to be able to care for his mother who suffered from insomnia, the cause unknown. He received orders to report to the office of General Leonard Wood, the Army chief of staff, who was a good friend of Douglas' mother and father. To this point in his career, Douglas had demonstrated an unwillingness to work at those duties he considered beneath him, and to use any and all connections to advance his career without completing those duties expected of him.

MacArthur's service in Vera Cruz, Mexico, in 1911 earned him recognition and a recommendation by General Wood for the Medal of Honor. Those officer's responsible for action on such recommendations refused to concur with the recommendation, and found MacArthur's actions presumptuous and arrogant.[9] The recommendation served more as a reprimand than a tribute.

MacArthur was promoted to major on December 11, 1915, and was subsequently ordered to the office of the Secretary of War, where he became the army's first public relations officer. On August 1, 1917, the secretary of war signed MacArthur's commission as a full colonel in the army, and gave him a choice of serving in the engineers or the infantry. The chief of engineers objected that he could not accept MacArthur with such a commission, so MacArthur chose the infantry.

MacArthur's first wife was Louise Brooks, the stepdaughter of a millionaire and well connected with the power brokers. They met while Douglas was superintendent at West Point. She did not like military duty and Douglas did not like the excesses associated with her wealth. It was not a good relationship, and resulted in a divorce in 1929 after seven years of marriage. They were separated for two years before the divorce. It was not an amiable divorce although money was not involved. She complained about her meddling mother-in-law and said Douglas was a failure as a lover.

Following his divorce, Douglas returned to the Philippines as commander of the army's Philippine department. During this period he became enamored of Elizabeth Cooper, a mixed Philippine and Scottish woman, 30 years his junior. When he was subsequently chosen to be chief of staff, he arranged to bring Elizabeth "Isabel" to Washington as his lover. He installed Isabel in an apartment and kept the relationship secret from his mother.

Douglas was named Army chief of staff in November 1930. He returned to Washington and moved into Quarters #1 at Fort Myer with his mother. According to MacArthur, the most poignant episode during his role as chief of staff took place when he was ordered to use military force to move 10,000 unemployed veterans from areas surrounding the capital and other federal buildings.[10] His troops destroyed the squatter's tents, used tear gas against them, and inflicted numerous casualties upon the veterans. Shortly after the "Battle of Anacostia Flats," as the displacement was called, Presidential candidate Roosevelt told his staff that MacArthur was one of the two most dangerous men in the country, the other being Senator Huey Long. Roosevelt went on to explain that many "Nazi minded" Americans wanted a symbolic strong man to lead them out of the depression. There was none so well endowed with charm, tradition, and majestic appearance as MacArthur. Roosevelt said he planned to tame such men and make them useful to the current administration.[11]

Following the Anacostia Flats action, journalists Drew Pearson and Robert Allen began to attack MacArthur's dictatorial leanings in their syndicated column, The Washington-Merry-Go-Round. In the spring of 1934, MacArthur sued them for $1,750,000, charging slander, and writing disrespectful things about his mother. This was a big mistake. MacArthur's first wife knew about Isabel Cooper, talked a lot at cocktail parties, and, as a result, it did not take the columnists long to find Isabel.

Douglas moved Isabel from an apartment to a hotel and then broke off their affair by mailing Isabel a one-way ticket to

Manila. Isabel refused to leave and was primed to make life miserable for the general. Isabel, in return for the journalist's promise of money, protection, and help in finding a job, provided boxes of MacArthur's love letters and a detailed diary of their affair.

MacArthur's lawyer was provided with copies of testimony that Isabel was prepared to make if the case went to trial. Her planned testimony included remarks that MacArthur allegedly made in her presence, such as denouncement of the secretary of war, calling Roosevelt, " that cripple in the white house," and other boastful and damning statements.

For at least once in his life, MacArthur turned tail. The journalists accepted MacArthur's offer to drop the suit, but only on condition that MacArthur pay all legal costs and provide for Isabel's future. Douglas paid $16,000 in legal costs and provided $15,000 directly to Isabel.[12]

The scandal became popular gossip in Washington but did not ruin MacArthur's career. Isabel was not so fortunate. She left Washington, worked at a series of jobs, including acting in Hollywood, and committed suicide in 1960.

The strain of the lawsuit, his mother's constant pressure for him to achieve more, and the demands of his job, nearly took a similar toll on Douglas. He feared that he might not measure up to the task as chief of staff, and rather than fail, confided to his friend, T.J. Davis, that he planned to commit suicide. He made the threats so often that Davis learned to ignore them. Once on a train, he told Davis, "I've done everything I can in the army and life, my term as chief of staff is ending. As we pass over the Tennessee River bridge, I intend to jump from the train. This is where my life ends Davis."[13] Davis wished him happy landings.

MacArthur's term as chief of staff was due to end in the fall of 1934. Roosevelt wanted to increase the military budget, and believed MacArthur could be helpful in steering his budget increase through a hostile congress. He extended MacArthur as chief of staff for another year. The one-year extension saw MacArthur primarily involved with legislation required to give the Philippines commonwealth status and later independence.

MacArthur saw an opportunity to avoid stepping down from his chief's position. He asked for and was given the position as head of the military mission to the Philippines. MacArthur believed he would keep his four star rank, and the commonwealth of the Philippines would pay his salary of $18,000 plus a $15,000 expense account, and a free luxury suite in the Manila Hotel. MacArthur expected to go to Manila while still in the status as chief of staff. Roosevelt had other ideas and named General Malin Craig as the new chief in October 1935. MacArthur was furious. No one in the White House seriously considered MacArthur's ego and what the demotion meant to him. This indifference can be blamed, at least in part, for the poor relations between MacArthur and Roosevelt in the years ahead.

During his shipboard passage to the Philippines with his mother and sister Mary, his sister arranged for Jean Faircloth, a woman she met on the ship that was going to Shanghai, to change her travel plans and visit Douglas in Manila. Jean was 19 years younger than Douglas, wealthy, and from Tennessee. His mother died a few weeks after reaching Manila, Mary returned home, but Douglas and Jean fell in love. Jean took up residence in Manila, and they both returned to New York City for a wedding at city hall in 1937. That was the last time either of them returned to the U.S. until MacArthur was relieved by President Truman in 1951. They had one son, Arthur, born in Manila. Jean MacArthur called her husband, "General," or "the General," but never by his first or last name. She seemed happy with military life, and performed her social functions with traditional southern courtesy.

As might be expected, MacArthur had serious disagreements with commissioner Frank Murphy in Manila. MacArthur criticized Murphy even before he arrived in Manila and continually tried to have Roosevelt appoint him (MacArthur) to both positions. When Roosevelt did not do so, MacArthur convinced Manuel Quezon, president-elect of the commonwealth, that Murphy played only a ceremonial role in the shaping of Philippine independence, further widening the area of disagreement between the two men.

In 1936, MacArthur submitted a defense plan for the Philippines to President Quezon. The plan called for the organization of an army of citizen soldiers led by a small regular army. This force, according to MacArthur, if armed with a small flotilla of torpedo boats and an air force, could deter or defeat any invader. Progress toward this goal, MacArthur said, already exceeded original anticipation.[14] The plan was appealing to Quezon, but not to the general staff in Washington. The staff had long ago decided that the Philippines could not be adequately defended and what defense could be offered lay in a quick retreat to a well-prepared Bataan Peninsula (code named War Plan Orange).

The staff also noted that that not a single conscript had been called into service, not one training camp existed, no weapons were available for the proposed army, and no military professionals (other than MacArthur) believed the plan to be practical. The Philippine Army was thought to be wholly ineffective in defending the country against an enemy like Japan.

Before retiring as commissioner in 1936, Frank Murphy warned his superiors of the menace of the military mission in Manila. Sending MacArthur was a mistake, he argued, and should be abandoned as soon as possible. Rather than fall back on the approved War Plan Orange which called for the defense of the Bataan Peninsula, MacArthur proceeded with his plan to defend the Philippines on the beaches. As a result, Bataan and Corregidor were not provisioned and equipped to feed and supply those men that finally did retreat there.

The loss of MacArthur's air force in the Philippines falls squarely upon MacArthur. After the war, he defended his lack of action to meet the Japanese attack on the Philippines by stating that he was told by Washington, "Not to initiate hostilities against the Japanese under any circumstances. The first overt move in the Philippines must come from the enemy."[15] He also states that Major Gen. Lewis H. Brereton, Commander of MacArthur's Far East Air Force in the Philippines, never discussed with him a preemptive raid against the Japanese bases on Formosa.[16]

MacArthur's first statement was partially true in that President Roosevelt wanted the Japanese to strike the first blow so Japan could not say their offensive actions were in response to American attacks. However, the actual message read, ". . . if hostilities cannot, repeat, cannot, be avoided the United States desires that Japan commit the first overt act." MacArthur knew that Japan had struck the first blow the previous day at Pearl Harbor because he had been so advised by Admiral Husband Kimmel in Hawaii at 3:30 A.M. December 8, (Manila time), and by Washington at 3:40 A.M. He was also advised that a state of war existed between the United States and Japan at 5:30 A.M.

His second statement is also partially true in that Major Gen. Brereton tried most of the morning to see MacArthur for approval to attack the Japanese bombers on Formosa. Colonel Richard Sutherland, MacArthur's chief of staff, refused to let Brereton see MacArthur, because MacArthur was too busy. Brereton had his pilots briefed and on short alert to launch. Finally, as the morning wore on and he was denied the opportunity to see MacArthur, Brereton realized that it would be impossible to gain tactical surprise over the Japanese and gave up on his attempt.

At 12:10 P.M., Manila time, 100 Mitsubishi bombers escorted by 84 Zero fighters roared across the Boshi channel and destroyed MacArthur's air force on the ground.[17] The Far East Air Force (FEAF) that MacArthur counted on so heavily for his defense of the Philippines, was effectively eliminated on the first day of the war.[18] Although the "unprepared" situation at Pearl Harbor became the subject of 19 separate investigations, the loss of MacArthur's air force in the Philippines did not produce a single inquiry. Commanders (such as Admiral Kimmel and General Short) were relieved for being unprepared for far less warning than that given to MacArthur.

Most military and civilian officials assumed that after the war, an appropriate investigation would be conducted to determine the reason for MacArthur's lack of preparedness. Francis B. Sayre, the Philippine high commissioner, assumed that "an official investigation would follow."[19] Lieutenant Gen. Claire Chennault told the war department that "If I had been caught with my planes on the ground ... I could never again have looked my fellow officers squarely in the eye."[20] Others considered MacArthur's actions as only short of treason, since MacArthur had the Magic (code-breaking) capability, nine hours of warning, and did nothing to save his aircraft. He was in a far better position than Admiral Kummel in Hawaii to have prevented the surprise attack.

Statements from Major Gen. Brereton, and Major Gen. Sutherland, after the war, did not solve the quandary of why the aircraft were destroyed on the ground. Brereton blames Summerlin. Summerlin blames Brereton, and MacArthur disclaims all knowledge of the issue. Due possibly to the situation in the Philippines, an investigation was never conducted. It is known that Sutherland had a reputation of arrogance and refusing to let high ranking officers see MacArthur promptly. He also had a reputation for interfering with orders and plans of MacArthur's air commanders. General George C. Kinney, MacArthur's air commander during 1942-1945, often clashed with Sutherland.

MacArthur takes great credit for the withdrawal of his forces from their defensive positions to Bataan, but, by his own words, it was a close thing. "It was close - just by a split-second, but split seconds are what win battles."[21] He fails to mention that if he had followed War Plan Orange, his forces would have been on the Bataan Peninsula two weeks earlier with enough food, equipment and supplies to last six months. If he had moved even one-fifth of the 50 million bushels of rice stored at the Cabanatuan rice storage facility, his troops would have been supplied for an entire year. Instead, by implementing his "defense on the beach strategy," not one grain of this rice was moved to Bataan or Corregidor.

While the responsibility for the loss of the FEAF has never been pinned to any one individual (except overall responsibility to MacArthur), the failure to provide sufficient food, medical supplies, ammunition, and defensive positions on Bataan, belongs to MacArthur. He waited for two weeks (December 23) to retract his "defense on the beach strategy" thereby eliminating any possibility of adequately supplying the troops that fell back into the Bataan Peninsula. Why he hesitated to make such a decision, despite the urgings of his staff, remains another of the mysteries associated with MacArthur.

When MacArthur's forces on Luzon retreated to Bataan, the troops on the main southern islands of Panay, Negros, Cebu, Leyte, Samar, Palawan, and Mindanao were left to fend for themselves. Supplies including ten million rounds of rifle ammunition on the dock at Cebu, were destroyed because there was insufficient time to move them to Manila.[22]

MacArthur and his family evacuated Manila on December 24, 1941, and issued a proclamation declaring Manila an open city. By so doing, he hoped to spare the people of Manila the ravages of an air and ground attack against the city.

On January 3, 1942, Philippine President Manuel Quezon issued a secret order transferring $640,000 in commonwealth funds to General MacArthur. One-half million dollars were to be given to MacArthur, the remainder divided among his top three staff members. The payment violated various army regulations and was kept secret by MacArthur.

MacArthur, his wife, son, and Ah Cheu, Arthur's Cantonese nursemaid, plus 13 senior members of his staff departed Corregidor on March 11, 1942. They left in four torpedo boats commanded by Lieutenant John D. Bulkeley, and arrived at Mindanao on March 13. They were flown to a field south of Darwin, Australia by two B-17s on March 16, and arrived in Melbourne on the 21st. Left behind on Corregidor with only a skeleton staff was General Jonathan Wainwright. MacArthur gave Wainwright orders not to surrender, but to fight to the last man.

President Quezon, was on the island of Negros when MacArthur decided to leave Corregidor. Once MacArthur was safely at Mindanao, he decided that Quezon and his family should also escape the Japanese and accompany MacArthur's group to Australia. MacArthur sent for Bulkeley, and ordered him to take his torpedo boat to Negros and bring back Quezon. "Hop over to Negros (one hundred miles northeast of Mindanao), find Quezon, and bring him and his whole tribe back here."[23] MacArthur added, "I don't care how you get him here - just do it. We're sending Quezon to Australia to form a Philippine government in exile, whether he likes it or not."[24]

President Roosevelt gave MacArthur a direct order to evacuate Corregidor on Feb. 22, 1942. MacArthur, his family, and his staff left Corregidor on March 11, and after a harrowing 560-mile trip on a PT boat like this one, he was flown to Australia in a B-17 bomber.

Real War Photos

Bulkeley's travels and troubles in locating and "kidnapping" a reluctant Quezon is a story unto itself.

Having said this much, there will be a later chapter on Admiral John Bulkley.

Wainwright passed the "no surrender" order to Major Gen. Edward King, commander of Luzon Force. King stated that he understood the no surrender instructions, but surrendered Bataan with its 70,000 sick, wounded and starving troops on April 9. General Jonathan Wainwright defended Corregidor until May 6, 1942. When faced with the destruction of the hospital and massacre of all forces on Corregidor, he surrendered all forces in the Philippines.

MacArthur, who was evacuated from the Philippines before either surrender, was awarded the Medal of Honor. He refused to permit the same honor to General Wainwright who stayed and defended the Philippines for two months following MacArthur's departure and spent the remainder of the war as a Japanese prisoner. It would be 1945, and the end of the war, before Wainwright would receive such an honor, despite MacArthur's refusal to support the award.

The Australians welcomed MacArthur as a savior, and he rapidly took to the idea. In Canberra, during a meeting with Prime Minister John Curtin, he said, "Mr. Prime Minister, you take care of the rear and I will take care of the front."[25] The United States sent 80,000 men to Australia by the time MacArthur arrived, and scheduled another 200,000 for later in 1942.

The MacArthurs occupied three suites in the private sector of the Lennox Hotel in Brisbane. An elevator serviced the floor and a guard was posted to keep uninvited persons from getting off at the floor. Most meals were provided by the hotel kitchen, although MacArthur's aide, Lieutenant Col. Sydney Huff, Ah Cheu (son Arthur's Chinese nurse), and a hotel maid prepared some of the meals in the quarters. Correspondent's that visited MacArthur in Melbourne and Brisbane observed that "MacArthur is just as remote as ever. He is rarely seen."[26]

Because Admiral Ernest J. King, chief of naval operations, refused to have the Pacific Fleet under army control, a separate land and water area was created for MacArthur to command. He was given the Southwest Pacific Area consisting of Australia, New Guinea, The Bismarck Archipelago, Solomon Islands, and Netherlands East Indies (less Sumatra). Admiral Chester Nimitz retained the Pacific Ocean Areas of the central and southern Pacific.

The decision to give MacArthur his own Pacific theater of operations was the result of public and political pressure. Roosevelt; General George C. Marshall, Army chief of staff; Dwight Eisenhower, former aide to MacArthur and second-in-command of the war plans division were all against his appointment. Since January, however, a MacArthur craze had swept America. MacArthur's own public relations team made MacArthur out to be a hero and the only force actually fighting the Japanese. Publications termed MacArthur as the "Lion of Luzon," and "Hero of the Pacific."[27] Buildings, streets and bridges throughout America were renamed after the General and members of congress strongly favored the nation's highest award for MacArthur. They also voiced support for him as a candidate for the next presidential election.

When they became aware, Roosevelt and his staff had grave concerns about Quezon's reported $500,000 "gift" to MacArthur. Many believed the "gift" was part of an agreement MacArthur negotiated with Quezon in order to go to the Philippines and plan for their defense. MacArthur never raised the issue with any one in Washington. When Quezon offered a similar, but much smaller, gift to Eisenhower, "Ike" promptly requested advice from General Marshall, who warned him to stay clear, lest it "destroy" him.[28] Ike carefully explained to President Quezon the reasons for his inability to accept the money. Quezon accepted the explanation and said that, under the circumstances, he would have done the same thing. One cannot help but wonder how Quezon (and anyone else) could then rationalize MacArthur's acceptance of the "gift."

Perhaps *Times* correspondent, Robert Sherrod, who was at Bataan and Corregidor during the fighting, best summed up the situation with MacArthur. "Outside his immediate headquarters," Sherrod reported, "most officers hated MacArthur almost beyond description." The troops called him Dugout Doug for his refusal to leave the protection of Malinta tunnel on Corregidor and visit the troops on Bataan. Only once did he do so. Sherrod described MacArthur as "brooding, aloof, and remote, a poser and extreme egoist."[29]

But, as Sherrod also put it, "The American people were hungry for a hero, and no one made better speeches than MacArthur, not Roosevelt, or even Churchill."[30] MacArthur had a sense of drama (ham acting) that appealed to the American public, and so, for no better reason, he became a central figure in the Pacific.

By May 1942, Roosevelt was complaining to his staff about the trouble MacArthur was making "with his constant and public demands for more troops, ships and a greater role in the Pacific war." He remarked to his press secretary about MacArthur's "constantly playing to the grandstand," and that he, MacArthur, "seems to have forgotten" that his record in Manila resembled that of Admiral Kimmel and General Short, who now "face court martial on charges of laxity at Pearl Harbor." "MacArthur's leadership at Corregidor," Roosevelt continued, "was criminal, not heroic."[31] General Robert Eichelberger, an army corps commander and later Eighth Army commander under MacArthur, found that the stealing of any publicity from MacArthur was like driving a dagger into his heart. A dagger wound MacArthur would never forget.

MacArthur decided that the Japanese fortress of Rabaul should be his first target on the way back to the Philippines. The joint staff knew better. Rabaul was much too strongly defended for the limited forces available in the Pacific. Instead, such additional forces as were available were sent to Midway and Guadalcanal. Both battles proved to be major American victories, although Guadalcanal took six long months to win.

Preempted by the successes of Admiral Nimitz at Midway, and Halsey at Guadalcanal, MacArthur shifted his attention from Rabaul to Buna, Papua New Guinea. Buna was a small mission station in the southeastern part of New Guinea. MacArthur wanted the area to construct a forward airbase to support his leapfrogging advance toward the Philippines. Naval Intelligence warned MacArthur that the Japanese also planned an assault on Buna to use the area as a base for an overland attack against Port Moresby.

The Japanese acted first. On July 21, they landed 16,000 troops and proceeded to drive the small militia and Australian force back over the Owen Stanley Mountain Range towards Port Moresby. Only a message from Imperial Headquarters to the Japanese commanding general, to stop his forward progress and return to Buna for evacuation, saved Port Moresby. Japanese Imperial headquarters mistakenly believed the large amphibious assault force approaching Guadalcanal was meant to cut off the Japanese force at Buna.

The Australians fought well at Milne Bay, another Japanese assault landing area intended to help seize Port Moresby. During a 14-day battle that drove a Japanese landing force back, the Japanese lost 600 dead to 161 Australians killed.

When the American forces did not arrive at Buna, landing instead at Guadalcanal, the Japanese dug in, and starting in November, fought a protracted battle against MacArthur's forces, most of them Australian. The Japanese were quick to grind the Australian advance to a complete stop. MacArthur, wanting a quick victory, sent a message to Major Gen. Edwin Harding on the 21st, "Take Buna today at all costs. MacArthur."[32]

Harding was astounded. His coastal force was pinned down by heavy enemy fire from fortified bunkers and his inland force bogged down in the savage swamps. Nevertheless, his attack continued the next morning. On November 30, MacArthur, convinced that his troops were not fighting, relieved Harding and sent Major Gen. Robert Eichelberger to take command with the orders to "take Buna or do not come back alive." He also told Eichelberger "If you capture Buna, I'll give you a Distinguished Service Cross and recommend you for a British decoration."[33] He then continued as if granting the ultimate acknowledgement, "I'll release your name for newspaper publication."[34] Months later when *Life* magazine did an article on Eichelberger with full-page photograph, MacArthur was incensed.

Eichelberger took until January 2, 1943, to take Buna, and was able to do so only because of substantial Australian reinforcements armed with bunker-busting weapons and tanks. The Japanese had been able to reinforce their defenses with troops from Rabaul, moved by destroyers to the beaches. Allied casualties were high, numbering 620 killed, 2,065 wounded, and 132 missing. The Australians took Gona on December 9, after losing 41 percent of the most combat experienced soldiers in the Australian army; 530 officers and men from the 21[st]Brigade and 39th Battalion. An additional 129 casualties were suffered in cleaning up the Sanananda area.

During one of MacArthur's conferences, attended by Admiral William Halsey, Australian General Thomas Blamey, and Army generals, Walter Kruger and George C. Kinney, the group was wrestling with the question of how to defeat Japanese strong points such as Rabaul, with a garrison of 100,000 men, with the limited resources available. MacArthur suggested that they don't take such strong points. "In fact, gentlemen," he said, "I don't want them."[35] He proposed instead, a series of island-hopping advances whereby they would leave Japanese strong points isolated and let them die on the vine.

The first such bypassed base was Lae on the northern New Guinea coast. General Kinney's aviation sunk convoys trying to supply Lae, and after sinking two such convoys during the Battle of the Bismark Sea, in March 1943, Lae fell without serious fighting.

MacArthur then landed forces on New Georgia, on New Britain, and in a 500 mile leap, at Hollandia, New Guinea. Rabaul, with its strong garrison, was left to rot as were other Japanese bases. In the summer of 1944, MacArthur moved his headquarters from Brisbane to Hollandia. Much has been written about the million-dollar "White House" that MacArthur had built for himself on Hollandia. In actuality, the house was well furnished, provided quarters for MacArthur and his staff, but his wife and son never did live in the quarters. MacArthur was promoted to five-star general on December 15, 1944.

One of the "interesting" stories to come to light during Macarthur's movement towards the Philippines was his insatiable need for publicity. His public relations officer, Brigadier Gen. Le Grande A. Diller, guarded MacArthur's publicity as though it were a gold mine, which indeed it proved to be. When Dwight Eisenhower returned from the Philippines as MacArthur's chief of staff, he was asked why he had left MacArthur. His reply was straightforward, "He thought I was stealing his publicity."[36]

MacArthur returned to the Philippines on October 21, 1944, wading ashore at Leyte Gulf. One of his major priorities was to free the prisoners at Santo Tomas and Cabanatuan prisons. When army forces liberated Santo Tomas, emaciated men and women dressed in rags approached their liberators. Hoarse sounds, not words came from many of their throats, and tears flowed from their faces. This was the best the prisoners could do to demonstrate their joy at being freed. Men who weighed 190 pounds when imprisoned now weighed 100 or less. The most requested thing they wanted was a piece of buttered bread.[37]

MacArthur had a need to create good news regardless of the immediate situation. He seemed to need to create a fantasy picture of the war wherever he was. On Christmas Day 1942 he sent a message back to America that "our activities are limited to routine safety precautions. Divine services were held."[38] But, as General Eichenberger recalled, the fighting at Buna was desperate on Christmas Day, and the outcome of the whole miserable, tortured campaign was in doubt."[39]

General Douglas MacArthur as a 5-star general after his promotion on December 15, 1944.

MacArthur Memorial

The Buna campaign seemed to set the pattern for MacArthur's version of the rest of the Pacific war. He eliminated the name of the general in charge of the actual fighting, leaving the reader to believe that it was MacArthur personally leading his troops in the field, but he started the practice of announcing victory well before it had been achieved. Due to this practice, some of the major battles of the Pacific were virtually unknown to Americans back home.

For example, MacArthur announced that the fall of Buna marked the end of the New Guinea campaign. His American and Australian forces in the field were well aware that the battle for Sanananda still lay ahead. They knew Sanananda would not be easy and feared for their careers if they could not match MacArthur's press releases.

After the war, some Pacific war veterans were reminiscing with General Eisenhower about the Pacific campaign, It turned out that Eisenhower had never heard of the Sanananda campaign. There is no reason why he should have known about it. It was merely a mopping up exercise in MacArthur's messages. Yet, more Americans and Australians were killed at Sanandana than died at Tarawa. The cost of lives during the Buna campaign was as great as the Battle for Guadalcanal.[40]

MacArthur declared imminent victory at Leyte on October 29, 1944 but Japanese resistance continued for another two months. Manila was declared secured on March 3, 1945. To liberate Manila, MacArthur used the same frontal tactics he criticized the marines for in the central Pacific. Instead of six weeks, it took six months to secure most of Luzon. Japanese losses were estimated as 17,000 killed, and as many as 3,000 escapees to the surrounding mountains. American casualties were 1,010 killed and 6,575 wounded. The citizens of Manila paid a terrible price in freeing the city of Japanese soldiers. An estimated 100,000 Filipinos died during the fighting for Manila.

Manila, and especially the old walled city of Intramuros within Manila, were virtually leveled. General Eichelberger reported that there was "practically nothing that hadn't been entirely knocked down and in ruins. It is all just graveyard."[41]

Another 8,000 Americans died "mopping up" the remainder of Leyte and Luzon with 29,000 wounded. Japan lost 200,000 soldiers and sailors. These operations were as costly in American lives as the battles waged by navy and marine forces in the central Pacific, battles MacArthur termed, "tragic and unnecessary massacres." [42]

General MacArthur at Morotai on Sept. 15, 1944.

MacArthur's public relations officer, Brigadier Gen. LeGrande A. Diller, failed to learn from the New Guinea campaign. MacArthur released information to Eichelberger and the press on Christmas Day, 1944, that only 6,000 Japanese were left on the Philippines for mopping up. It took the Eighth Army several more months and the killing of 27,000 more Japanese to finally secure Luzon.

When Davao City on Mindanao was captured, MacArthur announced victory on Mindanao. He told Eichelberger that there were not 4,000 Japanese left on Mindanao. After weeks of fighting, 23,000 Japanese soldiers finally surrendered. Corregidor was declared secure with thousands of Japanese casualties, and as many as 500 may have been buried in the tunnels under the island.

Another interesting aspect of MacArthur's messages back to Washington was his devotion to his army forces. As marine General Holland M. Smith wrote, "You will be unable to find a single reference to the marines in the Philippine campaign." A young marine that was wounded on Leyte and was being flown back to a rear area for treatment told Smith, "I don't mind losing my leg for my country, but at least MacArthur might have mentioned that marines were there."[43]

The famous marine poem did not do justice to their bitterness toward MacArthur, but the last verse remains a classic:

And while possibly a rumor now,
Some day it will be fact
That the Lord will hear a deep voice say,
Move over God, it's Mac.

MacArthur had General Yamashita tried, convicted, and executed for the Rape of Manila. In similar fashion, he had General Homma tried, convicted and executed for his responsibility for the Bataan Death March. These trials were more properly described as "rump courts," whereby MacArthur gained his revenge for the two Japanese generals that bested him. For a detailed summary of these trials, read chapters 30 and 33 of volume II of War in the Pacific.

MacArthur next proposed to invade the East Indies, but the joint chiefs refused to approve the operation. They believed the invasion of Java and other islands in the chain would be bloody and completely unnecessary. It was time to focus on the invasion of Japan. Thanks to the use of the two atomic weapons, invasion of Japan was unnecessary.

22

DOUGLAS MACARTHUR
SEPT. 2, 1945 - APRIL 5, 1964

General MacArthur (at right), with Admiral Halsey, Generals
Sutherland, Giles, Eichelberger and Chase, render salutes during the
flag-raising ceremony at the U.S. embassy in Tokyo Sept. 8, 1945.

US Army

MacArthur learned on August 10, 1945, that President
Truman selected him as Supreme Commander for the Allied Powers.
Once again, MacArthur's selection was based more on his high opinion
by the American public than by his relationship with the White House
or the joint chiefs. Admiral Nimitz was a candidate for the position,
but was eliminated due to the high casualties sustained during the

battle for Okinawa, and the first reports of the loss of USS *Indianapolis,* with possibly a thousand casualties. The American public wanted answers, not rewards for these tragedies.

MacArthur as commander-in-chief, Far East Command, aboard USS *Mount McKinley* during the Inchon landings, Sept. 15, 1950.

US Navy

MacArthur arrived in Japan on August 30, 1945, to find much of the country in ruins, millions of homeless refugees, and increasing shortages of food. MacArthur was 65 years old. Instead of retiring from military duty and seeking a position in civilian life, he became the ruler of 70 million Japanese. Insofar as the Japanese people were concerned, MacArthur personally ordered every occupation action, policy, and decision. To the Japanese, MacArthur "was" the U.S. government.

Yet, MacArthur had not been consulted on the use of the atomic bomb or postwar policies and procedures. He was given an advance copy of the "Initial Post-Surrender Policy for Japan," just before leaving Manila for Japan. Another document, transmitted to MacArthur from the joint chiefs, was the "Basic Directive for Post-Surrender Military Government in Japan Proper."[1] These documents outlined the policies and reform agenda MacArthur was to follow.

The acronym SCAP, for Supreme Commander of Allied Powers, was used for MacArthur personally as well as his administration. Moving quickly, in October 1945, SCAP issued orders for the release of all political prisoners, legalization of political parties, rights of free speech, and the right to assemble. The Japanese cabinet resigned in protest, warning that MacArthur had opened the floodgates to revolution.

Shortly after the New Year, SCAP presented Japan with a new draft constitution. The constitution stripped the emperor of divinity origins, opened voting to women, outlawed the creation of an armed force to conduct war, and increased the role of the Diet. Unless the draft was quickly accepted by the cabinet and Diet, SCAP warned, it would be presented directly to the Japanese people for a popular vote. Terrified by a popular vote on constitutional issues, the cabinet quickly approved the constitution.

Emperor Hirohito made the adoption of the constitution easier by publicly repudiating his divinity. A Texas senator suggested that the reason Hirohito said he wasn't God, "was because he found out MacArthur was."[2]

In rapid order, SCAP purged politicians, bureaucrats, military, and police that were in any way connected with the wartime policies of Japan. Land reforms were pushed through the Diet against strong Japanese opposition. Nearly a third of Japan's land changed hands and four million Japanese joined trade unions.

In 1947, amid speculation that he intended to run for the republican nomination for president, MacArthur pronounced the occupation complete. "Japan," he said, "was ready for a peace treaty, and he was available to host a peace conference." On March 12, Truman announced plans to continue the occupation until recovery seemed assured. MacArthur convened a press briefing to challenge Truman's decision, but few in Washington supported MacArthur. Since he had created a situation he could neither control nor win, MacArthur was forced to back down and follow Washington's instructions.

Perhaps MacArthur's attempt to drive through a peace treaty with its attendant publicity had much to do with his hope for the republican presidential nomination. He turned his wrath on General Eisenhower, following the "Ike for President" draft movement, calling Ike "a good time Charlie, and a New Dealer."[3] MacArthur was too shrewd to resign his military commission to run for the presidency. Only when he was announced as the republican candidate would he return to the United States to campaign for the election.

Eisenhower withdrew from the presidential race on January 22, declaring that he did not think military figures should seek political office. On March 9, MacArthur publicly announced his willingness to accept the nomination if offered. The Wisconsin primary scheduled for April 6, 1948, looked good for MacArthur, until the evening before the primary, when Joe McCarthy went public with his feelings:

> General MacArthur has been a great general. But he is now ready for retirement. He would be 72 years old before a term as President ended. Insofar as he being a favorite son of Wisconsin, the General was not born in Wisconsin, but rather in Little Rock, Arkansas. Neither of his marriages took place in Wisconsin nor did his divorce from his first wife. Neither of his wives ever resided in Wisconsin.[4]

Harold Stassen (of Minnesota) won 19 of Wisconsin's electoral delegates, and MacArthur eight. After a weaker showing in the Nebraska primaries, MacArthur's organization disbanded. At the republican convention in June, MacArthur received only the eight Wisconsin votes on the first ballot. The votes were switched to Tom Dewey for the second vote.

Following Truman's election, MacArthur's freedom to operate with SCAP was severely curtailed. Committees, strategic agendas, National Security Council directives, and special emissaries to implement the new policies were put into effect. MacArthur became a figurehead, but refused to step down. MacArthur told his Eighth Army commander, Lieutenant Gen. Eichelberger, that he refused to resign, " . . . that he planned to remain on the job and on the army's active list forever - until I die."[5]

For the next two years, most of MacArthur's time was consumed by the China-Taiwan issue and the industrialization of

Japan. Starting on June 25, 1950, with North Korea's invasion of South Korea, MacArthur's name became synonymous with Korea. His bold military advances in Korea routed the North Korean forces, but his lack of foresight brought the Chinese Communists into the war on the side of North Korea, eventually resulting in an armistice with boundaries at the 38th parallel.

MacArthur greets President Rhee at the ceremony marking the restoration of the government of South Korea at Seoul, Sept. 29, 1950.

US Navy

Korea, in 1950, was outside the American defensive perimeter in the Pacific. The joint chiefs of staff agreed with MacArthur's assessment that "anyone who commits the American army on the mainland of Asia ought to have his head examined."[6] On January 12, 1950, Dean Acheson, secretary of state, in a speech to the National Press Club, explained American policy in Asia to the world: "This country's defensive perimeter runs along the Aleutians to Japan, to the Ryukyus, to the Philippines." He went on to add " . . . So far as the military security of other areas in the Pacific is concerned, it must be clear that no person can guarantee those areas against military attack."[7]

The communist aggression in South Korea did not change American policy or make Korea vital to American interests or security. What did happen, according to MacArthur, was to make defense no longer a national issue, but rather an international issue. He was not so much concerned for the freedom of South Korea as he was in the possibility of millions of minds being swayed towards communism should the communists prevail there.

MacArthur was ordered to deploy forces to South Korea on June 26, 1950. It was too little, too late. Seoul, the capital of South Korea, fell on June 27 without a fight. By June 30, it became clear that if South Korea was to be saved, it would have to be by American ground troops. MacArthur's request was approved and a new American foreign policy towards South Korea began on that day.

As American and United Nations forces started to trickle into South Korea, the Allied forces were pushed rapidly to the southern end of the peninsula in and around the port of Pusan. Unless Pusan could be defended, there was little hope for reinforcements to enter South Korea. Pusan held for a month, and then MacArthur, against the advice of many military leaders, conducted the amphibious landing at Inchon, well in the rear of the North Korean forces.

U.N. warships pounded the defenses of Inchon for two days and navy carrier-based aircraft similarly pounded targets ashore. When the marines waded ashore on September 15, it took them only 40 minutes to capture Wohli Island, the key to the harbor's defense system. The U.N. troops that followed the marines ashore, turned and moved north, south and east to cut off the North Korean forces. Simultaneously, the forces bottled up at Pusan began to drive the enemy to the north. Seoul was retaken on September 27, 1950.

During July, MacArthur, without President Truman or UN knowledge, visited Chiang Kai-shek in Formosa. He spent a day-and-a-half there and provided little information regarding his visit. Shortly thereafter, however, Chiang began making public statements about "Sino-American military cooperation . . . and final victory in our struggle against communism."[8]

The visit to Formosa was the first major provocation on the part of MacArthur towards the administration, but it was far from the last. During August 1950, MacArthur angered President Truman and the National Security Council, and infuriated the joint chiefs for making statements contrary to existing policy on Taiwan and China, and for publishing classified materials. Truman repudiated the statements of MacArthur, saying they were in direct contradiction of administration policy. He also sent a personal letter to MacArthur drawing his attention to administration policies.

MacArthur met with Truman on October 15, 1950, at Wake Island to "alleviate certain strains" that existed between the two men. The meeting seemed to go well with MacArthur predicting fighting in Korea over by Thanksgiving and most of the Eighth Army back in Japan for Christmas. MacArthur told Truman he "saw very little chance of major (Chinese communist) intervention." Truman was pleased, gave MacArthur a box of candy for his family, pinned a medal on the general, and left for Washington.

By October 29, 200,000 Chinese troops had crossed the Yalu River and were driving the UN forces south. After a three-week lull, 300,000 Chinese and 65,000 North Koreans began a vicious counter attack that caused 11,000 casualties to U.N. forces. Seoul, the South Korean capital fell again in early January 1951.

The United States called for United Nations involvement to restore the boundaries of the divided Koreas, and the UN was quick to approve the request. As the Chinese pushed the U.N. forces southward, MacArthur advised Washington that he could only defeat the Chinese forces if provided with additional forces (including Chinese Nationalist forces from Taiwan), and given authority to bomb Manchuria.

The administration was unwilling to expand the war in this manner and suggested MacArthur withdraw his forces to an area in the south more suitable for defense. MacArthur was most inflexible on this issue and the joint chiefs lacked the courage to order him to do so. Truman later wrote that he "should have relieved General MacArthur then and there,"[9] but did not do so because it would give the impression that MacArthur was fired because of the Chinese offensive.

Truman, in his memoirs remarked that "MacArthur as usual has been shooting off his mouth," but felt it necessary to stand by his military subordinates. The President issued two directives on December 6, requiring all civil and military officials to clear their policy announcements in advance with the State and Defense departments. MacArthur's subsequent relief would be due to violations of these directives.

General Matthew Ridgeway took command of the Eighth Army in Korea on December 25, and reestablished a defensive perimeter further to the south. He stabilized the UN situation and improved morale of the UN forces. While the administration (and the UN) sought compromise and an end to fighting, MacArthur sought to escalate the war. On December 24, he submitted a list of targets that required the use of 34 atomic bombs. Unless the UN took offensive action against China, he said, ". . . the UN forces would be overrun."[10]

Thus began the debate, controversy and conflict associated with MacArthur's refusal to support the president's policy. MacArthur proclaimed that in war, there is no substitute for victory. He wanted to use Chiang Kai-shek's forces on Formosa to attack mainland China, thereby drawing away Chinese forces in South Korea. Truman's policy was to avert a third world war, with Russia on the side on communist China. He reiterated the limited goal of the UN forces in Korea: to restore the sovereign nation of South Korea.

On April 10, 1951, MacArthur bore the most impressive titles, trusts and responsibilities ever placed in a single individual. As Supreme Commander of the United Nations Forces in Korea, he was the first United Nations general in history, and the first leader of a major military action ever taken by the world body. He was also the Supreme Commander of Allied Powers in Japan, with the emperor of Japan as his deputy, and Commander-in-Chief of the United States Forces in the Far East.

On April 11, he was out of a job, relieved by the President of the United States for insubordination, although that word was not used. Harry Truman, as president, was entitled to the loyal service of his commanders, whether they shared his views or not. It had become apparent to everyone that for some time MacArthur did not share the views and plans of the administration, but that he was voicing public disapproval of the president's policy for Korea, China and Formosa. Someone had to go and it was not going to be Harry Truman.

MacArthur greets his wife at Haneda Airport, Tokyo, on his
return from Korea on Jan. 28, 1951.

US Army

Had Truman relieved MacArthur in December 1950, when
MacArthur failed to anticipate Chinese involvement in the Korean
War, public sentiment might have favored Truman. By April, the
disaster caused by MacArthur's blunder had long been forgotten
by the man on the street. MacArthur was not relieved for a military
blunder, but for failure to support administration policy. The
American public saw it as a whitewash and supported the general.

Truman was burned in effigy in many towns. In Los
Angeles, a man who did not like his wife's support for Truman, hit
her over the head with a radio.[11] In the first twelve days following
MacArthur's relief, the White House received 27,363 letters and
telegrams.[12] Almost all supported MacArthur and condemned
Truman, many in guttural and nasty terms.

MacArthur spoke to both houses of Congress on April 19, 1951. After 30 minutes of defending his strategy in Korea, wherein he held members of Congress and a radio audience enraptured, he said that after 52 years of military service, it was time to end his career. He said:

> I address you with neither rancor nor bitterness in the fading twilight of life, with but one purpose in mind: to serve my country. He then quoted an old army barracks ballad that claimed, Old soldiers never die, they just fade away. And like the old soldier of that ballad, I now close my military career and just fade away, an old soldier who tried to do his duty as God gave him the light to see that duty. Good bye.

One journalist reported that there was not a dry eye among members of Congress. MacArthur then traveled to New York City where eight million people cheered his ticker-tape parade. The police department estimated the trash from the parade weighed 16,600,000 pounds. In comparison, General Eisenhower returning in triumph from victory in WW II, drew four million people in New York City, amassing 3,600,000 pounds of trash.[13] We need not put too much faith in the trash figures, but perhaps the numbers do indicate the support and respect placed in MacArthur by the American people.

Douglas and his family moved into a luxury suite in the Waldorf Astoria hotel at the reduced price of $130.00 per day. Despite his "old soldier fading away" speech to Congress, MacArthur had no intent of fading away. He began a series of scathing attacks aimed at Truman, Truman's administration, and the Democratic Party.

Under the existing laws, a five-star general or admiral remained on the active duty list for the remainder of their life.[14] Neither congress nor the president could remove him from the active list. MacArthur continued to draw his salary of $18,761.00 per year, plus allowances, was supported by an eight-man staff, until Truman forced him to cut the staff to three men in February 1952, and was provided a three-room office with equipment and supplies in the Armed Services Building. Much to the discomfort of senior Pentagon officials and Truman, MacArthur continued to wear his military uniform while touring the country and denouncing the president and his administration.

MacArthur's quarters in the Waldorf Astoria hotel were lavish, to say the least. The towers where he lived had their own entrance and elevators with guards to screen all visitors. All telephone calls were also screened before they were put through to the apartment. The apartment consisted of ten rooms with a bedroom for Ah Cheu, Arthur's nurse. The drawing room measured 47 feet by 28 feet and provided a magnificent view of Park Avenue and the city.

Despite the size of the quarters, there was barely enough room for MacArthur's 49 tons of personal belongings that he had shipped from Japan. Gifts, including objects crafted in ivory, jade, ebony, silver, gold, and other souvenirs from all over Asia filled the rooms to overflowing. One woman remarked that the apartment looked like "a big, expensive curio shop."[15]

Jean MacArthur aged well, and continued to care for "the general" and to shield him from many of the distractions that would otherwise consume his time. Major Gen. Courtney Whitney continued to function as an aide, and described the MacArthur family ". . . as an idealistic one. Simple, of quiet elegance and of complete unity and devotion."[16] Credit for such an achievement must certainly go to Jean MacArthur.

MacArthur accepted the position of board chairman for the Remington Rand Corporation in July 1952. Whitney was given an executive position as MacArthur's assistant. Remington Rand was a multi-national corporation, with 22 plants and 23 factories in foreign nations, employing 36,000 people. They merged with Sperry Corporation in 1955, and became known as Sperry Rand. The corporate giant had sales in excess of $1.1 billion by 1960.

MacArthur received a starting salary of $45,000 per year. Eight years later his salary had risen to $68,800 and his Army pay to $20,543. Thanks in part to his "gift" of $500,000 from the Philippines, his estate was valued at $2,131,942 in 1964.[17]

MacArthur received respect and friendship among the corporate officers, many of whom shared his conservative political philosophy and aristocratic lifestyle. He spoke often in public and represented corporate America well. In 1945, MacArthur authorized the book, *MacArthur, 1941-1951*. The book was written by Willoughby and John Chamberlain, journalist friends of MacArthur. The book's purpose was to extol the leadership virtues of MacArthur, an issue about which not much had been written.

Reviews of the book were savage, as it painted MacArthur as winning the war by himself and being always right. McGraw-Hill Book Company decided against publication.

Two years later, Whitney, using much of the same material wrote *MacArthur: His Rendezvous with History*. Reviews by historians were consistently negative, but the book was published by Alfred A. Knopf. Truman followed with his *Memoirs* in 1955-1956, serialized in *Life* magazine, and in a book published by Doubleday. Truman was exceedingly blunt, charging MacArthur with insubordination.[18]

The book rekindled what is often described as the bitterest feud in the annals of modern time. Truman said he expected MacArthur to blowup because "when an egotist is punctured, a lot of noise and whistling always accompanies the escaping (hot) air." MacArthur fired back that Truman "was a vulgar little clown."[19] The controversy continued in the media even after MacArthur's death.

MacArthur with President Kennedy at a banquet in New York in 1961.

MacArthur Memorial

In 1962, certain southern congressmen attempted to secure passage of a bill to promote MacArthur to six-star rank. Only General of the Armies, John J. Pershing ever held such a rank. Truman responded that if he could have his way, he would demote MacArthur to four-star rank. The bill died in committee.

MacArthur, Jean, Whitney, and Ambassador and Mrs. Carlos Romulo visited the Philippines during July 1961, at the invitation of President Carlos P. Garcia to celebrate the 15th anniversary of Philippine independence. MacArthur's speech in Luneta Park in Manila was attended by one million people, the largest gathering in Philippine history.[20] The MacArthurs were escorted to Leyte, Cebu, Panay and Corregidor during their ten-day visit. At age 81, MacArthur was surprisingly active.

On May 12, 1962, MacArthur delivered his "duty, honor, country speech" to the cadets at West Point. Many observers thought he outdid his speech to congress 11 years earlier. Many of the tough cadets, that would not have shed a tear while being tortured, wept unashamedly as MacArthur expounded on the code of conduct and ethical behavior that followed the "Duty,. Honor, Country" oath taken by cadets.

In 1963, Whitney presented Henry R. Luce, editor-in-chief of Time, Inc., a 220,000-word manuscript titled, *MacArthur Reminiscences*. Time agreed to pay MacArthur $900,000 for the work which was published in serial and book form. Once again, historians were critical of the book due to the self-glorification, inaccuracies, and similarity to the earlier works by Whitney. One noted historian wrote, "This is a sad book. . . . Hard as he may try, even General MacArthur cannot destroy his own place in history."[21] Other critics noted that MacArthur was his own worst enemy and kindly stated that his autobiography added nothing to his reputation.

MacArthur was admitted to Lenox hospital in New York City on January 29, 1964, for treatment for a kidney infection. On March 19, he underwent prostate surgery. MacArthur returned to the Waldorf, became active in work with Rand, but postponed follow-up medical checks. During the next year, visitors became increasingly concerned over his poor physical condition. On March 6, 1964, (against his will), he was flown by military aircraft to Walter Reed Army Medical Center in Washington, D. C. His spleen was removed on March 23, and a portion of his intestines on March 29. He sank into a coma and died on April 5, 1964.

President Lyndon Johnson ordered the nation's flags to be flown at half-mast in tribute to the old warrior, and he was buried with all the honors a grateful nation can provide. The MacArthur Museum Memorial opened in Norfolk in January 1964. The remains of Douglas and Jean are interred in the rotunda of the museum.

There will be no summarization to this chapter. After reading and researching thousands of pages of print, tapes, and videos for several years, this author, like many others, feels there is something more to the man than can be adequately expressed on the written page. Certainly, he was not a simple man. MacArthur provided his own best epitaph in a speech in 1951, when he said, "Could I have but a line a century hence crediting a contribution to the advance of peace, I would gladly yield every honor which has been accorded by war."[22]

The rotunda of the MacArthur Memorial Museum in Norfolk, Va. MacArthur's grave is on the left; the other is reserved for his wife.

MacArthur Memorial

23

JOHN D. BULKELEY:
THE PACIFIC THEATER

One would have to search a long time to find someone with a more exciting 59 years of military service than that of John D. Bulkeley, U. S. Navy. I admit to being partial to Admiral Bulkeley's career, since I was part of his Guantanamo Bay Defense Force during the Cuban missile crisis and the fresh water crisis at Guantanamo Bay in the 1960s. Bulkeley's career consists of much more than the Guantanamo experience, but it was one of the more memorable experiences of my career to be associated with him at that time.

Vice Adm. John D. Bulkeley, "The Sea Wolf."

US Navy

This chapter examines Bulkeley's contribution to attacks on enemy shipping during the Japanese conquest of the Philippines; the evacuation of General MacArthur, his family and staff from Corregidor; and the kidnapping of Philippine President Manuel Quezon. A following chapter will describe his spy running for the OSS in Europe; reconnaissance of Utah Beach before the Normandy invasion; and the Cuban missile crisis.

John Bulkeley was born in New York City on August 19, 1911. He came from an old navy family and at age 12, served aboard the Columbian merchant freighter *Baracoa* as an ordinary seaman. Upon graduation from Hackettstown, New Jersey, in 1928, his class predicted that one day he would become a sailor. Bulkeley received his appointment to the U. S. Naval Academy in 1929.

In 1936, two years after his commissioning as an Ensign in the U.S. Navy, Bulkeley was traveling between Norfolk, Virginia, and Washington D.C. on a coastal steamer when he learned that the four Japanese men on board included the ambassador to the United States and other senior Japanese officials. At dinner in the wardroom, Bulkeley saw the bulging briefcase of the ambassador on the floor next to his table. Bulkeley decided it was his duty to obtain the briefcase and deliver it to the Office of Naval Intelligence.

Bulkeley waited until the ambassador went to his stateroom and took a position on the deck where he could observe the stateroom without being seen. When the ambassador left his stateroom to go to the men's room at the end of the deck, Bulkeley climbed through the porthole to the stateroom, grabbed the briefcase, and climbed back through the hatch. It wasn't long before the ambassador returned to his room and found the briefcase missing.

The ambassador and the other Japanese began screaming and the ship's company responded to find out what was happening. Bulkeley leaped over the side of the ship and dropped into the Potomac River, still clad in his dress white uniform with white shoes, and began to sidestroke, holding the briefcase clear of the water, toward the Maryland shore of the Potomac River. Once ashore, he hitchhiked a ride to Washington, D.C., where he took a room in a cheap hotel until naval intelligence opened their offices on Monday.

When naval intelligence opened for business, Bulkeley had been waiting for more than an hour. His banging on the unmarked door was finally answered by an old gentleman in civilian clothes. When Bulkeley told him his story and presented the briefcase, the old man turned ashen and slammed the door in his face. After a few minutes, the door was suddenly opened, the briefcase was snatched from his hands, and he was told to report immediately to his ship. When Bulkeley reported aboard USS *Indianapolis,* he was told to keep his mouth shut and report to the transport *Chaumont,* due to sail in 24 hours for Shanghai, China. The U.S. Navy was suddenly intent on sending Bulkeley as far from Washington, D.C. as they could. Bulkeley never did learn what was inside the briefcase.

Upon arrival in Shanghai, Bulkeley transferred to the coastal gunboat *Sacramento,* anchored in the Whangpoo River, along the banks of the international settlement. During the next few months, Bulkeley witnessed and was sickened by the sight of Chinese civilians being terrorized, raped, and murdered by the Japanese military. Chinese males were dragged into the city, bound hand and foot, to have their heads chopped off by Japanese officers with their long swords. Other Chinese men, women, and children were beaten with rifle butts by Japanese soldiers while the Chinese population was forced to watch.

When Admiral Thomas Hart, commander of the U.S. Naval Forces in the Far East, asked Bulkeley to become a civilian spy and take photographs of Japanese tanks, artillery, troops, and warships in the Yangtze River, Bulkeley jumped at the opportunity. His photographic mission was a great success, but Bulkeley fell into trouble when he refused to bow to the Japanese sentry on duty at the bridge leading into Japanese occupied Hongkew. According to Bulkeley, he had crossed the bridge many times and never bowed to the Japanese "son-of-a-bitch" sentries that manned the gate post.

One sentry took exception and Bulkeley was hustled off, under guard, to see the Japanese Admiral Hasegawa. Hasegawa was an Annapolis graduate, an American exchange student, and spoke English fluently. Additionally, according to Hasagawa, he was a personal friend of Admiral Hart. Hasagawa asked Bulkeley to go back to the bridge, bow and apologize to the sentry and all would be forgiven, including Bulkeley's possession of a forbidden camera. Bulkeley refused and was returned to the brig.

For the next four days Bulkeley was brought before Hasagawa each morning. Hasagawa asked him to write 1,000 times that he must bow before the sentries that represent the Imperial Majesty of Japan. Bulkeley refused and was returned to the brig. By the fifth day, the writing was reduced to 100 times. Bulkeley, fed up with the lack of food, the bug-infested straw bed, and the stinking water, wrote out the detested sentence 100 times and was released. He turned over several hundred photographs to the fleet intelligence officer, but his revenge was not complete.

Shortly after his release from imprisonment, Bulkeley was the officer of the deck on the *Sacramento* one night, when he observed a pair of Chinese torpedo boats approaching the anchored flagship of Admiral Hasagawa. Bulkeley was supposed to warn the Japanese ship by a blast on his ship's whistle, but curiously, there was no steam in the ship's whistle.[1] The Chinese fired four torpedoes into the Japanese flagship and sunk it into the mud of the Whangpoo River. When Hasagawa called Admiral Hart to complain about the lack of warning, Hart did not bother to mention it to Bulkeley.

On July 1, 1937, the British warship *Dianna* was anchored nearby *Sacramento* in the mouth of the Foochow River. Bulkeley was sent to call on the captain of *Dianna* to extend an invitation to be Admiral Hart's guest for a celebration of Independence Day aboard *Sacramento* on July 4. To Bulkeley's surprise, the British commander responded, "American Independence Day, wasn't that one of those Indian wars in the colonial days?" "Why you son of a bitch!" Bulkeley responded, "Do you remember the battle of Bunker Hill?"[2] Bulkeley was escorted off *Dianna* by two British enlisted men.

Bulkeley fell in love with 25-year-old Hilda Alice Wood, the daughter of a British citizen with business in Swatow. Alice, as she was better known, graduated from the University of Hong Kong and was a star athlete in track and field. She was the confidential secretary for a shipping firm in Swatow. After a 13-month romance, Bulkeley and Alice were married on November 10, 1938 by the American consulate in Shanghai.

Following the wedding, Bulkeley and his bride took a boat 20 miles down the Whangpoo River to the *Sacramento* where they had the evening meal with ship's officers. After dinner, Bulkeley told his wife that he was the duty officer that evening and escorted her to a vacant house where she spent the night alone in the basement. There was a cot, a washroom, and a 45-caliber pistol that Bulkeley insisted on leaving with Alice in case she needed it. Alice had never fired a pistol in her life. She stuck it under her pillow and, except for a few gunshots, slept quite well.

Bulkeley left China in the spring of 1939, but Alice had to remain behind since she was not an American citizen. In mid May, *Sacramento* reached New York and went into dry dock. Alice said goodbye to her parents and sailed to New York to join her husband. She would never see her father again.

Bulkeley remained with USS *Sacramento* until December, when he reported aboard USS *Saratoga*, one of the navy's largest and most powerful aircraft carriers. In February 1941, he was ordered to Naval Air Station Pensacola, Florida, for flight training as a naval aviator. Enroute to Pensacola, Bulkeley stopped in Washington, D.C., where he was asked if he would volunteer for a new and exciting branch of the naval service - patrol torpedo boats (PTs for short). Bulkeley was not enamored at the opportunity but realized he was expected to comply, and agreed to the change in his orders.

He was ordered to the Brooklyn Navy Yard where he was given command of Submarine Chaser Division Two, an experimental unit whose PT boats were equipped to find and sink enemy submarines. The PT boats were 70 feet long, had depth charge racks, sonar, and four torpedoes. The craft was powered by three Packard engines that could drive the boat at 55-knots. In March, Bulkeley took the four boats to Key West, Florida, for training. At Key West, he broke and lost all four of the sonar devices in rough water. Upon returning to Brooklyn, he recommended that the sub chaser role for the PT boats be abandoned. The navy agreed and Bulkeley was ordered to Manila with six of the newer 77-foot boats, each armed with four torpedoes, two pairs of .50-caliber machine guns, and two .30-caliber automatic weapons. They arrived at Manila on September 28, 1941, and set up shop at Cavite Naval Yard on the eastern shore of Manila Bay.

On the morning of December 8, 1941 (Manila time), Bulkeley was issued his war orders by Rear Adm. Francis W. Rockwell, commander of the 16th Naval District. Bulkeley was to take his PT boats across Manila Bay to Marivales Harbor, and be prepared to attack the Japanese fleet. Bulkeley and his small command spent the rest of day arming and loading 24 torpedoes, machine gun ammunition, and preparing the boats for battle. Three of the boats were armed and sent to Mariveles, but the remaining three PTs were still in Manila Bay when the Japanese attacked. The PTs were credited with shooting down three Japanese planes with their .50-caliber machine guns.

Following the Japanese attack, Bulkeley took his three boats back to Cavite to search for fuel. He found thousands of drums of high-octane gasoline destroyed, and hundreds of dead and wounded sailors and civilians. What fuel he did find was contaminated with water, rust, and wax. The water and rust could be filtered but the wax would build up and clog the carburetor jets in the engines. Bulkeley and his men loaded the seriously wounded survivors aboard the PTs and made repeated trips to the hospital at Canacao. Later, Bulkeley surprised two Filipino saboteurs aboard a fuel barge in the bay. They had a large supply of wax and were busy putting it in the fuel supplies. Bulkeley took them to naval headquarters with recommendation that they be shot. All fuel barges were then put under guard.

Admiral Thomas Hart departed the Philippines on Christmas Day. He left three old minesweepers, five old tugboats, three gunboats, and Bulkeley's six PT boats to Admiral Rockwell to defend the Philippines. A week later when the Japanese were already in Manila, Bulkeley was given the mission of scuttling the old ships to keep them from the Japanese. Slowly and quietly the PTs slipped into Manila harbor and Bulkeley and his men boarded the old boats. They bashed in the bottoms of the smaller boats and set delayed charges in the bottom of the larger boats. The eleven old boats were all sunk and Bulkeley's boats made it safely to Bataan.

On the morning of January 18, 1942, Bulkeley was issued orders to attack Japanese shipping in Subic Bay. He was told that the Japanese force included a destroyer and large transport. At midnight, Bulkeley and the crews of two PTs entered Subic Bay. As they did so, the blackness was broken by a powerful searchlight and shells began to impact close to Bulkeley's boat. He turned the boat away and was immediately engaged by searchlights and artillery from shore.

Bulkeley turned the boat again and headed for Binanga Harbor, the reported location of the Japanese ships. Suddenly, there was a huge ship less than 500 yards ahead. Before Bulkeley could launch his torpedoes, his boat was lit up in blinding light by a searchlight from the Japanese vessel. Bulkeley fired two torpedoes, ordered a hard right turn and roared off into the night.

Moments later a huge fireball erupted at the enemy ship's waterline. One torpedo had found its mark. The other torpedo failed to clear its tube and its propellers were whirling madly as it completed the arming cycle. Once armed, it could explode, blowing the PT to pieces. Torpedo Man First Class John Martino grabbed a handful of toilet tissue, climbed aboard the "hot" torpedo, and jammed the paper between the vanes of the propeller. The blades stopped turning and the PT lived for another day. It was subsequently reported that Bulkeley's boat destroyed a 5,000-ton Japanese ship.

The Manila Bay region

Presidio Press

The second PT went aground and had to be destroyed by its crew. All but three of the crew washed ashore at Bataan and were rescued by American soldiers. Another boat also went aground. Bulkeley now had only four PTs to defend the Philippines. On the night of January 23, Bulkeley again entered the hotbed of Subic Bay. He found a 50-foot long motorized barge loaded with Japanese soldiers. His gunners opened up on the barge with their

.50- and .30-caliber machine guns and sank it. Near dawn, Bulkeley's crew spotted another vessel, raced in to machine gun range, and managed to hit the ship's fuel tank. The Japanese vessel stopped, its engines silent, and fire mushroomed upward. Bulkeley ordered his PT to pull alongside of the enemy craft, "I'm going aboard," he said.[3]

Bulkeley threw several hand grenades aboard the craft and then, armed with a sub machine gun, jumped into the drifting craft. A quick search revealed many dead and three wounded Japanese, including the ship's captain. Bulkeley took them all prisoner, and then retrieved all the documents, papers, briefcases and charts he could find. He scrambled back aboard the PT just as the Japanese vessel sank.

On the evening of January 24, Bulkeley and one of his PTs spotted what appeared to be a large Japanese transport in Subic Bay. As they began a high speed run towards the ship, a crewman spotted and warned of wires and entanglements floating in the water just ahead. The obstacles had been laid by the Japanese to foul the propellers of the PT boats. Once clear of the obstructions, the PT raced to within 400 yards, fired one torpedo, and then raked the enemy ship with .50-caliber machine gun fire. As the ship responded with their own machine gun fire, shore batteries began firing on the PT. Suddenly, the transport lit up as she was rocked by a blast from the torpedo. Bits of the ship began falling all around the PT as the ship began to sink. The PT went towards deep water as fast as possible and escaped.

Bulkeley's heroics were appreciated and back in the states he was being described in newspapers and by the radio as a hero. Closer to his base, however, he was described somewhat differently. This is how Captain Malcolm Champlain, aide to Admiral Rockwell, described Bulkeley.

> Bulkeley was a wild man. Daring, courageous, and admirable in many ways, but still a wild man. He reminded one, on first glance, of a swashbuckling pirate in modern dress. He wore a long, unruly beard and carried two ominous looking pistols at his side. His eyes were bloodshot from constant night patrols and lack of sleep, but his nervous energy was tremendous and never seemed to give out. He walked with a cocksure gait, and one could always count on him to raise particular hell with any Jap

he met. John Bulkeley was one of the most colorful figures in the Philippine campaign.[4]

General MacArthur called for Bulkeley to bring his PT boats to the pier at Corregidor on February 28. While there, MacArthur pinned the Distinguished Service Cross on Bulkeley and then explained in confidence that he had been ordered by President Roosevelt to leave Corregidor and go to Australia to take command of an army that would liberate the Philippines. MacArthur explained that he would like Bulkeley to take him, his family and staff to Mindanao, where he would be met by aircraft from Australia. When asked if he thought he could pull it off, Bulkeley responded, "General, it will be a piece of cake."[6]

Bulkeley was young, cocky, and brash. When asked in 1987 if he would still answer MacArthur in the same manner, Bulkeley said he would answer, "No way." To navigate, mostly at night, through 600 miles of uncharted waters, with jagged coral reefs capable of ripping the thin-skinned-wooden boats apart, would be near impossible.

On the morning of March 4, MacArthur sent for Bulkeley and told him they would leave at 7:30 P.M. that day. Bulkeley quickly briefed his crews. He would carry the general in his boat, PT 41. All boats were to remain together, but if they had to separate due to Japanese intervention, it was important that the other three boats attack the pursuers and MacArthur's boat continue to Mindanao. Everyone understood.

Lieutenant Bulkeley and the crew of PT 41 tied up to the pier at Corregidor at 7:21 P.M. MacArthur's wife Jean, son Arthur, and Ah Cheu, Arthur's nursemaid, were the first to board. The general boarded last. Their baggage was minimal, and MacArthur carried only a toothbrush in his pocket. As he stepped aboard, he told Bulkeley to cast off when ready.

Bulkeley rendezvoused with the other three PTs just outside the Corregidor minefield. The other boats, following in single file, carried 16 members of MacArthur's staff, plus each boat had 20 steel drums containing 50 gallons of high octane gasoline. The sea was violent, causing the boats to pitch while waves 15 to 20 feet tumbled over the bows, drenching everyone.

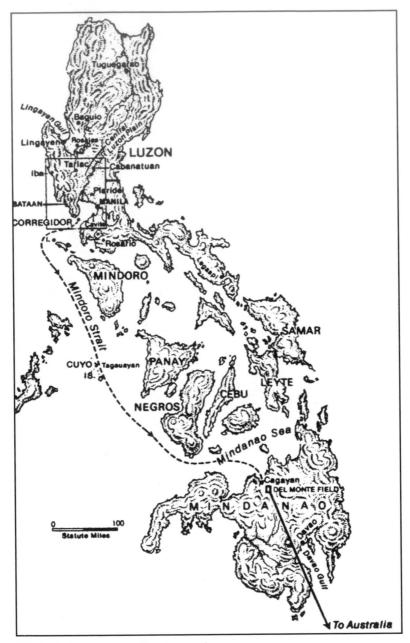

MacArthur's escape route from Corregidor.

US Navy

At 3:00 A.M., the engines of the last PT in line went dead. While mechanics cleaned wax and rust from the carburetors, the other boats surged ahead. That was the plan; no boat was to stop to assist a disabled boat unless it was the boat with MacArthur aboard. After 40 minutes, the engines started and the last PT boat moved ahead.

The other three PTs were unable to remain together in the darkness and heavy seas. Each boat was on its own to reach an agreed rendezvous point in the Cayo Islands, halfway to their destination at Mindanao. Three of the four boats arrived by midmorning, but the fourth boat did not appear. Later, Bulkeley learned that the boat had repeated engine breakdowns, but did make its way to Mindanao by itself.

General MacArthur was sick most of the trip as was his wife. Heavy angry waves swamped the boats, tossing the passengers around violently and nearly washing several people overboard. One of the generals being evacuated refused a sailor's offer to take him below by saying, "No, no, let me die here."[6] As the sun rose in the morning, after 35 hours in the pounding sea, the lighthouse at Cagayan Point, their destination, became visible. When they reached the dock, MacArthur told Bulkeley, "Johnny, you've taken me out the jaws of death-and I wont forget it."[7] MacArthur then called the crew together and awarded each of them the Silver Star Medal for gallantry.

Later in the afternoon, as the PT crews were patching their battered boats, MacArthur called Bulkeley to his quarters. Although Bulkeley had been without sleep for 40 hours, he found MacArthur's appearance worse than his own. "His shirt and trousers, usually immaculate, were soiled and wrinkled, and he had heavy beard stubble. His eyes were bloodshot from lack of sleep and illness from the rough trip."[8]

MacArthur had been informed that Manual Quezon's loyalty to the United States was wavering. Quezon was reported to have told, Carlos Romulos, his aide, that the fight between Japan and the United States was not their fight and that they must try to save themselves. MacArthur told Bulkeley that he had another mission for him. Bulkeley was to go to Negros Island (halfway back to Cayo), find Quezon and his tribe, and bring him back to Mindanao. "We're sending Quezon to Australia to form a Philippine government in exile," MacArthur roared, "whether he likes it or not."

As Bulkeley prepared to depart, MacArthur reminded him, "Don't forget to bring him back, by whatever means is necessary."[9] After dark, Bulkeley cast off with his two boats, and after evading a Japanese destroyer, arrived at the little port of Dumaguete on Negros. He went ashore quickly looking for Quezon, and when he could not find him, asked a constable where he was. The constable replied that he was not supposed to tell anyone where Quezon and his family had gone. Bulkeley cocked his Tommy gun, stuck the muzzle end against the constable's head, and suggested he tell him where Quezon had gone. The constable replied that he was at a village about 25 miles up the coast.

When Bulkeley arrived at the suspected location, a native informed him that Quezon was in a house a few miles inland. Bulkeley stole two old automobiles and several of his crew drove to the nipa hut (native thatched roof hut) on the side of a hill. They called for Quezon, who shortly appeared in the doorway. He was a small lonely figure, coughing from tuberculosis, clad only in his nightclothes. Bulkeley told Quezon he was there to take him to MacArthur. Quezon said he wasn't going. Bulkeley had heard enough.

Bulkeley was an ominous sight, clad in an oilskin, muddy boots, unruly black beard, with long hair tied around his head with a bandana. Embellishing the pirate look were the two pistols and a nasty looking knife in his belt, and the Tommy gun in his hand. He minced no words. Quezon was going with him, with his family or by himself, but he was going and right now. Shaking in fear, Quezon replied that he was ready to go.

Quezon's family was rousted out of bed and into the two cars. The group included Quezon, his wife, two daughters, Vice President Sergio Osmena, a Philippine general, and two cabinet officials. When they reached the pier, Bulkeley learned that one of his boats had struck a submerged object and could not proceed. To compound his problems, seven more of Quezon's cabinet arrived at the dock. Included in their baggage were huge sacks of American currency worth nearly 15 million dollars. Bulkeley told everyone to get in the one remaining boat and to leave all their baggage at the dock. Everyone scrambled aboard except Quezon, who told Bulkeley he was not going. Quezon was convinced, not very tactfully, to get into the boat.

On the way back to Mindoro, a heavy wave snapped the shear pins of two torpedoes causing the arming of the firing mechanism. A sharp slap by a wave could detonate the torpedo and blow the boat to pieces. Bulkeley and two of his crew succeeded in moving the torpedo from its tube and into the water and raced away. Quezon used this interruption to tell Bulkeley that he wanted to return to Negros. Bulkeley responded that he would have to walk on water to do so.

As the PT boat arrived at the Mindoro pier, a U.S. Army honor guard was on hand to meet America's staunch ally.[10] When MacArthur reached Australia; President Roosevelt announced his escape from Corregidor and Bulkeley was once again acclaimed a hero. As a parting gesture to Bulkeley, MacArthur issued orders that navy lieutenant Bulkeley and his command were to be independent of all commanders in the Philippines and to report directly to MacArthur in Australia.

Bulkeley and his small unit of two remaining PT boats continued to attack Japanese shipping in the Mindanao Sea and around Cebu, to include a near fatal attack on a heavy cruiser on April 18. The two boats made a surprise night attack on the cruiser and fired four torpedoes, none of which exploded. A searchlight from the cruiser illuminated Bulkeley's boat and large shells began exploding around the boat. Both boats attacked again and launched their last two torpedoes. The torpedoes from PT 34 scored two hits at the waterline of the cruiser. The cruiser's searchlight dimmed and then went out.

The PTs had poked a hornet's nest. Japanese destroyers appeared in numbers, boxed the two ships and began shelling the PTs as well as trying to ram them. Bulkeley's PT 41 managed to escape the ramming attempt, eluded two more destroyers, and found shelter in a shallow inlet as the sun rose. Lieutenant Bob Kelly's PT 34 was not so fortunate. The shrapnel and bullet- ridden boat limped into the 400 foot wide Cebu City channel just as the sun came up. Four Japanese fighters located them immediately and bombed and staffed the boat until all the PTs guns were disabled and many of its crew killed. Two of the engines quit and the boat started to sink. Kelly helped move as many of the dead and wounded through the coral to land before the next flight of aircraft arrived to finish the boat. That left only Bulkeley's PT 41 as the remaining U.S. Navy in the Philippines.

There were no more torpedoes at Cagayan or anywhere else for the PT boat. After determining that the beaches around the mouth of the Cotaboto were not suitable for MacArthur's return to the Philippines, Bulkeley was ordered to leave the Philippines and fly to Australia aboard a B-17. As the bomber taxied from the Del Monte plantation airstrip on Negros with Bulkeley aboard, it was strafed by Japanese fighters and one of its engines damaged. The B-17 continued to Australia with one inoperable engine.

Thirty-eight of the 83 crewmembers of Bulkeley's unit eventually became Japanese prisoners of war. Only Lieutenant Kelly, Ensign Cox, and Ensign Akers were able to be evacuated to Australia by air before the Japanese attained air superiority over the country. One other officer, Lieutenant Hank Brantingham eventually made his own way to Australia. On May 8, Bulkeley, Cox, Kelly and Aker were flown to the United States to a heroes' welcome. Bulkeley was awarded the Medal of Honor, the nation's highest award for bravery in combat.

A massive parade awaited Bulkeley and the other PT officers in New York City, where 250,000 people welcomed them. Later, Bulkeley met with President Roosevelt where he was presented the Medal of Honor. That night he was the guest at a large function where he told why the Philippines fell and what needed to be done about it. Bukeley pulled no punches and could not have pleased many of the senior officers in the room. When he finished, Roosevelt said simply, "Thank you John."[11] Bulkeley strode from the oval office ignoring the sober-faced aides that glared at him.

Bulkeley was now America's most decorated serviceman. He had been awarded the Medal Of Honor, the Navy Cross, two Army Distinguished Service Crosses, the Army Silver Star Medal, the Army Distinguished Unit Badge, and the Philippines Distinguished Service Star. He was also very weary of going on war bond drives, recruiting trips, and speaking engagements. He wanted to get back to the war.

During October 1942, Bulkeley's new Torpedo Squadron-7 was commissioned at the Brooklyn Navy Yard. Bulkeley chose PT 131 as his flagship because it was the 100th PT boat manufactured for the war. The PTs motored to the Panama Canal and were then loaded aboard the Esso tanker, *White Plains*. On Christmas Eve, the tanker left Balboa Harbor unescorted for the 24-day journey to Brisbane.

About halfway through the journey, on a clear night, lookouts sighted a blacked-out ship moving past the *White Plains* in the opposite direction. Bulkeley immediately had all the .50-caliber guns on the PT boats manned and made ready to fire. He asked the skipper of the tanker to challenge the mystery ship, and if the ship did not respond properly, he would blast it to pieces with his .50-caliber guns. The tanker's skipper refused the request. Bulkeley was outraged. For at least an hour, he stormed around the deck, loudly denouncing the "gutless" captain who may have allowed a Japanese vessel to escape unharmed.

Three weeks after departing Panama, the *White Plains* arrived at Noumea, New Caledonia. Noumea was about 750 miles east of Australia and was being used as a navy anchorage. Bulkeley reported to the senior navy officer ashore, a rear admiral who told him that his ships were to be diverted to the South Pacific Theater of operations commanded by Admiral Nimitz. It did not take Bulkeley long to warm to the argument. He insisted that he was specifically ordered to MacArthur's Southwest Pacific Theater and that if he was sent elsewhere, it would have to be with MacArthur's approval. The admiral backed down and permitted Bulkeley and his squadron to proceed to Australia.

From Brisbane, Bulkeley was ordered to a boat base at Kana Kopa on the southeastern end of Papua New Guinea. In late February, MacArthur learned that a fleet of eight Japanese transports with 6,912 troops aboard and escorted by eight destroyers was bound for Lae and Salamana, Papua, 350 miles northeast of Kana Kopa. On March 2, American search planes reported the convoy in the Bismarck Sea, approaching the Huron Gulf in Papua.

MacArthur sent every aircraft at his command (207 bombers and 129 fighter planes) to attack the Japanese convoy. All but one transport and one destroyer were sunk. Seven of the eight transports and seven of the eight destroyers were sunk. Hundreds, perhaps thousands of Japanese survivors were reported to be adrift in rafts, life preservers and clinging to debris following the attack. Now it was time for the PT boats. For the next two days, the PTs blasted life rafts and machine-gunned Japanese soldiers and sailors. No mercy was asked or given. The PT crews were following the rules set by the Japanese at the beginning of the war.

A story about Bulkeley in the Southern Pacific was told by Bill McGovern, a professor of political science at Northwestern University. McGovern was flown to the Pacific to see if he could gain intelligence from Japanese prisoners that might be induced to surrender. He was told to accompany John Bulkeley's PT squadron because they came face to face with more Japanese than anyone else. During a patrol with Bulkeley, the PTs shot up and then boarded a large Japanese troop barge. Seeing a Japanese that was still alive, McGovern threw himself across the wounded Japanese in order to prevent him being killed. Bulkeley came running by, saw the Japanese was not dead, and yelled, "The son of a bitch is still alive."[12] He pulled McGovern away from the Japanese and used his Tommy gun to riddle the Japanese. McGovern decided he needed to look elsewhere to find live Japanese.

Bulkeley accompanied his PTs nightly on their 12 hour patrols of the New Guinea coast. On the night of August 28, Bulkeley was aboard one of his two PTs when they found three long, low-slung Japanese barges close to the Papua coast. Bulkeley's boats charged the barges, firing all guns as they approached. One barge sank but their bullets ricocheted off the other two. PT 152 raced in alongside the two barges and dropped a depth charge along each one, but the steel-plated barges sailed on. PT 142 rushed in and depth-charged the two barges, sinking one. Now it was Bulkeley's turn. "Pull up alongside the bastard,"[13] Bulkeley shouted, jumping onto the barge when the PT was close enough. A helmeted figure was spotted slipping out of the wheelhouse and Bulkeley squeezed off a shot. The man fell dead with a round in the forehead. Twelve other Japanese lay dead on the barge. Bulkeley sank the barge, and the two PTs raced back to their base.

By late summer, Bulkeley was 30 pounds lighter and wracked by jungle malaria, a foe he could not beat. He was ordered to San Francisco for treatment and could not prevent the orders from being executed. He was treated at Oak Knoll Hospital in Oakland. In late November, 1943, Bulkeley still weak from malaria, was ordered to Washington to discuss his next assignment.

24

JOHN D. BULKELEY:
THE ATLANTIC THEATER

Following his colorful and highly successful tour of duty in the Pacific, Bulkeley, now a commander, was called to Washington for further orders. He was told that he would form and lead a squadron of PT boats to England where they would insert Allied spies, saboteurs, and other secret material into German-occupied France, and to recover agents and intelligence to bring back to England. In command of this secret operation in England, named Operation of Strategic Services, was the legendary WW I figure, "Wild Bill" Donovan.

In April 1944, Bulkeley's three PTs were loaded aboard a tanker in New York harbor, and arrived in England on April 24. Less than a week later, Bulkeley was summoned to British naval headquarters and given a mission to cross the channel at night and bring back buckets of sand scooped up at 50-yard intervals from Utah Beach. Bulkeley was not aware that Utah had been selected as one of the landing beaches and swore loudly that this was the most ridiculous mission he had ever received. But, he went.

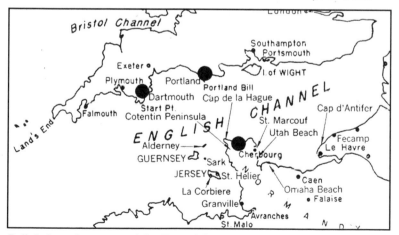

Bulkeley's spy boats crossed the Channel from their base at Dartmouth.

PT Boats, Inc.

Upon reaching the designated beach, the crew collected buckets of sand. Bulkeley was about 100 yards from the boat and had just scooped up the final bucket of sand when he was stopped by a helmeted German soldier. The soldier shone his flashlight into Bulkeley's face, but did not speak or shout an alarm. Bulkeley threw his bucket of sand into the German's face, overpowered and threw him down on his back, straddled and strangled him. Once he was sure the German was dead, he ran as fast as he could back to the boat, made certain they had the necessary sand samples, and headed back to England. Years later it was revealed that Bulkeley's sand samples resulted in Utah Beach being utilized as one of the main landing beaches.

During June, Bulkeley was given command of all PTs for Operation Overlord, the code name for the invasion of Europe. Bulkeley's command was to escort four groups of minesweepers as they swept Utah beach in advance of the amphibious landing ships. Their primary mission was to preclude the German E-boats from interfering with the minesweeping operation. After the six channels to the beaches had been swept, the PTs were to return to England, refuel, rearm, and return to the landing area. At least 20 PT boats would be in position at any given time, the remainder refueling and rearming as required.

As the landing progressed, the PTs were kept busy rescuing survivors from ships that were sunk by mines or German shore batteries. PT 505 hit a mine while chasing a German U-boat and had to be towed to shore for repair. Bulkeley's four boats saved 69 men from the destroyer escort USS *Rich,* before it sank, including the captain and executive officer, both of whom had broken legs and were bleeding badly from the explosion. Both men were determined to go down with their ship, and threatened everyone who tried to carry them off the ship with their .45-caliber pistols. Bulkeley talked to the two men for a few moments, grabbed them, and had them carried off the ship. Of the *Rich's* complement of 215 men, 27 were killed, 73 wounded, 52 were missing,

Shortly thereafter, destroyer *Glennon* was struck and cut in half by shells from a German shore battery. Bulkeley raced his PT to the sinking ship and rescued all the crew that could be found. *Glennon* sank a few minutes later leaving 25 dead and 38 wounded. In mid-August, Bulkeley was given command of the destroyer *Endicott,* and, with a force of his PTs, directed to conduct a decoy operation off Naples. During the operation, Bulkeley's small boats were attacked by two enemy corvettes and were in danger of being sunk. Bulkeley pleaded with his boats to hold on until he could get there and then proceeded to sink both corvettes. For his action, he was awarded a second Silver Star Medal.

Bulkeley captained USS *Endicott* on its way back to the United States in late 1944. The ship stopped at Tangiers, French Morocco, to refuel, and Bulkeley gave part of his crew liberty to explore Tangiers. While ashore, two of his men were badly beaten by a pair of local thugs. When he heard of the incident, Bulkeley put on civilian clothes, went ashore with a sailor that could identify the locals, found them and "beat the hell out of them."[1] This incident perhaps explains Bulkeley's method of handling problems.

In May 1948 Bulkeley returned to his first love, sea duty as executive officer of USS *Mount Olympus*, flagship of Amphibious Group Two. His reporting senior described Bulkeley in this manner: "This officer is the finest leader and most competent officer I have ever served with in over 23 years of service in the U.S. Navy. He leads by his superior example of tireless energy and selfless devotion to duty."[2]

Following sea duty Bulkeley completed the Armed Forces Staff College and received orders to report to the Atomic Energy Commission (AEC) in Washington. He was less than excited about his orders. He knew nothing about atomic energy and had no desire to learn. When he told his wife that he would be working with Dr. E.L. Lawrence, Dr. J. Robert Oppenheimer, Dr. Edward Teller, and navy captain Hyman Rickover, his wife, Alice, responded, "That's wonderful dear, but please allow them to express their opinions before telling them where they can go."[3]

During September 1952, Bulkeley was promoted to captain, his first promotion in eight years, and, according to some of his contemporaries, his last one. The feeling was that the navy no longer needed swashbuckling sailors, but rather diplomats to deal with foreign nations. A month after his promotion, Bulkeley was in command of a destroyer division in the Far East, and deployed to the Sea of Japan. Following the Korean War, Bulkeley became the morning briefing officer for Admiral Arthur W. Radford, Chairman of the Joint Chiefs of Staff.

Bulkeley found his Pentagon assignment fascinating and exciting. He was among the first to be aware of events taking place around the world, and was allowed to voice his opinions on such matters. Next, Bulkeley received shor-term orders to USS

Tolovana, a Pacific Fleet oil tanker based at Long Beach, California. The *Tolovana* was described by senior naval officials as a disaster waiting to happen. Bulkeley concurred. Equipment and machinery had been neglected and were ready for operational failure. Crew morale was at rock bottom due to poor leadership. Bulkeley assembled the ship's officers in the wardroom and thundered that, "You are a disgrace to the navy uniform. None of you will leave this ship until your division or department is brought up to my standards, and those standards are g———— high."[4]

Six months later, Bulkeley reported that *Tolovana* was ready for unrestricted operations with the fleet. Then followed a tour of duty with the navy Bureau of Personnel and finally, command of Destroyer Squadron-12 in the Atlantic Fleet, where the squadron won the coveted "E" award for battle efficiency. Bulkeley was stunned upon receipt of his next set of orders, command of the super secret Nuclear Modification Center near Clarksville, Tennessee. This was about as far from the ocean as a sailor could get.

Bulkeley was able to solve disciplinary and security problems within the complex, and improve relations with the civilian community off base. In mid-August 1963, Bulkeley was selected for promotion to rear admiral, and shortly thereafter was sent to command the naval base at Guantanamo Bay, Cuba, where Fidel Castro was demanding the United States to get out of Cuba. Castro's actions followed the "Bay of Pigs" abortive invasion of Cuba.

President Kennedy was assassinated on November 22, 1963. Less than two weeks later, John Bulkeley arrived at Guantanamo to take command. His assignment was due to the efforts of Bobby Kennedy who wanted someone in charge at Guantanamo that could stand up to Castro. A few days after Bulkeley took command, he received a note delivered to the main gate which said that 1,100 yards of chain-link fence along the base fence line would be bulldozed down later that day. The note was signed by Major Ramiro Valdez and warned that it would be imprudent for the Americans to try to restore the fence.

Bulkeley knew exactly what the Castro government was trying to do. He studied the Guantanamo Treaty on his way to Cuba and found the part that said if any portion of the fence went down and was not repaired or replaced immediately by the United States, the base would be considered abandoned and revert to

Cuban ownership. Castro was gambling that Bulkeley and his staff were not aware of this part of the treaty.[5]

That afternoon, Cuban soldiers bulldozed a portion of the fence that divided the naval base and Cuba. Within an hour, Bulkeley sent a message to Valdez "that the fence is going back up at ten o'clock in the morning."[6] The next morning, Bulkeley attired in Marine Corps fatigues, a .357 Colt magnum pistol and three hand grenades attached to his belt arrived to supervise the fence reconstruction. With him were 2,000 marines dug in along the three-quarter-mile stretch of bulldozed fence, with machine guns, rifles and rocket launchers. In the sky were armed jet aircraft and helicopters ready for action, and in the bay four destroyers were at battle stations.

Seabees arrived with the fencing, cranes, and survey equipment. By 4:00 P.M., the fence was reestablished. Not a single Cuban soldier was seen throughout the entire process. The message was clear; Castro had met a worthy adversary. One that would not shrink from armed confrontation when necessary.

Bulkeley decided to take the next step. For as long as anyone could remember, some 3,500 Cuban workers entered the base each morning and left at the end of the day. Not only were many of these workers spies, but they provided an important source of income for Castro. If Castro wanted the United States out of Cuba, Bulkeley rationalized, he did not need the income from these workers. Immediately, a large number of suspected spies and potential saboteurs were weeded out and terminated from base employment. Those that remained were identified and required to wear an identity tag at all times. Their movement about the base was severely curtailed. Over time, all Cuban workers were terminated including the maids who had been one of the "perks" of duty at Guantanamo. Some of these workers were replaced by contract labor from Jamaica or other Caribbean islands.

During January 1964, Cuban soldiers at the boundry fence leveled their weapons at marines and threw stones at them trying to provoke retaliation. The author can attest to being a bit nervous while inspecting sentry posts along the fence line at 3: 00 A. M. in the morning as the Officer of the Day. The Cubans were always on the high ground since the terrain sloped uphill from the bay to the mountains surrounding the base. Each sentry would ease into a firing position and aim his rifle at me as I drove the fence line alone inspecting posts. I did not mind the prospect of being shot at, but the distance was so close that I disliked the idea of being killed at close range and not being able to respond.

Admiral Bulkeley appreciated this fact and after marines started throwing rocks back at the Cubans, directed Colonel George Killen, the commander of the Marine Barracks and Guantanamo Defense Force, to move his sentry posts 100 yards back from the fence and to build trenches and fighting positions. Killen took the "pull back" order to be tantamount to retreat and reacted to Bulkeley's order with stone-faced silence. His marines had been on the short end of exchanges with the Cubans, and Killen had no desire to retreat. Bulkeley understood Killen's chagrin and said, "Colonel, my job is to protect this base without touching off WW III. That I intend to do."[7]

A weak point in the defense of Guantanamo naval base had always been the lack of fresh water. All fresh water for the 10,000 people at Guantanamo (about 2,000,000 gallons per day) was pumped from the Yateras water plant, four-and-a-half miles in Cuban territory. The United States paid $14,000 monthly for the water. A Cuban from the water plant collected the bill for the water each week. During the Cuban Missile Crisis, I was assigned to lead a platoon of marines with gun and flame tanks and a self-propelled 155-mm howitzer to seize and defend the Yateras water plant to keep the water flowing. We were pleased that a nuclear war did not erupt, and that the situation returned to normal, but were disappointed at not being able to leave the base and seize the water plant.

On the morning of February 6, 1964, the Cuban from the water plant delivered a message that said the water would be shut off at noon on that day. Castro had played his trump card, blaming the water cutoff on the American seizure of his fishing boats. Bulkeley responded to the water cut off by declaring "water condition Apha" which reduced the amount of water available to base personnel. Castro, in an organized press meeting, announced that he would allow the water to flow one hour each day —for the women and children. Bulkeley responded by saying, "To hell with the bastard and his water. We'll furnish our own water."[8]

Congressmen called for the president to send in the marines to turn the water back on, but President Lyndon Johnson said he did not have to send in the marines. He had a navy admiral there that was fully capable of handling the situation. Bulkeley arranged for fresh water to be immediately barged from Jamaica and Norfolk, and had a shuttle service established between Port Everglades, Florida, and the naval base. In addition, the water barge, *Abatan*, was moored at Guantanamo with the capability of distilling 200,000 gallons of seawater per day.

Water condition Alpha decreased the base consumption from two million to less than one million gallons per day. Swimming pools were closed and salt water was used for flushing toilets. Paper plates and cups became fashionable and marine fatigues were worn by base personnel because they required less washing and pressing. A plan was announced by the president on February 10 to construct a ten-million dollar plant at Guantanamo to convert seawater to freshwater.

Castro's plots to drive the United States from Guantanamo had backfired. Fidel needed some face-saving device. On February 13, he went on Havana television to announce that Bulkeley had secretly been using suction pumps to draw off 114,000 gallons of water per day from the Yateras water pipeline. "Hogwash," responded Bulkeley. "The mains are sealed tightly closed and anyone is welcome to inspect them." As Castro continued with his accusations, Bulkeley got mad. Not only was Castro calling him a liar, but our own state department began to question him as to how the base could continue to function without Cuba's water.

"That's it," decided Bulkeley, "I'm going to cut the damned pipe and prove to the world that we are not stealing Castro's water." On February 17, near dusk, a 300-pound section of 14-inch pipe, 38-inches long was cut and hoisted from the evacuation. Newsmen were invited to inspect the pipe and declared it dry. No water had been flowing through the pipe. Castro was a liar and Bulkeley had called his bluff.

I was privileged to be at the site when the pipe was raised from the ground and remember well the excitement that accompanied the visiting newsmen's announcement that the pipe was dry. Bulkeley, satisfied that no water was coming from Cuba began an inspection of all the marine positions at both sides of the base (Guantanamo was divided into a leeward and windward side, separated by the bay). The admiral was satisfied with the marine's responsiveness and we returned from the inspection at 3:00 A, M. I was subsequently told that after two hours of sleep in his uniform and boots, Bulkeley was back at work in his office.

A comic captioned "Full Speed ahead" captured the spirit of Bulkeley's dealings with Castro.

US Navy

Later, the water pipe was prominently displayed near the front gate as a constant reminder to the Cubans not to try to bluff the defenders of Guantanamo. Bulkeley, understanding the concern of some civilians, offered transportation back to the states for any dependents and civil service employees that wanted to leave. Not a single military dependent left, but 200 civil service employees packed their bags and departed.

American newspapers again made a hero of Bulkeley. His large sign near the main gate proclaimed, "U.S. answer to Castro...Gitmo water liberated from Cuba at this point" and it became front page material in newspapers all over the world. The navy was proud of Bulkeley; the nervous Nells in the state department were shocked. Those were proud times at Guantanamo. We were proud of our defense force of marines, sailors, and Seabees, and proud of our admiral. President Johnson was quick to say that he was pleased with the way the Cuban challenge was handled. "We believe it is far wiser to send an admiral to cut off the water than a battalion of marines to turn it back on."[9]

Rear Adm. Bulkeley (at right) explains his triumph over Castro to Chief of Naval Operations Adm. McDonald.

US Navy

On February 25, Castro met with foreign newsmen in Havana and said that the water could be restored to Guantanamo. Of course he added, restoring the water supply depends upon the United States government requesting it. Bulkeley responded, "Mr.

Castro can go straight to hell."[10] State Department officials were appalled. One did not use such language when referring to the leader of another nation. It was suggested to the navy that they send an expert in international relations to serve as Bulkeley's political advisor. "I'll be my own political advisor," responded Bulkeley.

Bulkeley had souvenirs of the water pipe sliced from the pipe and sent to President Johnson and Castro. Castro retaliated by placing a $50,000 dead or alive bounty on the admiral's head. I have enough bodyguards Bulkeley responded. I have my marine driver and my .357 magnum. The Gitmo marines coined the nickname "Big Iron" Bulkeley as the result of the huge pistol he kept strapped to his hip.

On the evening of June 28, four Cuban searchlights began to illuminate a large area near the main gate. The marines standing post in the area were blinded as a result of the strong light. Bulkeley spent two nights in a concrete structure near the gate and decided the Cubans were just engaging in harassment. Later in the day, Bulkeley supervised the construction of a huge Marine Corps insignia of the eagle, globe and anchor. The insignia was painted in Marine Corps colors, was thirty feet in diameter, six inches thick, and placed right in the center of the light from the Cuban searchlights. A day later, the Cubans shut off their searchlights.

On June 26, the anniversary of Castro's 26th of July movement, several thousand service personnel, families, and civilian workers assembled at the new water evaporation plant to celebrate the day that fresh water started to flow from the plant. Fireworks exploded, bands played, hamburgers, chicken, beer, soft drinks, and fresh water were consumed, and a proper celebration was conducted to celebrate the event that changed forever the need for the base to rely upon Cuba for its fresh water. Bulkeley bottled and sent a container to Castro. By December, the final unit of the plant was operational and provided the capability to supply 2,250,000 gallons of fresh water per day.

Bulkeley was enjoying the challenge at Gitmo, but after two-and-a-half years, it was time for him to go back to sea to command cruiser-destroyer Flotilla 8, and a fast-attack carrier task Group as part of the Sixth Fleet in the Mediterranean. After his year at sea, Bulkeley returned to Washington for perhaps his most challenging career assignment.

Few seagoing sailors relish the idea of a tour in the inspection and survey business. The reason has historically been because it is a lose-lose proposition. If you find too many things wrong, the research, development and operations side of the navy labels you as an obstructionist. If you do not find and report the things that go wrong before they go wrong, you are labeled incompetent and unnecessary.

Bulkeley would be labeled with both titles, and it is doubtful if he could have accomplished his mission of ensuring that navy ships were ready for sustained combat without the support of the senior echelons of the navy. He was selected for the job by Paul H. Nitze, secretary of the navy, and he reported directly to the chief of naval operations (CNO). Bulkeley was told that he would receive no efficiency reports while on the job and no promotions. He could speak out and report deficiencies candidly and without fear of retaliation by those senior to him.

Adm. Bulkeley and his inspectors check a switchboard during an inspection in 1988.

US Navy

According to Bulkeley, "I inherited a collection of misfits. Several officers were alcoholics, one was undergoing psychiatric treatment, most were unprofessional, unmotivated, and simply did not give a damn."[11] Bulkeley was quick to clean house. Thirty-four officers were relieved for cause, and most of the remainder were given the option of immediate retirement or court martial. Most chose retirement.

Bulkeley then used the support of Secretary Nitze to gain approval to select his own replacements. In short order, the Board of Inspection and Survey (InSurv) was recognized as one of the most professional organizations in the navy.

Bulkeley personally established an inspection schedule for navy ships that kept him on the road 46 weeks each year. In his first year, he traveled 150,000 miles to inspect navy ships regardless of their location. Depending on the size of the ship to be inspected, Bulkeley would take between two and 100 of his staff to assist. His engineering officer accompanied him on 244 ship inspections in the first eight months.

Instead of trying to inspect a ship for material readiness while it was tied up at the pier, Bulkeley ordered that all such inspections would be conducted during a three-day at-sea deployment with all equipment and machinery operating. Everything from anchors to guns and engines were inspected.

Predictably, it wasn't long before senior navy officials and navy contractors were calling for Bulkeley's scalp. Bulkeley realized it was not going to be a publicity contest when he was assigned the job and simply responded that his charter was to ensure victory rather than defeat, and life for the navy's sailors, rather than death. "If they don't like that," he quipped, "they can go to hell."[12]

There were many navy seniors who wished to see Bulkeley relieved, but none had the authority to do so. The ultimate challenge came when the navy was about to accept the new aircraft carrier, *John F. Kennedy*. The ship could not be accepted by the navy nor the contractors paid until Bulkeley conducted his inspection. After several days at sea, Bulkeley submitted his inspection report to the secretary of the navy.

The report contained a long list of inadequacies and inefficiencies that cut through the entire design and construction process. While Bulkeley was reviled by contractor's offices and navy research offices, Secretary Nitze's office directed the commander of Naval Ships System Command to take immediate action to put the ship into satisfactory condition for acceptance. A crash program was implemented, and several months later the ship took her place in the fleet.

In the spring of 1973, Bulkeley was approaching his 62nd birthday and mandatory retirement from the navy. Well before his retirement date, the new secretary of the navy, John W. Warner, notified Bulkeley that he would be retired in accordance with navy regulations but recalled immediately to active duty. Bulkeley simply knew more about navy ships that anyone else alive, and the navy could not afford to lose him. According to Warner who knew Bulkeley well, "he (Bulkeley) is a rare combination of professional dignity, humility, tenacity, and firmness. ...he will go down in history as a truly remarkable sailor. He is a sailor's sailor in every sense of the word."[13]

Many of Bulkeley's initiatives had to do with the safety of the sailors. One example was his decision to join the below-deck crew in the boiler room where temperatures reached 184 degrees. Four hours after working alongside the sailors, Bulkeley collapsed in 190 degree heat. As a result, Bulkeley won a five-year battle with the navy and major changes to the boiler rooms followed immediately.

Another example was Bulkeley's insistence that emergency escape breathing devices (EEBDs) be installed on all ships. This small apparatus provided only three minutes of air but that could be enough time for many sailors to escape the smoke and fumes from fires aboard ship. After a long period of procrastination, the EEBDs were installed on all ships. Hundreds of sailors have been saved over the years because they had a EEBD to use. Few know that they owe their life to John Bulkeley.

Late in 1977, the navy was about to install 40,000-horsepower propellers on the new Spruance class destroyers. Bulkeley took a look at the new propellers and advised the chief of navy material, Admiral Isaac C. Kidd, Sr., that, as designed, the propeller would throw a blade. Kidd took Bulkeley's advice seriously, and had one of the new propellers installed on USS *Barbey*, then undergoing sea trials. Not long into her sea trials, *Barbey* threw a propeller blade, and then in rapid succession, the remaining three blades. Almost a year and millions of dollars later, corrected propellers were installed on the Spruance class destroyers.

In 1984, Prince Phillip, the Duke of Edinburgh, visited the naval base at San Diego. Phillip automatically became a five-star admiral in the Royal Navy when he married Queen Elizabeth II. Because Phillip and Bulkeley's friendship went back to WW II, Bulkeley was invited to join the Queen and Phillip for lunch aboard USS *Ranger* at San Diego.

During dinner, Bulkeley quipped, "Say, Prince, in WW II you and I were both navy Lieutenants, we both married English women, and now you are a five-star admiral and the best I could do is two stars. Where did I go wrong?" Prince Phillip smiled broadly and replied, "You married the wrong English woman."[14]

On August 25, 1988, John Bulkeley was promoted to vice admiral and awarded his third Distinguished Service Medal. He retired in 1988, after serving on active duty for 59 years (including his time at the naval academy). He died on April 6, 1995.

25

RETURN TO GUAM, SAIPAN AND TINIAN: JUNE-JULY 1944

Guam, Puerto Rico, and the Philippines became American possessions following the Spanish-American war. The United States paid Spain 20 million dollars for the colonies, and Spain sold the remainder of the Marianas group to Germany in 1899. Following the end of WW I, Japan was given a mandate over the German-owned Micronesian group by the League of Nations, and began secretly to build fortresses on the mandated islands. Guam remained virtually defenseless, and surrounded by Japanese military bases. It is no surprise that Guam has the distinction of being the first American possession to fall to the Japanese in WW II.

During December 1941, the American garrison on Guam consisted of 153 marines, 271 navy personnel, 308 Guamanian militia, three small patrol vessels, and an old oiler. The garrison had no artillery or fixed defenses and little communication capability. Japan used planes from Saipan to bomb the patrol vessels, and the cable and wireless stations on December 8, and the marine barracks the following day.

Major Gen. Tomitara Hori landed his 5,500-man invasion force at 2:30 A.M., on December 10, and the fighting was over by 5:45 A.M. The island governor, Navy Captain C. J. McMillin, was forced to publicly surrender the island in his underwear. The American defenders were shipped to Japan to toil as POWs, and the Japanese conquerors departed for Rabaul and more fighting. General Hori met his death on the Kokoda Track in Papua New Guinea, on October 21, 1944.

When the Allies landed in the Marianas in early summer 1944, readers found newspaper headlines focused on the Normandy invasion and the Allied attack in Europe. Little was said about the capture of the southern Marianas and the Allied return to Guam. Also unsaid, was the fact that with the fall of these islands, Japan lost their last chance for victory in the Pacific. Japanese leaders knew well the strategic importance of the islands. On May 4, 1944, Admiral Soemu Toyoda, commander-in-chief, combined fleet, warned the Japanese military that "The war is drawing close to the lines vital to our national defense. The issue of national existence is unprecedentedly serious; an un-precedented opportunity exists for deciding who shall be victorious and who shall be defeated."[1]

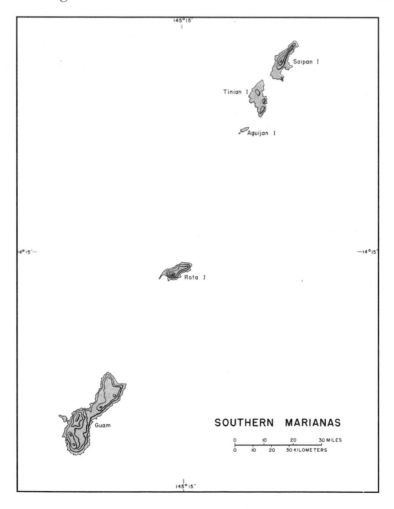

Southern Marianas

US Army

Strategically, the Marianas Islands were important for three reasons:
1. Army air corps B-29s would be able to launch attacks against
mainland Japan from the airfields that currently existed on these
islands. Tokyo was 1,260 miles away. 2. Guam would provide a
submarine refueling and supply point much closer to Japan; and 3.
Apra harbor at Guam, would provide an excellent anchorage for
an advanced naval base that could control the sea lines of
communication in the western Pacific. Before Guam could be
invaded, Saipan and Tinian would have to be isolated or captured.

Saipan

As the invasion date for Saipan approached, Admiral Marc
Mitscher's Task Force 58 (TF 58) with seven aircraft carriers
bombed Truk, the western Caroline Islands, the Palaus, Marcus,
and Wake Islands to ensure that there would be no intervention
from Japanese bases at these locations. Task Force 58 then returned
to the objective area and began bombing Saipan, Tinian, Rota,
and Guam. On June 11, 1944, a Japanese convoy of 20 ships
attempted to flee Saipan but was found 160 miles northwest the
following day. Carrier aircraft sank 14 of the ships including a
torpedo boat, three subchasers, and ten transport craft. In addition,
the *Bokuyo Maru* and *Keiyo Maru* were sunk at Saipan. (Maru are
transport craft.)

On June 14, the old battleships of the Pacific Fleet relieved
the new "fast battleships" and began bombardment of Saipan and
Tinian. The following day, two marine divisions landed on Saipan.
The landing brought an immediate response from the Japanese
navy who sailed their carrier task force to defeat the amphibious
assault. Planes from U.S. carriers met the Japanese on June 19 and
20, and in the action that followed (termed the Battle of the
Philippine Sea), destroyed much of the Japanese fleet.

Japan lost nine ships including carrier *Hiyo*, 402 planes, two
attack oilers, and suffered damage to four carriers, a battleship,
and an oiler. While carrier air was destroying Japanese naval
aviation, American submarines sank the carriers *Taiho* and *Shokaku*.
The U.S. Navy lost 130 aircraft.

419

Lieutenant Gen. Holland M. Smith

Vice Adm. Richmond Kelly Turner

US Marine Corps

US Army

Tactical command of troops ashore on Saipan belonged to Lieutenant Gen. Holland M. Smith, USMC. He was responsible to Vice Adm. Richmond K. Turner, the expeditionary force commander until the amphibious phase of the assault was completed. Smith had two marine corps divisions, an army corps of artillery, and the army 27th Infantry Division in reserve for the capture of Saipan and Tinian, a total of 66,779 troops. Another 39,080 troops would be added for the capture of Guam.[2]

Lieutenant Gen. Yoshitsugo Saito, commander of the 43rd Division, commanded Japanese forces on Saipan, with 12,939 men. In addition, artillery, engineer, and tank units increased the total personnel strength to nearly 30,000 troops, plus 48 tanks.[3] Saito utilized numerous land-based naval guns to cover the entire beach area with interlocking fire and dedicated another twenty-four 105-mm howitzers and thirty 75-mm field pieces to defend the beachhead. The weapons were pre-sighted and took a heavy toll of the personnel on the landing beaches. It would be six days before marines would secure the beachhead.

The landing on Saipan took place on June 15 (D-day) at 8:43 A.M., against heavy Japanese resistance. The plan to move 300 yards inland with amphibious tanks and tractors (LVT (A)'s was a failure because the LVT (A)'s lacked the armor and armament to close against the Japanese artillery and supporting weapons. Troops were pinned down on the beach, which rapidly became enemy artillery concentration points. After a full hour of fighting ashore, one marine battalion had advanced 12 yards. By noon, regimental casualties were estimated at 35 percent. By nightfall, division casualties were reported at 1,575, but a beachhead 1,000 yards deep and 10,000 yards long had been established.

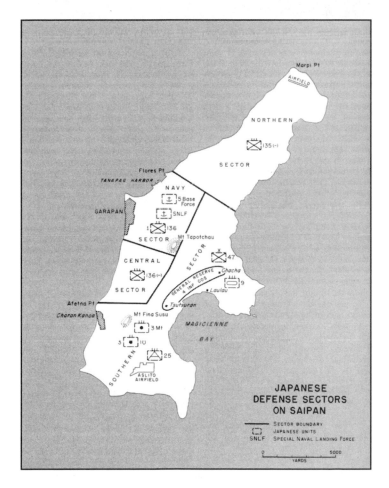

Japanese defense sectors on Saipan.

US Army

421

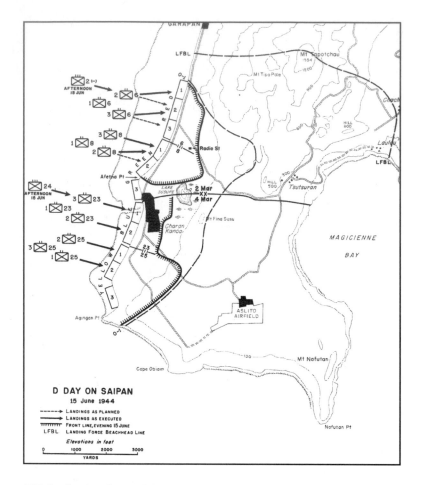

U.S. landing beaches on Saipan

After dark on D-day, the Japanese defenders, supported by tanks, began their counterattack against the marine positions. The marines lacked artillery to stop the charge but received illumination and 5-inch naval gunfire support. The naval gunfire plus rifle and machine gun fire stopped the first attack. Another counterattack developed at 3:00 A.M., and a final charge at daybreak on D-day +1. None of the attacks succeeded and 700 Japanese were killed in the assaults.

On June 17th, General Saito tried again to counterattack and drive the marines into the sea. This attack included 1,000 troops and 37 tanks, and was directed against the 6th Marine Regiment to the north of the marine lines. The Japanese attack was stopped with organic artillery, machine guns, mortars, bazookas, and rifles. Twenty-four of the tanks were destroyed and the Japanese fell back with heavy casualties.

The army's 165th Regimental Combat Team (RCT) landed on the 16th, and was positioned on the right of the marine line of attack. The RCT landed at night, established contact with the marines, and began the assault of Aslito airfield at 7:30 A.M. the next morning. Shortly thereafter, the decision was made to land the 105th Regimental Combat Team, the remainder of the 27th Army Division.

On the 18th, General Saito attempted to conduct an amphibious raid against the beachhead. At 4:30 A.M, a battalion of infantry in 35 small boats approached the beachhead but were intercepted and destroyed by U.S. Navy gunboats. Most of the Japanese infantry were killed.

Aslito field (3,600 feet of runway) was captured on June 18, and renamed Conroy Field, in honor of Colonel Gardiner J. Conroy, former regimental commander of the 165th RCT, who was killed at Makin Island. Later, the field was renamed Isely Field, after Commander Robert H. Isely, whose plane was shot down over Saipan. U.S. Army P-47s began flight operations from Isely on June 22.

The Japanese position on the evening of the 18th was precarious at best. The island had been cut in two, thus isolating some forces in the south. All artillery had been destroyed and, as if needed, the following message was received from the emperor: "Although the front line officers are fighting splendidly, if Saipan falls, air raids on Tokyo will take place often, therefore you absolutely must hold Saipan."[4]

Two marine divisions began a turning movement to the north to begin the attack on the Japanese main force near Garapan. The two army RCTs were directed to eliminate the Japanese stragglers, estimated as 1,050 mixed troops near Nafutan Point in the southern sector.

Due to the slow movement of the two RCTs, the disorganized Japanese had not been eliminated in the south. Major Gen. Ralph Smith, division commander, requested that the 105th RCT be left to conduct operations. Holland Smith agreed, but stipulated that only two battalions could be used for the mopping up exercise. The other battalion was to be held in reserve.

Ralph Smith met with Holland Smith late on June 22 to explain the reasons for the lack of progress in the south and why the 2nd Battalion had not been released to corps reserve. Holland Smith told Ralph Smith that the 105th RCT could not be permitted to delay. The troops were needed in the north. "If the commander of the 105th could not do the job, send somebody who could."[5] One hour later, Ralph Smith issued orders to the 2nd battalion to continue operations against the Japanese near Nafutan Point. The following morning, Holland Smith warned Ralph Smith that the 2nd Battalion 105th RCT was under Corps command as a reserve unit and should not be included in Ralph Smith's tactical orders.

Major Gen. Ralph Smith

US Army

Ralph Smith now had a single infantry battalion, six tanks, and naval gunfire support to eliminate the estimated 300 to 500 Japanese remaining in the south. Instead of continuing operations on the morning of the June 23, as directed, the battalion did not conduct offensive operations until the afternoon, and made no advance whatsoever. No progress was made on June 24.

On June 25th, the battalion reached Ridge 300. This high ground was the main Japanese defensive position that had posed such a problem for the attackers. After midnight on June 26, an estimated 500 Japanese led by Captain Sasaki, penetrated the army positions and attacked Isley airfield and marine artillery positions. All Japanese infiltrators were killed by morning with the loss of 33 marine artillerymen killed or wounded.

The army division was inserted between the two marine divisions for the assault against Japanese forces in the north of Saipan. The initial assault began at 5:30 A.M., on June 23. One army company was three hours late for the assault and held up the entire division. Progress of the division was disappointing on the 23rd, and, as a result, Holland Smith, the corps commander, registered his complaint with Major Gen. Sanderford Jarman, the island commander and senior army general on Saipan. The following morning, Holland Smith sent a stern dispatch to Ralph Smith, to advance and seize objectives as ordered.

By noon on the 24th, both marine divisions had moved well ahead of the army division and had to stop their advance due to lack of contact with the army division. At that time, Holland Smith relieved Ralph C. Smith as commander of the 27th Army Division. Relief was for lack of aggressive action on the part of the army division and for Smith's contravening orders of the corps commander. Historians still debate the appropriateness of the relief, but from June, 1944, through the remainder of the Pacific war, the issue divided the army and marines at a time when close cooperation was essential.

The army and marines had different philosophies and trained in different tactics in regard to island fighting in the Pacific. The army philosophy was to advance slowly, behind a creeping artillery or naval gunfire barrage. They expected to suffer fewer casualties, take a longer time to complete their mission, and have less mopping up to do. The marine, and navy philosophy was to press the attack quickly, bypassing strong points of resistance, leaving them for reserve elements to eliminate. Such tactics resulted in more casualties in the short term, but accomplished the mission sooner, thus decreasing casualties in the long term and freeing the naval support ships much earlier.

Saipan and Okinawa provide excellent examples of the different tactics. In both places, coral atolls and caves pockmarked the country. The enemy could hide inside the caves and tunnels, and move in and out at will. Artillery and naval gunfire were largely ineffective. The enemy had to be overrun quickly and eliminated with bayonets, flame-throwers, and explosives. Marines liked to keep the enemy moving on the defensive, for fear that if given time; he would dig in deeper or surface behind them. They were determined not to let the offensive bog down, as happened with the army on Munda.

Both philosophies and associated tactics worked well when only one service was involved. When army and marine units fought side by side, marine units would advance much faster than their army counterparts, thus exposing their flanks to the enemy. This is not to suggest that there was any lack of courage by the infantrymen, or even lack of experience. The army 27th Division fought well at Makin and Eniwetok.

Ralph Smith's relief did nothing to change the lack of aggressiveness of the army division, but did serve to highlight differences in tactics on the part of the army and marine corps. These same differences were illuminated during the battle for Okinawa, when the navy was suffering tremendous ship and personnel casualties from the *kamikazes,* due to lack of aggressiveness on the part of the ground forces. Admiral Nimitz again gave serious consideration to relief of the army corps commander.

Major Gen. Jarman assumed command of the 27th Division on June 24. After two days of fighting, forward progress was stalled. The marine divisions had suffered 1,145 casualties and the army division 277. The line of advance sagged as much as 1,500 yards in the 27th division zone, and six days of hard fighting remained.

General Saito tried another amphibious raid on June 25. An infantry company from Tinian was loaded on 11 barges and sent to conduct a landing on the east coast of Saipan. Destroyer USS *Bancroft* intercepted and sank one barge, and sent the remainder fleeing for Tinian. Later on the same morning, two more barges loaded with infantry departed Tinian. Two patrol boats sank one barge and damaged another before they reached Saipan.

On June 26, General Jarman visited the army front lines at 10:00 A.M., and found that there had been no advance from the assembly area. Jarman relieved the regimental commander and assigned his chief of staff to command. He also issued orders to the 105th RCT that they must hold their positions at all costs. On June 28, Major Gen. George W. Griner relieved Jarman as 27th division commander.

On June 30, physical contact was established among all three divisions for the first time since June 22. Throughout the day few Japanese were seen and only stragglers and civilians were flushed from caves and ravines.

Early on the morning of July 6, about 3,000 Japanese and a few tanks made their final *banzai* charge against the army division. The Japanese overran the 105th and engaged in hand-to-hand combat over a wide area. The following morning, Holland Smith relieved most of the army units, and directed the 2nd Marine Division to "mop up" the Japanese pockets of resistance. On July 9, Saipan was declared secure.

Vice Adm. Chuichi Nagumo, leader of the Japanese carrier task forces during the attacks on Pearl Harbor and Midway, committed ritual suicide on Saipan, followed by the suicide of Lieutenant Gen. Yoshitsugu Saito on July 6. Allied forces reached Marpi Point at the south end of Saipan on July 9, resulting in the mass suicides of Japanese civilians at Marpi Point, Suicide Cliff, and *Banzai* Cliff. At times, the waters below the point were so thick with the bodies of men, women, and children, that small craft were unable to rescue the few living amongst them.

American casualties were 14,111 or 20 percent of the landing force. This is about the same percentage of casualties suffered at bloody Tarawa and Pelileu. The entire 30,000-man Japanese garrison was killed.

Tinian

At daybreak on July 24, the two marine divisions embarked for Tinian, landing on the northeast coast. Marines were supported by artillery fire from Saipan, naval gunfire, and by close air support from navy carriers and Isely field on Saipan. By nightfall, the marines had established a beachhead 2,900 yards wide and a mile deep.

The expected Japanese counterattack occurred at 2:00 A.M. the following morning in three separate thrusts, one of which was supported by five tanks. The attack continued for five hours, failed to penetrate the marine's lines, and the Japanese lost about 1,241 men.[6]

By July 31, the Japanese had been forced to the southern tip of Tinian and once again counterattacked. Colonel Takashi Ogata, commander of the Japanese garrison, led the attack. Ogata started the defense of Tinian with 8,500 men but casualties decreased his forces to a thousand men for the last counterattack. Ogata was killed by machine gun fire, and by 6:00 A.M., the final *banzai* charge was exhausted with about 700 dead.[7]

Tinian was declared secure that evening. Marine casualties were 328 dead and 1,571 wounded. During the period July 1944, until January 1945, another 542 Japanese were killed during "mopping up" exercises. The Tinian operation is considered by most historians and military personnel to be the most brilliantly conceived and executed amphibious operation in the Pacific. Holland Smith termed it, "a perfect amphibious operation."[8]

Tinian would become one of the best airfield complexes in the Central Pacific. Ushi Point and Gurguan Point airfields supported most of the bombing attacks against Japan, and the *Enola Gay* departed Ushi Point to deliver the first atomic bomb on Hiroshima.

A concrete pillbox at Gaan Point on Agat Beach, Guam. The fallen section of log is in place to represent a field artillery piece.

J.T. Hagen

Guam

Guam is located 100 miles south of Saipan and comprises an area 34-miles long and five to nine miles wide. Life had become difficult for the civilians (Chamorros) on Guam since Japan captured the island in 1941. Many Chamorros were interned in concentration camps while others died on forced marches and massacres committed by the Japanese.

The beaches on Guam are wide and deep enough to permit troops to get ashore and consolidate before moving inland. At least that was what Admiral Richmond Kelly Turner, the expeditionary force commander, and Major Gen. Roy Geiger, commander of the landing force, were counting on. To liberate Guam, Geiger would have the 3rd Marine Division, a marine brigade, the 77th Army Division, and amphibious corps artillery, a force of about 55,000 men.[9]

A 25cm antiaircraft gun like the one shown here at Gaan Point on Agat Beach, Guam could fire 300 rounds of HE ammo per minute.

J.T. Hagen

Guam was defended by the 29th Japanese Division, commanded by Lieutenant Gen. Takeshi Takashina, and the 11th Infantry Regiment, commanded by Major Gen. Kiyoshi Shigematsu. The infantry plus several thousand navy personnel brought the total strength to about 30,000.

For 13 days before the amphibious assault, six battleships, nine cruisers, and numerous escorting destroyers saturated Guam with 28,764 shells of assorted sizes. Naval aviation flew 4,303 missions against Japanese positions on Guam during the last three days before the landing. The intense fire support convinced many that the landing on Guam would be uneventful. The night before the scheduled landing, Major William Gilliam, Geiger's naval gunfire officer, reported that, "The assault troops would meet little resistance." navy staff officers were heard to say that, "Not one fixed gun was left in commission on the west coast (of Guam) that was of greater size than a machine gun."[10]

The first armored amphibian vehicles, landed on Guam at 8:29 A.M., on July 22, 1944. Within a few minutes, similar landings took place at all the designated beaches. The 3rd Marine Division landed at Asan, the 1st Provisional Marine Brigade and the 77th Army Infantry Division at Agat. The euphoria concerning the destruction of all Japanese weapons lasted until Japanese mortar fire started falling among the landing forces. Mortar fire, anti-boat guns, and artillery scored direct hits on many of the landing craft. Despite strong opposition that caused 697 casualties, the 3rd division secured a foothold on Guam by nightfall.

At the Agat beachhead, the brigade casualties numbered 350. The brigade had moved as much as 2,000 yards inland before sunset, and was prepared to attack at first light the following morning. The brigade took many of their casualties from preregistered artillery and mortar fire while they were still in the slow amphibian tractors (24 tractors were destroyed), as they approached the beach. More punishment came from 37-mm and 75-mm guns firing from concrete blockhouses in the center of the beaches. Despite overextended lines, shortages of ammunition and fuel for those vehicles that were ashore, Brigadier Gen. Lemuel Shepherd, brigade commander and a future commandant of the marine corps, radioed General Geiger, "I think we can handle it."[11]

The high humidity, lack of fresh water, and inactivity of long shipboard life took a toll on U.S. troops. Many fell from sheer exhaustion and the difficulty of moving through the mud and jungle. Due to 30 inches of rain in June and July, and the heavy naval bombardment, Asan beachhead was a sea of deep mud. The tangled jungle growth, jagged limestone, boulders, and rubble made any movement difficult and tiring.

Shortly after sunset, Japanese began to probe the brigade defenses. Finally, from 2:30 to 4:00 A.M., they launched three major attacks against the beachhead. Following mortar barrages four Japanese tanks and infantry closed the brigade defenses. Bazooka fire and some Sherman tanks that Shepherd had hidden in the foliage quickly destroyed the Japanese tanks. Next followed the traditional *bushido* charge by Japanese infantrymen armed with rifles, bayonets, grenades and demolitions. Marines heard the Japanese preparing for their charge. Through the noise of a steady rain came the laughter, merriment, and crash of broken saki bottles that signaled confidence-building for a charge. To the marines, the noise sounded like New Years eve at the zoo.

When the Japanese were ready, Commander Asaichi Tamai sent them charging toward the Allied position. Life and death, hand-to-hand combat followed with a few Japanese breaking through the defensive lines to engage U.S. forces in the rear areas. By morning, 659 Japanese bodies were counted. Shepherd's brigade, tired and battered, reported they were ready to continue the attack. After four days of tough fighting, a regiment of the army division was landed to move through the marine front lines and take over the left half of the perimeter. The marine brigade turned north to attack Orote Peninsula.

In the north, the marine division fought through tangled brush, up steep slopes, and a series of ridges, to defeat the defensive positions of General Takashima. As the division approached, Takashima committed seven of his best battalions to a counterattack on the evening of July 26, to drive the marines into the sea. Two major attacks developed. One struck the right center of the marines' forward line, and penetrated the defensive positions. The second attack penetrated rear areas in an attempt to destroy logistic installations near the beachhead.

Wave after wave of fanatical Japanese plunged through the marine lines and their rainwater-filled foxholes. The Japanese shouted, "Wake up Americans and die."[12] Close, bitter, hand-to-hand combat ensued. Service troops, support troops, and bandaged patients that could operate a rifle or use a bayonet were rushed into the melee. Slowly, the Japanese were isolated into pockets, and killed. Sunrise favored the Americans as artillery support could be used to annihilate the remaining pockets of Japanese. By noon, 3,500 Japanese bodies were counted within the division perimeter. The division suffered 845 casualties, of which 166 were killed in action (KIA). The loss of these Japanese battalions and infantrymen in the charge against the brigade would cost General Takashima dearly in the days to come. The backbone of Japanese resistance had been broken.

Shepherd's brigade captured Orote Peninsula on July 29, after four days of hard fighting. American aircraft began using the airfield the next day. General Geiger then placed the brigade in reserve and turned both divisions north to capture the Japanese-held high ground. Tank-infantry assaults permitted the 77th Division to capture Barrigada and Mount San Rosa while the marines suffered heavily, advancing through thick jungles near Finegayan, killing 700 Japanese defenders. General Takashima was killed on July 26, and Lieutenant Gen. Hideyoshi Obata succeeded him.

The Japanese made their last organized defensive stand at Yigo, in the Mount Santa Rosa area. On August 7 and 8, the 77th Infantry Division, supported by heavy artillery and tanks, achieved a final victory there, thus ending organized Japanese resistance. Japanese casualties at Santa Rosa were 500. Lieutenant Gen. Obata died at the battle for Yigo.

Guam was declared secure on August 10, 1944. Although Japanese stragglers continued to survive on Guam for years to come, eventually the entire garrison was killed or captured. American casualties numbered 7,800, of which 6,943 were marines.[13] Guam became the forward operating base for the U.S. Pacific submarine force and the headquarters for the Commander in Chief Pacific, Admiral Chester Nimitz.

The Guam World War II Memorial

J.T. Hagen

434

26

VICE ADMIRAL CHUICHI NAGUMO

"Ships are attacked by torpedoes, land bases by bombs."

"Let us be buried here together in Saipan! We are beaten, but we shall die here with honour."[1] Shortly after Vice Adm. Chuichi Nagumo spoke these words on July 6, 1944, he killed himself with his service revolver. His body was never recovered from the coral caves of Saipan; many closed forever by marine corps bulldozers, dynamite, artillery, and naval gunfire.

Vice Adm. Chuichi Nagumo

AP/Wide World

Vice Adm. Nagumo was commander of the *Kido Butai* (Carrier Striking Force), and hero of the Japanese carrier attack on Darwin, the surprise attack on Pearl Harbor, the raid into the Indian Ocean, the Battle of the Coral Sea, the defeat at Midway, and fleet actions off Guadalcanal. But, what was he doing on Saipan near the end

435

of the war? Nagumo's success and failures in the Pacific and his position on Saipan make an interesting and compelling story.

Chuichi Nagumo was born in Yomezawa City in Yamagata prefecture (north of Tokyo) on March 25, 1887. He decided in the seventh grade that he wanted to join the Imperial Navy because Japan was an island nation and would need a strong navy.[2] He excelled in his studies, was always rated at the top of his class, and became adept at judo. Nagumo graduated number five from his naval academy class at Etajima and served on several destroyers, and the battleship *Hirado* before attending the Naval Staff College in 1910. As a lieutenant commander, he commanded destroyer *Momi* and served on the staff of the First Torpedo Squadron and the naval general staff.

He was promoted to commander in 1924 and served as an instructor at the Naval Staff College. He was promoted to captain and commanded the light cruiser *Naka*, the First Destroyer Flotilla; cruiser *Takao;* and battleship *Yamashiro.* In 1935, at age 48, Nagumo was promoted to rear admiral and assigned command of the Eighth Torpedo Squadron. He was subsequently principal of the Torpedo School, and in April 1941, eight months before the attack on Pearl Harbor, Nagumo was named commander-in-chief of the First Carrier Division.

At the time of his assignment, Nagumo was a highly respected expert on torpedo warfare. However, he knew virtually nothing about aerial warfare or carrier operations. He was gruff, conservative, and unimaginative. He was also suspicious of the potency of air power and was assigned commander of the carrier division solely because of his seniority and against the wishes of Admiral Isoroku Yamamoto, commander of Japan's Combined Fleet. Neither Nagumo nor Yamamoto wanted Nagumo to command the carrier division, yet neither was able to prevent it. From a superb career involving important staff and operational command positions, Nagumo now entered a phase of his life that would lead downward and end in his suicide on the lonely island of Saipan. Regardless of one's opinion of Admiral Nagumo's leadership ability, one cannot help but be impressed by the combat activity of Nagumo's carrier fleet during the next seven months.

Pearl Harbor, Hawaii

Admiral Yamamoto's orders to Nagumo were simple and concise. "Destroy the U.S. Fleet at Pearl Harbor by a surprise attack." Besides his six carriers, Nagumo had a fleet of 33 warships to accomplish his mission. Shortly before midnight on November 25, 1941, Nagumo's six carriers and 15 escort vessels slipped quietly out of Hitokappu Bay in the Kurile Islands. They headed west, toward the International Date Line with the remainder of their refuelers and other support ships.

Three days later, Nagumo's task force encountered heavy fog, rain, and freezing temperatures. The refueling tankers became separated from the task force, and, with total radio silence, Nagumo had to detach his destroyers to find them and bring them back. Shortly thereafter, rain and sleet turned the flight deck of carrier *Kaga* into a huge skating rink. It was not a time for the fainthearted. Nagumo, still very much unsure of himself, struck up a conversation on the bridge with his chief of staff, Rear Adm. Ryunosuke Kusaka. "Mr. Chief of Staff, What do you think? I feel that I have undertaken a heavy responsibility. If only I'd have held out and declined it." (command of the carrier strike force). Kusaka replied somewhat nonchalantly, "Don't worry Sir. Everything will turn out all right."[3]

Kusaka, however, was shocked to hear such indecisiveness from Nagumo and reported the conversation to Commander Mitsuo Fuchida, commander of the flying corps, and to Commander Minoru Genda, a close confidante of Yamamoto.

On December 1, Nagumo received the radio message, *"Niitaka Yama Nobore,"* meaning, climb Mt. Niitaka. The message directed Nagumo to proceed with the attack on Pearl Harbor. Early on the morning of December 7, 1941, Nagumo hoisted the same battle flag on the signal mast of his flagship *Akagi* that Admiral Heihachiro Togo flew at the battle of Tsushima in 1905. The flag meant that, upon this one battle rests the fate of our nation. Let every man do his utmost. Immediately thereafter, Nagumo's six carriers launched 366 planes against Pearl Harbor.

Mitsuo Fuchida, leader of the first wave, arrived at Pearl Harbor at 7:50 A.M., and sent the now famous message, *"Tora, Tora, Tora,"* meaning we have achieved complete surprise. The Japanese attacked from three directions, and when they departed at 9:45 A.M., they left behind sunken and broken battleships, and burning docks. Nagumo's aircraft sank or damaged eight battleships, three light cruisers, three destroyers, and four support ships. They destroyed 311 army and navy aircraft and killed 2,330 military personnel, wounding another 1,178. Nagumo lost 29 planes and 55 airmen. It was a great victory, was it not?

As the pilots returned to their carriers, they expected to be refueled, rearmed, and sent back for a second strike. Both Fuchida and Genda argued with Nagumo and Kusaka that a second attack should take place at once. Fuchida told Nagumo that, "We must carry out another attack as there are still destroyers and factories that are undamaged." Fuchida was far more than a chance selection to lead the air attack on Pearl Harbor. He was Japan's most experienced aviator with more than 3,000 hours of flight time. His recommendation could not be ignored. Genda recommended that Nagumo call in his refuelers, and spend several days attacking bases in Hawaii and seeking the U.S. carriers. Rear Adm. Kusaka was concerned about heavy losses if they made another attack, and Nagumo was worried about U.S. submarines and the three missing aircraft carriers.[4] It was Nagumo's decision to make and he made it. "We may conclude that the anticipated results have been achieved," he announced, and ordered the task force to withdraw.

Fuchida would later say of Nagumo, "Nagumo's leadership as

a commander was always conservative and he would never take the initiative. In the end he would always agree with the staff officer when making decisions."[5] Historians with the benefit of 60 years of hindsight tend not to focus upon Nagumo's conservatism as much as they do his misunderstanding of Yamamoto's strategy. Yamamoto expected to lose one-third to one-half of his fleet including two carriers in the Pearl Harbor attack, but deemed such losses justifiable if the U.S. Pacific Fleet was completely destroyed. Nagumo treated the mission like a raid, and believed that he had scored a great victory without even scraping the paint of one of his ships.

Yamamoto wanted at least six months of non-interference from the U.S. Pacific Fleet in order to consolidate Japan's gains and establish a defensive barrier. He saw Nagumo's results as a hollow victory. Yamamoto was proven correct in that Pacific Fleet carriers attacked Japanese outposts in the Pacific in less than three months after Pearl Harbor.

Darwin, Australia

During the evening of February 18, 1942, four carriers of Nagumo's *Kido Butai* (carrier striking force) arrived at a position 200 miles from Darwin. A bit before 10:00 A.M., the following morning, 188 Japanese aircraft roared out of the northwest and devastated Darwin. For 10 weeks Australians had been aware of Japanese aggression to the north of Australia, but were not ready for such an attack. The North Australian Worker's Union had paralyzed the Darwin docks with wildcat strikes. As a result, the harbor was crammed with fully loaded ships; much of the cargo needed for Allied troops. For 30 minutes the Japanese bombers and fighters led by Lieutenant Cmdr. Mitsuo Fuchida, attacked ships, harbor installations, and the city. They sank eight ships, including the destroyer *USS Peary*, damaged 13 more, cratered the runway, and destroyed the hangars, harbor, and port facilities. At noon, 54 more Japanese planes attacked Darwin to finish off the job. Casualties were 240 killed and 300 injured.

It was the greatest loss of life in one day in Australia. The people were so certain that an invasion would follow the bombing that they fled south any way they could. Commander-in-Chief, Home Forces, Major Gen. Sir Iven MacKay, put into effect defense plans that would abandon vast areas of north Australia to any invading Japanese force. Over the next 21 months, Darwin was bombed 62 times, but never with such devastating results as that inflicted by Nagumo. [6]

The Indian Ocean

Although the success of the attack on Pearl Harbor elevated Admiral Nagumo to hero status in the eyes of the Japanese people, he continued to be criticized by Yamamoto and Admiral Matome Ugaki, chief staff officer of the Combined Fleet, for his failure to make a second attack on Pearl Harbor. Three months after the Pearl Harbor attack, Yamamoto sent Nagumo's carrier division to the Indian Ocean to disrupt British bases at Colombo (now Sri Lanka) and Trincomalee, Ceylon.

Nagumo left the Celebes Islands near Borneo on March 26, 1942, with five large carriers, four modern battleships, three cruisers and nine destroyers. At the same time, another force commanded by Vice Adm. Jisaburo Ozawa, consisting of a light carrier, six cruisers, and eight destroyers, sailed from Malaya to attack shipping in the Bay of Bengal. The Japanese forces were challenging the British Royal Navy, which had controlled the Indian Ocean for 150 years.

On April 5, 1942, Nagumo's aircraft attacked Colombo, where they inflicted losses on ships and land-based facilities. They destroyed 20 British aircraft and sank heavy cruisers *Dorsetshire* and *Cornwall*. Four days later Nagumo attacked Trincomalee, where he sank two light cruisers, several destroyers, and 10 freighters. Off the southeast coast of Ceylon, Nagumo discovered the British carrier *Hermes*, a destroyer, and a large merchant vessel traveling without escort. The Japanese pilots sank all three in less than 15 minutes. In a five-day period, Ozawa's forces sank a thousand tons of shipping in the Bay of Bengal.

Nagumo's force returned to Japan without loss of ships or aircraft. As impressive as their results seemed, they did come at a price. His ships, crews, and pilots were weary, overconfident, and boastful. Rest would take care of the weariness. Maintenance time would take care of the ships, but there was something else more difficult to explain. The Japanese would later call it, "The victory disease."

The Battle of the Coral Sea

Admiral Chester W. Nimitz, commander-in-chief of the Pacific Fleet since December 31, 1941, could do little more than "hit and run" with his remaining forces in the Pacific. He had Admiral "Bull" Halsey with the USS *Enterprise* raid Kwajalein in the Marshalls, and Admiral Willard Brown's *Lexington* carrier group raid Rabaul. On March 10, Brown's *Lexington* group was joined by USS *Yorktown*, commanded by Rear Adm. Frank J. Fletcher, and attacked Japanese land forces on the north coast of Papua New Guinea. These raids accomplished a bit more in material damage than would Lieutenant Col. Jimmy Doolittle's raid on Tokyo, but were not in the same league when it came to psychological impact.

On April 18, 1942, Lieutenant Col. James H, Doolittle led 16 army B-25 bombers from the deck of the carrier USS *Hornet* on a 650-mile raid on Tokyo. The physical damage inflicted was small, but psychologically the results were huge. The homeland and the emperor were threatened by enemy bombing. A decision was made to extend Japan's defensive perimeter to preclude future attacks. All opposition to Admiral Yamamoto's Midway plan ceased, and Admiral Shigeyoshi Inoue was told to seize Port Moresby in Papua New Guinea. Thanks to "Station Hypo," the code-breaking and traffic analysis facility at Pearl Harbor, Pacific Fleet intelligence knew that the Japanese were preparing for an offensive in the South Pacific with Port Moresby as the objective.

Admiral Nimitz rushed the carrier *Lexington* from Pearl Harbor to join Rear Adm. Frank Fletcher's *Yorktown* force already in the Coral Sea. The USS *Hornet* returned to Pearl Harbor from the Doolittle raid on April 25, and was also sent to join Fletcher. On May 2, Fletcher's forces attacked and threw back the Japanese landing at Tulagi. The Japanese carrier strike force was under command of Rear Adm. Takeo Takagi and consisted of two carriers, *Shokaku* and *Zuikaku*, two heavy cruisers, and six destroyers. The Main Force, commanded by Rear Adm. Arimoto Goto, included the light carrier *Shoho*.

In the first naval battle where the opposing forces never saw each other, the United States lost carrier *Lexington*, and oiler *Neosho*. Japan lost the small carrier *Shoho*. Japan won the battle, but lost far more in the longer term. *Shokaku* was damaged so badly that she would be unable to participate in the Midway battle. *Zuikako* was undamaged, but lost so many aircraft and aircrews that she also would not participate at Midway. More importantly, the Port Moresby invasion was defeated and was not again attempted.

The Battle for Midway

Admiral Isoroku Yamamoto wanted to attack Midway to lure the Pacific Fleet, and especially its carriers from Pearl Harbor and destroy them. The Battle for Midway was a clear example of the forcefulness of Yamamoto. No one else wanted to attack Midway. Nagumo's forces were drained. He and his chief of staff, Admiral Kusaka, strongly opposed Yamamoto's strategy as did the general staff in Tokyo. The general staff argued that it would be difficult to supply and support Midway once it was captured, and the American's could return anytime to recapture it. Commander Genda and Admiral Tamon Yamaguchi from the First Air Division protested vigorously against the attack, but in the end, Yamamoto got his way. In actuality, Yamamoto's cause was advanced by the Doolittle raid on the Japanese homeland. Following Doolittle's bombing of Tokyo and its suburbs, the general staff became determined to prevent a reoccurrence, and decided to extend

Japan's outer defensive perimeter. Midway would provide such an extension.

Yamamoto's plan was to draw the U.S. Pacific Fleet from Hawaii and defeat it in a "decisive battle." The striking force of six carriers would destroy the defenses of Midway, then destroy the American carriers when they sortied from Pearl Harbor. Yamamoto would have a cordon of submarines posted north of Hawaii to alert him when the American fleet was enroute to Midway, and would have search aircraft to keep him informed when the fleet left Pearl Harbor. Yamamoto's main body of battleships and cruisers would wipe out any remaining American naval forces.

Japan's report of the Coral Sea Battle had the carrier *Lexington* sunk and *Yorktown* as possibly sunk, or at least heavily damaged. Japan lost the light carrier *Shoho* and the service of their damaged carrier *Shokaku*. Japan also lost their carrier *Zuikaku* for the Midway battle because there was insufficient time to replace her aircraft and train new aircrews. The situation was not alarming. Yamamoto reasoned that four Japanese carriers could easily take care of the one or two American carriers that might make it to Midway.

Nagumo's forces left the port of Hashira Jima in the Inland Sea of Japan on May 27, heading for Midway. He had four large aircraft carriers with 261 aircraft, two battleships, two heavy cruisers, 12 destroyers, and eight large tankers. Despite the power contained in Nagumo's force, he was only part of a much larger force. Yamamoto commanded a fleet of 127 warships and established his flagship with the eight battleships of the main force.

Enroute to Midway, Nagumo and his staff decided that their mission to support the amphibious landing at Midway and to destroy the American Fleet would interfere with each other. Since the Americans couldn't possibly know about the Midway operation, and since their submarines had not reported any movement of the American Pacific Fleet, Nagumo decided that there was adequate

443

time to support the landing first, and then deal with the enemy fleet when it arrived.

Nagumo struck Midway early on the morning of June 4, by sending 72 "Kate" and "Zero" bombers armed with 1,170-pound contact-fused bombs and 550-pound armor-piercing bombs. They were escorted by 36 Zero fighters. He prudently kept half his remaining aircraft loaded with torpedoes to attack enemy ships when contact was established. The remaining aircraft were fighters used for combat air patrol over the carriers. When the first wave of aircraft failed to destroy the runway and facilities at Midway, Nagumo, perhaps remembering his criticism at Pearl Harbor, ordered a second strike. Fate would now intervene to turn what was a sound decision into a catastrophe.

Since his scout planes had not reported any enemy surface forces, Nagumo made a decision to download the torpedoes from his reserve aircraft, reload them with bombs, and send them to attack Midway on the second strike. Shortly after downloading commenced, a scout plane reported 10 ships 200 miles east of Nagumo's force. No carriers were reported so Nagumo continued downloading the torpedoes from his reserve aircraft. At 8:09 A.M., the scout plane reported that there were five cruisers and five destroyers in the enemy force. Nagumo vacillated and ordered the aircraft rearmed with torpedoes. Admiral Nagumo was from the old school where he was taught that, "ships are attacked by torpedoes, land bases by bombs." The bombs that were on the aircraft could have created substantial damage to the American carriers had Nagumo launched them at that time. But now, the aircraft from the first attack on Midway were returning and had to be recovered aboard the carriers.

At 8:20 A.M., the scout plane reported what appeared to be a carrier in the enemy force. The scout plane had sighted USS *Yorktown*. Nagumo had a problem. If he delayed landing the first strike bombers and their fighter escorts while he launched planes against the enemy force, his planes would have to go without fighter escort since his fighters were returning with the bombers or overhead the carriers with low fuel state. He asked the scout plane to confirm the presence of an enemy carrier.

Since no enemy carrier planes had been confirmed. Nagumo doubted that there was one and delayed launch of his torpedo bombers until his first-strike aircraft could be recovered. *Yorktown,* like *Hornet* and *Enterprise,* began launching aircraft at 8:30 to strike Nagumo's carriers.

By 10:00 A.M., Nagumo's carriers had recovered the Midway strike aircraft and their fighter escorts. Nagumo turned the fleet north to put some distance between him and the enemy fleet before launching his aircraft. The carrier's hangar and flight decks were covered with planes, torpedoes, bombs, and gasoline hoses. At that moment, destroyer *Arashi* returned to the fleet from pursuing the U.S. submarine, *Nautilus. Arashi* returned at flank speed, leaving a wide and highly visible wake.

At 9:55 A.M., Commander Wade McClusky's attention was focused on the huge wake being generated by *Arashi.* McCluskey and his 37 SBD Dauntless dive-bombers had searched for the Japanese carriers in vain, and were now short on fuel. McCluskey had a hunch that the destroyer moving so fast must be headed for larger game, and followed *Arashi* for several minutes. At 10:00 A.M., McCluskey spotted three carriers and American torpedo bombers attacking the Japanese fleet. He put his plane in a 70-degree dive from 14,500 feet, accelerated to 280 knots, and placed four bombs on *Kaga.* The remainder of Bombing Six Squadron, and then Bombing Three Squadron from *Yorktown,* followed and scored direct hits on *Akagi* and *Soryu.* As the American dive-bombers departed, the three Japanese carriers were burning fiercely. Within a span of five minutes, Nagumo lost three of his four carriers.

Only *Hiryu* remained, and she promptly launched 40 aircraft at 30-minute intervals against the American carriers. Eight of

445

Hiryu's first wave of aircraft penetrated *Yorktown's* fighter shield and placed three bombs into *Yorktown*. One bomb damaged the flight deck, one went squarely inside the funnel, putting out five of the six boilers, and the third penetrated the carrier's flight deck, exploded on the fourth deck, and at 12:20 P.M., caused *Yorktown* to go dead in the water, burning fiercely.

The damage control team repaired *Yorktown's* boilers and by the time *Hiryu's* second attack wave arrived, *Yorktown* was cruising at 20 knots and refueling aircraft. Five Japanese aircraft were shot down, but the survivors flew a well-coordinated torpedo attack from four different directions and put two torpedoes into *Yorktown*. The ship was abandoned at 3:00 P.M. In the meantime, *Enterprise* launched 24 SBD dive-bombers against *Hiryu*. Lieutenant Earl Gallaher led the strike that found *Hiryu* at 6:50 P.M. Gallaher's SBDs dove from 19,000 feet and placed four bombs on the carrier that started massive fires. By 9:23, *Hiryu* was dead in the water, the fourth and last carrier of Admiral Nagumo's *Kido Butai*. It was one of the most stunning losses in the history of naval warfare. For the first time in the war, the naval odds in the Pacific now favored the United States.

Admiral Yamamoto blamed the defeat upon the failure of his cordon of 16 submarines to alert him of the approach of enemy carriers. The blame, of course, fell on Yamamoto for placing the submarines where he thought the Pacific Fleet should be rather than where it was. In similar fashion, Japanese aerial surveillance of Pearl Harbor was precluded by Nimitz stationing naval craft in the area where the surveillance craft were to refuel.

Once again, there appeared to be a lack of understanding of Yamamoto's strategy on the part of Nagumo. Yamamoto was using Midway as bait to draw Nimitz's fleet to Midway, where he could destroy it. Nagumo's focus was on the invasion of Midway, which he supported with little regard for the possibility of enemy surface forces. Perhaps Nagumo had the "victory disease."

The Battle for Guadalcanal

Following Japan's disaster at Midway, the Japanese general staff dismantled the *Kido Butai,* and formed two new divisions. The Third Carrier Division consisted of 29 ships including six carriers and was commanded by Admiral Nagumo with Rear Adm. Ryunosuke Kusaka as his chief of staff. The Eighth Carrier Division consisted of 13 ships, all cruisers and destroyers, and was commanded by Vice Adm. Mikawa.

When Admiral Yamamoto became aware of the landing of the First Marine Division on Guadalcanal in August 1942, he sent Nagumo's Third and Mikawa's Eighth Carrier Division to Guadalcanal to support Vice Adm. Kondo's assault scheduled for August 25. Kondo was landing only 1,500 men on western Guadalcanal, but Yamamoto provided three carriers, three battleships, nine cruisers, 13 destroyers, 36 submarines, and support ships to ensure success. Nagumo sent light carrier *Ryujo* ahead with *Mikawa* on August 24.

At a point 250 miles north of Guadalcanal, early on August 24, an American PBY spotted *Ryujo.* Fletcher launched 38 aircraft and shortly thereafter received sighting reports of *Shokaku* and *Zuikaku.* Fletcher tried to divert his aircraft to the large carriers, but could not communicate with them. *Ryujo* was sunk while Nagumo launched 73 aircraft in his first wave and 36 more in the second. In this battle, Nagumo lost light carrier *Ryujo*, destroyer *Mutsuki*, and 90 aircraft. Fletcher lost 15 aircraft and suffered heavy damage to *Enterprise.*

Battle of Santa Cruz (Oct 25-27, 1942)

The two fleets located one another on October 25. This time the opponents were Nagumo and Admiral Thomas A. Kinkaid. Nagumo, with four large carriers, launched 75 aircraft to attack USS *Hornet. Hornet* took seven bombs and two torpedo hits, became inoperable, and was later sunk by Japanese destroyers. Nagumo's second attack wave consisted of 48 aircraft launched one hour later to attack *Enterprise*. *Enterprise* escaped with three bomb craters on her flight deck. The first wave of American aircraft scored a single hit on *Chikuma*, a heavy cruiser, and placed four bombs on Nagumo's flagship, the carrier *Shokaku*.

Admiral Nagumo clearly bested Kinkaid in the Battle of Santa Cruz. Nagumo lost 69 aircraft to enemy action, and 23 more were forced to ditch in the ocean when they ran out of fuel. *Shokaku* was able to return to Truk for repair. Kinkaid lost *Hornet*, and 74 aircraft. The Pacific Fleet was down to two carriers, *Saratoga* and *Enterprise*, both needing repair.

During November 1943, Vice Adm. Jisaburo Ozawa relieved Nagumo as commander of the carrier striking force. Ozawa was also designated as commander of the First Mobile Fleet, which comprised 90 percent of Japan's remaining surface vessels. In December 1943, a new Mid-Pacific fleet was created for the defense of the Marianas and Caroline Islands. Nagumo was appointed to command the newly formed fleet based in Saigon with orders to repel the anticipated Allied invasions of Iwo Jima, Palau, Truk, Guam, and the other islands of the Marianas.[7]

Nagumo moved his headquarters to Saipan, to better direct his forces against the anticipated Allied invasion.

Nagumo, normally an outgoing person, became an introvert on Saipan. He was used to leading men and ships, but was now in a far corner of the Pacific without either ships or men to command. As the senior officer on Saipan, he had few friends and led a lonely life. He missed his wife and children.

Nagumo's life changed one afternoon during March 1944, when he was sipping a beer at the officers' club. Nagumo was alone with his thoughts when his attention turned to a group of young men and women playing tennis. They seemed so happy and enthusiastic that Nagumo went home, changed into athletic attire and returned to the club. He asked the young people if he could join them. They had no idea who Nagumo was or his rank, but accepted him as a part of the group.[8]

Nagumo was not a very good tennis player but he practiced and played with the young people at every opportunity. Soon, he was playing doubles with Shizuko Sugano, an 18-year-old nurse in the army field hospital. Shizuko was from Nagumo's prefecture of Yomigata in Japan. The two had much in common and enjoyed each other's company. In time, Nagumo began to discuss his family with Shizuko. She recalled that he always seemed sad that he could not be with his family. Nagumo obviously enjoyed his time with Shizuko, describing their time together as some of the best while on Saipan.[9] Shizuko last saw Nagumo on June 10, five days before the Allied invasion of Saipan. He seemed nervous and had no time to talk with her.[10]

Saipan

Following the battle of Santa Cruz, Nimitz reorganized the Pacific Fleet. Admiral "Bull" Halsey commanded the Third Fleet as did Admiral Raymond A. Spruance. One would plan and train while the other fought. Vice Adm. Marc A. Mitscher's Fast Carrier Force operated continuously, designated TF-58 when under Spruance, and TF 38 when under Halsey.

The battle for Saipan began early on June 15. The Allied Fleet was under the command of Admiral Spruance, who still held a personal vendetta against Nagumo for his surprise attack of Pearl Harbor. When Spruance arrived at Pearl Harbor the day after Nagumo's attack, he is reported to have wept at the loss of the Pacific Fleet and his many friends. Although he defeated Nagumo at Midway, he now intended to take final vengeance.

To do so, Spruance had 14 battleships, 25 carriers and carrier escorts, 26 cruisers, 144 destroyers, and hundreds of transports and supply ships. For two days his battleships fired thousands of 15-inch shells into the Japanese fortifications. Lieutenant Gen.

Holland M. "Howlin Mad" Smith commanded the V Amphibious Corps consisting of two marine divisions and one army division in reserve, with a total of 71,034 troops.

Nagumo did not believe that the Americans would be so bold as to invade Saipan, 3,500 miles from Pearl Harbor, and 1,000 miles from their nearest supply base at Eniwetok. Saipan was crucial to Japan, being only 1,200 miles from Tokyo. Aircraft and submarines based on Saipan would control the sealanes south of Japan, with the ability to deny all surface resupply. Nagumo's plan was to have Lieutenant Gen. Yoshitsugo Saito stop the marines on the beach, and then to counterattack and drive them into the sea. The Japanese waited patiently inside their bunkers and caves for the landing to occur.

On the first day of the assault, the old battleships, *California* and *Tennessee,* fired from their 14-inch guns. They also took some casualties; *California* had 98 dead and *Tennessee* five. Not bad for two ships sunk by Nagumo's *Kido Butai* on December 7, 1941. By the end of the first day, 20,000 marines were ashore with 2,000 casualties.

At 10:00 P.M., 2,000 Japanese infantry supported by tanks and artillery led the first counterattack. Destroyers fired star shells for illumination, while California and other "ghosts" from Pearl Harbor fired salvo after salvo into the charging Japanese. The marines' lines held in most places and when the sun rose, five marine tanks stopped the final charge. Marines counted 700 Japanese dead on the approach to the beachhead. The following evening, the Japanese launched another counterattack with 44 tanks. The marines held their positions, and in the morning counted 24 smoldering tanks. General Smith made the decision to start landing elements of the reserve army division.

Near the center of Saipan, towering 1,554 feet above the marines was Mount Tapotchau. The terrain was "a nightmare of ravines, caves, hills, valleys, and cliffs; all fortified and defended to the death by the Japanese." Well up the side of the mountain were the observation posts and the bunkers housing Admiral Nagumo and the ground force commander, Lieutenant Gen. Saito.

450

Spruance's naval gunfire cut the communication lines between Nagumo, Saito and the operational forces on Saipan. For the present, Nagumo could only count on the powerful Japanese fleet with its numerous aircraft to drive the Americans back.

Spruance had other ideas. In what became the greatest carrier battle of the Pacific war, "The Battle of the Philippine Sea," submarine *Cavalla* torpedoed and sank *Shokaku*. Submarine *Albacore* sank *Taiho*, newest and largest Japanese carrier, with a single torpedo, and Avenger torpedo bombers sank the carrier *Hiyo*. The principal phase of this battle became known as, "The Great Marianas Turkey Shoot." Admiral Ozawa lost 401 planes on June 19 and 20. American losses were 130 aircraft, 76 airmen, and no ships. Following the debacle, Ozawa's Mobile Fleet reached Okinawa on June 22, with only 35 operable aircraft out of the 430 he had on the morning of June 19. With the loss of the Mobile Fleet, Nagumo and Saipan were doomed.[11]

On June 18, marines and army forces overran the Aslito airfield (renamed Isely). Marine and some army aviation units could now move ashore. By July 6, the remaining Japanese were pushed into a small pocket in the northern part of Saipan. Lieutenant Gen. Smith, commander of the land forces, warned that a *"banzai"* charge was likely. He was right. At 4:45 A.M., on July 7, bugles announced the charge of 3,000 Japanese. The Japanese forced a gap between two army battalions and drove the soldiers into the attack, but the army and marine lines held. Artillery commanders set fuses for four-tenths of a second and fired point blank into the charging Japanese. Three howitzer battalions fired an average of 44 rounds per minute for more than an hour during the peak of the attack. In the morning, 4,311 Japanese bodies were counted. American losses were 406.

After ordering the *banzai* charge, General Saito drew his own blood with his samurai sword and was then shot in the back of his head by his adjutant. A similar fate awaited Admiral Chuichi Nagumo, a good man, and a good sailor. Marines purified the caves with napalm and sealed them with dynamite, bulldozers, and artillery fire. Nagumo's remains were never recovered.[12]

Shizuko, left on the tennis courts of Saipan by Nagumo, tried to take her own life by pulling the pin on a hand grenade held to her chest. She was attempting to remove the safety pin when the grenade was taken away from her by an American. She survived and periodically comes to Saipan to visit the cliff where many of her friends leaped to their death.[13] Known Japanese dead totaled 23,811 during the Japan battle. Thousands more were sealed in the caves of the island. U. S. Marine and Army killed totaled 3,225.

View from the entrance to Admiral Nagumo's command post on Saipan (top). Note the large hole in the command post wall caused by a naval shell (left).

Digital American Heritage

ADDENDA
TO CHAPTER 2

Internment of Japanese-Americans

during WWII

Additional information about some of the U.S. camps

Assembly Centers	Evacuees
Puyallup, WA.	7,400
Portland, OR.	3,700
Marysville, CA.	2,400
Walegra/Sacramento, CA.	4,700
Stockton, CA.	4,300
Turlock, CA.	3,600
Merced, CA.	4,500
Pinedale, CA	4,800
Fresno, CA.:	5,100
Tulare, CA.	5,000
Tanforan, CA.	7,800
Salinas, CA.	3,600
Santa Anita, CA.	18,000
Pomona, CA.	5,400
Mayer, AZ.	250
Manzanar, CA.	9,600

War Department Internment Camps

Topaz, UT.	Max 8,130
Tule Lake, CA	Max 18,789
Poston, AZ.	Max 17,814
Gila River, AZ.	Max 13,348
Heart Mountain, WY.	Max 10,767
Granada, CO.	Max 7,318
Manzanar, CA.	Max 10,046
Minidoka, ID.	Max 7,318
Rowher, ARK	Max 8,475
Jerome ARK.	Max 8,497

Total # of evacuees from assembly centers: 90,150
Total # of internees (max): 110,502
Justice Department Internment Camps: Missoula, MN, Bismarck, ND, Santa Fe, NM, Crystal City, TX.

Jerome, Arkansas

The camp at Jerome was used to hold German POWs, although as many as 8,497 Japanese were housed at the facility from October 6, 1942, when it opened, until June 30, 1944 when the remaining internees were moved to Rohwer, Arkansas. The 634 days of operation were the shortest of any camp.

There were no guard towers at Jerome, and the perimeter fences were low. Security was provided by swamps and four species of the deadliest snakes in America. Jerome had a single sawmill that produced lumber for local use.

Rohwer, Arkansas

The camp at Rohwer was opened on September 18, 1942, and closed on November 30, 1945. Most of the Japanese came from the Los Angeles and Stockton areas. The camp had a peak population of 8,475 internees during March, 1943.

Two-hundred-seventy-four (4.7%) AJA from Rohwer were inducted directly into the military services. Early in 1942, some of the Japanese clearing brush outside of the camp were arrested and taken to the local jail because they were suspected of being Japanese paratroopers.

Minidoka, Idaho

The Kooskia Relocation Center was in a remote area of north central Idaho on Canyon Creek. The camp was opened on August 10, 1942, to house enemy aliens and closed on October 28, 1945. The camp was unique in that its inmates were volunteers from other camps and received wages for their work. A total of 265 male Japanese, 24 male and three female Caucasians, and two male German internee doctors occupied the camp between May 1944, and May 1945. Most Japanese came from the Puyallop camp,

455

Portland, Washington, and northwestern Oregon. Twenty-seven Japanese-Latin Americans from Peru, eleven Mexican-Americans, and two Panamanian-Americans were also detained at the camp.

Minidoka was regarded as one of the "best" of camps, due to its lighter security, and benevolent administration. Peak population of the camp was 9,397. Seventy-three of the Minidoka AJA that volunteered for military service died during WW II.

Heart Mountain, Wyoming

Heart Mountain opened August 12, 1942. It had a peak population of 10,767 Japanese internees from the Los Angeles and central Washington areas. Heart Mountain gained some notoriety from the "walk out" of Japanese-American hospital workers due to pay discrimination, and in July 1944, 63 AJA in the camp who refused to be drafted were convicted and sentenced to three years in prison.

The camp consisted of 468 buildings of six rooms each, ranging in size from 16-feet by 20-feet to 20-feet by 24-feet. Each block had two laundry/toilet buildings. The Heart Mountain camp maintained a security force of 124 soldiers and three officers. The camp was enclosed by barbed wire, illuminated with search lights, and soldiers were stationed in nine guard towers along the perimeter.

Amache (Granada), Colorado.

The camp was opened on August 24, 1942 and closed on October 15, 1945. Peak population was 7,318, most from the northern California coast. Thirty-one AJA from Amache volunteered for military service and lost their lives during WW II. During April 1944, thirty-six AJA draft resisters from Amache were sent to the federal prison camp at Tucson, Arizona.

Gila River, Arizona

The two camps at Gila River (Butte Camp and Canal camp) opened on July 20, 1942, and closed on November 10, 1945. More than 1,100 AJA from both camps served in the U.S. military during WW II, and a plaque at the site of the Canal camp lists 23 AJA who lost their lives in WW II.

The state of Arizona accredited the schools in both camps, and 97 students graduated from high school in 1944. Most detainees worked in the 8,000 acres of farmland around Canal camp, growing vegetables and raising livestock.

Salinas and Poston, Arizona

The Salinas Assembly Center was officially opened on May 8, 1942, when sixty-three Santa Cruz, California Japanese-Americans arrived. By the end of May, 700 Japanese were in residence at the camp. During the summer, internees began moving to the larger camp at Poston, which was divided into three camps, with a total population of 17,814. Most of the internees came from the Sacramento and Southern California area. Twenty-three AJAs from Poston volunteered for military service and lost their lives during WW II.

During November 1942 a general strike was conducted by 8,500 Japanese internees at Poston. The problem was reported to be the physical assault of internees by other internees. Fifty internees were gathered and questioned as part of the subsequent investigation. As a result of the investigation, two of the suspects were scheduled for trial in an Arizona State Court. A protest by the internees and a general strike followed.

This resembled incidents at other relocation camps, such as Tule Lake, where militant groups of Japanese sought to protest the government's forced relocation of Japanese from the west coast, and to prevent AJA from enlisting in the U.S. military. Poston was closed on November 28, 1945.

Camp Harmony, Puyallop, Washington

In late April 1942, Japanese-Americans from the Seattle area were sent to Camp Harmony in northern Washington. By the end of May, the population had grown to 7,000 internees. The plan was for the internees to stay at the Puyallop camp for four months, and be moved to Minidoka, Idaho.

On April 21, the Japanese were informed that they must be registered by April 25, and would leave a week later for the camp at Puyallop for internment. Processing and movement of the internees from the Seattle and Tacoma areas was well planned and coordinated with the Japanese Citizen Leagues. Many of the internees drove their own vehicles to Puyallop and then turned them into the assembly area for safekeeping during their internment.

Despite friendly and courteous treatment during their processing, the evacuation from their homes to the internment camp was difficult at best. The internees were required to stand in line, first to register, then for physical examinations, and then to make last-minute arrangements to sell, store, and dispense with their possessions.

The last night before evacuation was spent packing and getting ready for the early morning departure. The few hours of sleep were done on hard floors, in a home empty of furniture, either sold or stored. By 6:00 P.M., everyone was up, dressed in their best clothes, and standing in a cold rain, waiting for buses, or the approval to drive their own vehicle to Puyallop.

Camp Harmony was located at the local fair grounds as was true for most of the west coast assembly areas. The Japanese from the Seattle and Tacoma areas were joined with similar groups from Alaska. Most of the internees brought blankets, linen, silverware and dishes. They carried as much clothing as they were allowed, as well as personal necessities such as tooth brushes, razors and lotions.

Six mess halls served three meals a day to each individual. Long tables and benches replaced the family tables, and initially, food consisted of Vienna sausages, boiled potatoes, stewed tomatoes, hash, beans, and bread. Later, fresh vegetables, fruit, and milk were provided. There was always enough canned food if one missed the regular serving because of the long lines. Bread and pastry products were baked at the camp. Without question, the meals most Japanese would have preferred, (rice, rice cakes, fresh fish, soup, soy sauce, sukiyaki, and sushi), were seldom served. During 1942, more fresh vegetables, and rice were provided.

A view of the barracks at Heart Mountain Relocation Center, Wyoming.

National Archives

Japanese-Americans wait to be processed at Poston Relocation Center.

National Archives

NOTES

Chapter 1 The Merchant Marine in WWII

1. Middlebrook p. 1.
2. Williams p. 17.
3. Wright p. 58.
4. Middlebrook p. 8.
5. Greatest U-boat Commanders p. 1.
6. Kaplan p. 61.
7. Middlebrook p. 27.
8. Kaplan p. 23.
9. Kaplan p. 28.
10. Reminick p. xi.
11. Williams p. 54.
12. Williams p. 54.
13. Riesenberg p. 22.
14. Riesenberg p. 25.
15. Riesenberg p. 133.
16. Riesenberg p. 136.
17. Riesenberg p. 137.
18. Kaplan p. 142.
19. Kaplan p. 147.
20. Middlebrook p. 39.
21. Middlebrook p. 43.
22. Kaplan p. 26.
23. Middlebrook cover.
24. Middlebrook p. 105.
25. Middlebrook p. 105.
26. Middlebrook p. 111.
27. Middlebrook p. 232.
28. Middlebrook p. 281.
29. Middlebrook p. 328.
30. Reminick p. 178.
31. Reminick p. 194.
32. Reminick p. 177.
33. Hagen Volume I, Ch 19.

Chapter 2 Internment of Japanese-Americans during WWII

1. Inada p. 32.
2 Inada p. 71.
3. Inada p. 72.
4. Obata p. 17.
5. Obata p. 41.

6. Inada p. 106.
7. Inada p. 168
8. Obata p. 93.
9. Inada p. 125.
10. Knaefler p. 46.
11. Knaefler p. 72.
12. Wright p. 1.
13. Marquez p. A11.

Chapter 3 Internment of Japanese-Canadians during WWII

1. Broadfoot p. 24.
2. Broadfoot p. 27.
3. Broadfoot p. 58.
4. Broadfoot p. 87.
5. Broadfoot p. 100.
6. Broadfoot p. 64.
7 Broadfoot p. 264.
8. Broadfoot p. 295.

Chapter 4 Internment of the Aleut People in Alaska

1. Fuchida 1955, p. 258.
2. Castanza 2004, p. 17.
3. Garfield 1969, p. 92.
4. Castanza 2004, p. 17 and Cohen 1981, p. 100.
5. Garfield 1969, p. 93.
6. Kohlhoff 1995, p.59.
7. Castanza 2004, p. 21.
8. Castanza 2004, p.22.
9. Castanza 2004, p. 24.
10 Castanza 2004, p.24.
11. Jones 1980.
12. George 2003.
13. George 2003.
14. Kirtland 1981.
15. Aleutian/Priblof Islands Association (APIA) 1992,
16. Aleutian/Priblof Islands Association (APIA) 1992,

Chapter 5 Salvage of the Battleships at Pearl Harbor

1. Madsen 2003, p.9
2. Madsen 2003, p. 10.
3. Madsen 2003, p. 12-13.
4. Madsen 2003, p. 30.

5. Madsen 2003, p. 36.
6. Bartholomew 1990, p. 58.
7. Submarines *Gudgeon* and *Plunger* left Pearl Harbor on December 11, *Pollack* on the 13th, and *Pompano* on the 18th.
8. Madsen 2003, p. 36.
9. Wallin 1968, P. 204-205. The tug Sotoyoma was not a Japanese name, but a name from the war-like tribe of Sioux Indians from the Dakotas.
10. Wallin 1968, p. 235.
11. Madsen 2003, p. 92.
12. Bartholomew 1990, p 60.
13. Wallin, 1968, p. 251.
14. Madsen 2003, p. 216.

Chapter 6. General Hideki Tojo, Premier of Japan: 1941-1947

1. Hagen 1996, p. 5.
2. Butow 1961, p. 91.
3. Hagen 1996, p. 17.
4. Butow 1991, p. 103.
5. Hagen 1996, p. 14.
6. Butow 1961, p. 159.
7. Butow 1961, p. 224.
8. Butow 1961, p. 453.
9. Butow 1961, p. 468.
10. Butow 1961, p. 469.
11. Brackman 1967, p. 379.
12. Brackman 1967, p. 381.
13. Butow 1991, p. 526.
14. Butow 1991, p. 535.
15. Hagen 1996, p. 302.
16. Butow 1961, p. 540.

Chapter 7. Subhas Chandra Bose

1. Rediff 1997, p. 2.
2. Rediff 1997, p. 3.
3. Maikap 1998, p. 133.
4. Sherer 1962, p. 1102.
5. Sopan 1946, p. 313.
6. Rooney 1992, p. 18.
7. Bose, S.K. 1973, p. 143.
8. Bose, S.K. 1973, p. 203.
9. Lebra p. 190.
10. Yadav 1996, p. 97.
11. Maikap 1998, p. 306.
12. Maikap 1998, p. 286.

Chapter 8 Stilwell's Retreat from Burma

1. Rooney p. 162 (back cover).
2. Rooney p. 25.
3. Dorn p. 86.
4. Dorn p. 85.
5. Dorn p. 85.
6. Dorn p. 157.
7. Dorn p. 243.

Chapter 9 The Battle for Imphal: April 1945

1. Lucas 1966, p. 33.
2. Fergusson 1945, p. 8.
3. Lucas 1966, p. 37.
4. Slim 1956, p.287.
5. Latimer 2004, p.48.
6. Latimer 2004, p.51.
7. Allen 1984, p.211.
8. Rooney 1992, p. 54.
9. Slim 1956, p. 300.
10. Allen 1984, p. 214.
11. Rooney 1992, p. 56.
12. Slim 1956, p. 329.
13. Slim 1956, p. 300.
14. Slim 1956, p. 300.
15. Slim 1956, p. 349.
16. Allen 1984, p. 314.

Chapter 10 The Seige of Kohima

1. Campbell 1956, p. vii.
2. Moser 1978, p 103.
3. Campbell 1956, p. 120.
4. Rooney 1992, p. 71.
5. Campbell 1956, p. 194.
6. Campbell 1956, p. 174.
7. Campbell 1956, p. 176.
8. Campbell 1956, p. 188.
9. Rooney 1992, p. 105.

Chapter 11 Victory in Burma

1. Allen 1984, p. 368.
2. Allen 1984, p. 445.
3. Rooney 1992, p. 183.

4. Allen 1984, p. 457.
5. Slim 1956, p. 398.
6. Allen 1992, p. 430.
7. Allen 1992, p. 442.
8. Allen 1992, p. 454.
9. Allen 1992, p. 474.
10. Rooney 1992, p.189.
11. Allen 1984, p. 480.
12. Allen 1984, p 488.
13. Allen 1984, pp. 520-523. Allen lists the strength of Sakurai's forces as 30,872 before the breakout from the Pegu Yomas, and the number of Japanese forces remaining after the breakout as 16,919. Of this number of 16,919, 4,000 were listed as missing and 2,000 as sick. Japanese records list 185,149 Japanese as dying in Burma. Allen 1984, p. 640.
14. Slim 1956, p.534.
15. Slim 1956, p. 533.
16. Allen 1984, p. 640.
17. 17th century Japanese poet.

Chapter 12 Masanobu Tsuji

1.Ward 1992, p. 52.
2. Harries 1991, p. 343.
3. Harries 1991, p. 343 and 402.
4. 25,000 dead.
5. Ward 1992, p. 195.
6. Hagen 2003, p. 326.
7. Ward 1992, p.161.
8. Ward 1992, p. 239.
9. General MacArthur was evacuated from Corregidor on March 11, 1942.
10. Ward 1992, 246.
11. Ward 1992, p. 240.
12. Ward 1992, p. 256.
13. Ward 1992, p. 303.
14. Ward 1992, p. 305.
15. Ward 1992, p. 307.
16. Ward 1992, p. 319.
17. Ward 1992, p. 322.

Chapter 13 Joe Foss

1. http://www.acepilots.com/usmc-foss.html
2. http://www.acepilots.com/usmc-foss.html

Chapter 14 Bougainville: November 1, 1943

1. Gailey 1991, p. 21.
2. Oliver 1970, p. 94.
3. Oliver 1970, p. 94.
4. Hagen 2003, pp. 125-132.
5. Oliver 1970, p. 131.
6. Gailey 1991, p. 29. Most of the troops were from the Army 25th Division.
7. Gailey 1991, p. 30.
8. Gailey 1991, p. 30.
9. Gailey 1991, p. 45.
10 Gailey 1991, p. 59.
11. Gailey 1991, p. 69.
12. Monks 1945, p.9.
13. Gailey 1991, p. 68.
14. Gailey 1991, p. 73.
15. Gailey 1991, p. 77.
16. Gailey 1991, p. 95.
17. Morison 1950, p. 342.
18. Gailey 1991, p. 109.
19. Gailey 1991, p. 117.

Chapter 15 Bougainville: The Consolidation Phase

1. Walker 2004, p. 85.
2. Gailey 1991, p. 139.
3. Morison 1950, p. 428.
4. Walker 2004, p. 93.
5. Walker 2004, p. 94.
6. Gailey 1991, p. 155.
7. Gailey 1991, p. 166.
8. Gailey 1991, p. 178.
9. Gailey 1991, p. 183.
10 Gailey 1991, p. 123.
11. Charlton 1983, p. 37.
12. Gailey 1991, p. 186.
13. Gailey 1991, p. 201.
14. Hagen 1996, p. 248.
15. Hagen 1996, p. 252.

Chapter 16 Tarawa: November 20, 1943

1. Shaw p. 32.
2. Wright p. 21.
3. Wright p. 21.
4. Morison p. 154.

5. Morison p. 61.
6. Wright p. 31.
7. Morison pp. 162-163.
8. Wright p. 41.
9. Alexander p. 9.
10. Shaw p. 83.
11. Morison p. 173.
12. Morison p. 173.
13. Wright p. 49.
14. Shaw p. 147 and Morison p. 134.
15. Wright p. 81.

Chapter 17 Peleliu: September 1944

1. Manchester 1979, p. 373.
2. Manchester 1979, p. 354.
3. Manchester 1979, p. 357.
4. Manchester 1979, p. 358
5. Ross 1991, p. 87.
6. Ross 1991, p. 106.
7. Ross 1991, p. 133.
8. Ross 1991, p. 146.
9. Ross 1991, p. 154.
10 Ross 1991, p. 158.
11. Ross 1991, p. 159.
12. Ross 1991, p. 159.
13. Ross 1919, p. 163.
14. Ross 1991, p. 156.
15. Ross 1991, p. 156.
16. Ross 1991, p. 182.
17. Ross 1991, p. 215.
18. Ross 1991, p. 212.
19. Ross 1991, p. 261.
20. Ross 1991, p. 262.
21. Ross 1991, p. 268.
22. Ross 1991, p. 277.
23. Ross 1991, p. 323.
24. Ross, 1991, p. 331.
25. Ross 1991, p. 346.
26. Ross, 1991, p. 347.

Chapter 18 William F. "Bull" Halsey Jr.

1. Potter 1985, p. 27.
2. Potter 1985, p. 32.
3. Potter 1985, p. 126.

4. Potter 1985, p. 87.
5. Cressman 1989, p. 3.
6. Cressman 1989, p. 3.
7. Potter 1985, p. 13.
8. Carrier *Saratoga* was on the West Coast undergoing scheduled maintenance, USS *Lexington* was at Midway Island offloading personnel, aircraft, and supplies.
9. Potter 1985, p. 36.
10. Potter 1985, p. 38.
11. Hagen 1996, p. 80.
12. Potter 1985, p. 74.
13. Halsey memoir unpublished, p. 364.
14. Griffith 1963, p. 164.
15. Potter 1985, p. 179.
16. Morison 1949, p. 222.
17. Potter 1985, p. 186.
18. Potter 1985, p. 193.
19. Potter 1985, p. 193.
20. Potter 1985, p. 201.
21. Potter 1985, p. 216.
22. Potter 1985, p. 320.
23. Potter 1985, p. 322.
24. Potter 1985, p. 323.
25. Potter 1985, p. 301.
26. Potter 1985, p. 303.
27. Y'Blood 1987, p. 242.

Chapter 19 Sir Edward "Weary" Dunlap: 1942-1945

1. A Buddhist belief.
2. Dunlop p. 414.
3. Dunlop p. 414.
4. Dunlop p. 5.
5. Dunlop p. 5.
6. Dunlop p. 17.
7. Dunlop p. 17.
8. Dunlop p. 158.
9. Dunlop p. 183.
10 Ebury p. 381.
11. Dunlop p. 226.
12. Dunlop p. 246.
13. Kinvig p. 32.
14. Dunlop p. 289.
15. Dunlop p. 346.
16. Ebury p. 460.
17. Ebury p. 464.

18. Ebury p. 475.
19. Ebury p. 484.
20. Dunlop p. 376.
21. Dunlop p. 395.
22. Dunlop p. 398.
23. Dunlop p. 435.

Chapter 20 Marc A. Mitscher

1. Taylor 1954, p. 162.
2. Taylor 1954, p.162.
3. Taylor 1954, p.311.
4. Coletta 1997, p. 1.
5. Coletta 1997, p. 7.
6. Coletta 1997, p. 33.
7. Coletta 1997, p.18.
8. Taylor 1954, p. xxiii.
9. Taylor 1954, p. xxiii.
10. Taylor 1954, pp. 136-137.
11. Morton, 1943, p. 186.
12. Potter 1985, p. 240.
13. Potter 1985, p. 240.
14. Taylor 1954, p. 179.
15. Coletta 1997, p. 197.
16. Taylor 1954, p. 186.
17. Taylor 1954, pp. 188-189.
18. Taylor 1954, p. 194.
19. Taylor 1954, p. 227.
20. Taylor 1954, p. 236.
21. Coletta 1997, p. 259.
22. Coletta 1997, p. 291.
23. Coletta 1997, p.259.
24. Coletta 1997, p. 311.
25. Coletta 1997, p. 324.
26. Taylor 1954, p. 332.
27. Taylor 1954, pp. 339-340.
28. Taylor 1954, p. 342.
29. Taylor 1954, pp. 343-344.

Chapter 21 General Douglas MacArthur: Jan. 26, 1880 to Sept. 2, 1945

1.Gunther p. 31.
2. Gunther p. 34.
3. Gunther p. 33.
4. Gunther p. xiv.

5. James p. 96.
6. James p. 98.
7. James p. 99.
8. James p. 100.
9. James p. 126.
10. MacArthur p. 92.
11. Schaller p. 16.
12. Schaller p. 20.
13. Schaller p. 20.
14. Schaller p. 33.
15. Schaller p. 56.
16. MacArthur p. 120 and Morton pp. 80-87.
17. Hagen, Volume 1, p. 31.
18. James p. 4.
19. James p. 5.
20. James p. 5.
21. MacArthur p. 126.
22. James p. 17.
23. Breuer p. 16.
24. Breuer p. 16.
25. MacArthur p. 151.
26. James p. 248.
27. Schaller p. 61.
28. Schaller p. 64.
29. Schaller p. 65.
30. Schaller p. 65.
31. Schaller p. 65.
32. Mayo p. 115.
33. Revere p. 71.
34. Revere p. 71.
35. Huff p. 92.
36. Revere p. 70.
37. Huff p. 98.
38. Schaller p. 97.
39. Schaller p. 98.
40. Schaller p. 123.
41. Schaller p. 128.
42. Schaller p. 146.
43. Schaller p. 154.

Chapter 22 General Douglas MacArthur: September 2, 1945 to April 5, 1964

1. Schaller p. 123.
2. Schaller p. 128.
3. Schaller p. 146.
4. Schaller p. 153.

5. Schaller p. 154.
6. Revere p. 98.
7. Revere p. 99.
8. Revere p. 126.
9. Schaller p. 218.
10. Schaller p. 224.
11. Revere p. 18.
12. Revere p. 8.
13. Revere p. 10.
14. James p. 640.
15. James p. 656.
16. James p. 660.
17. James p. 662.
18. James p. 670.
19. James p. 672.
20. James p. 677.
21. James p. 685.
22. James p. 690.

Chapter 23 John D. Bulkeley: The Pacific Theater

1. Breuer p. 13.
2. Breuer p. 15.
3. Breuer p. 48.
4. Breuer p. 52.
5. Breuer p. 54.
6. Breuer p. 64.
7. Breuer p. 74.
8. Breuer p. 68.
9. Breuer p. 69.
10. Breuer p. 72.
11. Breuer p. 104.
12. Breuer p. 115.
13. Breuer p. 115.

Chapter 24 John D. Bulkeley: The Atlantic Theater

1.Breuer p. 166.
2. Breuer p. 174.
3. Breuer p. 175.
4. Breuer p. 178.
5. Breuer p. 187.
6. Breuer p. 190.
7. Breuer p. 195.
8. Breuer p. 202.
9. Breuer p. 216.

10. Breuer p. 217.
11. Breuer p. 253.
12. Breuer p. 257.
13. Breuer p. 262.
14. Breuer p. 279.

Chapter 25 Return to Guam, Saipan and Tinian: July 1944

1. Lodge 1954, p. 1.
2. Crowl 1985, p. 36.
3. Crowl 1985, p. 65.
4. Crowl 1985, p. 117.
5. Crowl 1985, p. 150.
6. Crowl 1985, p. 294.
7. Crowl 1985, p. 302.
8. Crowl 1985, p. 269.
9. Asan Beach Guide 1994, p. 7.
10. Crowl 1985, p. 325.
11. Hoffman n.d., p. 1873.
12. Hoffman n.d., p. 1874.
13. Crowl 1985, p. 446.

Chapter 26 Vice Admiral Chuichi Nagumo

1. Howarth 1993, p. 277.
2. Matsushima 1967, p. 35.
3. Lippman 2000, p. 1.
4. Howarth 1993, p. 6.
5. Lippman 2000, p. 1.
6. Wright 1989, p. 157.
7. Matsushima 1967, p. 264.
8. Matsushima 1967, p. 267.
9. Matsushima 1967, p. 267.
10. Morrison 1963, p. 276.
11. Chapin 1994, p. 12.
12. Chapin 1994, p. 36.

Addenda to chapter 2: Internment of Japanese-Americans during WW II

1. Watsonville Register, November 23, 1942, p.1.

BIBLIOGRAPHY

Aleutian/Priblof Islands Association (APIA), *Aleut Evacuation, The Untold War Story.* Anchorage: APIA, 1992.

Alexander, Joseph H. *Utmost Savagery: The Three Days of Tarawa.* New York: Random House, 1995.

Allen, Louis. *Burma: The Longest War 1941-45.* London: J. M. Dent and Sons, 1986.

Amrine, Michael. *Great Decision,* The Secret History of the Atomic Bomb. New York: G. P. Putnam and Sons, 1959.

Anderson, Christopher J. *The Marines in World War II: From Pearl Harbor to Tokyo Bay.* Mechanicsburg, PA: Stackpole Books, 2000.

Atkins, David. *The Forgotten Major: In the Siege of Imphal,* West Sussex: Toat Press, 1989.

Baker, Leonard. *Roosevelt and Pearl Harbor.* New York: MacMillan, 1970.

Bartholomew, C.A. *Mud, Muscle, and Miracles.* Washington, D.C.: Naval Historical Center, 1990.

Beamish, John. *Burma Drop.* London: Elek Books, 1958.

Beck, John Jacob. *MacArthur and Wainwright: Sacrifice of the Philippines.* Albuquerque: University of New Mexico Press, 1974.

Belote, James H. and William M. Belote. *Corregidor:* The Saga of a Fortress. New York: Harper and Row, 1967.

Bergerud, Eric. *Touched with Fire: The Land War in the South Pacific.* New York: Penguin Books, 1996.

_____, *Fire in the Sky.* New York: Westview Press, 2000.

Bernstein, Marc D. *Hurricane at Biak.* Xlibris, 2000.

Blake, Robert W. *From Belleau Wood to Bougainville.* Bloomington, IN: AuthorHouse, 2004.

_____, *Bayonets and Bougainvilleas.* Bloomington, IN: Author House, 2001

Bond, Charles R. and Terry H. Anderson. *A Flying Tiger's Diary.* College Station: Texas A&M University Press, 1984.

Brackman, Arnold C. *The Other Nurenberg.* New York: William Morrow, 1987.

Brereton, Lewis H. *The Brereton Diaries.* New York: William Morrow, 1946.

Breuer, William B. *MacArthur's Undercover War.* New York: John Wiley, 1995.

_____, Sea Wolf: *A Biography of John D. Bulkeley, USN.* Novato, CA: Presidio Press, 1989.

Brimner, Larry Dane. *Voices from the Camps.* Internment of Japanese Americans During World War II. New York: Franklin Watts, 1994.

Broadfoot, Barry. *Years of Sorrow, Years of Shame.* The Story of the Japanese Canadians in World War II. Don Mills: Ontario, 1979.

Buell, Thomas B. *Master of Sea Power: A Biography of Fleet Admiral Ernest J. King.* Boston: Little Brown, 1980.

Bulkley, Robert J. *At Close Quarters: PT Boats in the United States Navy.* Annapolis: Naval Institute Press, 2003.

Butow, Robert J.C. *Tojo and the Coming of War.* Stanford: Stanford University Press, 1961.

Campbell, Arthur. *The Siege: A Story from Kohima.* London: George Allen and Unwin, 1956.

Castanza, Gordon E. *Aleut Internment in World War II.* Unpublished Manuscript, July 2004.

Catanzaro, Francis B. *With the 41st Division in the Southwest Pacific.* Indianapolis: Indiana University Press, 2002.

Chan Won Loy. *Burma-The Untold Story.* Novato, CA: Presidio Press, 1986.

Chapin, John C. *Breaching the Marianas: The Battle for Saipan,* Washington: Marine Corps Historical center, 1994.

Charlton, Peter. *The Unnecessary War.* Melbourne: MacMillan, 1983.

Chennault, Claire Lee, *Way of a Fighter.* New York: G.P. Putnam's Sons, 1949.

Chwialkowski, Paul. *In Caesar's Shadow.* The Life of General Robert Eichelberger. Westport, CT: Greenwood Press, 1993

Clayton, James D. *The Years of MacArthur 1880-1941.* Boston: Houghton Mifflin, 1970.

_____, *The Years of MacArthur 1941-1945.* Boston: Houghton Mifflin, 1975.

_____, *Triumph and Disaster: 1945-1964.* Boston: Houghton Mifflin, 1985.

Cohen, Stan. *The Forgotten War.* A pictorial history of World War II in Alaska and Northwestern Canada.vol.4. Missoula, MT: Pictorial Publishing, 1981.

Coletta, Paolo E. *Admiral Marc A. Mitscher and U.S. Naval Aviation.* Lewiston, NY: The Edwin Mellon Press, 1997.

Collier, Basil. *The War in the Far East.* New York: William Morrow, 1969.

Craig, William. *The Fall of Japan.* New York: Dial Press, 1967.

Craven, W.F. *The Army Air Forces in World War II.* Chicago: The University of Chicago Press, 1948.

Cressman, Robert J. and Michael Wenger. *Steady Nerves and Stout Hearts.* Missoula, MN: Pictorial Histories,1985.

Crowl, Philip A., *The War in the Pacific: Campaign in the Marianas,* Washington, DC: United States Army, 1985.

Daniels, Roger. *Concentration Camps USA: Japanese Americans and World War II.* New York: Holt, Rinehart and Winston. 1971.

Deacon, Richard. *A History of the Japanese Secret Service: Kempai Tai.* New York: Berkerly Books, 1963.

Dear, I.C.B. *The Oxford Companion to World War II.* New York: Oxford, 1995.

Dencker, Donald O. *Love Company: 96th Infantry Division in WW II.* Manhattan, KS: Sunflower University Press, 2002.

Devlin, Gerard M. *Back to Corregidor.* New York: St. Martin's Press, 1992.

Dexter, David. *The New Guinea Offensives.* Canberra: Australian War Memorial, 1968.

Dunlop, E.E. *The War Diaries of Weary Dunlop: Java and the Burma-Thailand Railway: 1942-1945.* New York: Penguin, 1986.

Dunn, William J. *Pacific Microphone.* College Station: Texas A and M University Press, 1988.

Ebury, Sue. *Weary: The Life of Sir Edward Dunlop.* Ringwood, Australia: Penguin, 1994.

Eichelberger, Robert L. *Our Jungle Road to Tokyo.* New York: The Viking Press, 1950.

Fahey, James J. *Pacific War Diary: 1942-1945.* New York: Houghton Mifflin, 1963.

Falk, Stanley. *Palaus: Bloodiest Victory.* New York: Random House, 1974.

Farwell, Byron. *The Gurkhas.* New York: W.W. Norton, 1984.

Feis, Herbert. *The China Triangle.* New York: Antheneum, 1967.

Fergusson, Bernard. *Beyond the Chindwin.* London: Fontana Books, 1945.

Franks, Norma. *The Air Battle of Imphal.* London: William Kiber, 1985.

Fuchida, Mitsuo. *Midway: The Battle that Doomed Japan.* Annapolis: Naval Institute Press, 1955.

Gailey, Harry A. *The War in the Pacific.* Novato, CA: Presidio Press, 1997.

_____, *Bougainville: 1943-1945*. Lexington KY: University Press of Kentucky, 1991.

Garfield, Brian. *The Thousand Mile War*. World War II in Alaska and the Aleutians. New York: Ballantine, 1969.

George. http://www.alaskasoutheaster.com/archives/March 2003/aleut.ntml.

Girdner, Audrie and Anne Loftis. *The Great Betrayal*. The Evacuation of the Japanese-Americans During World War II. London: Macmillan, 1969.

Goldstein, Donald M. and Katherine V. Dillon. Ed. *The Pearl Harbor Papers: Inside the Japanese Plans*. New York: Brassey's, 1993.

Gordon, Beate Sirota. *The Only Woman in the Room*. Tokyo: Kodansha, 1997.

Greatest U-boat Commanders. http://uboat.net/Men/accs/top.ntm.

Green, Michael. *MacArthur in the Pacific*. Osceola, WI: Motorbooks, 1996.

Griffith, Samuel B., *The Battle for Guadalcanal,* New York: J. B. Lippincott, 1963.

Gunther, John. *The Riddle of MacArthur*. New York: Harper, 1950.

Hagen, Jerome T. *War in the Pacific*. vol I, *America at War*. Honolulu: Hawaii Pacific University, 1996.

_____, *War in the Pacific,* vol II, *People and Places*. Honolulu, J.T. Hagen, 2003.

Hanley, Fiske II. *Accused American War Criminal*. Austin: Eakin Press, 1997.

Hart, Peter. *At the Sharp End.* The 2nd Royal Norfolk regiment 1940-45, South Yorkshire: Pen and Sword Books, 1998.

Hartog, Rudolf. *The Sign of the Tiger: Subhas Chandra Bose: His Indian Legion in Germany 1941-1945*. New Delhi: Rupa Co., 2001.

Hawaii Nikkei History Editorial Board. *Japanese Eyes American Heart*. Honolulu: Tendai Educational Foundation, 1998.

Hickam, Homer H. *Torpedo Junction*. New York: Random House, 1989.

Howarth, Stephen, ed, *Great Naval Leaders of WW II*. New York: St. Martin's Press, 1992.

Hoyt, Edwin P. *Storm over the Gilberts*. New York: Mason and Charter, 1978.

Huff, Sid. *My Fifteen Years With General MacArthur*. New York: Paperback, 1964.

Hull, Cordell. *The Memoirs of Cordell Hull*. Vol. 1, New York: The MacMillan Company, 1948.

_____, *The Memoirs of Cordell Hull*, vol. II, New York: The MacMillan Company, 1948.

Huston, James A. *Out of the Blue: U.S. Army Airborne Operations in World War II*. West Lafayette, IN: Purdue University Press, 1998.

77th Infantry Division. *Ours To Hold It High*. Nashville: The Battery Press, 1947.

Inada, Lawson F. Ed. *Only What We Could Carry*. The Japanese Internment Experience. Berkeley: Heyday Books, 2000.

Ireland, Bernard. *Jane's Naval History of World War II*. London: Harper Collins, 1998.

Irons, Peter. *Justice at War:* The Story of the Japanese American Internment Cases. New York: Oxford Press, 1983.

Ito, Masanori. *The End of the Japanese Navy*. New York: MacFadden Books, 1965.

Joe Foss-American Hero, The Log Book: Miramar CA: The newsletter of the Flying Leatherneck Historical Foundation, Winter 2003.

Jones, Dorothy K. *Century of Servitude: Priblof Aleuts under U.S. Rule*. Lanham, MD: University Press of America, 1980.

Jones, F.C. *Shanghai and Tientsin, Studies of the Pacific, No. 5*. New York: American Council Institute of Pacific Relations, 1940.

Kaplan, Phillip and Jack Currie. *Convoy: Merchant Sailors at War 1939-1945*. Annapolis: Naval Institute Press, 1998.

Kenney, George C. *General Kenney Reports.* New York: Duell, Sloan and Pearce, 1949.

Kimball, Warren. *Forged in War.* London: Harper Collins, 1998.

Kimm, Samuel. *Cries of the Korean Comfort Women.* USA: Samuel Kim, 2003.

Kirtland, J.C. and Coffin, D.F. Jr. *The Relocation and Internment of the Aleuts during World War II.* Aleutian/Priblof Islands Association, Seattle: University of Washington Press, 1981.

Knafler, Tomi. *Our House Divided.* Honolulu: University of Hawaii Press, 1991.

Kohlhoff, D. *When the wind was a river: Aleut Evacuation in World War II.* Seattle: University of Washington Press, 1995.

Latimer, Jon. "Battle of the Admin Box." *World War II.* vol. 19, 8 (December 2004) 48-53.

Leahy, William D. *I Was There.* London: Victor Gollancz Ltd, 1950.

Lebra, Joyce C. *Jungle Alliance: Japan and the Indian National Army.* Singapore: Asia Pacific Library, 1971.

Leckie, Robert. *Wars of America.* New York: Castle Books, 1998.

Lightfoot, Keith. *The Philippines.* New York: Praeger, 1973.

Lippman, David H. *Pearl Harbor Revisited.* http://www.centuryinter.net/midway/intro.html.

Liria, Yauka Aluambo. *Bougainville Campaign Diary.* Victoria, Australia: Indra Publishing, 1993.

Llewellyn, Bernard. *From the Back Streets of Bengal.* London: George Allen and Unwin, 1955.

Lodge, O.R. *The Recapture of Guam.* Washington, DC: U.S. Marine Corps, 1954.

Lucas Phillips, C.E. *Springboard to Victory,* London: Hindemann, 1966.

MacArthur, Douglas. *Reminiscences.* New York: McGraw-Hill, 1964.

Madsen, Daniel. *Resurrection: Salvaging the Battle Fleet at Pearl Harbor.* Annapolis: Naval Institute Press, 2003.

Maikap, Satish Chandra Dr. *Netaji Subhas Chandra Bos.* The Indian Wars of Independence. Calcutta: Sandip Nayak, 1998.

Manchester, William. *American Caesar: Douglas MacArthur 1880-1964.* New York, Dell, 1972.

_____, *Goodbye Darkness.* New York: Dell, 1979.

Marquez, Sandra. *"500 travel to former camp to mark WW II internment of Japanese."* *Honolulu Advertiser,* 28 Apr. 2002: p. A11.

Matsushima, Keizo. *The Tragedy of Admiral Nagumo.* Tokyo: Tokuma Books, 1967.

Mayer, S.L. *Encyclopedia of World War II.* Greenwich, CN: Longmeadow Press, 1977.

Mayo, Lida. *Bloody Buna.* New York: Doubleday, 1974.

Mee, Charles L. Jr. *Meeting at Potsdam.* New York: M. Evans, 1975.

Middlebrook, Martin. *Convoy.* New York: William Morrow, 1976.

Miller, Edward S. *War Plan Orange: The U.S. Strategy to Defeat Japan, 1897-1945.* Annapolis: Naval Institute Press, 1991.

Miller, John Jr., *The United States Army in World War II: The War in the Pacific: Cartwheel: The Reduction of Rabaul.* Washington, D.C.: Center of Military History, U.S. Army, 1984.

Miller, Thomas G. *The Cactus Air Force.* New York: Harper and Rowe, 1981.

Millis, Walter, ed., *The Forrestal Diaries.* New York: The Viking Press, 1951.

Monks, John Jr. *A Ribbon and a Star.* New York: Henry Holt, 1945.

Morison, Samuel Eliot. *History of United States Naval Operations in World War II,* Edison, NJ: Castle Books, 2001.

Morison, Samuel Eliot. *The Struggle for Guadalcanal,* Annapolis: Naval Institute Press, 1949.

_____, *Vol. 6, Breaking the Bismarck's Barrier: 22 July 1942-1 May 1944.* Edison, NJ: Castle Books, 1950.

_____, *History of United States Naval Operations in World War II. Vol. 7, Aleutians, Gilberts and Marshalls: June 1942-April 1944.* Edison, NJ: Castle Books, 1951.

Morris. Eric. *Corregidor: The End of The Line.* New York: Stein and Day, 1981.

Nakasone, Edwin M. *The Nisei Soldier.* White Bear Lake, MN: J-Press, 1999.

Noli, Jean. *The Admiral's Wolf Pack,* New York: United Press International, 1974.

Obata, Chiura. *Topaz Moon:* Art of the Internment. Berkeley: Heyday Books, 2000.

Odgers, George. *Air War Against Japan 1943-1945.* Canberra: Australian War Museum, 1957.

Oliver, Douglas. *Bougainville.* Clayton, Victoria: Wilke and Company, 1973.

Petilo, Carol Morris. *Douglas MacArthur: The Philippine Years.* Bloomington IN: Indiana University Press, 1980.

Pinck, Dan. *Journey to Peking: A Secret Agent in Wartime China.* Annapolis: Naval Institute Press, 2003.

Potter, E.B. *Nimitz,* Annapolis: Naval Institute Press, 1976.

_____, *Bull Halsey,* Annapolis: Naval Institute Press, 1985.

Prados, John. *Combined Fleet Decoded.* Annapolis: Naval Institute Press, 1995.

Reminick, Gerald. *Patriots and Heroes: True Stories of the U.S. Merchant Marine in WW II.* Palo Alto: Glencannon Press, 2000.

Rentz, John N. *Bougainville and the Northern Solomons.* Washington, D.C.: Headquarters U.S. Marine Corps, 1948.

Reports of General MacArthur. Japanese Operations in the Southwest Pacific Area, volume II-part I, Washington DC: Government Printing Office, 1966.

Revere, Richard H. and Arthur M. Schlesinger, Jr. *The General and the President.* New York: Farrar, Straus and Young, 1951.

Riesenberg, Felix Jr. *Sea War: The Story of the U.S. Merchant Marine in WW II.* New York: Rinehart and Company, 1956.

Rhodes, Richard. *The Making of the Atomic Bombs.* New York: Simon and Schuster, 1986.

Rooney, David. *Burma Victory: Imphal and Kohima.* London: Arms and Armor Press, 1992.

_____, *Stilwell,* New York: Ballantine Books, 1971.

Roosevelt, Elliott. *As He Saw It.* New York: Duell, Sloan, and Pearce, 1946.

Ross, Bill D. *Peleliu: Tragic Ttriumph.* New York: Random House, 1991.

_____, *A Special Piece of Hell.* New York: Random House, 1991.

Schaller, Michael. *Douglas MacArthur. The Far Eastern General.* New York: Oxford University Press, 1989.

Shaw, Henry I. Jr. Tarawa: *A Legend is Born.* New York: Ballantine, 1969.

Sledge, E. B. *With the Old Breed.* Oxford: Oxford University Press, 1981.

Slim, William. *Defeat Into Victory.* Hong Kong: PAPERMAC, 1972.

Spector, Ronald H. *At War At Sea,* New York: Penguin, 2001.

"Stand easy." *Australian War Memorial,* Canberra, 1945.

Sweeney, Charles W. *War's End.* New York: Avon Books, 1997.

Stilwell, Paul. Ed. *The Golden Thirteen.* Annapolis: Naval Institute Press, 1993.

Tateishi, John. *And Justice For All.* An Oral History of the Japanese American Detention Camps. New York: Random House, 1984.

Taylor, Theodore. *The Magnificent Mitscher.* Annapolis: Naval Institute Press, 1954.

Teller, Edward with Allen Brown. *The Legacy of Hiroshima.* Garden City, NY: Doubleday, 1962.

Thomas, James O. *Trapped with the Enemy.* Xlibris Corp, 2002.

Tsuji, Masanobu. *Singapore: The Japanese Version.* New York: St. Martins Press, 1960.

_____, *Japan's Greatest Victory-Britain's Worst Defeat.* New York: Sarpedon, 1997.

_____, *Underground Escape.* Tokyo: Robert Booth and Taro Fukuda, 1952.

Wales, Ken and David Poling. *Sea of Glory.* Nashville: Broadman and Holman, 2001.

Walker, Charles H. *Combat Officer: A Memoir of War in the South Pacific.* New York: Ballantine Books, 2004.

Wallin, Homer N. *Pearl Harbor: Why, How, Fleet Salvage and Final Appraisal.* Washington, DC: Naval History Division, 1968.

Ward. Ian. *The killer they called a god.* Singapore: Media Masters, 1992.

Wells, Arthur W. *The Quack Corps: A Marine's War-Pearl Harbor to Okinawa.* Chico, CA: Dol An, 1992.

Wheal, Elizabeth-Anne. *Encyclopedia of the Second World War.* Secaucus, NY: Castle Books, 1989.

White, W.L. *They Were Expendable.* New York: Penguin, 1942.

Williams, Andrew. *The Battle of the Atlantic.* New York: Basic Books, 2003.

Willoughby, Malcolm F. *The U.S. Coast Guard in World War II.* Annapolis: Naval Institute Press, 1957.

Wright, Derrick. *Tarawa 1943.* Oxford: Osprey Publishing, 2002.

Wright, Michael, ed. *The World at Arms.* The Readers Digest Illustrated History of World War II. London: The Readers Digest Association Limited, 1989.

Wright, Walter. *"Sculpture took wing through Sand Island Camp Heritage".* Honolulu Advertiser, 22 Oct. 1999: p. 1.

Yadav, K.C. and Akiko Seki. *Adventure into the Unknown: The Last Days of Netaji Subhas Chandra Bose.* Mayapuri, New Delhi: Hope India Publications, 1996.

Y'Blood, William T. *The Little Giants,* Annapolis, Naval Institute Press, 1987.

INDEX